Edith Wharton's Writings from the Great War

Florida A&M University, Tallahassee
Florida Atlantic University, Boca Raton
Florida Gulf Coast University, Ft. Myers
Florida International University, Miami
Florida State University, Tallahassee
University of Central Florida, Orlando
University of Florida, Gainesville
University of North Florida, Jacksonville
University of South Florida, Tampa
University of West Florida, Pensacola

Edith Wharton's Writings
from the Great War

Julie Olin-Ammentorp

University Press of Florida

Gainesville · Tallahassee · Tampa · Boca Raton

Pensacola · Orlando · Miami · Jacksonville · Ft. Myers

09 08 07 06 05 04   6 5 4 3 2 1

Library of Congress Cataloging-in-Publication Data
Olin-Ammentorp, Julie, 1959–
Edith Wharton's writings from the Great War / Julie Olin-Ammentorp.
p. cm.
Includes bibliographical references (p.) and index.
ISBN 0-8130-2730-6 (cloth: alk. paper)
1. Wharton, Edith, 1862–1937—Criticism and interpretation.
2. Women and literature—United States—History—20th century.
3. Wharton, Edith, 1862–1937—Knowledge—History. 4. World War,
1914–1918—Literature and the war. 5. World War, 1914–1918—
Literary collections. I. Title.
PS3545.H16Z755   2004
813'.52–dc22   2004044187

The University Press of Florida is the scholarly publishing agency
for the State University System of Florida, comprising Florida A&M
University, Florida Atlantic University, Florida Gulf Coast University,
Florida International University, Florida State University, University
of Central Florida, University of Florida, University of North Florida,
University of South Florida, and University of West Florida.

University Press of Florida
15 Northwest 15th Street
Gainesville, FL 32611-2079
http://www.upf.com

For my father, David Burton Olin,

and in memory of my mother, Jane Ott Olin

Contents

List of Illustrations   ix

Preface and Acknowledgments   xi

Introduction   1

1. Edith Wharton and the Literary Legacy of the Great War   6

2. A Shaken Reality: Writings from Early in the War (1914–1915)   28

3. Work, Escape, and the Loss of Ambiguity: Writings from Later in the War (1916–1918)   56

4. Elegies and Satires: Works from the War's End (1919)   90

5. Monument Building: *A Son at the Front*   115

6. Writing in the Wake of the War   154

Conclusion: Glancing Back at the War   212

Appendix A: War-related Poems by Edith Wharton   235
   "Belgium"   235
   "Beaumetz, Feb. 23rd. 1915."   235
   "The Great Blue Tent"   236
   "The Tryst"   238
   "Battle Sleep"   239
   "'On Active Service'"   240
   "Elegy"   240
   "You and You"   241
   "With the Tide"   243

Appendix B: Selected War-related Prose by Edith Wharton   245
   "My Work Among the Women Workers of Paris"   245
   "Preface" to *The Book of the Homeless*   252
   "Edith Wharton Tells of German Trail of Ruin"   257

"Talk to American Soldiers" 261
"Capt. Ronald Simmons Dies on Active Service" 272
"How Paris Welcomed the King" 273
"Christmas Tinsel" 276

Notes 279
Bibliography 291
Index 299

Illustrations

1. Cartoon of Edith Wharton and Walter Berry at the front, by Abel Faivre   17

2. Sketch of his son, by Pierre-Auguste Renoir   119

3. Photograph of Newbold Rhinelander in uniform   120

4. "A French palisade." Edith Wharton at the front   171

5. Sketch done by a French soldier, "Pour Mrs. Edith Wharton"   231

Preface and Acknowledgments

Writers of fiction sometimes say that they do not choose their subjects; rather, their subjects choose them. That has been much my experience with the topic of this book. Fifteen years ago, though I could easily imagine writing a book about Edith Wharton, I could not have imagined it would be a book about Edith Wharton and war. And yet, about ten years ago, thanks to a series of coincidences as well as much help and encouragement, I began work on the manuscript that grew into this book.

Like any work of scholarship, this book is not exhaustive: far from it. My work on it has suggested to me, and I hope will suggest to others interested in the work of Edith Wharton and the literature of World War I, a host of new topics: for instance, comparative studies of Wharton and other writers of the Great War, both male and female; studies of the nature of women's writing about war, including fiction, nonfiction, and poetry, traced through history, particularly through the twentieth century; the relationship between women, war, and literature; and a further pursuit of the relationship between Wharton and politics.

Acknowledgments

Works by Edith Wharton that are still under copyright are reprinted by permission of the Estate of Edith Wharton and the Watkins/Loomis Agency. I appreciate their cooperation. Wharton's poem "Beaumetz, February 23, 1915," is used courtesy of the Lilly Library, Indiana University, to whom I am grateful; I am also grateful to *Studies in American Fiction* for permission to reproduce material on Wharton's war-related short stories, which I published in an earlier version as an article in that journal. I also extend thanks to the Bibliothèque Historique de la Ville de Paris, the source of the Abel Faivre cartoon of Edith Wharton, and to the Yale Collection of American Literature, Beinecke Rare Book and Manuscript Library, the source of all quotations identified *"Wharton Collection* Yale," as well as the source of the photograph of Newbold Rhinelander and the sketch captioned "Pour Mrs. Edith Wharton." I have made every attempt to obtain appropriate copyright clearance for materials in this book that are not in the public domain; if I have inadvertently overlooked any copyright holders, I urge them to contact me.

This book never would have been completed without the assistance of a great many people, and one of the pleasures of working on it has been discovering how many receptive and truly helpful friends and colleagues I have. At Le Moyne College, I owe thanks to many people. Within the English Department, Julie Grossman carefully read and commented on the manuscript at its penultimate stage; Lib Hayes, whom I succeeded as department chair, served an extra year in that position, partly to give me more time to work on this project; David Lloyd read and commented on Wharton's war-related poems; Ann Ryan read some of the earliest work on this project and encouraged me to persevere; Patrick Keane made valuable comments about my prospectus for the book; Paul Campbell, S.J., happily discussed French idioms with me. I owe thanks to many others in the college as well. John McMahon, Leonard Marsh, F.S.C., and Jim Dahlinger, S.J., all provided information on translations; John Langdon of the History Department cheerfully answered innumerable questions about the Great War, suggested essential readings, and regularly asked about the well-being of "Edith"; Harold "Hap" Ridley, S.J., formerly of Le Moyne, kindly loaned me several books on the literary history of the war. Librarian Gretchen Pearson was invaluable on research and copyright matters, and interlibrary loan expert Wayne Stevens efficiently filled many, many requests. Ellen P. Smith, Annabeth Hayes, and Melissa Lee carefully checked quotations and did other detailed work on the manuscript. I also thank Nancy Ring, then Interim Dean of Arts and Sciences, for a course load release in Spring 2002 and the Le Moyne Committee on Research and Development for course load releases, summer stipends, and several grants that helped make this book a reality.

There are many outside Le Moyne who have also been vital to the work on this book. The librarians at the Beinecke Library, Yale, were most helpful during my research visits, as well as in letters and e-mails. Jean Frantz Blackall, Kristin Boudreau, Hildegard Hoeller, Melissa Pennell, Lyall Powers, Carole Shaffer-Koros, Abby Werlock, Sarah Bird Wright, Annette Zilversmit, and the late Scott Marshall gave many kinds of assistance. Eleanor Dwight generously provided me with information about, and a slide of, the Abel Faivre cartoon of Wharton. Irene Goldman-Price, Alan Price, and Frederick Wegener all provided detailed and extremely useful comments on the manuscript, as well as good advice on other book-related matters. I owe a particular debt of gratitude to Elsa Nettels, who inadvertently set me on the path to this book many years ago; she has read and commented on every chapter of the manuscript, some of them in multiple forms, and has encouraged me every step of the way. I am also grateful to Linda Pennisi for her unflagging friendship and her enthusiasm for writing in all its forms.

Many members of my family have also been a great help. My parents-in-law, Janet and Lee Ammentorp, successfully scoured estate sales for copies of out-of-print books by Wharton. My father, David Olin, has encouraged me in all my endeavors, and my sisters Susan Olin and Sara Olin Codrea have regularly asked about the progress of the book; Sue has also shared her knowledge as an editor and proofreader on several occasions. My children, Jane and Wilkie, who were much younger when this work was begun, have been patient and interested; I'm sure neither can remember a time in their lives when they did not know the name "Edith Wharton." Finally, I wish to thank my husband, Warren, for his excellent memory and encyclopedic knowledge, which encompasses not only literature and military history but computer management. His help and companionship over many years have helped bring this book into being.

Introduction

> One of the fascinating themes in literary history is the impact of a
> great war upon the creative imagination—its capacity to galvanize
> or to crush, and the oddly varying pace at which either process
> works; all this dependent to some extent upon the writer's actual
> involvement in the conflict.
>
> **R.W.B. Lewis, *Edith Wharton: A Biography* (393)**

There can be no doubt at this point in literary history that Edith Wharton is a major American author. Many of her novels have remained constantly in print; she is read by the general public, taught in high school, college, and graduate level courses, and has had her novels adapted for television specials, films, plays, and operas.[1] In the last twenty-five years alone over eight hundred scholarly books and articles have been written about Wharton and her work; recently, scholars have brought new approaches to her work and analyzed an increasingly wide range of her writings, including short stories, novels, nonfiction, and even poems that were overlooked a decade ago. A substantial body of Wharton's work, however, has gone largely ignored: her writings related to World War I. R.W.B. Lewis's implied call in 1975 for a study of "the impact of a great war upon the creative imagination" of Edith Wharton has, so far, gone largely unheeded.[2] Critical interest in Wharton's war-related writings is only beginning; this book is the first extended study devoted primarily to these writings, bringing them to the attention of scholars and general readers alike. Further, it examines the wartime and war-related writings as a coherent and crucial part of Wharton's oeuvre.

Although Wharton protested in her memoir, *A Backward Glance,* that her literary output declined during the war years, she actually wrote a good deal in this period—though not always in the genres, novel and short story, that had established her literary success before the war. Between December 1914 and November 1918 she published thirty-seven magazine and newspaper items, including war-related poems, newspaper articles about the charities she was responsible for administering and funding, and essays describing Paris in wartime and Wharton's several trips to the front;[3] some of these articles would be collected in *Fighting France: From Dunkerque to Belfort* (1915) and *French Ways and Their Meaning* (1919). Wharton also edited *The Book of the Homeless*, a collection of literature, artwork, and musical scores with an impressive list of contributors, to raise money for the charities she administered. Her first war-related short story, "Coming Home," was published in *Scribner's Magazine* in December 1915. In 1916 she wrote a novel, *Summer*, set in rural New England, on its surface it seems as remote as possible from the situation in which Wharton wrote it, yet it holds significant echoes of the war years. Wharton quickly returned to the war as her primary subject, and the end of the war engendered a number of pieces of fiction: a short novel entitled *The Marne*, published in 1918, and two short stories, "The Refugees" and "Writing a War Story," both published in 1919. Her war-related writings continued, as did the effects of the war, beyond the November 1918 Armistice. Wharton composed a number of elegiac poems in late 1918 and 1919; her final portrait of the war years, the novel *A Son at the Front*, was begun in 1918 but not completed until 1922.[4]

Although *Son* was Wharton's last work focused on the Great War, that epoch continued to influence her work. A number of works written after *Son* make brief references to the war to establish chronology or use wartime events as catalysts for postwar plots; the war informed her later work in more profound ways as well. The Great War changed the world in which Wharton lived; inevitably, it affected matters as diverse as her choice of subject, her tone, her sense of her role as a novelist, memoirist, and public figure, as well as her view of the past—and, correspondingly, her view of the postwar world in which she found herself. In short, her experience of the Great War influenced not just her literary output during the war years, but also the remainder of her life and career.

Taken together, Wharton's war-related writings exhibit great consistency in many ways. Wharton's love of France pervades the writings, as does her commitment to the war despite its huge human cost; letters, fictions, and essays alike suggest her desire to know the truth about the war, including conditions of life at the front. Reading her works chronologically reveals her deepening understanding of the war—and her changing attitude toward it. Wharton found the war profoundly interesting, declaring it at some points "thrilling" and at others utterly disheartening. By following the writings in the order they were written, this book charts Wharton's shifting reactions to the war as well as the war's influence on her creative life.

Chapter One, "Edith Wharton and the Literary Legacy of the Great War," analyzes the reasons for the neglect of Wharton's war-related writings both by general scholars of World War I literature like Paul Fussell and Samuel Hynes, and by feminist scholars, who, despite Wharton's stature as a writer, have generally dealt only briefly with her war-related writings. In addition, the first chapter establishes Wharton's intersections with both of these traditions of scholarship on Great War writing. It also introduces the vexed question of gender and genre: how does a woman legitimately write about an experience from which she is, by definition, excluded? Chapter Two, "A Shaken Reality: Writings from Early in the War," discusses Wharton's early reactions to the war as expressed in her letters, in *Fighting France*, in "Coming Home," and in a number of poems, focusing on her fascination with the war and her tendency to see and depict it in romantic terms, even as she was coming to grips with the horrors it presented.

Summer, *The Marne*, and *French Ways and Their Meaning* are all treated in Chapter Three, "Work, Escape, and the Loss of Ambiguity: Writings from Later in the War," which argues that the war became normalized for Wharton (as for others) after the first two years of the war had passed. Her work from this period suggests both the longing to escape the war and her commitment to propaganda, or at least polemic, in favor of U.S. involvement in the war. The Armistice in November 1918 allowed Wharton to assume different tones: Chapter Four, "Elegies and Satires: Works from the War's End" explores a number of poems she wrote, their elegiac tone contrasting sharply with the two satirical short stories also discussed in this chapter, "The Refugees" and "Writing a War Story."

Chapter Five, "Monument Building: *A Son at the Front*" is devoted to a discussion of that complex, if flawed, novel, Wharton's last and most thoughtful portrait of the war years. Chapter Six, "Writing in the Wake of the War," looks at the long-term influence of the war on Wharton's writing both in terms of her turn to the prewar period in works like *The Age of Innocence* and *Old New York,* and in terms of the subject and style of her other postwar fiction. The final chapter analyzes Wharton's presentation of the war in her memoir *A Backward Glance.*

Each of these chapters presents a number of issues.[5] In addition to following the continuities and discontinuities of Wharton's attitude during the war, I trace the close ties between her daily life in those years and her literary output; examine the complex relationship between gender and art in this complex writer, whose attitudes toward gender (and particularly toward the position of women writers) are often surprising and elusive; discuss choices of style, subject, and tone in her writings; consider these works in the context of her literary career as a whole; and bring critical awareness to the existence and importance of a number of texts frequently overlooked. Several chapters discuss material that has scarcely been touched by Wharton scholars, in part because it has been out of print for decades; the appendices include these materials, including the texts of all Wharton's war-related poetry and a sampling of her war-related prose.[6] In addition, this book has much to suggest about the canon of literature of World War I, including the long-established classics by male authors as well as the increasingly available works by female authors;[7] about the complex, and sometimes surprising, differences and overlaps between men's and women's writing about the Great War; about the process of canonizing authors or specific works by authors in the context of a particular historical event, like World War I; about the relationship of women authors to events seen exclusively, or nearly exclusively, as masculine; and about women and war. A study of Wharton's experiences in World War I and her writings about them allows readers nearly a century later to see how much—or perhaps how little—the relationship between women, writing, and war has changed.

The tragic events of September 11, 2001, and the months immediately following had sometimes uncanny echoes for the student of World War I, including those familiar with Wharton's war-related writings. When the German army first crossed Belgium's boundaries, later burning the great library at Louvain and bombing Reims Cathedral, citizens of France, England, and the United States were outraged, claiming that such acts constituted an attack not just on those places and buildings but on all of civilization. Much the same rhetoric emerged in the wake of the attack on the Pentagon and the destruction of the World Trade Center towers; American and European leaders expressed their belief that civilization itself was under attack.[8] In the Great War, France and England responded quickly to the invasion of Belgium by mobilizing their armies and urging potential allies to do the same in order to defeat the barbaric Hun; in fall 2001, the United States moved quickly into military action with President George W. Bush urging other nations to join the United States in what he presented as a justified war of civilization against evil. There are, of course, obvious contrasts between the two situations as well; but the rhetoric of wartime, with all of its grandeur, its sense of purpose, and its oversimplifications, is very much with us today, perhaps allowing readers some additional insight into Wharton's reactions, both personal and literary, in time of war.

Specific comparisons between the two situations, however, are not the focus of this work. The most fundamental purpose of this study is to ask its readers to reread (or, in many cases, to read for the first time) and consider Wharton's war-related writings. Her works from this period have often been ignored, brushed off as propagandistic, or worse: one scholar, for instance, refers to *The Marne* as combining "gentility with bloodthirst" (Cooperman 41). As we will see in more detail in chapter one, some of Wharton's writings from this period—perhaps particularly *The Marne* and *French Ways and Their Meaning*—strike scholars today as embarrassingly polemical and aesthetically weak. Yet, as I will argue, aesthetics are themselves profoundly shaped by the political beliefs of scholars and writers; Wharton's particular personal and historical circumstances have rarely been taken into account when negative judgments of her war-related writings have been made. I am not claiming in these pages that general readers and literary scholars have overlooked any lost masterpieces; nevertheless, many of Wharton's works from this period have not only intrinsic worth but biographical and historical value, and deserve far more study than they have received. The war-related works taken together—the poems, essays, short stories, and novels—reveal not only how Wharton shaped the war for her readers, but how a great war—*the* Great War—shaped Wharton's own particular creative imagination.

1

Edith Wharton and the Literary Legacy of the Great War

> Some months ago I told you that you could count on the completion
> of my novel by the spring of 1916; but I thought then that the war
> would be over by August. Now we are looking forward to a winter
> campaign and the whole situation is so overwhelming and
> unescapable that I feel less and less able to turn my mind from it.
> May I suggest, during the next six months, giving you instead four
> or five short stories, not precisely war stories, but on subjects sug-
> gested by the war?
>
> **Edith Wharton to Charles Scribner, June 28, 1915 (*Letters* 357)**

I.

Edith Wharton's letter to Charles Scribner in June 1915 would come to
epitomize much of her writing, and indeed much of her experience, during
the Great War. Like millions of others, Wharton initially believed the war
would be short and conclusive, but gradually realized that it would be long
and drawn out, "overwhelming and unescapable." Normal routines were
disrupted; in Wharton's case, this meant—among many other things—the
drastic alteration of her writing plans. Instead of completing the novel she
mentions here (*Literature*, which she never finished), Wharton turned her
hand to a wide variety of projects, including a number of charitable endeavors. Three weeks after the mobilization of France on August 1, 1914,
Wharton had established a workroom for seamstresses put out of work by
the war; in later months and years she undertook the administration of
and fund-raising for an array of war-related charities, including hostels for
Belgian refugees and sanitaria for tubercular soldiers as well as infected
women and their children. "Mrs. Wharton's charities," as they came to be
known, aided thousands of French and Belgian citizens during the war.[1]
Her efforts were so impressive that the French government awarded her

the Legion of Honor in March, 1916 (Benstock, *No Gifts* 324). Other projects were literary, though often not in the genres Wharton had preferred before the war. Even fiction, Wharton's area of greatest literary expertise, raised genre-related issues. Her phrase "not precisely war stories" suggests the negotiations she would have to make during the war: her writing both was and was not "war writing," fell both into and outside the definitions of war writing—as it still does today. Further, the war created subjects for writing that Wharton could not have anticipated. As she continued to Scribner, "So many extraordinary and dramatic situations are springing out of the huge conflict that the temptation to use a few of them is irresistible" (*Letters* 357). The years between 1914 and 1919 constitute a major period in the life and career of this major writer. Collectively, the writings from this period tell us not only about Wharton's life and imagination during the First World War, but about how the war would influence her work in the nearly twenty years that remained between the end of that war and her death in 1937.

II. The Myth of the War

Given Wharton's stature as a writer and given the historical and literary prominence of World War I, it initially seems odd that there exists no extended treatment of Wharton's wartime work. When people think of Great War writers, they rarely think of Edith Wharton; when they think of Edith Wharton, they rarely think of her war-related writings. Yet the reason for this omission, though complex in its details, is simple in its central import: Wharton's war works do not adhere to the basic attitudes and styles that most readers since World War I have come to expect in writings related to that war.[2]

Indeed, most literary discussions of the Great War have either ignored Wharton's work or, when they discussed it, have gotten it significantly wrong.[3] For instance, neither Paul Fussell's *The Great War and Modern Memory* (1975) nor Samuel Hynes's *A War Imagined: The First World War and English Culture* (1990) even mentions Wharton. It is not simply a question of nationality: both authors focus on English writers, but neither hesitates to discuss American Ernest Hemingway and expatriates Ezra Pound and T. S. Eliot. Nor is it a matter entirely of gender: Fussell mentions Virginia Woolf, and Hynes discusses several women authors, including May Sinclair and Edith Sitwell. And yet, regardless of their exclusion of Wharton, Fussell's and Hynes's studies provide a great deal of insight into Wharton's war writings—as well as suggesting a great deal about the causes for their neglect.

To a large extent, Wharton is excluded from the canon of Great War writers because her work does not adhere to what Fussell and Hynes define as "The Myth of the War." Both authors make convincing cases that post–World War I generations (in England and the United States) have had their war-view and indeed their worldview shaped by the debacle of the Great War. Fussell writes that Thomas Hardy's volume of verse, *Satires of Circumstance*, largely composed before the English entered the war, "establish[ed] a terrible irony as the appropriate interpretive means" for understanding the war (3). Prewar idealism, epitomized by capitalized abstractions like Honor and Glory, failed as soldiers experienced high casualties and the brutal realities of trench warfare.

Hynes states that the basic myth of the war "can be reduced to two terse propositions: the old betray the young; the past is remote and useless" (xii). These two propositions comprise a number of other elements: "the idealism betrayed; the early high-mindedness that turned in mid-war to bitterness and cynicism; the growing feeling among soldiers of alienation from the people at home for whom they were fighting; the rising resentment of politicians and profiteers and ignorant, patriotic women; the growing sympathy for the men on the other side, betrayed in the same ways and suffering the same hardships; the emerging sense of the war as a machine and of all soldiers as its victims; the bitter conviction that the men in the trenches fought for no cause, in a war that could not be stopped" (439). These beliefs inevitably required a change in literary style: "the old high rhetoric of war had been emptied of its meaning and its values, and . . . the truth about war could only be told in the plainest, most physical words" (439). Writing during the war and certainly in the postwar period had to change. The prewar literary tropes, those of idealism, romanticism, and the pastoral, had all been shattered. The use of irony by soldier-authors like Siegfried Sassoon and Wilfred Owen was one literary response to the disillusionment of the war; the high modernism of Ezra Pound, T. S. Eliot, Virginia Woolf, and others, despite their status as noncombatants, was another.[4]

Although Wharton was an ironist and a satirist almost from the beginning of her career—certainly her first great success, *The House of Mirth* (1905), is both satirical and ironic—her irony differs from the kind employed by the World War I writers generally admired today. At the base of *The House of Mirth*, as Wharton wrote, is a tragedy—the ability of "a frivolous society" to "debas[e] people and ideals" (*Backward Glance* 207). The story is a tragedy because, under somewhat different circumstances, Lily Bart could have lived; because she who loved art (and was in some ways an artist) is destroyed by those who love only money and a pointless exercise of social and economic power. Lawrence Selden asks in his famous conversation with Lily on the hills above Bellomont, "Why do we call all our generous ideas illusions, and the mean ones truths?" (*House of Mirth* 70). The "generous ideas"—the ideals—existed for Wharton before, during, and after the war, though they had been destroyed for many other writers during the war—particularly for younger writers just being formed during those years.

While Wharton eventually abandoned the capitalized Ideals of the prewar period, she never sacrificed ideals with a lowercase "i" for the anti-idealism and irony of other wartime writers. And she never believed that the war was pointless—even as she saw it drag on and on and as she suffered the deaths of one relative and several friends in the war. The "old high rhetoric" of war emerges unscathed in *The Marne*, despite the fact that the novel was published at the end of the war; its initial popularity suggests that Wharton was not the only one who still clung to ideals. Similarly, among the chapter headings of *French Ways and Their Meaning* stand four high-sounding ideals—"Reverence," "Taste," "Intellectual Honesty," "Continuity"—the very sort of language the war had supposedly outmoded.

One line that echoes through literary history epitomizes Wharton's adherence to ideals even in a world that had largely abandoned them: Horace's "Dulce et decorum est pro patria mori" ("It is sweet and fitting to die for one's country"). The Great War poet Wilfred Owen reworked this line in a heavily ironic way in his famous poem "Dulce et Decorum Est." After sixteen lines describing in detail the horror of war and the agonies of one soldier who, in a gas attack, cannot put on his mask in time, Owen addresses his reader:

If in some smothering dreams you too could pace
Behind the wagon that we flung him in,
And watch the white eyes writhing in his face,
His hanging face, like a devil's sick of sin;
If you could hear, at every jolt, the blood
Come gargling from the froth-corrupted lungs,
Obscene as cancer, bitter as the cud

Of vile, incurable sores on innocent tongues,—
My friend, you would not tell with such high zest
To children ardent for some desperate glory,
The old Lie: Dulce et decorum est
Pro patria mori.

For Fussell, this poem epitomizes the change war wrought for English writers. He notes that Owen's "tag from Horace" would be "familiar to every British schoolboy"—a familiarity necessary to establish fully the poem's irony (Fussell 158). This poem represents a new kind of writing—succinct, detailed, ironic, anti-idealistic—that became, for many, the only kind of writing palatable in light of the realities of the war.

By way of contrast, Wharton also quotes Horace's "dulce et decorum est" in both *The Marne* and *A Son at the Front*, as we will see in later chapters. But in each instance she quotes it sincerely, unironically, as a way of explaining why young men were willing to die in a long and terrible war. By the very terms of Fussell's definition of the effect of the Great War, Wharton is excluded: her attitude, by this standard, remains naively "pre-war," idealistic and unironic. Judging from this sort of literary example, Wharton seems like one of the much-despised "Old Men," as they became known—the men who conducted and, many believed, mismanaged the war—or like one of the women who blithely sent men off to deaths they believed to be glorious, but that were in actuality often slow, meaningless, or ignominious. Emphasizing the difference between the horrific knowledge of men at the front and the glorifying ignorance of women at home appears to have been one of Owen's points in writing "Dulce et Decorum Est": it was first called "To Jessie Pope" and then "For a Certain Poetess" (Gilbert and Gubar, *No Man's Land* 284), apparently as a rebuke to Pope and other women like her who, through their writings, enthusiastically supported the war.[5]

Indeed, many of Wharton's literary choices put her in the camp of the Old Men. As we will see in more detail in chapter two, Wharton alluded to the *Chanson de Roland* and other literary models in her attempt to comprehend the war. So, Fussell notes, John Masefield's *Gallipoli* (1918), a work about what has come to be seen as one of the most disastrous campaigns of the war, "argued not just the thrilling 'adventure' but . . . the triumph (at least moral triumph) of the campaign. To assist this argument Masefield prefaced each chapter with a quotation of heroic tendency from *The Song of Roland*" (Fussell 87). Similarly, Lord Northcliffe, in charge of

British government propaganda during the war (Fussell 87), employed "the rhetoric of heroic romance" in his writing. In a newspaper report about the first day of battle on the Somme—a day that resulted in "appalling loss of life" for British soldiers, most of them killed on their own ground (Keegan, *The First World War* 295)—Northcliffe wrote, "There is a fair field and no favor, and we have elected to fight out our quarrel with the Germans and to give them as much battle as they want" (Fussell 88). To contrast postwar, nonelevated diction, and the elevated, "essentially feudal language" often used in military reports, Fussell creates a "table of equivalents." In the category of elevated diction are such examples as "A horse is a *steed,* or *charger.* . . To be earnestly brave is to be *gallant* . . . Not to complain is to be *manly* . . . Things that glow or shine are *radiant*[;] The army as a whole is *the legion*[,]" and so on (21–22). While Wharton never quite employs such full-blown medieval rhetoric, she often makes choices that are on the side of that rhetoric—particularly in works like *Fighting France* and *French Ways and Their Meaning.*

The general trend of language as the war went on was that "essentially feudal language" became more and more outmoded, less and less used, while bolder, franker, and less idealistic or even anti-idealistic language became more and more common. But such a simple trajectory is misleading. As Hynes reports, the romanticism of Rupert Brooke remained popular with soldiers throughout the war (300); even the cynical Wilfred Owen "kept a newspaper photograph of Brooke's grave tucked into his copy of [Brooke's book,] *1914*" (Hynes 300). Similarly, Wharton's choice between romantic and factual language follows no simple trajectory. The earliest works—for example, *Fighting France* and her poem "The Great Blue Tent"—use romantic rhetoric, but so do some later works like *The Marne* and *French Ways and Their Meaning.* By the same token, realistic writing appears at different points in Wharton's work throughout the war years. While some passages in *Fighting France* are romantic, others are realistic; "Coming Home," Wharton's first war-related short story, does not employ "elevated" language. Never a mindless follower of merely fashionable writing styles, Wharton seems to have selected her language, realistic or romantic, as her writing task or intended audience required.

With the end of the war, however, Wharton abandoned exaggerated romanticism and high Ideals—though lowercase ideals remained a quiet part of *A Son at the Front.* There is a decided break between her works written during the war and those written after, but about, the war. Yet she never turns to bald statement or abandons ideals in the way that became popular—or necessary for literary survival—after the war. In 1929, Ernest Hemingway's *A Farewell to Arms* described the new literary standard: "Abstract words such as glory, honor, courage, or hallow were obscene beside the concrete names of villages, the numbers of roads, the names of rivers, the numbers of regiments and the dates" (Hemingway 185).[6] But, as Alan Price has pointed out, Hemingway was not the first to make such an observation. As early as March 1915 Henry James remarked that "The war has used up words: they have weakened, they have deteriorated like motor-car tires; . . . we are now confronted with a depreciation of all our terms, or, otherwise speaking, with a loss of expression" (qtd. in Price xiii–xiv). Wharton, like James, was aware of the war's effect on language, though she would never rule out abstractions and ideals to the extent that Hemingway did.

It is Wharton's use of the old high rhetoric in some of her war-related writings (and even her clinging to a very tempered idealism in *A Son at the Front*) that has made her "read" wrong to modern audiences, that is, to audiences whose literary tastes and expectations have been shaped by a wholly ironic, wholly disillusioned view of the war. As Samuel Hynes has written, Siegfried Sassoon "rejected [the old high rhetoric] not because it is inadequate, but because it is wrong" (Hynes 156). Hynes further explains the "two qualities" that came to be seen as necessary to accepted war writing: "The first is its prose style, which is bare, direct, exact, and unmetaphorical . . .: war is not like anything except itself, and the meticulous witness will not interpret it, or place it in some order of perceptions that gives it meaning, but will simply tell what it is. The second is its structure, which is the formal expression of the same point: there is no order in war except chronology, event followed by event without evident reason" (Hynes 95).[7] Wharton's phrase "not precisely war stories" may have been all too predictive of her work, as well as of its exclusion from the canon of Great War writings. To some extent her fictions, particularly the short stories and *A Son at the Front*, do adhere to the criteria Hynes describes here: events are narrated in simple chronological order, "event followed by event without evident reason"; focalizers may provide their own interpretation of events, but there is no omniscient narrator to tell the reader what the "right" interpretation is. Their language is "bare, direct, exact," and generally "unmetaphorical." But they are not soldiers' stories; hence, they are not quite war stories, and have been neglected.

Related to this point is another reason for the neglect of Wharton's later works: a certain sense that, for all Wharton's native intelligence and ability, for all the nuance and skill of prewar works like *The House of Mirth, Ethan Frome,* and *The Custom of the Country,* Edith Wharton missed the literary boat at the war's end. Literature and all the big literary lights—Virginia Woolf, D. H. Lawrence, James Joyce, Ezra Pound, T. S. Eliot—went on to create modernism, which has since come to be seen as the only viable artistic response to a world shaken by the war. Wharton, like others, questioned the limits of genre in a postwar world. But in the end she adhered to an earlier mode of writing, becoming a literary traditionalist like some of her contemporaries in England, a topic that will be further discussed in chapter six. As Peter Buitenhuis has written, the work of Wharton, John Galsworthy, Rudyard Kipling, Arnold Bennett and others "has seemed somehow irrelevant because it does not appear to be in harmony with the prevailing view of 'the lost generation,' as it came to be called" (148). Paradoxically, the "lost generation" has come to dominate literary history, while many of those authors who were well known in 1914 have been largely relegated to the position of footnotes in the received history of twentieth-century literature.

Feminist approaches to the literature and history of the Great War have yielded other insights, some more useful than others in the analysis of Wharton's war-related works. In what may be the best-known approach to women's writings about the Great War—that developed by Sandra Gilbert and Susan Gubar—the war that was so crippling and disillusioning to men was rewarding for women, providing them with new opportunities and a new sense of liberation. Some women authors, Gilbert and Gubar write, "recount[ed] their feeling that the Great War was the first historical event to allow (indeed, to require) them to use their abilities and to be of use, to escape the private 'staves' of houses as well as the patriarchal oppression of 'high towers' and to enter the public realm of roads, records, maps, machines" (297). Their work in *No Man's Land: Vol. 2, Sexchanges* documents many such cases. But, although they include Wharton in their argument, Wharton's war-related works do not adhere to their paradigm any more fully than they do to the myth delineated by Fussell and Hynes.

In noting Wharton's enthusiasm for the war in works such as *Fighting France* and *The Marne,* Gilbert and Gubar suggest that Wharton was among the women who—thanks to the Great War—finally found a purpose in life (296). But they make certain significant errors in their estimation of Wharton. For instance, they place a discussion of Wharton's establishment of "the first paying workroom in Paris" in a discussion of how previously unpaid women at last found paying work during the war (277)—apparently unaware that Wharton's *ouvroir* employed women who had been working when the war began, but who were put out of work when fashionable ladies began doing for charity what working-class women had previously done for pay (Lewis, *Edith Wharton* 365). Similarly, they note that "even wartime Paris, far from actual combat, made [Wharton] feel as though she were 'reading a great poem on War'" (296)—when in fact Wharton uses this phrase in *Fighting France* to express her awareness that such a sensation, however tempting, was spurious (*Fighting France* 15). They also claim that "Edith Wharton depicted the satisfactions of having 'a son at the front' in her novel of that name" (283). But when Wharton does portray Julia Brant, the mother of the "son at the front," as taking satisfaction in the photograph of her son in uniform, it is only to satirize that satisfaction: Mrs. Brant is posing as the mother who admires her son's bravery under fire, even while she believes that her son George is really at a safe desk job. These points may be minor, but they suggest again that Wharton's position vis-à-vis the war is little understood even when she has been included in major discussions of the war. Noncombatant, she does not fit into Fussell's and Hynes's analyses; and, by her own declaration "not of the number" of women who "found their vocation in nursing the wounded, or in other philanthropic activities" (*Backward Glance* 356), Wharton fails to fit into the Gilbert and Gubar paradigm.

In many ways this is hardly surprising. Although Wharton has been a fascinating subject for feminist critics, she herself was in no easily definable way a feminist. She opposed higher education for women, and when she endowed a scholarship, "specified that the recipient be a male" (Benstock, *No Gifts* 387). She described herself as "entirely out of sympathy with woman-suffrage" and apparently never voted (Benstock, *No Gifts* 265). Although Wharton admires the Frenchwomen she describes in *Fighting France* and *French Ways and Their Meaning*, the English and American women in Wharton's war-related fiction are usually unsympathetic, foolish, and even counterproductive in terms of the war. In fact, Wharton's literary depictions of women in and after the war are often what Gilbert and Gubar expect of male authors. For instance, Gilbert and Gubar write of the "horrors" for male authors of "unleashed female sexuality" resulting from the war (292). Wharton expresses similar fears in her war-related fiction—for example in the character of Mrs. Talkett in *A Son at the Front.* Wharton's attitudes, particularly her attitude toward women, were not liberalized by the war; if anything, they became more conservative.

Nevertheless, much of what Gilbert and Gubar have to say about the war has a place in understanding Wharton's war work. For instance, *A Son at the Front* suggests "the guilt of the female survivor . . . [and] a half-conscious fear that the woman survivor might be in an inexplicable way a perpetrator of some unspeakable crime" (Gilbert and Gubar, *No Man's Land* 264). Even so, Wharton portrays such guilt not through women, but through the characters of older men, men who could not fight. Similarly, the work of some other theoreticians on the relationship between women and war is useful, even when their readings of Wharton are less than insightful. In her 1987 work *Women and War,* for instance, Jean Bethke Elshtain's brief comments on Wharton are dismissive and uninformed,[8] and yet she provides useful analyses of the stereotypes of women and men in wartime, some of which resonate with Wharton's work. She also notes that "Whatever else it may be, war is *interesting.* . . . The soldier has been to hell and back, and that fascinates. . . . Peace does not enthrall as does war" (166). Wharton, too, understood the fascination of war: the events of the war interested her deeply; she was also aware of the war as subject, as material that could fascinate her reading public.

Particularly useful in thinking about the place of Wharton's war-related writings is the work of Dorothy Goldman, Jane Gledhill, and Judith Hattaway. In their study *Women Writers and the Great War,* they note that "when the experiences of two groups"—in this case, men's experience in war and women's—are compared, "two pitfalls to full understanding appear. The first is the temptation to contrast, rather than compare, the experiences. The second is to prioritize one experience as the central, the authentic, the real, and to make the other just that, 'the other'" (26–27). *Women Writers and the Great War* avoids these pitfalls; the authors' consistently astute analysis of Wharton's war-related writings places her work in the context of that of a host of other women writers and emphasizes the validity of women's narratives about the war. Yet even in this context, Wharton's work is something of an anomaly; unlike other women writers, for instance, Wharton's topics were rarely "the predictable ones of the home, childbirth and childcare, and nursing" (Goldman et al. 32). As we will see in chapter two, Wharton navigated her own, rather unusual way between the conventions of men's war writings and those of women.

III. Combatant and Noncombatant, Male and Female

In general, Wharton's war works, like other war-related writings by women, have been overlooked on other grounds besides the aesthetic; or rather, the aesthetic grounds have been inextricably linked to the requirement that Great War authors be male combatants. Hynes has argued that "The notion that only those who had fought could speak the truth about war is one that old soldiers have always had, but it had never been the basis of an aesthetic until the Great War, when for the first time the soldiers who fought it were also the artists who rendered it" (Hynes 158). Because the earliest war poems and war paintings were done by noncombatants, they reflected not the realities of the Great War itself, but rather "inherited images of war" (Hynes 34). As soldiers—particularly British soldiers— came back from the front, they began to decry these images and the civilians who had created them. Hynes notes "the intensity of the loathing that Sassoon expressed for all the people who were not directly engaged in the fighting" (173).

In writing an introduction to the catalog of a soldier-painter's works, Robert Graves seems also to have described what may have been, from a soldier's perspective, Wharton's civilian weakness for the spectacle of war: "'This is no series of superficial war impressions that Mr. Kennington has recorded: here is no genteel amusement at the gaudy slap-dash camouflage on a big howitzer; no discreet civilian wonder at distant shells bursting along a chalk ridge or the long procession of ammunition lorries moving along the pavé road; no old-maidish sympathy for convalescents at the base hospital'" (qtd. in Hynes 199). While Wharton's experiences at the front were far more comprehensive than those mentioned here, Graves nevertheless captures Wharton's tone at points. In her letter of February 28, 1915, to Henry James, Wharton certainly displays "civilian wonder" when she writes: "Suddenly we heard the cannon roaring close by, & a woman rushed in to say that we could see the fighting from the back of a house across the street. We tore over, & there, from a garden we looked across the valley to a height about 5 miles away, where white puffs & scarlet flashes kept springing up all over the dark hillside" (*Letters* 349). Wharton's "rush" not to avoid but to witness battle (albeit at a safe distance) may well have seemed ludicrous to those who fought in the war. This letter expresses not the hardships and horrors of battle, but instead suggests that war is an exciting spectacle, a colorful show. Even when she goes on to remark about the probable casualties, Wharton seems unrealis-

Fig. 1. Edith Wharton and her friend Walter Berry at the front. Abel Faivre cartoon used by permission of Bibliothèque Historique de la Ville de Paris.

tically detached: "And so we saw the reason why there are to be so many wounded at Clermont tonight!" (*Letters* 349). Abel Faivre's cartoon of Wharton and Walter Berry in a chauffeur-driven car at the front (fig. 1) depicts a Wharton much like the civilians Graves describes. With a town standing in ruins behind her, she is well-dressed, stout, and idly curious as she watches distant warfare through her lorgnette. The cartoon's caption, "Ce n'est que ça!" [Is that all?], brands her as uncomprehending.

Although Wharton was better informed than the average civilian—and herself scorned those who felt uninvolved in the war, or who watched it almost as spectators—the belief that "only those who have suffered can imagine truly" (Hynes 199) has caused her war writings to be overlooked. Until quite recently, most discussions of the literature of war have excluded women's writings. Historically, war has been carried on exclusively by men—at least when "war" is, as Claire Tylee explains, defined in the usual terms: "While war was taken to mean 'armed conflict,' with the assumption that physical combat is natural (and even desirable) between males, since to be truly masculine is to be prepared to kill other men, women would hardly be able to write about war. They would be specifically excluded from direct acquaintance with it" (Tylee 13). Some women writers, like Mrs. Humphry Ward, seemed to accept their exclusion and even to glory in the difference of the feminine perspective. After touring munitions factories in England and traveling near the English army's front in France, Mrs. Ward exclaimed "For a woman—a marvelous experience!" (*England's Effort* 9), and told her readers that she hoped to "describe some of its details, and some of the thoughts awakened by them in *a woman's mind*" (9, emphasis added). She accepts the idea that women will think differently from men and, moreover, takes the "woman's" angle as her particular perspective in writing. But Wharton, as we will see, was unwilling to express only "a woman's mind"; she wanted to describe the war, and thus faced what seemed an insurmountable problem: how to write about a topic from which she was "specifically excluded."

Even for male authors the link between war and masculinity could prove vexing. As two military doctors observed, the suppression of emotion required in battle was "an exaggeration of male sex-role expectations in civilian life" (Smith and Pear, qtd. in Showalter 65). Soldiers were expected to be courageous and unemotional; as Elaine Showalter has illustrated, Siegfried Sassoon, during a period in which he had become a pacifist, was persuaded to return to the front by a "delicate and subtle intensification of his fears that pacifism was unmanly and cowardly" (Showalter 66). Pacifism, intellectual doubts about the war, or even a lack of enthusiasm for battle could brand men as unmasculine—an attitude illustrated in some of Wharton's own works. Boys under eighteen were encouraged to look forward to the day they could enlist; men too old to fight sometimes perceived themselves as emasculated or feminized.

For women the situation was both simpler and more complex. Although many women served as nurses or in other positions, their role was clearly secondary: they were largely excluded from what would become a defining event of their century.[9] For, while the Myth of the War held that the war itself was meaningless, it also held that experience of the war—frontline experience in particular—was essential. It seems that many women would have agreed with what Hemingway would write: the war was "one of the major subjects . . . and those writers who had not seen it" were simply missing out on "something quite irreplaceable" (qtd. in Higonnet et al., *Behind the Lines* 14). Many women voiced their belief that they were excluded from a significant, even transcendent, experience solely because of their gender. In *A Journal of Impressions in Belgium*, May Sinclair depicts women who were accepted for an ambulance detachment; rather than shying away from battle, these women, certain that the real experience of war lay at the front, constantly competed for the opportunity to be "under fire"—an experience romanticized as thrilling (see, for example, 49). She writes enthusiastically of war, shelling, and the attraction of "the Greatest Possible Danger" (115) and of "the sheer excitement of the rush through the danger zone" (151). Sinclair confirms that "of all the things that can happen to a woman on a field ambulance the worst is to stay behind" (36). Hynes notes that even members of the English Volunteer Aid Detachment (VAD) felt not so much freed by their opportunities as frustrated because of their sex and their lack of formal nursing education: "The impression that one gets from women's accounts is of self-doubt and self-denigration, of being women who can't do what the trained nurses can do, and who feel inferior to men because they can't be *in* the war as men can" (Hynes 91–92). Even highly qualified women were discouraged from any activity too close to the front lines. When, in 1914, a Scottish doctor named Elsie Inglis offered "fully staffed medical units" to the War Office, she and "the other women doctors were told 'To go home and keep quiet' for the commanding officers 'did not want to be troubled with hysterical women'" (Tylee 7).

Such frustration is further voiced in Rose Macauley's *Non-Combatants and Others*, illustrating that male noncombatants—in this case, a clergyman—often felt the same frustration as women: "War's beastly and abominable to the fighters: but not to be fighting is much more embittering and demoralising, I think. Probably largely because one has more time to think. To have one's friends in danger, and not to be in danger oneself—it fills one with futile rage" (qtd. in Hynes 127). As we will see, such frustration with inactivity was one Wharton expressed herself, both directly, in letters to friends, and indirectly, through the attitudes expressed by a number of her fictional characters. Hynes summarizes the problem faced by women in wartime: "There is nothing like a war for demonstrating to women their inferior status, nothing like the war experiences of men for making clear the exclusion of women from life's great excitements, nothing like war casualties for imposing on women the guiltiness of being alive and well" (379).

For Wharton, the desire to see battle, even to be under fire, expressed itself in almost all her war works—which often portray the front as a semi-mystical place where otherwise impossible transformations occur. As we will see, her view of the front became increasingly realistic as the war dragged on and on, but even in her final war work, *A Son at the Front*, the protagonist John Campton not only sees the maturing and enriching effect the war has on his son George, but also glimpses what his son's life at the front must be like: seeing George with acquaintances from the front, John perceives George as almost radiant. Wharton accepted the fact that she could not fight at the front, but—consonant with her refusal to give up ideals—never gave up the belief that the war could be an ennobling, even transcendent, experience.

In this way Wharton has, again, something in common with a more conservative view of war. English leaders and writers of the period often referred to the "condition of England," a belief that Edwardian England had become too "soft," too pampered, too materialistic—and that the war would purify the English and English culture as a whole (Hynes 13). While Wharton never takes such a large view of the situation, she too believed in the power of the war to shape and ennoble the individuals, both men and women, involved in it. In this way she once again deviates from the standard Myth of the War, which insists on the meaninglessness of the war and its utter failure to provide heroism, much less a transcendent or ennobling experience.

IV. "Not Precisely War Stories"

The passage of time—nearly a century since the outbreak of the Great War—has also had an impact on readers' responses to Wharton's wartime writings. A century that has experienced not only the First but also the Second World War and, in the United States, the tragedy of Vietnam, is unlikely to take the same heroic view of war that many, including Wharton, took in August 1914. The military historian John Keegan's recent history of the Great War opens by stating that "The First World War was a tragic and unnecessary conflict" (3). Wharton would have agreed with "tragic," but certainly would have taken exception to the adjective "unnecessary." In her view, the war was absolutely necessary: Germany had inexcusably invaded Belgium and parts of France and had to be repulsed. Such a view, though simple, was not merely the thought of an oversimplifying civilian: British Field Marshall French and France's General Joffre "had but one thought: to drive the invader from the national territory" (Keegan, *First World War* 190).

Nor would Wharton entertain the notion that the English or French might in some way have contributed to the situation that brought about the war. She was indignant at any such suggestion, and relayed with dismay her friend Walter Berry's sense that "the whole of Germany believes, as one man, the war to have been forced upon it by English ambitions" (*Letters* 344). Her exasperation voiced itself in letters to other friends: to Sally (Sara) Norton, daughter of Harvard professor Charles Eliot Norton, she recommended "'The Anglo-German Problem' by Prof. Sarolea" (*Letters* 339), and to Bernard Berenson she enthused, "Sarolea is A1!" (*Letters* 341). Her excitement is hardly surprising: *The Anglo-German Problem* supported her view of the war as being entirely the fault of Germany (Sarolea 4–5). Moreover, it corroborates her view of the war as a conflict between good systems of government and bad ones. Sarolea writes, "*The present conflict between England and Germany is the old conflict between liberalism and despotism, between industrialism and militarism, between progress and reaction, between the masses and the classes.* The conflict between England and Germany is a conflict, on the one hand, between a nation which believes in political liberty and national autonomy, where the Press is free and where the rulers are responsible to public opinion, and, on the other hand, a nation where public opinion is still muzzled or powerless and where the masses are still under the heel of an absolute government, a reactionary party, a military Junkerism, and a despotic bureaucracy" (xii). Sarolea's book, published in 1912, urged a peace to be "achieved by hard thinking" (276). Further, it described France in terms Wharton would echo in *French Ways and Their Meaning*: "the French people will only fight if they are attacked. No doubt they will fight with grim determination if they are driven into war; . . . but it is certain that France will never be the aggressor" (Sarolea 115).

Wharton's admiration of France in wartime was matched by her frustration, almost from the time of French mobilization, with the United States' refusal to enter the war. After the sinking of the *Lusitania* in May 1915, Wharton was deeply disappointed in the United States' failure to declare war. She could not understand American pacifism, writing to friends that "it is indeed hard for some of us to 'accept America as it seems to be today'" (*Letters* 373). To Sally Norton she wrote, "France continues to be magnificent, & one envies the people who have a real 'patrie.' I'm glad your father didn't live to see what America has become" (*Letters* 380). Wharton, like Henry James, felt so strongly about the war that she commiserated with him in March 1915 about their difficulties with those who did not share the same views: "Yes—I suffer as you do from the inability to communicate with people who are not vibrating to my tune" (26 March 1915, *Wharton Collection* Yale).[10] During a winter coal shortage she parodied President Wilson's stance on the war: "I've adopted as my motto a variant of Wilson's 'Too proud to fight' which runs 'Too cold to sleep'" (*Letters* 389). Much of her wartime writing, including virtually all of her nonfiction and many of her poems, was intended to build U.S. support for military involvement. When President Wilson finally broke off relations with Germany in February 1917, Wharton was both relieved and enthusiastic. She wrote to Berenson, even adopting (half-mockingly, half-affectionately) an American twang: "I 'kinder feel' that intelligent Americans have a right—since last Sunday—to be in the centre of things" (*Letters* 391). After the United States declared war in April 1917 she wrote to Sally Norton, "let us embrace on the glorious fact that we can now hold up our heads with the civilized nations of the world" (5 May 1917, *Wharton Collection* Yale).

As the international character of the list of recipients of Wharton's letters might suggest, her stance in the war also made her somewhat anomalous in terms of her national identity. A resident of France since 1909,[11] she was still a U.S. citizen. As an American citizen living in Paris when the war broke out, she was not required to report for military service; as an American woman, she did not have the opportunity an American man would have had to volunteer his services. She was passionately interested and involved in the war effort from the time of French mobilization—unlike most Americans at home and many expatriates abroad. And she cannot be classed with her literary friends across the Channel. Her life in France was directly and immediately impinged upon in a way that the life of the English was not. She cannot even easily be classed with a majority of other civilians in wartime. Her charitable work not only put her in direct contact with wounded soldiers and refugees; it also allowed her the trips to the front that she describes in vivid letters and in *Fighting France*. Unable to fight in the war, she nevertheless came as close to the war—to seeing, hearing, and experiencing the war—as any noncombatant could come.

One study of the home front during the Great War, however—Jean-Jacques Becker's *The Great War and the French People*—suggests that Wharton's attitudes were more akin to those of the French than to those of the American or the English. Shari Benstock and others have argued her affinity with France;[12] the beginning of the war made clear how fundamentally her attitudes had become permeated by the French view of things—or, at least, by an idealized version of the French perspective. Becker's study suggests that, in many ways, Wharton idealized and simplified the French response to the war. Particularly in *French Ways and Their Meaning*, Wharton presents the French people as unflaggingly heroic, stoic, and united in their efforts to withstand Germany's assault. Becker shows that the French were not always so united: labor strikes occurred during the war; people were distressed emotionally and, as inflation hit hard later in the war, financially; not all women were as willing to sacrifice as Wharton suggests, nor were they unchanged by their experiences of higher wages in the munitions factories during the war.

Yet overall Becker's study confirms the "Frenchness" of Wharton's attitude toward the war and toward the French people themselves. For instance, her finding the war "thrillingly interesting" at its outset (*Letters* 333) may sound cold-hearted in retrospect; but it reflects the French attitude early in the war, when most people assumed that the war would "turn out to be an adventure, cruel perhaps, but of short duration" and that "this martial interlude would be no more than a brief interruption of the normal course of events" (Becker 3). Similarly, Wharton's sense that the Germans were invading *her* home territory accounts for her sense of involvement in the war from its outset; for her unmitigated hostility toward both Germans and German-Americans in *French Ways and Their Meaning*;[13] and for the fact that, with the majority of the French, she never questioned the importance and the necessity of the war—despite France's terrible losses: figured in both absolute and relative terms, France's casualties were the highest of the countries involved in the war (Becker 6). For Wharton, as for the French, there was no English sense of disillusionment as the war dragged on—perhaps because they had fewer illusions to begin with, but more significantly because they knew that the only choice other than continuing the war was to give up their own *patrie*. And, although Becker does not rely on the abstract idealization of France as Wharton does in *French*

Ways, he nevertheless (and in the context of a very focused, frequently statistical analysis of home front morale) concludes that France held out during the Great War because of "the intellectual, spiritual and political leadership of the people" (326). The French "accepted the war because they were part of one nation and they tolerated it for the same reason" (327). Like Wharton, he relies in the end on a sense of the solidity and even the stoicism of French national character. Yet for all this Wharton was not French; although Becker mentions her friend Paul Bourget's literary efforts during the war, Wharton is not cited in his history any more than she is in books treating the English reaction to the war.

Issues of gender, opportunity, and national identity, though important to literary history, did not consciously trouble Edith Wharton during the war. Her concerns were more immediate: the settlement and care of refugees; the maintenance of her own establishment; and as the war went on, the periodic arrangement of restful travel. But as a writer, she was encountering obstacles in some ways new to her. Some stories from early in her career evince what Gilbert and Gubar have entitled "anxiety of authorship," a basic fear many women writers face about their ability to pen anything worthwhile; stories like "April Showers" and "The Pelican," while mocking their heroines' attempts to write publishable novels or deliver intelligent lectures, also demonstrate fears of gender-related incompetence that haunted Wharton in the period of her apprenticeship.[14] Similar fears seem to have re-emerged for Wharton during the war.

As we have seen, women's exclusion from battle led women writers to various solutions. Mrs. Humphry Ward handled this exclusion by emphasizing what she perceived as a woman's perspective of her visits to munitions factories, the British fleet, and sites near the front. Others emphasized their experiences on the home front. For instance, Mildred Aldrich's popular *A Hilltop on the Marne* recounts the activity around her little house in the fall of 1914, focusing on her domestic situation and her occasional interaction with soldiers. Similarly, *Scribner's Magazine* published Mary King Waddington's "In War Times" in January 1915; this nonfiction account tells the story of an American expatriate woman's retreat from Paris to the countryside when Paris was threatened by the Germans. Such accounts, though interesting in themselves, did not seem to attract Wharton as material for her own pen. In fact, she specifically dismisses the work of Mary King Waddington in letters to friends, protesting to Henry James at the end of one of her letters describing a trip to the front that "This reads like one of Mme. Waddington's letters . . . but I'm so awed by all I've seen I can only prattle" (*Letters* 350). In a letter describing the

Fourth of July, 1918, to Minnie Jones, she throws off the remark that "I can only hope that old Mary Waddington isn't one of your regular correspondents, & hasn't intervened *here* too!—" (*Letters* 406). Waddington's work, Wharton implies, is stylistically weak, her writing akin to the "prattle" Wharton fears she has produced; the letter to Minnie Jones implies that Waddington is something of a competitor for her sister-in-law's attention. In either case, Wharton was not impressed with such women's writing.

More importantly, however, Wharton seems to reject the idea that women's accounts of life on the home front might constitute war writing. By the same token, she seems to accept the standard definition of "war" as fighting in battle or in the trenches, or the strategizing that went on at headquarters. Indeed, as we will see in the next chapter, the "real business" of war was something she felt excluded from—but also respected profoundly. Apart from her occasional articles about her charities for newspapers, in which she wrote from her perspective as the head of those charities, she generally wrote from a position that was as close to the lines of battle as she could get without actually stepping over them. *Fighting France* emphasized her close contacts with the front; her three short stories, like *A Son at the Front*, would approach the front itself, but always remain the story of civilians—American expatriates, to be specific—who themselves had no battle experience. Only in *The Marne* would she venture in imagination into battle; but even that venture is a short one, and most of that tale, like her other work, focuses on American expatriates in wartime France. In this way she negotiated between the demands of her profession and those of her conscience: she came as close to battle as she, a female noncombatant, could without intruding into territory from which she sensed herself excluded, both literally and, to a large extent, psychologically. Her respect for the trenches and the front lines, and for the men who fought there, was such that she seems to have felt that she could not have written about that territory either authentically or authoritatively.

While respecting the unstated definition of war writing, Wharton came close to challenging it when describing her war-related works. Writing to Charles Scribner, for example, she hedges: the "four or five short stories" are "not precisely war stories, but on subjects suggested by the war" (*Letters* 357). Wharton's phrase "not precisely" creates ambiguity: the stories are not what most people might consider war stories; but certainly stories "suggested by the war" could logically, if not conventionally, be called war stories. Similarly, in correspondence with her editor Rutger B. Jewett of Appleton, she noted that *A Son at the Front* "was never intended to be a 'war novel,' in the military sense of the term" (24 July 1920, *Wharton*

Collection Yale). Here she seems first to accept the term "war novel," though she also challenges it implicitly by putting it in quotation marks and by further defining what is usually meant by that expression: a military novel. She goes on to explain what *A Son at the Front* is, and in doing so perhaps suggests a broader definition of the term "war novel": "It is ... a study of Americans living in Paris during the war and re-acting to it in various ways" (24 July 1920, *Wharton Collection* Yale). Claire Tylee has suggested that "women's literary responses to war ... tend to be much wider and more subtle in scope than battle-tales, since they are interested in the social context of belligerence and its connection with personal relations and the quality of ordinary life" (13). Through her depiction of war's "connection with personal relations" and "ordinary life," Wharton was helping to create what might be called the "home front novel"—perhaps as important a subgenre of the "war novel" as the more recognized "military novel." Only recently have literary critics begun to pursue the question of what, exactly, defines a "war novel." One critic has asked, "At what point does a novel which takes account of the war become a novel *of* the war? ... Should novels which concentrate primarily upon aspects of the war's effect at home be included, or novels concerned with how the war shaped post-war life?" (Parfitt, qtd. in Goldman et al. 93). While some critics have asserted that "the response" to these questions "must be a resounding yes" (Goldman et al. 93), Wharton herself was less sure. Certainly there is, as yet, no generally accepted widening of the definition of the "war novel," however arbitrary its traditional boundaries have been.[15]

The war was a watershed not only in Wharton's life but in her career as a writer. Even in terms of the literary stature of Wharton's works, the war marks a sharp divide. Her most-studied works are *The House of Mirth, Ethan Frome, The Custom of the Country, Summer,* and *The Age of Innocence.* The first three are from before the war years; *Summer* is from the middle of the war; *The Age of Innocence* is the only postwar work that receives considerable analysis, and that is rarely in terms of the war. The works from the postwar period—a period both productive and lucrative for Wharton—have not garnered the same critical attention nor the same kind of admiration as those from before the war; her style and choice of subject matter changed in the postwar period, and her later writing has often been charged, overtly or tacitly, with lacking subtlety. Several reasons have been offered for this: Wharton's long residence in France, which caused her to be out of touch with the Americans she portrayed; her writing at greater speed to keep up with her increased expenses, including the demands of the new income tax.[16] But it is also likely that her experience of the war years led her to alter her choice of subjects and the manner in which she treated them.

Wharton herself may have been surprised at her productivity in the postwar years. In her memoir she wrote: "After 'A Son at the Front' I intended to take a long holiday—perhaps to cease from writing altogether. It was growing more and more evident that the world I had grown up in and been formed by had been destroyed in 1914, and I felt incapable of transmuting the raw material of the after-war world into a work of art" (*Backward Glance* 369–70). How did one write in the wake of a war so devastating that some, Wharton included, believed it had nearly obliterated civilization? And if one chose to go on writing, were there advantages to topics that were less subtle, more obvious—or more important than, say, the death of a Lily Bart or the emotional paralysis of an Ethan Frome? In Wharton's 1915 story "Coming Home," a character named Macy Greer exclaims, "Hang it! This war's going to teach us not to be afraid of the obvious" (244). To some extent the postwar works can be described in Greer's terms: Wharton turned her hand to topics and styles that were more "obvious," which may account both for her financial success in this period and for the later disregard of literary critics.

Edith Wharton's writings from the war reveal the struggles she underwent in those years—a struggle between an old, romantic vision of war and a new antiheroic one; between a sense of the need to change and a reluctance or even inability to do so; between the need to depict the fine and subtle and the need to describe the situation of France in terms that would move her readers to action; between a need to hold on to a comfortable and increasingly idealized old world and the need to accept a new world in which the old standards no longer seemed to matter. As early as November 1914 Wharton glimpsed the vast changes the war would bring about. To Gaillard Lapsley she wrote, "There are so many people who seem nowadays like left-overs—dead flies, shaken down out of a summer hotel window curtain! We shall never lodge in *that* summer hotel again" (*Letters* 342). As the war dragged on years longer than anyone had anticipated, she knew that the old reality would not simply reassert itself once the war had ended. On the contrary, she noted in *A Backward Glance* that the Great War had obliterated the world of her youth—a world which, as harshly as she had satirized it in the prewar period, she now regretted and mourned. No writer could live through such experiences without being profoundly changed.

2

A Shaken Reality

Writings from Early in the War (1914–1915)

It is all thrillingly interesting, but very sad to see one's friends going to the slaughter.
There is so much to say that I won't begin now—but, oh, *think* of this time last year! Hasn't it shaken all the foundations of reality for you?
Edith Wharton to Bernard Berenson, August 11, 1914 (*Letters* 333)

I.

Writing to Bernard Berenson ten days after the mobilization of France on August 1, 1914, Wharton revealed much about her early reactions to the war. The first sentence quoted above exhibits her ambivalence: enthusiasm mixed with fear of loss. At the outset of the war she finds it not simply interesting but "thrillingly interesting"—perhaps to the point that makes the remainder of the sentence ("but very sad . . .") impossible to take at face value. Indeed, Wharton's use of the stock phrase "going to the slaughter" reflects the fact that Wharton had not yet felt any personal sense of loss.

If the first part of this letter sounds the note of war-interest, the next sounds the ground-note for much of Wharton's writing from early in the war: "Hasn't it shaken all the foundations of reality for you?" Both a sense of shaken reality and a disturbed sense of the simultaneous unreality of war manifest themselves repeatedly in the different works Wharton wrote during the year after the mobilization of France. During this period Wharton's usual life was disrupted; like many others, she had to come to terms with the fact that the war was going to be a long interruption in her normal life, rather than the brief, glorious episode many at first expected it to be. In August 1914 she found the war "thrillingly interesting"; by October

1915, following the death of her former servant Henri, she cried out, "Oh, this long horror!" (*Letters* 361). These two letters mark Wharton's gradual acceptance of the reality of war, as well as her shift from excitement to horror and fatigue; during the fourteen months that separated them, Wharton saw much that moved her to write and to act. Her observation of the French under mobilization and the staunchness of French civilians in wartime led her to write "The Look of Paris" in the early months of the war for *Scribner's Magazine*; as Belgian refugees flooded into Paris during the fall of 1914, she became intensely and intimately involved in the organizations that would care for thousands of displaced people.

As Wharton's daily activities altered, so did her writing: the well-known novelist and short story writer turned her hand successfully to journalism, occasional poetry, and the writing of charitable reports in her attempts to help the refugees and to promote American involvement in the war. Wharton's writings from this period are various in genre and tone, unlike the more decidedly propagandistic works—*French Ways and Their Meaning* and *The Marne*—that she would produce later in the war. Wharton's poems from 1915 would generally express the idealism that Wharton felt in the early months of the war—as well as the sorrow. Other early writings, particularly *Fighting France* and the short story "Coming Home," reflect Wharton's sense of a shaken reality that, as she progressed through 1914 and 1915, gradually gave way to a sense of an altered reality. This, in turn, raised for Wharton, as it did for so many others, the questions of how and what one could write in light of the devastation that had occurred.

II. Fascination and Horror

Fighting France: From Dunkerque to Belfort was first published serially in *Scribner's Magazine* and then in book format in November 1915 (Benstock, *No Gifts* 315). Ninety years after the events it describes, *Fighting France* remains a vivid and evocative record of the war—perhaps largely because, although it is decidedly pro-French, it is not a doctrinaire work but a descriptive one: one that describes both the scenes Wharton witnessed and her own reactions to life at and near the front during the early months of the war.

Prominent within the book is the sense of the "shaken . . . reality" she described to Berenson. The unreality of war pervades *Fighting France*; Wharton describes vividly the numerous instances that created this unsettling feeling. In one case, driving back toward Paris from the eastern front, Wharton notes that all mileage posts had been defaced, whether by French natives or German soldiers she could not say. She remarks, "It was the strangest of sensations to find ourselves in a chartless wilderness within sixty or seventy miles of Paris" (83). Perhaps the most acute moment of unreality comes when she and her companions find themselves in the town of Châlons after curfew, without lodgings on a cold dark night. Wharton chances upon an army staff attaché whom she happened to know from the Paris literary world, Jean-Louis Vaudoyer.[1] When he whispers the password to her she reflects, "I stood there in the pitch-black night, suddenly unable to believe that I was I, or Châlons Châlons, or that a young man who in Paris drops in to dine with me and talk over new books and plays, had been whispering a password in my ear to carry me unchallenged to a house a few streets away!" (*Fighting France* 88–89) Recounting this incident in a letter to Henry James, Wharton remarks more directly, "I suddenly refused to believe that *any* of it was true, or happening to *me*, or that a nice boy who dines with me & sends me chocolates for Nouvel An, was whispering a *pass-word* to me, & adding, "Quand vous le dites au chauffeur, prenez garde qu'une sentinelle ne vous entende pas" [when you say it to the chauffeur, be careful that a sentinel doesn't hear you]—It was no use trying to keep up the pretense of reality any longer!" (*Letters* 353) Continuing her public version of the incident in *Fighting France*, Wharton remarks that this new reality seems so unreal that "for a blissful moment . . . the whole huge and oppressive and unescapable fact of the war . . . slipped away like a torn cobweb" (89). The prewar reality reasserts itself: the unreal seems real, while the real seems insubstantial. Yet "The next morning dispelled that vision" (89). The old reality is clearly gone, yet the new one, the war-reality, persists in seeming fundamentally unreal.

In fact, Wharton's sense of altered reality is so difficult for her to accept that she relates experience after experience where she must learn anew that the old reality no longer obtains. For instance, after a glimpse of German soldiers, she writes that "The wooded cliff swarmed with 'them,' . . . yet all about us was silence, and the peace of the forest. Again, for a minute, I had the sense of an all-pervading, invisible power of evil. . . . Then the reaction of unbelief set in, and I felt myself in a harmless ordinary glen" (133). Even Wharton's conclusion here illustrates the difficulty of grasping the changes war had wrought. If "the sense of an all-pervading, invisible power of evil" is an exaggeration, so too is her sense that she is "in a harmless, ordinary glen"—the glen may be ordinary, but it is not harmless. A similar scene emerges later in *Fighting France*, when the prewar Wharton who loved her picnic luncheons attempts to settle down to eat on a grassy slope. After Wharton and her companions seat themselves, a French soldier tells them they must move out of sight of "the lines": "We retreated hurriedly and unpacked our luncheon-basket on the more sheltered side of the ridge. As we sat there in the grass, swept by a great mountain breeze full of the scent of thyme and myrtle, while the flutter of birds, the hum of insects, the still and busy life of the hills went on all about us in the sunshine, the pressure of the encircling line of death grew more intolerably real. It is not in the mud and jokes and every-day activities of the trenches that one most feels the damnable insanity of war; it is where it lurks like a mythical monster in scenes to which the mind has always turned for rest" (200). This scene exemplifies the unreality of the war: an ordinary picnic—complete with luncheon-basket, mountain breezes, and the natural life of the hillside—which abruptly threatens to bring German military might down on the French forces. Here Wharton's sense of unreality manifests itself as the "damnable insanity of war," the insanity that, at the very point at which she acknowledges that it is "intolerably real," turns a pastoral scene into the lair of a "mythical monster."

In choosing the trope of the "mythical monster," Wharton illustrates the extent to which her mind, even in wartime, is imbued with literary models. Within the unreality of war Wharton turns to mythology and to romance—a genre that by definition describes the unreal, and yet that provides a reassuringly familiar model for contextualizing and thus comprehending the war. The romantic model emerges repeatedly in her descriptions of war activity behind the lines.

In fact, one central tension within *Fighting France* is that between the unremittingly realistic and horrible on one hand and the reassuringly romantic on the other. In the first chapter, for instance, Wharton remarks that after Paris had undergone six months of war, the nights were pitch-black, and "the days are less remarkable and less romantic" (31). She notes that "Almost all the early flush and shiver of romance is gone" (31). Yet the passage that precedes this conclusion is an extremely romantic, even mysterious description of the city at night: "In the narrow streets of the Rive Gauche the darkness is even deeper, and the few scattered lights in courts or 'cités' create effects of Piranesi-like mystery. The gleam of the chestnut-roaster's brazier at a street corner deepens the sense of an old adventurous Italy, and the darkness beyond seems full of cloaks and conspiracies" (30). Wharton remarks that "observers from other countries" may still find that the city appears romantic, but judging from her description it seems that a vestige of romance remains even for her—despite her claims to the contrary.

In other passages as well Wharton depicts the war as a romantic endeavor. She tells how the war has succeeded in "transforming [one] lifeless little town into a romantic stage" (146), a sense of romance that, apparently, is not altered by her equally clear vision of "all the sordid shabby rear view of war" (149). Watching a "river of war" wind down a road, Wharton describes it in decidedly romantic terms: "Cavalry, artillery, lancers, infantry, sappers and miners, trench-diggers, road-makers, stretcher-bearers, they swept on as smoothly as if in holiday order. Through the dust, the sun picked out the flash of lances and the gloss of chargers' flanks. . . . Close as the men were, they seemed allegorically splendid: as if, under the arch of the sunset, we had been watching the whole French army ride straight into glory . . ." (139–40). Numerous details here—the "holiday order," the "gloss of chargers' flanks," the sense of allegory and of immortal splendor and glory—can only be called romantic. Wharton's literary sensibility even leads her to describe riders as looking as if they had come from some "wild northern legend" and to compare the sound of bugles to "the call of Roland's horn" (176). It was doubtless reassuring to view scenes of war not as reality but as illustrations of Nordic legends or the *Chanson de Roland.* Yet at the far end of the spectrum from these reassuringly romantic visions was the reality of war, which, Wharton found, was often a reality of horror.

Like the conservative English poet John Masefield and the British propagandist Lord Northcliffe, as we have seen, Wharton used medieval and romantic imagery to make the war understandable, familiar, comfortable, and heroic. But Wharton was also aware of the danger of believing that what she saw was only an illustration of some "great poem on War"—a different matter from "facing its realities" (15). Other passages in *Fighting France* acknowledge that war itself, or at least this war, was different from romantic literary representations. Though Wharton often employs terminology suggestive of romance and myth, she also insists that her readers "picture" a visual reality that had nothing to do with the supposed romance of war. In describing the activity in a little town held partly by the French and partly by the Germans, for instance, she remarks that "It was one of those strange and contradictory scenes of war that bring home to the bewildered looker-on the utter impossibility of picturing how the thing *really happens*" (208–9).

Yet even as Wharton insists on the language of "seeing" the war, she rarely depicts the horrors of war in detail; even more difficult than describing to others what she has herself seen is "picturing" what she has not. Wharton repeatedly approaches imagining the details of war, particularly its effect on civilians, only to retreat. She writes, for instance, of French civilians who had lived "under the menace of reprisals too hideous to picture" (193). Of one group of refugees she notes, "Their faces are unmistakable and unforgettable. No one who has ever caught that stare of dumb bewilderment—or that look of concentrated horror, full of the reflection of flames and ruins—can shake off the obsession of the Refugees" (33). Similarly, she writes later of a long line of refugees: "[I]t is a grim sight to watch them limping by, and to meet the dazed stare of eyes that have seen what one dare not picture" (50). That "look of concentrated horror," those "eyes that have seen what one dare not picture"—Wharton is both aware of the grim realities of war and reluctant to "picture" completely what war victims have experienced: not because such a thing is beyond imagination, but because, as her verb choice points out, one "dare not"—an issue she would return to in her story "Coming Home."

As these examples illustrate, Wharton's contact with the realities of war diminished the initial enthusiasm that she had expressed in her letter to Berenson. Yet within *Fighting France*—that is, within the early months of the war—that fascination recurs as she returns repeatedly to a sense of the romance and heroism of war. One passage in *Fighting France* illustrates this vividly. Immediately after describing the horror of seeing the "éclopés" (refugees), Wharton returns to the war as romantic vision. She remarks, "If one could think away the 'éclopés' in the streets and the wounded in the hospitals, Châlons would be an invigorating spectacle" (50). She then proceeds to do such "think[ing] away," going on to describe the "inexhaustibly interesting" (51) scene at the best Châlons restaurant. Putting the refugees firmly behind her, she describes in detail the variety of officers' uniforms and the lively activity of the restaurant in a way that seems almost heartless, considering what she has just described. At moments, the war remains "thrillingly interesting" to Wharton.

The tension between romanticism and realism, fascination and horror is mirrored further in Wharton's attitude toward her trips to the front. Although Wharton shies away from the horrors of war, she often expresses a desire to witness, even experience, the war firsthand. The "reprisals too hideous to picture," the events "one dare not picture" did not deter Wharton from traveling as close to the front as she could and from glorying in such travel. In a June 1915 letter to Charles Scribner, Wharton refers to her travels to the front as "eight days of wonderful adventures" (*Letters* 356). In the words of one critic, Wharton "was a lifelong, inveterate, and insatiable traveler."[2] She opened her 1908 travelogue *A Motor-Flight Through France* with the enthusiastic declaration that "The motor-car has restored the romance of travel" (1); only six years later, the motor-car was carrying her toward the horrors of war, and yet her enthusiasm for trips to the front equaled her enthusiasm for travel in times of peace.

III. The "Real Business" of War

Fighting France reveals that Wharton felt a constant, almost nagging fear not of war itself, but of missing out on some kind of "real" experience of the war. In Wharton's 1913 novel *The Custom of the Country*, a minor character remarks that American women miss out on "the real business of life" in America: money and financial affairs. In a wartime letter to her sister-in-law Minnie Jones, Wharton remarked similarly that "People in America don't seem to understand that at the most critical period of a terrible war it is hard to get the attention of the War Office for any matter outside the real business of the nation" (*Letters* 366). For Wharton, the "real business" of war was on the front lines, and her war writings reflect her fear that, as a woman and a civilian, she was excluded from this epoch-making event. Wharton, like many other women writers—among them May Sinclair, Enid Bagnold, and others—experienced not liberation but frustration during the war years. As we saw in chapter one, even women in the Volunteer Aid Detachment, women taking some of the most active roles available to them during the war, felt a sense of "self-doubt and self-denigration" and of "inferior[ity] to men because they can't be *in* the war as men can" (Hynes 91–92). For many women, Samuel Hynes concludes, "the war brought feelings of helplessness, uselessness, and guilt" (92).

Wharton's war-related writing, both fiction and nonfiction, is haunted by such feelings, despite the fact that she describes herself repeatedly as the exception to the rule that women and civilians must keep away from the front. In one letter to Henry James she temporarily elides her civilian status, boasting that she is going "off again to see other military scenes inaccessible to the civilian" (*Letters* 356). In another, she notes that she is going "to see the little corner of reconquered Alsace, which no one has been allowed to visit as yet" (*Letters* 356). She is thrilled at being told at Verdun "Vous êtes la première femme qui soit venue à Verdun" [You are the first woman who has come to Verdun] (*Letters* 350). Wharton's thrill in these situations demonstrates her fear of missing "the real business" of war—that is, she is thrilled to find herself such an exception because it means that she is *not* missing the real thing. In 1917, in response to Bernard Berenson's praise for *Summer*, she would write to him, "And, oh, how it does agreeably titillate the author's vanity to have his pet phrases quoted to him!" "Him" here refers to herself, and at the foot of the letter she has written "You see I'm getting a little confused about my sex!" (*Letters* 398–99). So here, as she goes off to "military scenes inaccessible to the civilian," Wharton has implicitly turned herself into a member of the military she seems to long for.

Wharton's exclusion from the war not only caused her personal frustration; it also created problems for her as a writer. The individual chapters in *Fighting France* were first published as articles in *Scribner's Magazine*, and examining the articles in their original context suggests that war-related writing was, for Wharton, a matter of careful navigation between the Scylla of women's sentimental writing and the action-packed, "I was there" Charybdis of men's war writing. In the May 1915 *Scribner's*, the issue that carried the first of the articles that would become *Fighting France*, the only other war-related item is a story entitled "Sinews of War." Although the title might lead readers to expect a tough nonfiction tale about combat at the front, the story is instead a rather sentimental piece of fiction about the Austrian army's mistreatment of a peasant's two fine horses. The story includes no account of the war—even the horses die of neglect offstage—and it concludes with the peasant exclaiming of his horses, "So! They were good enough to be killed . . . but not to feed nor to water." He goes on to "lift up an exceeding bitter cry and curse the lord of war" (635). Though it is possible that the author—a woman named Annie Eliot Trumbull—meant this story to echo the war's huge human losses, it is far more about the mistreatment of animals than it is about the war: it addresses none of the issues the war had so rapidly created.

Wharton's second war-related article came out in *Scribner's* the next month, June 1915. Again, the only other war-related item was a short story by a woman: "Made in Germany," by Temple Bailey. This story does mention some details of the war—the tales of atrocities, the burning of Louvain, the bombing of Reims Cathedral. But the story itself is set in Boston and concerns the war's effect on the budding romance of a New England shopkeeper, Dorothea Dwight, and her German boarder, Otto von Puttkamer. The mounting tension between the two is exacerbated by

Dorothea's friendship with a Frenchwoman, Mme. Papin. In the end, however, the romance is saved by Dorothea's sense of historical relativism. She reflects that in the Revolutionary War "England had been wrong, dead wrong. And as for France, had there ever been any war-madness to equal the war-madness of Napoleon! Should Germany stand alone among the nations in the scarlet of military sins?" (718). The well-timed death of Herr von Puttkamer's beloved brother also helps mend the rift between the two—a mending on which even Mme. Papin gives her blessing, as she tells Otto: "[Dorothea] will comfort you. She loves you. And where death is—there are no—enemies" (718). Clearly we are a long way from the front lines here. Indeed, the war begins to seem like nothing more than a device for separating and reuniting lovers—a staple of sentimental fiction.

Since Wharton had long disdained sentimental fiction, such models appealed little to her. But neither could she write in the vein taken up by most men writing about the war. Even before the publication of famous realist works like Henri Barbusse's antiheroic novel *Le Feu* in 1916, male authors were writing in detail about the front lines. Besides carrying the series of war-related articles by Wharton, *Scribner's* carried regular articles by two male correspondents, Richard Harding Davis (son of Rebecca Harding Davis) and E. Alexander Powell. Although Wharton would eventually travel to the front lines, she would be allowed to do so only where there was no real danger of shelling. By contrast, Davis and Powell were frequently on the front lines. Their writing has nothing to do with sentimental fiction, but instead bursts with facts, communiqués, adventures, and tales of the truth about the war.

In "'To Be Treated as a Spy,'" for instance, Davis recounts his adventures on the German side of the front lines when he pursues a lead for his story too far. Even today, his narration of this event is exciting. It also emphasizes what would become the *sine qua non* of war writing accepted as such: the belief that the author "had to be there" to understand what the war was really about because the truth was, essentially, unbelievable. Davis stresses at one point that the circumstances under which he traveled back to Belgian soil were so bizarre that they created "a situation I would not have used in fiction" (714). Similarly, Powell writes of the British army in his article "On the British Battle Line": "you cannot appreciate what it is like or what it is accomplishing by reading about it; you have to see it for yourself, as I did" (457). In May 1915, the cover of *Scribner's* highlighted "The Look of Paris in War Time by Edith Wharton"; in the October 1915 issue—which also carried an article by Wharton—pride of place went to

"'Joffre'—by Captain X—of the French Staff." "Captain X" was the ultimate insider, and of necessity male: a man who had met Joffre personally,
who could recount choice military anecdotes, who could speak with authority on the French situation and the movements of the French army. He
too implicitly emphasizes the exclusively masculine nature of war, writing
of the first Battle of the Marne: "Those were soul-thrilling days. We who
lived through them, in actual contact with them, knew that they marked a
dividing line in our experience, and that henceforward all we did and were
would gravitate about that central moment of our lives" (396).

Because Wharton generally accepted the idea of war as that which was
carried out on the front lines, her idea of war writing did not permit her to
settle for sentimentalized tales—in fact, she would satirize such sentimentality after the war in her short fiction "Writing a War Story." Moreover,
she seems to have accepted as well the unstated principle that only those
who had seen the front lines could legitimately write about them; on only
one occasion—at the end of The Marne—would she deviate from that
principle. Yet her impulse was that of the reporter: to go to the scene of
action—the same impulse that drove Davis to return to Reims Cathedral
during its destruction "to see if during the night it had been further mutilated" regardless of the fact that "Around it shells were still falling" (With
the Allies 133). In August 1914, Wharton was in England when the Germans nearly succeeded in capturing Paris. Rather than feeling relief at her
escape from danger, Wharton bemoaned her absence from the French capital: "I regret very much not having been in Paris during the week of panic,"
she later wrote to a friend (Letters 339). For Wharton the challenge was to
write as legitimately as she could about the war without sentimentalizing—and without claiming experience she had not had. Her choice of
genre in Fighting France—nonfiction prose—indicates the kind of war
writing that seemed most important and most authentic to her.

Wharton's first article about the war, "The Look of Paris," sets the pattern that Wharton would follow in most of her other war-related writings.
The article describes life in a Paris where soldiers are mobilized and tour-
ists immobilized. Wharton's abilities as a sharp observer of the social scene
helped her create an evocative portrait of the city in wartime, yet her article is haunted by absence: the absence of the army that is, she knows, off
fighting—carrying on the real war—in a location neither she nor any
other Parisian can see. She avoids the errors of other women writers: she
does not sentimentalize the war. But, sagely, she makes little attempt to
relay news from the front. The closest she comes is in her description of

Belgian refugees, the "great army of the Refugees" (*Fighting France* 33) as she calls them, perhaps aware that this is as close as she will come to seeing an army in action. She takes the risk of using her imaginative powers to re-create the details of war that the refugees have experienced, writing of their "memory of burning homes and massacred children and young men dragged to slavery, of infants torn from their mothers, old men trampled by drunken heels and priests slain while they prayed beside the dying" (34).

Such a passage may seem to transgress the unwritten law that women not depict war. But even here the description is secondhand, drawn probably from early reports of atrocities. Nor does Wharton linger long on this half-imagined scene. She quickly returns her discussion to events she has herself seen, and within three pages she is cheerfully reporting that Parisian women—"however valiant, however tried, however suffering and however self-denying"—are "begin[ning] to shop again" (37). This she reports not sardonically—as Wilfred Owen or Siegfried Sassoon might do—but as an index of the health and morale of the French. Her essay closes with a glimpse of wounded French soldiers, their faces "not gay. Neither are they sad, however. They are calm, meditative, strangely purified and matured" (41). As she would do in much of her fiction, Wharton is laying out her own line here. She is not sentimentalizing the war, but neither is she claiming the kind of experience to which she could not have access. Avoiding the typically female literary treatment of the war, she also skirts the masculine treatment—respecting the unwritten rule that only those who had seen combat (or stalemate in the trenches) had the right to write about it.

For Wharton, writing about the war meant getting as close to war zones as she could and depicting what she saw for her readers. In some cases, her reports were not news to readers of *Scribner's:* her depiction of the bombed and burned Reims Cathedral, for instance, was published only after Richard Harding Davis's report written from his experience of being in Reims during the bombardment—and after another author had written a general article deploring the destruction of the cathedral. Surprisingly, Wharton does not use the vision of a shattered Reims as a soapbox for lambasting the Germans, but instead depicts the cathedral as having a strange beauty: "in the dull provincial square there stands a structure so strange and beautiful that one must search the Inferno, or some tale of Eastern magic, for words to picture the luminous unearthly vision. . . . The interweaving of colour over the whole blunted bruised surface recalls the metallic tints, the peacock-and-pigeon iridescences, the incredible mingling of red, blue, umber and yellow of the rocks along the Gulf of Aegina. And the wonder of the impression is increased by the sense of its evanescence; the knowledge that this is the beauty of disease and death. . . . [T]he Cathedral of Rheims is glowing and dying before us like a sunset . . ." (*Fighting France* 185–86). This powerful piece of descriptive prose relies, like other passages we have examined, on literary models—in this case, Dante's *Inferno* and unspecified "tale[s] of Eastern magic"—which make the unfamiliar familiar, or at least strangely comprehensible. Moreover, this passage, like Wharton's portrait of soldiers' faces "strangely purified and matured" (41), suggests that although Wharton did not sentimentalize the war, she did believe in its transformative power—its strange ability to ennoble.

Wharton's belief in the war's power to ennoble pervades *Fighting France;* as we will see, it is a belief that resurfaces in many of her other war-related writings. Wharton frequently notes such transformations by emphasizing the changes in people's faces: "I often pass in the street women whose faces look like memorial medals—idealized images of what they were in the flesh. And the masks of some of the men . . . look like the bronzes of the Naples Museum, burnt and twisted from their baptism of fire" (38–39). Wharton implicitly stresses both the similarity of women's and men's experiences and the difference: the women's faces are "idealized images[,]" ennobled by their deprivation and sacrifice at home; the men's, showing the marks of their experience at the front, have undergone a "baptism of fire." Yet both are museum pieces, beautiful and fascinating, as well as tokens of a heightened spiritual state. Wharton frequently portrayed the war as an ennobling force in both her fiction and her nonfiction—perhaps most notably in her portrayal of George Campton in *A Son at the Front.*

While such a view seems naive to many readers at the beginning of the twenty-first century, for Wharton it is part of the structure that helped her grasp and accept the war. She deplored the huge human cost of the war, but like most people undergoing trials, she managed to find a paradigm for what had been previously unthinkable, but which now had come to seem inevitable, unalterable. Wharton presents this transformation as the inevitable effect of the nature of war itself: "War is the greatest of paradoxes: the most senseless and disheartening of human retrogressions, and yet the stimulant of qualities of soul which, in every race, can seemingly find no other means of renewal" (*Fighting France* 53). Turning to yet another literary model—*War and Peace*—Wharton reassures herself of the validity of this paradox: "It is one of the most detestable things about war that everything connected with it, except the death and ruin that result, is such a heightening of life, so visually stimulating and absorbing. 'It was gay and terrible,' is the phrase forever recurring in 'War and Peace'" (*Fighting France* 146). Had she written *Fighting France* a year later, she might have quoted William Butler Yeats as well: "All changed, changed utterly: / A terrible beauty is born." For Wharton, the French took on a "terrible beauty," a beauty that allowed her to make sense of the war, as soon as the Great War began.[3]

Some of the transformations Wharton describes are more eerie than noble. Wharton writes of a curé at a church in Ménil-sur-Belvitte, a town near Nancy. There, she notes, the curé has turned one room of the parsonage into a chapel:

> everything in it has something to do with the battle that took place among the [local] wheat-fields. The candelabra on the altar are made of "Seventy-five" shells, the Virgin's halo is composed of radiating bayonets. . . . But the chapel-museum is only a surplus expression of the curé's impassioned dedication to the dead. His real work has been done on the battle-field, where row after row of graves . . . have been fenced about, symmetrically disposed, planted with flowers and young firs, and marked by the names and death-dates of the fallen. . . . This particular man was made to do this particular thing: he is a born collector, classifier, and hero-worshipper. In the hall of the "presbytère" hangs a case of carefully-mounted butterflies, the result, no doubt, of an earlier passion for collecting. His "specimens" have changed, that is all: he has passed from butterflies to men[.] (114–15)

Wharton seems genuinely to admire this man, whom she introduces as "the happiest being on earth: a man who has found his job" (113). Yet the macabre details—the halo of bayonets, the mentality of a collector of dead men—depict the strangeness of the altered reality the war had created.

Reading *Fighting France* nearly a century after its composition and, more significantly, after literary views of World War I writing have been firmly established, one is struck by the fact that it is very much a book without a thesis. It does not declare "war is glorious," but neither does it declare "war is horrible." Paradoxically, this very inconsistency is what keeps a reader reading. One has the sense of Wharton describing what she saw and felt without leaping on her soapbox to editorialize, as she would in

French Ways and Their Meaning, a book in which France represents all things good, Germany all things evil, and U.S. soldiers had best appreciate the culture they had come to defend. The tone of *Fighting France* is richer and more varied. Wharton's responses to the aspects of the war she witnessed were fresher, less doctrinaire than they would be later in the war.

Even Wharton's attitude toward the Germans varies somewhat in *Fighting France;* she cannot establish a new reality that contains her reactions toward them. Largely, she tends simultaneously to romanticize and vilify the Germans. She refers to them as "the Beast" (see 94, for example), calling the destructiveness of their advance through France "a piously planned and methodically executed human deed" (98). In another passage she observes the destruction of the house of General Lyautey, whom she describes as "Germany's worst enemy in Africa" (116). In the village of Crévic only his house was destroyed, and Wharton describes the destruction sardonically as "this typical tale of German thoroughness and German chivalry" (116).

Yet occasionally Wharton seems surprisingly neutral about German soldiers. Touring trenches and abandoned farmhouses being used as military outposts, Wharton comments again on the fundamental unreality of the landscape she is covering. But she also implies the basic similarity of French and German soldiers: "I only knew that we had come out of a black labyrinth into a gutted house among fruit-trees, where soldiers were lounging and smoking, and people whispered as they do about a death-bed. Over a break in the walls I saw another gutted farmhouse close by in another orchard: it was an enemy outpost, and silent watchers in helmets of another shape sat there watching on the same high shelves. . . . And then, little by little, there came over me the sense of that mute reciprocal watching from trench to trench: the interlocked stare of innumerable pairs of eyes, stretching on, mile after mile, along the whole sleepless line from Dunkerque to Belfort" (215–16). In this passage the Germans, although the enemy and even another "race" as she styles them at times, seem remarkably like the French: in similar outposts, in similar orchards, helmeted, staring, and waiting. Paul Fussell has written that as the war dragged on, French and English soldiers began to think of German soldiers not as "the Beast," but rather as simple soldiers who, like themselves, were only carrying out the orders of their superiors. Fussell writes of a widespread legend of "half-crazed deserters from all the armies, friend and enemy alike, harbored underground in abandoned trenches and dugouts and caves, [and] living in amity" (123). Such a legend "conveys the point that

German and British are not enemies: the enemy of both is the War" (Fussell 124). Wharton never forgets that the Germans are the enemy, but here, suspended for a moment in time, the enemy seems remarkably like the French Wharton so admired. For the moment, the old reality has vanished, and the new reality is suspended.

IV. The Poetry from 1915

Wharton's poetry from 1915 suggests that even with the new reality of war, Wharton adhered to the idealism she had expressed at its outset. She continued to see war as "the stimulant of qualities of soul which . . . can seemingly find no other means of renewal" (*Fighting France* 53); the war still moved her deeply and stirred her to articulate some of her deepest-held convictions. These poems are unified in their emphasis on nobility and idealism. The first of them is called "Belgium"; it was included in *King Albert's Book. A Tribute To The Belgian King And People*, published in 1915. Wharton's typescript of the poem is dated January 1915, a few short months after the invasion of Belgium; it carries the epigraph "La Belgique ne regrette rien" [Belgium regrets nothing], a phrase, Wharton wrote, which was "used soon after the fall of Liège by Belgium's Foreign Minister" (*Fighting France* 154).

> Not with her ruined silver spires,
> Not with her cities shamed and rent,
> Perish the imperishable fires
> That shape the homestead from the tent.
>
> Wherever men are staunch and free,
> There shall she keep her fearless state,
> And, homeless, to great nations be
> The home of all that makes them great. (Jan. 1915, *Wharton Collection* Yale)[4]

This poem leaves no doubt of Wharton's admiration for Belgium's self-defense under German attack. Through her use of paradox, Wharton emphasizes Belgium's transcendence of any merely military defeat. Belgium appears here as the spirit of civilization—"the fires / That shape the homestead from the tent"—and as the "home," however displaced, of "all that makes [great nations] great." Although Wharton's view of the war would be less lofty as the war continued, even the last of her war works, *A Son at the Front,* would echo the same idea: that a nation is not so much a geographical entity as a spirit, an idea.

"The Tryst" is a second poem Wharton composed in response to the plight of the Belgians. Written for inclusion in *The Book of the Homeless,* the poem, like her introduction to that book, uses a specific incident to help readers—especially distant American readers—to "pictur[e] how the thing *really happens*" (*Fighting France* 209). By focusing (as journalists still do) on a single individual, Wharton must have hoped to give a human face to a tragedy too large for American readers to absorb.

"The Tryst" is written as a dialogue between an unidentified "I," speaking from a position of safety, and a Belgian refugee. In response to the speaker's questions, the refugee explains that her town has been destroyed and her family killed. While Wharton avoids details of atrocities in much of her wartime writing, here her fictional refugee speaks in detail:

> They shot my husband against a wall,
> And my child (she said), too little to crawl,
> Held up its hands to catch the ball
> When the gun-muzzle turned its way.

The refugee refuses a permanent home in "countries far from here," despite their attractive peacefulness. Wharton understood that the refugees' desire was not to settle elsewhere, but to return to their own countries, however devastated:

> I shall crouch by the door till the bolt is down,
> And then go in to my dead.
> Where my husband fell I will put a stone,
> And mother a child instead of my own,
> And stand and laugh on my bare hearth-stone
> When the King rides by, she said.

Though Wharton dismissed "The Tryst" as "doggerel" (Benstock, *No Gifts* 319), it is an effective poem, one that works through the force of its detail, its strong rhythm and rhyme, and its simple diction. Unlike the poems submitted to *The Book of the Homeless* by Thomas Hardy—"the jolly Hardy malediction," as Henry James called it (Powers 349)—and William Dean Howells, and unlike the approach Wharton herself would take in parts of *French Ways and Their Meaning,* this poem proceeds not by vilifying the Germans but rather by portraying the plight of the Belgians.[5]

It was, thus, a perfect contribution to a book meant to raise money for the Belgian homeless. It is also somewhat of a departure in tone from the majority of Wharton's other war writings: simple, spare, and concrete, it adheres more closely than many of her works to the standards for language and theme that the war was beginning to generate. At the same time, the poem delineates the noble attitudes Wharton admired: the refugee faces facts head on; she persists even in the wake of the destruction of her village and the deaths of her family; she is determined to return home and begin anew with whatever may be left her, both memorializing her past ("Where my husband fell I will put a stone") and moving into the future ("And mother a child instead of my own").[6] The refugee looks toward the day when she can "stand and laugh . . . / When the King rides by."

Two other poems of 1915, "Battle Sleep" and "The Great Blue Tent," return to the nobler, more idealistic diction of "Belgium." "The Great Blue Tent," published in the August 25, 1915 *New York Times,* is a poem Wharton wrote to urge U.S. involvement in the war. In it, the American flag speaks, offering "warmth and sleep / And a table largely spread" to those coming "From ravaged town, from murdered home, / From your tortured and your dead." But this offer of merely bodily comforts (representative of the U.S. aid to refugees) is not enough, and a "cry" asks, "Where did you learn that bread is life, / And where that fire is warm—[?]" The Flag, reminded of its fight for freedom in the Revolutionary War, now "wake[s] and shake[s] at your cry" and pleads "to be off on the old fierce chase / Of the foe we have always fought."

The poem, an attempt to shame the United States into a war that had already lasted over a year, relies heavily not only on its central symbol— the American flag—but on the idealistic diction that the war was beginning to make obsolete. The general shift away from the idealistic language Wharton uses in this poem and toward more concrete, even crude, language, is illustrated by the poem's placement on its page in the *New York Times:* directly to its right is an article entitled "When the Mask of Civilization Slips" and subtitled "War is to Win and to Win Is to Kill—Why Talk Ethics to a Man Whose Head You Mean to Blow Off?" That article's author deplores the "dead language of morality." Far from agreeing, Wharton continued to work in the "language of morality" throughout the war and even, though in a more tempered way, in her postwar work.

"Battle Sleep" is a poem not so much about idealism as about the already-vanishing prewar world. A common refrain after the war was that the war had abruptly closed the curtain not only on an idyllic summer, but even more importantly on an idyllic way of life. Paul Fussell, for instance, notes that "For the modern imagination that last summer [i.e. the summer of 1914] has assumed the status of a permanent symbol for anything innocently but irrecoverably lost" (24). Samuel Hynes, though he points out that the years immediately before the war included political unrest as well as remarkable developments in the arts, reiterates Fussell's basic point: "later writers referred nostalgically to those years as the 'Edwardian summer'" (5). It is that summer idyll, that near-Arcadian pastoral, that Wharton evokes in "Battle Sleep," both through her choice of images—the sun setting over the rural landscape and the ocean, as one last boat "leans westward"—and through her prewar, romantic diction:

> Somewhere, O sun, some corner there must be
> Thou visitest, where down the strand
> Quietly, still, the waves go out to sea
> From the green fringes of a pastoral land.

Until the poem's final stanza, there is no indication that this is a war-related poem—nothing to explain its title. But in those final lines the poem takes on its poignant meaning:

> Giver of dreams, O thou with scatheless wing
> Forever moving through the fiery hail,
> To flame-seared lids the cooling vision bring,
> And let some soul go seaward with that sail!

The "fiery hail" of battle, the "flame-seared lids" of soldiers—it is in contrast with these that the vision of the sea, the "orchard-bloom," the "brown sheep," and the slow twilight take meaning: as an escape, as a restful vision for those in "battle sleep," or even those who may be dying ("let some soul go seaward"). Wharton asks that their resting or their final moments be blessed with this peaceful vision rather than that of the horrors around them—even though that peaceful world was vanishing.

In some ways a reprise of "Belgium," "Battle Sleep" also foreshadows Wharton's claim in *A Son at the Front* that France—even the idea of France—was worth fighting and dying for, despite the horrific cost. Belgium, though geographically homeless, will be "the home" of great nations; the pastoral world, though vanishing, gains its greatest value even at the moment of its disappearance. Similarly, life in "The Great Blue Tent" is more than mere bread—an idea Wharton would return to both in *The Marne* and *A Son at the Front*.

Wharton's idealism, however, was soon interwoven with sorrow. In August 1914 she had used the stock phrase "going to the slaughter," but three deaths in 1915 led her to a far more personal sense of loss and grief. The earliest blow was the death of her friend Jean du Breuil de Saint-Germain. In a eulogy for him published in the *Revue Hebdomadaire*, Wharton described him enthusiastically as a man both sympathetic and intellectual, as deeply interested both in art and in social justice. His death, rather than leading her to question the war, only confirmed her sense of the glory that war could confer. In her eulogy she concluded that Jean du Breuil "had the 'good fortune' to die for his country, on a morning already lit by the next French victory . . . [L]isten to this description of his death and tell me if he had not accomplished all" (*Uncollected Critical Writings* 203). Wharton then quotes an account of du Breuil's death: "'He took a bullet in the heart and another under the shoulder-blade'" as he was attempting "'to look for one of his wounded men close to the Germans'" (*Uncollected Critical Writings* 203). Such a death in action fit the heroic mold of soldiery still adhered to by many, and James's response to Wharton's report of du Breuil's death confirms her sense of his heroism: "your account of the admirable manner of his end makes one feel that one would like even to have just beheld him" (Powers 331).

Wharton's sorrow for du Breuil's death elicited her first war-related elegy. Apparently never published, the poem exists in typescript. It is entitled simply "Beaumetz, February 23rd 1915."—the place and date of Jean du Breuil's death;[7] beneath this typed title is his name, written in Wharton's hand. The poem begins with the grim notion of burial: "So much of life was sudden thrust / Under this dumb disfiguring dust[.]" The first stanza, however, quickly turns to commemorating the mental energy and intellectual scope of a friend whose companionship Wharton had enjoyed on a trip to Spain:

> Such ardour for things deep and great,
> Such easy disregard of fate,
> Such memories of strange lands remote,
> Of solitudes where eagles float. . .

The second, shorter stanza recounts obliquely yet clearly what du Breuil meant to Wharton herself:

> All this—and then his voice, his eyes,
> His eager questions, gay replies,
> The warmth he put into the air—

And, oh, his step upon the stair!

These lines both recall Wharton's joy at hearing "his step upon the stair" and tacitly acknowledge that she will never again experience that particular joy. The poem returns to its initial focus on the burial—now on the grave itself—only to pity that grave for its inability to "Efface the sense of what he was[.]" Wharton writes,

Poor grave!—for he shall burst your ties,
And come to us with shining eyes,
And laughter, and a quiet jest,
Whenever we, who loved him best,
Speak of great actions simply done,
And lives not vain beneath the sun. (Lilly Library, Indiana
     University)

"Beaumetz" established the pattern that Wharton would follow in later elegies as well (particularly in "'On Active Service,'" discussed in chapter three): the expression of grief and loss, followed by an assertion of the power to keep the dead alive through memory. In "Beaumetz" such recollections are not individual, but collective ("whenever *we* . . . / Speak," emphasis added). Moreover, spoken memories of Jean du Breuil would, Wharton implies, not only revive the fallen friend but reaffirm the cause in which he died. In "Belgium" Wharton had called that nation the home of all "great nations"; that glory also shines around Jean du Breuil and his "great actions simply done[,]" as well as around Wharton's assertion that his life—like his death—was "not vain" but purposeful.

At the foot of the manuscript of this poem are typed Wharton's name and the date, "Easter. 1915." While the poem does not suggest du Breuil as a Christ figure, it would be impossible not to see overtones of Christ's resurrection in Wharton's declaration, "Poor grave!—for he shall burst your ties[.]" Appropriately for an Easter poem, "Beaumetz" ends on that triumphant note of resurrection. Grief itself is buried as Wharton asserts the power of memory to resurrect the dead; the poem's final line ends not on "*deaths* not vain," as it well might have done, but rather on "lives not vain." Later elegies, though they would also ascribe a crucial role to memory, would be less triumphant in tone.

Indeed, Wharton's attitude toward death seemed to modify even as 1915 continued. In June 1915 her friend and translator Robert d'Humières died in the war; her former footman Henri was killed in September 1915. At the time of Jean du Breuil's death Wharton's adherence to the notion of the glory of war exceeded that expressed by du Breuil's own commanding officer, the Comte de Séguier. In a letter to Wharton he stated that "My sadness, I confess, remains indifferent to what is called the glory of his dying. His personality alone was in my eyes sufficient to crown him with glory"; du Breuil's death made him aware of his own unrealistic optimism: "I stupidly thought, if you can imagine, that he would be spared, and that all these brutalities unleashed by civilization and human progress would treat him gently" (Powers 393). Although the deaths of Robert d'Humières and Henri did not affect Wharton's belief in the importance of the war, her response to them was simpler and more personal. After Henri's death she wrote to Bernard Berenson, "Just a line to tell you that our poor little Henri was killed on the 30th. One of his friends has just brought us the news, & all my servants are crying their eyes out. Oh, this long horror! It comes home with a special pang when an obscure soldier drops out of the lines, & one happens to know what an eager spirit beat in him" (*Letters* 361). Wharton's idealism and her sense of war as a stirring and noble conflict persisted, but they were accompanied by a growing understanding that, if the war had to be fought to save France and even civilization, it would inevitably bring loss and sorrow in its wake.

V. "Coming Home"

As Alan Price has observed, the war pushed Wharton not only into new activities but into new genres, even "genres and literary voices she once condemned" (*End of the Age* xii). In the first year and a half of the war, most of Wharton's writing was nonfiction; her only work of fiction from this period is a short story entitled "Coming Home." This tale has generally been ignored; when it has been mentioned at all, it is only to be dismissed as "a trifle" (Lewis, *Letters* 331) or criticized as overconstructed (White 86). Yet "Coming Home" reflects a number of issues that arose for Wharton during the early months of the war: questions not only of historical import—the destructiveness of the Germans, the atrocities committed—but of other matters: how the war had affected morality, the role of women, and even the nature of fiction.

With the exception of *The Marne*, "Coming Home" is Wharton's closest approach to the front in fiction. In it she drew on the details she observed on her own trips to the front, incorporating, for instance, the nonfictional description of altered signposts and leveled villages in *Fighting France* into the fictional landscape of "Coming Home." This story, moreover, reflects her own responses to the war, though she divides her various responses among three characters, creating what one might call a triply narrated or a doubly framed plot.

"Coming Home" has a Chinese-box sort of structure: the initiating or external narrator "opens" to reveal Macy Greer; Macy Greer in turn "opens" to reveal Jean de Réchamp who—though ostensibly the central character of the narrative—is not actually present as a witness to the most "interior" events of the story, events related only by innuendo and unreliable testimony. Thus Wharton puts a terrific distance not only between herself and the events on the front, but between her readers and those events; even as she uses each of the three narrators to articulate and reflect her own opinions about and experiences of the war, she implicitly acknowledges the nonparticipant's inability to know fully the experiences of war.

The initiating narrator of the story is never named. He is, however, clearly a male version of Wharton: an affluent American living in Paris but not directly involved in the war. Not only does he share Wharton's city of residence and her lack of direct involvement in the war, he also shares her passion for good food and her love of good conversation (230). It is he who draws the central story out of visiting ambulance driver H. Macy Greer, but only after reflecting, in a most writerly manner, on Greer's persona as a narrator, on the war as a possible source of narrative interest, and on the genre of war stories themselves. He notes, "I can't say that . . . all the members of the Relief Corps have made the most of their [story-collecting] opportunity. Some are unobservant, or perhaps simply inarticulate; others, when going beyond the bald statistics of their job, tend to drop into sentiment and cinema scenes; and none but H. Macy Greer has the gift of making the thing told seem as true as if one had seen it" (230). Like Wharton, the initiating narrator is shaken by the war; as his phrase "as if one had seen it" implies, he is also like her in his wish to "pictur[e]" what has occurred at the front. Again reflecting Wharton's interests, he is of such a writerly or even scholarly turn of mind that he ponders a taxonomy of war writing, observing that "Some of [Greer's] tales are dark and dreadful, some are unutterably sad, and some end in a huge laugh of irony. I am not sure how I ought to classify the one I have written down here" (230). In this, he reflects Wharton's own uncertainty about how to handle the tales emerging from war; they often defy the genre classifications of the prewar world.

Wharton's central narrator for the story is Macy Greer, but much of

Macy's story relies on the words and reflections of yet another man, Jean de Réchamp. It is he who most echoes Wharton's outrage over the devastation of French villages and the French countryside, and who most represents Wharton's frustration at her own inability to participate more actively in the war. Like a number of Wharton's other male characters in war works, Jean de Réchamp has a bad leg that precludes his taking part in active combat. Réchamp began the war as a capable officer, but by the time he is introduced—that is, by the time he is of narrative use to Wharton—he "had had a leg smashed, poor devil, in the first fighting in Flanders" (231) and has been reduced to driving an ambulance behind the front lines, the kind of work that Wharton viewed extensively on her visits to the front. Réchamp, like Wharton, is as active as he can be for a person excluded from the front lines.

Jean de Réchamp further reflects Wharton's own sense of frustration during periods of inactivity. As we have seen, Wharton had been at Stocks, Mrs. Humphry Ward's country house in England, when the war broke out (Benstock, *No Gifts* 302–4); upon her return to the Rue de Varenne she opened her lingerie workshop and soon wrote to Sally Norton that "All this keeps me busy & interested so that I feel the oppression of war much less than I did in England" (*Letters* 339). Her sense that activity relieves the frustration of passivity is reflected by Jean: "'Of course,' he explained with a weary smile, 'as long as you can tot up your daily bag in the trenches it's a sort of satisfaction . . . But lying here staring at the ceiling one goes through the whole business once an hour, at the least: the attack [on his home village of Réchamp], the slaughter, the ruins . . . and worse . . .'" (232). The attempt to visualize horrors, the obsession caused by the inability to help, the sense of the distance from home now that home is in crisis—all reflect Wharton's attitudes.

But it is Greer who suggests Wharton's determination, her interest in (and her shying away from) atrocities, and her awareness that war was affecting narration. Paradoxically, the initiating narrator describes Greer as exactly the sort of American Wharton often looked down on: he "has a voice like thick soup, and speaks with the slovenly drawl of the new generation of Americans" (230). Greer has, however, the quality that might redeem almost anyone for Wharton: "his eyes see so much that they make one see even what his foggy voice obscures" (230). He also reflects Wharton's own determination to get to the front: twice in the story he remarks that he is "not sure if we could get through [to Réchamp], but bound to, anyhow!" (240; compare 234). And, like Wharton, he somehow manages to "get through" to a place previously considered inaccessible. It is Greer, not the initiating narrator nor Jean de Réchamp, who is really the story-teller here; like Wharton in *Fighting France,* he tells the story he saw with-out embroidering on it, allowing facts to speak for themselves—the minimalist style the war was making increasingly popular.

More profoundly, however, Macy Greer reflects both Wharton's desire to know the worst and her desire to shy away from it, to not quite imagine it. In the story, Oberst von Scharlach is the merciless German officer who has passed through Jean's home village of Réchamp; his reputation and deeds are so villainous that Jean overhears one of Scharlach's own soldiers saying that he wishes he had been "struck dead" before he had a chance to carry out Scharlach's orders (235)—though what these orders are we never learn. The portrayal of Scharlach is further developed through re-ports—but not depictions—of his burning an old woman's "half-wit" son, and through a report that he carries painting materials so as to paint the scenes of devastation he leaves behind him. In short, the story repeatedly suggests wartime atrocities without actually depicting them.

Further, the central action of the story is left unnarrated and is only implied. Given Scharlach's reputation, Jean is understandably concerned about his family when he learns that the German general has taken his town. As it turns out, the Germans have spared both his family and their ancestral home, thanks to the clever intervention of Jean's fiancée, Yvonne Malo. The story suggests—but only through Yvonne's unwillingness to spend time alone with Jean, and the absence of other likely explanations—that Scharlach spared the family, house, and village because Yvonne Malo allowed him to have sexual relations with her.[8] But this scene, assuming it occurs, is never recounted. The story implies more strongly that Jean de Réchamp is responsible for the death of the wounded Scharlach: while Greer and Réchamp are driving the wounded Scharlach to a hospital, their ambulance runs out of fuel. Given Réchamp's bad leg, Greer returns to the front lines to get some gas; before leaving, he instructs Réchamp to give Scharlach a hypodermic if the German officer should take a turn for the worse. When Greer returns, however, Scharlach is dead; Réchamp says that there was "[n]o time to" administer the medication; "He died in a minute" (255). Scharlach's death—his possible murder, or at least his death as a result of criminal negligence—also goes undepicted. In this way, the story—and Macy Greer as storyteller—do exactly what Wharton and *Fighting France* do: tell of atrocities without actually describing them. Greer's and Wharton's story-telling parallels their wartime activity: both are behind the lines figuratively as well as literally, and the story's triple-box narration increases the sense of distance between the narrators and the narrated events, between the reader and the fictionalized historical events related. When all the boxes are opened, there is nothing visible inside.

Yet this absence, this reticence, is not necessarily a flaw in Wharton's work, but perhaps its very strength. For many the war was not something directly witnessed, but only heard about; the oral quality of "Coming Home" is illuminated by Paul Fussell's observation that, as printed accounts of the war became increasingly untrustworthy, the orally communicated tale became more common and more widely believed (115). At the time the story was published, a *New York Times* reviewer noted that the "tragedy" of the story was "the more appalling because it is only suggested, never fully told" (Tuttleton et al. 228). The very absence of detail at the story's center created the story's impact; "the descriptions are wonderful, biting deep into the memory," the reviewer stated (Tuttleton et al. 228).

The story reflects the agony of those who both want to know the worst and who dread to learn it, those who want to be aware of atrocities and yet whose humanity, and perhaps sanity, flinches from the prospect of actually witnessing or even fully imagining such acts—particularly when they cannot intervene or prevent them. "Coming Home" suggests the abysmal frustration of the incapacity to act; why should Wharton, or for that matter her fictional male counterparts, tell in detail—or even imagine in detail—the horrors they were unable to stop? Yvonne Malo asks, "Why brood on other horrors—horrors we were powerless to help?" (251) The story even implies the probability that, should Jean de Réchamp and Yvonne Malo carry out their plan to marry (and there is no suggestion that they will not), they would still keep silent about their separate encounters with Scharlach.

The title suggests the way in which war altered every aspect of reality it touched: even in "coming home" to find his family and household physically safe, Jean de Réchamp finds a home profoundly changed from the place that he left. The story suggests other deep changes as well. Although Wharton would declare pointedly in a chapter of *French Ways and Their Meaning* entitled "The New Frenchwoman" that "there is no new French-woman" (98), asserting that Frenchwomen were fundamentally unaltered by the war, her portrait of Yvonne Malo suggests otherwise. It is one of the few flattering portraits of the "new woman" that Wharton ever painted. Before the war, Yvonne Malo lived alone in Paris as a musician (232) and did not get along well with Jean's very traditional provincial family. Yet Yvonne's quick thinking with the German soldiers has convinced even the family matriarch that "there is something to be said for the new way of bringing up girls" (246)—though her naive assumption is that Yvonne has simply provided the soldiers with good food and entertainment. As Macy Greer counsels Jean, at least the war has made his family "worship" the girl they earlier rejected (252). The war altered standards, sometimes for the better.

If war made more liberated gender roles acceptable—at least at times—it also altered, perhaps less happily, morality. While killing an enemy soldier in combat is by the nature of warfare acceptable, fatally neglecting a wounded prisoner of war under one's supervision is a different matter. Macy Greer, the narrator and perhaps the representative American reader as well, has some reservations about the manner of Scharlach's death; he mentions twice that "the man wasn't anywhere near death when I left him" (255, compare 254). Yet Greer reassures himself that Scharlach may have died a natural, if sudden, death, remarking, "Well, I'm not a doctor, anyhow. . . ." (255). Further, he notes that Jean's conscience seems untroubled: "he had somehow got back, in the night's interval, to a state of wholesome stolidity" (255).

While this observation seems to reassure Greer that his friend is innocent of murder, the reader may understand it differently. Perhaps it is the very killing of Scharlach that has eased Réchamp's mind, as it has balanced the score between them: he reclaims Yvonne's chastity (viewed implicitly as the possession of her fiancé) through his taking of Scharlach's life, or, as an act of omission, by his failure to save it. His last words to Greer before the latter goes off to fetch more gas are ambiguous: he promises to "do my best" regarding Scharlach (254). In the context of war—a war here made very personal—Réchamp may reason that the "best" he can do is to exact as even a revenge as he can. In fact, the "wholesome stolidity" Jean exudes may testify not to his innocence but to his role in Scharlach's death: it has eased his conscience.

By the story's conclusion, Greer seems to have regained his own "stolidity" as "arm in arm we started off to hunt for the inn" and a good "café complet" (256). Jean comes to accept Yvonne's (assumed) sexual encounter with Scharlach not as infidelity, or even as the tragic pollution of a previously pure French maiden—a symbol of the German invasion of France—but rather as an action acceptable, even necessary, under the specific circumstances of the war. So too Jean may accept a role in Scharlach's death, and Macy Greer may, in turn, accept Jean's (assumed) killing of Scharlach not as murder, but as the settling of a score with a man who threatened not only his fiancée but his family, his home, his village, and his country. The story suggests that, disturbing as it may be—and Wharton's story trails off in an ellipsis, never returning to the opening narrator for a contextualizing or normalizing remark—war alters moral standards that, before the war, seemed inalterable. Wharton's cry to Berenson echoes: "Hasn't it shaken all the foundations of reality for you?"

For Wharton, the war also altered what she could write and how she would write it. The war suggested subjects she would not previously have considered, or perhaps rather subjects that, a few months earlier, did not exist as subjects. As the opening narrator of "Coming Home" suggests, the war shook up the question of genre; one hardly knew how to categorize some of the stories emerging from the war. Macy Greer has more to say in this line as well. While telling the opening narrator of Jean's reunion with an "old family servant," he relates, there were "tears and hugs and so on. I know you affect to scorn the cinema, and this was it, tremolo and all. Hang it! This war's going to teach us not to be afraid of the obvious" (244). Greer is conscious of genre; shortly after this remark he returns to his narration, saying, "[Yvonne] went back to 'prepare' the parents, as they say in melodrama" (244). In much of her work before the war, Wharton rigorously avoided the melodramatic and the obvious. Yet the war was teaching her to reassess these modes, to see that they had their uses when, in fact, life itself became melodramatic or "obvious." An altered reality requires an altered prose. As Alan Price has written, Wharton learned "to hit and hold 'the tremolo note' when its effects served her ends" (*End of the Age* xiii).

Wharton used "the tremolo note" to express her disdain for the tone that, she had learned, she needed to achieve in order to persuade reluctant donors to give more generously to the costly and important charities she administered. But "the tremolo note" has a corollary, "the illuminating incident," which she viewed much more positively: as an essential ingredient of evocative writing. Writing to Mary Berenson of Walter Berry's letters to her from Germany, Wharton complained, "so far [he] has totally failed to do for me what Mr. Hazen has: give me a picture. I can't *see* anything he has seen . . . & what I call (in novel-writing) 'the illuminating incident' doesn't seem to have caught his attention" (*Letters* 344). What makes Wharton's war writing effective (when it is effective, as in *Fighting France*) is her use of "the illuminating incident." Although later she would claim that writing journalistically had become a chore, her novelist's sense of "the illuminating incident" served her well as she sent her first reports to the United States. She employs it well in other works as well as in *Fighting France;* her November 1915 article for the *New York Times,* "My Work Among the Women Workers of Paris," her introduction to *The Book of the Homeless,* and "The Tryst" also rely on such illumination.[9] If at times her examples verge on the cliché, at other times they still surprise with their freshness and their unpredictability. Her preface to *The Book of the Homeless,* for instance, opens with an anecdote about a child refugee. While the choice of a child as subject might seem obvious—the plight of children seems almost guaranteed to stir sympathy—Wharton's particular choice is surprising. She tells the story not of some destitute waif made happy by the ministrations of her charity, but instead about "a little acrobat from a strolling circus" who has grown up among "mummers and contortionists" (xix) and who has been separated from his family. Though the Children of Flanders Rescue Committee provides him both a sympathetic ear and a job as a page in a hotel, the child does not prove a success story. Instead he is caught for theft. Yet the things he has stolen—"the spangled dresses belonging to a Turkish family, and the embroidered coats of a lady's lap-dog" (xix)—indicate how much he has missed his circus family. It is a perfect example of Wharton's use of "the illuminating incident"; Wharton has recounted it, she explains, to point up "the fact that we workers among the refugees are trying, first and foremost, to *help a homesick people*" (xx).

Wharton's need to "hit and hold 'the tremolo note'" or—to use her more positive term—to employ "the illuminating incident" explains some of the shift in tone in Wharton's war writing. The war's beginning both fascinated and horrified her; it led her into a variety of genres and topics she could not have projected even a month before mobilization. The articles comprising *Fighting France,* though in some ways building on her earlier travel writing, were also a new departure for her as she located a voice and style that allowed her to depict the male world of war. Her idealism expressed itself through her poems, and in her single fiction of the period she examined shifting social mores, gender roles, and the ways in which the war was already beginning to alter the possibilities of fiction itself. The war had "shaken all the foundations of reality" for her; her writings show not only the ways in which the war was influencing her imagination but also the ways in which her creative imagination was shaping the war—in order to express her personal grief, to express her deeply held convictions, and, in some cases, to influence her readers.

Work, Escape, and the Loss of Ambiguity

Writings from Later in the War (1916–1918)

> After two years of war we all became strangely inured to a state which at first made intellectual detachment impossible. It would be inexact to say that the sufferings and the suspense were less acutely felt; but the mysterious adaptability of the human animal gradually made it possible for war-workers at the rear, while they went on slaving at their job with redoubled energy, to create within themselves an escape from the surrounding horror.
> **Edith Wharton,** *A Backward Glance* **(355–56)**

> If truth is the main casualty in war, ambiguity is another.
> **Paul Fussell,** *The Great War and Modern Memory* **(79)**

I.

As *Fighting France* and "Coming Home" attest, the early months of the war—the fascination and horror, even the novelty of war—stimulated Edith Wharton. As we have seen, she initially believed, like many others, that "the war would turn out to be an adventure," a "martial interlude" in "the normal course of events" (Becker 3). But she would never repeat her early stock phrase "gone to the slaughter" about those who died in the war. The deaths of her friend Jean du Breuil de Saint-Germain in February 1915, of her friend and translator Robert d'Humières in June 1915, and of her former footman Henri in September 1915 made her painfully aware of the lives the war destroyed.

The year 1916 brought more deaths, including those caused by illness and old age: Henry James in February, her life-long friend Egerton Winthrop, and her long-time servant Anna Bahlmann in March (Benstock, *No Gifts* 322, 325). In mid-June Wharton wrote to Sally Norton that "I can't

rally from the double blow of Henry James's death, & then Egerton Winthrop's, one so soon after the other—& followed so quickly by poor little
Anna's!" (*Letters* 379). The war would add still further to Wharton's grief
by claiming two more close to her. Her young cousin Newbold ("Bo")
Rhinelander was shot down over Germany on September 26, 1918, and
was eventually pronounced dead. A few weeks before that, the war produced the death Wharton felt most acutely: that of Ronald Simmons, a
young American who had been studying at the Ecole des Beaux-Arts and
who had become close to Wharton. On August 13, 1918, she wrote of his
death to Bernard Berenson, her fragmented letter reflecting her deep grief:

> Simmons is dead. He died in the Engl. Hospital in Marseilles yester-
> day morning of double pneumonia. It is all I know as yet.
>   This breaks me down to the depths. I really loved him dearly—&
> he had a great sort of younger brotherly affection for me—& we
> understood each other so completely! . . .
>   . . . this news has paralyzed me.
> He was coming to Paris next week. . . .
> J'ai le coeur meurtri. [My heart is broken.] (*Letters* 409)

Here Wharton employs no rhetoric about noble deaths or sacrifice for a
noble cause: there is only grief, the grief that would motivate—though it
would not pervade—the two novels Wharton would dedicate to Simmons,
The Marne and *A Son at the Front*. The war had become a reality for
Wharton.

While news of the deaths of friends jarred and saddened Wharton, she
also adjusted to living in a state of war. The sense of a shaken reality evaporated, and the reality of wartime became the new background against
which her life was lived: she became "strangely inured to a state which at
first made intellectual detachment impossible." While she still felt the
plight of the refugees (and continued her considerable and varied efforts to
care for them), she was no longer obsessed with "that look of concentrated
horror" (*Fighting France* 33). As early as November 1915 she wrote to a
friend from Hyères that "it is delicious just to dawdle about in the sun, &
smell the eucalyptus & pines," adding casually that "I long to send you
some flowers, but I'm afraid it's no use in war time" (*Letters* 361–62). Her
sense of humor returned. In November 1916 she sent a parrot as a birthday
present to six-year-old William Tyler, the son of her good friends Elisina
and Royall Tyler, with an accompanying letter: "As I cannot come [to your
party], however, I am sending a little pet to replace me, and as he is very

handsome and most beautifully dressed I am almost sure he will remind you of me" (*Letters* 382). Even her Legion of Honor award was one she wore lightly. In December 1916 she opened a letter to her former lover with the salutation "Dear Mr. Morton Fullerton (vide yr. signature!!)"— and signed herself "Mrs. E. Wharton / Chevalier de la Légion d'Honneur" (*Letters* 383). In January 1917 she wrote to Berenson of her delight at receiving his new book, proclaiming: "I've just chucked the refugees & read on—I couldn't help it" (*Letters* 388). In another letter to Berenson about three weeks later, she indulged herself in a brief literary discussion only to halt herself with the remark, "Dear me—what a flight! Now I must plump down to refugee-land again.—" (*Letters* 393). While Wharton continued to be engaged in refugee work, and while she continued to track with the greatest interest the turns in the war, the war-reality had come home to her; the horror and fascination of the first months of the war had worn off. The "early flush and shiver of romance" (*Fighting France* 31) were finally gone, and "refugee-land" had become her place of abode.

From 1916 through 1919, Wharton wrote three significant works: the novel *Summer* (1917), the novella *The Marne* (1918), and a series of articles that would be republished in 1919 as *French Ways and Their Meaning*. While *Summer* has been, if anything, more popular in recent years than it was at the time of its publication, the other two works of this period have generally been ignored.[1] From an aesthetic standpoint, this may not be surprising; of *The Marne* Blake Nevius wrote in 1953, "In no other work has she limited her effects to such broad strokes or so abused the medium of the long tale by compelling it to absorb so many issues" (163). More recent critics and biographers tend simply to mention that she wrote *The Marne*, that it received good initial reviews, then fell into neglect.[2] Initial reactions to *French Ways* were mixed, with the enthusiastic writing that "Mrs. Wharton's volume is deliciously entertaining and exquisitely salutary" (Tuttleton et al. 275) and the more outraged asking, "Can it be possible that America will survive this apologist and France this defender?" (Tuttleton et al. 273).

What may be most notable about *The Marne* and *French Ways*—which are, in their exhortation to Americans to appreciate and defend French culture, a fictional and a nonfictional expression of the same impulse—is their lack of literary ambiguity, their lack of any complicating moral issues. While this seems a great loss in Wharton's writing, so rich in irony and moral ambiguity before the war, their absence in the context of the war, and in particular in the writing of an inhabitant of an invaded country, is hardly surprising. Wharton's vision in *Fighting France* of symmetrical, nearly identical French and German lines has disappeared; in its place was the simple fact that France—*her* France—was being invaded by the German army. "If truth is the main casualty in war," Paul Fussell has written, "ambiguity is another" (79). And yet *French Ways and Their Meaning* and *The Marne*, works that are in some ways simple, didactic, and unambiguous, nevertheless reveal the multitude of forces at work on Edith Wharton and within her writings during the later part of the war.

II. Escape: *Summer*

Before plunging into the unambiguously pro-French *The Marne* and *French Ways and Their Meaning,* however, Wharton demonstrated—for the first time since the war's beginning—her ability "to create within [herself] an escape from the surrounding horror" (*Backward Glance* 356). For Wharton, the escape was literary: the composition in 1916 of *Summer.* As she wrote to her friend Gaillard Lapsley, "I don't know how on earth the thing got itself written in the scramble & scuffle of my present life: but it *did*" (*Letters* 385); to Robert Grant she wrote that "It is such a relief to get away from refugees and hospitals" through her writing (qtd. in Price 95). By the time she wrote her memoir in 1934, she remembered writing *Summer* "at a high pitch of creative joy," and, despite the interruptions her writing suffered, she added, "I do not remember ever visualizing with more intensity the inner scene, or the creatures peopling it" (*Backward Glance* 356).

In many ways the "inner scene" provided Wharton with a necessary escape, for there is little on the surface of *Summer* connecting it with Wharton's other wartime writings. The short novel tells the story of Charity Royall, the daughter of two people from "the Mountain," an only partially civilized settlement. She is adopted by Lawyer Royall, the most prominent citizen of North Dormer, a small and sleepy town in the Berkshires, and his wife. After his wife's death, Lawyer Royall makes advances to the teen-aged Charity, which she repulses. When a summer visitor, the young architect Lucius Harney, comes to town, he and Charity begin a romance that leads to their sexual involvement and Charity's pregnancy. But Charity does not tell Harney she is pregnant; he returns to New York and his engagement to another young woman. Hearing that her mother is dying up on the Mountain, Charity journeys there, thinking she will settle on the Mountain with her own child. But her mother's death is shocking rather than redemptive; the Mountain and its inhabitants appall Charity; Lawyer Royall rescues Charity from the Mountain settlement, returns her to civilization, and proposes to her again, knowing that she is pregnant. Charity accepts him, and the end of the novel finds her back in Lawyer Royall's house in North Dormer, now as his wife.

Summer is far more often compared to *Ethan Frome*, its wintery New England counterpart, than to any of her war works. Wharton nicknamed *Summer* "Hot Ethan" (*Letters* 385) and described it as being "as remote as possible in setting and subject from the scenes" around her when she wrote it (*Backward Glance* 356). There is no mention or even hint of the Great War in the novel, whose time setting is indeterminate—possibly several years before the events of 1914.

Yet the novel's very remoteness from scenes of war gives it a special wartime status for its readers as well as its author: that of escape. As Paul Fussell has written, literary works have provided an important imaginative respite for generations of soldiers as well as for their relatives and other civilians at home. Fussell notes that Geoffrey Keynes "pored over Courtney and Smith's *Bibliography of Samuel Johnson*. . . . Eighteenth-century writing was popular [during World War I]. . . . It offered an oasis of reasonableness and normality, a place one could crawl into for a few moments' respite from the sights, sounds, and smells of the twentieth century" (162). A letter from Joseph Conrad to Edith Wharton suggests that her gift copy of *Summer* had provided him with just such a respite. Conrad had just come home from returning his son to the front when, as he wrote to Wharton, "I saw the summer-blue book on my table." He praised the novel ("no matter where one opens it presents itself en beauté, toujours en beauté"), and he particularly appreciated its "rhythms." These he specified as creating the refuge he found in the novel: "On opening the book I let myself be carried away by them and I must tell you in all sincerity that it wasn't difficult even under the circumstances" (1 Oct. 1917, *Wharton Collection* Yale). While one could argue that the rather claustrophobic world of North Dormer would not, in peacetime, be the epitome of "reasonableness and normality," in wartime it might have looked relatively appealing both to Conrad and to its creator. The ending of the novel—despite the troubling undertones of incest as Charity marries her guardian—is far more optimistic than the perpetual death-in-life of Ethan Frome.[3] In any case, Charity's situation—bad as it may be—must have seemed reassuringly manageable and domestic in a world at war. And although *Summer* is certainly set in the early twentieth century, it has none of the more disturbing twentieth-century innovations Wharton was witnessing, reading about, and hearing of in Paris: the massive German siege guns, the nerve gas, the mud and immobility of trench warfare.

Summer resonates with issues that surface in Wharton's works from before the war: like many of her other works, it examines the situation of women in society; Charity's expected baby is the flesh-and-blood version of the imagined infant cradled by Lily Bart at the end of *The House of Mirth;* and the socially conscious Charity may be a small-town (and less successful) version of Undine Spragg. But *Summer* is deeply shaped by the war, echoing issues and images from the two wartime works that preceded it, *Fighting France* and "Coming Home," and anticipating issues Wharton would handle more harshly in the two war works directly following it, *The Marne* and *French Ways and Their Meaning.*

Many ties, linguistic, imagistic, and thematic, connect *Summer* with *Fighting France* and "Coming Home." Candace Waid has noted the resonance between the dilapidated huts of the Mountain people in *Summer* and the ruined homes in *Fighting France* (*Edith Wharton's Letters* 81); she has also pointed out Wharton's use of the same imagery—flowers in the night sky—to describe bombs falling in *Fighting France* and the Fourth of July fireworks display in *Summer* ("Introduction" vii). An earlier critic, Blake Nevius, commented on the war's influence on Wharton's description of the corpse of Charity's mother: "It is as if the grim realities of the war in France had momentarily cast their shadow over the countryside of *Ethan Frome.* The dead woman lying on the mattress 'like a dead dog in a ditch,' her face 'thin yet swollen, with lips parted, in a frozen gasp above the broken teeth,' stresses the physical ugliness of death in a manner appropriate to the combat diary" (169–70). Nowhere else in Wharton's writing did Wharton portray death so gruesomely. Fulvia Vivaldi in Wharton's first novel, *The Valley of Decision,* is shot, yet she dies without blood: "no wound showed through her black gown. She lay as though smitten by some invisible hand" (Vol. II, 286). Lily Bart is lovely even in death. And although Wharton describes Ralph Marvell's thought process preceding his suicide—he shoots himself in the head—she does not describe his horribly mutilated body in *The Custom of the Country.* Even one postwar portrayal of a shooting victim—Nona Manfort in Wharton's 1927 novel, *Twilight Sleep*—is less graphic; readers are told merely that "Nona's blood spatter[ed] the silvery folds of the rest-gown, destroying it forever as a symbol of safety and repose" (354). There can be little doubt that the description of Charity's mother, a poor, rural, American woman, carries the horror of many of the deaths in World War I. The "inner scene," so "intense," was not wholly separated from the outer scene of war.

The Mountain people themselves, shabby and poor, are reminiscent of the refugees Wharton describes in *Fighting France*. There are significant differences between the two groups: the refugees are hard-working people displaced by the German army, while, Wharton implies, the Mountain people are degenerate; the refugees are homeless, while the Mountain people suffer from having lived too long in the same place. Yet Wharton's recollection of the refugees' "look of concentrated horror" (*Fighting France* 33) is mirrored in the situation of the Mountain people. Wharton describes the rector who gave her the story on which she based the funeral of Charity's mother as "coming back" from a Mountain burial "with his eyes full of horror and his heart of anguish and pity" (*Backward Glance* 294). Indeed, the "savage misery of the Mountain farmers" (173) has much in common with the plight of the refugees, who "receive, in return for the loss of everything that makes life sweet, or intelligible, or at least endurable, a cot in a dormitory, a meal-ticket—and perhaps, on lucky days, a pair of shoes . . . " (*Fighting France* 35). Of the refugees Wharton writes "it is a grim sight to watch them limping by, and to meet the dazed stare of eyes that have seen what one dare not picture" (*Fighting France* 50). The same is implied of the inhabitants of the Mountain, leading a life that Charity thinks about assuming—but which she instinctively rejects once she realizes its horrors.

Further, Charity suffers, like her creator, from a sense of a shaken reality. After dark one evening she spends an hour or more "crouch[ing] on the steps" of the house where Lucius Harney is staying (67), watching him move about his lighted bedroom; the intense emotions of the evening give her the sense of "floating high over life," not euphorically but rather "on a great cloud of misery beneath which everyday realities had dwindled to mere specks in space" (70). Her trip up the Mountain serves as the metaphorical equivalent of Wharton's trips to the front, "shak[ing] all the foundations of reality" for her: "As she approached the door [of the house where her mother lay dead] she said to herself: 'This is where I was born . . . this is where I belong . . . .' She had said it to herself often enough as she looked across the sunlit valleys at the Mountain; but it had meant nothing then, and now it had become a reality" (164). That reality is the body of her dead mother in the horrible attitude already described. Though Charity has tried to convince herself that this is her new reality—"where I belong"—she only manages to stay the night before concluding that "Anything, anything was better than to add another life to the nest of misery on the Mountain. . . ." (174).

In another passage, Charity finds that the formal words of the Episcopal burial service "sooth[e] the horror" (168) of her mother's death. Only her acceptance of Lawyer Royall's marriage proposal keeps reality from slipping away: "The clergyman opened a book and signed to Charity and Mr. Royall to approach. Mr. Royall advanced a few steps, and Charity followed him . . . she had the feeling that if she ceased to keep close to him, and do what he told her to do, the world would slip away from beneath her feet" (185). For Charity, as for Wharton in the war zone, the new reality is elusive at best. Despite Charity's sense that Mr. Royall prevents the world from "slip[ping] away," it is not until a few hours after the marriage ceremony that Charity fully comes "to a realization of what she had done" (187). So, too, for Wharton in Châlons, reality itself slips away so that she was "unable to believe that I was I" (*Fighting France* 88–89). Wharton eventually came to accept the oppressive new reality of war; Charity finally accepts a life in North Dormer, a town that, at the novel's outset, she found dreary, even hateful.

In other ways as well the "inner scene" of *Summer* mirrors the outer scene in which Wharton composed it. A picnic scene in *Summer*, for instance, reflects the one in *Fighting France* in which Wharton and her companions are warned back from the lines by a French soldier just as they are about to settle down to eat. The details of this luncheon—"the flutter of birds, the hum of insects" (*Fighting France* 200)—are reminiscent of Charity and Harney's picnics in the Berkshires: "they unpacked their basket under an aged walnut. . . . The sun had grown hot, and behind them was the noonday murmur of the forest. Summer insects danced on the air, and a flock of white butterflies fanned the mobile tips of the crimson fireweed" (50). These scenes are significant both in their parallels and in their differences. Wharton surely drew on her memories of the Berkshires in composing this scene, yet it also echoes the Alsatian picnic described in *Fighting France*. In both a menace lurks, though the menace in Alsace is of greater magnitude: "the damnable insanity of war" (*Fighting France* 200). The menace at the edge of Charity's picnic is far more manageable: "disquieting thoughts stole back on her" (50); an oncoming storm (51), not the German Army, disturbs her picnic. The menaces threatening Charity are relatively minor—worries, bad weather; ultimately, an unexpected pregnancy:

all problems quite small in the context of war. The "inner scene" copies the outer, but also serves as refuge and escape: its problems are comparatively normal and comparatively manageable.

Similarly, *Summer*, like "Coming Home," suggests a shift in moral values, though less is at stake in *Summer*. Even one factor of the central scene is the same: North Dormer (in the person of Miss Hatchard) suspects an inappropriate sexual liaison between Charity and Mr. Royall; a servant in Réchamp starts rumors that Yvonne Malo had a sexual liaison with her older male guardian.[4] In both cases the rumors are wrong; Miss Hatchard is incorrect, and Jean de Réchamp discredits the source of the rumors about Yvonne. Yet both works challenge conventional moral codes: "Coming Home," as we have seen, by suggesting that Yvonne Malo—whatever her ruse may have been—is heroic, not victimized, and by suggesting that Jean de Réchamp's possible murder of Scharlach (or at least his responsibility for Scharlach's death) is morally acceptable. Similarly, *Summer* does not condemn Charity for her youthful sexuality, nor does it condemn her—or Lawyer Royall—for a marriage many have seen as "figuratively incestuous" (Ammons 137). In the context of the war, Royall's treatment of Charity can be seen as generous: Charity is twice homeless—twice a refugee—and he twice provides her a home, first as his ward and then as his wife. The sheer emphasis on physical comforts, on Royall as providing them—not as foolish luxuries, but as the basic creature comforts of human existence—may be an outgrowth of Wharton's experience with the displaced and homeless refugees she served.

While Royall has been faulted for proposing to Charity while she is at her weakest (Ammons 137), it is also possible to see that the very comforts he provides are what make it possible, first, for Charity to survive, and second, for her to regain her social position. On the return trip from the Mountain Lawyer Royall stops at a rural house to provide some breakfast for Charity; "she was conscious only of the pleasant animal sensations of warmth and rest" (179)—essentials of which Wharton had seen so many refugees deprived. It is only after eating and drinking that Charity "began to feel like a living being again," even if she finds "the return to life . . . painful" (179). If Charity follows Royall to be married in Nettleton "as passively as a tired child"—a phrase Ammons quotes to suggest that Royall is maneuvering Charity into marriage in her moment of weakness—Charity also finds strength in him, noting in his look "the same steady tranquil gaze that had reassured and strengthened her" (183). Only with her marriage to Royall can she be saved from a destitute life on the

Mountain or a degraded one as a town prostitute. Like the refugees, Charity is "someone to whom something irreparable and overwhelming had happened" (183), and she must make the best of the scant possibilities open to her. As Lawyer Royall and Charity prepare to return to North Dormer, she concedes at last, "I guess you're good, too" (194).

If the Mountain is the psychological and experiential equivalent of the front lines, *Summer* suggests that Wharton understood that, much as she longed to see and be part of the "real business of the nation," that business was devastating and better left behind. After each of her trips to the front, Wharton returned to the realms of civilization to administer her charities and write articles—and *The Marne*—to encourage the U.S. entry into the war; her role was not on the Volunteer Aid Detachment or near the trenches any more than Charity's was on the Mountain. Seeing those horrors was enough; Charity's world, like Wharton's, was profoundly changed by that glimpse. For Charity, the "menace" was "like looking out over the world as it would be when love had gone from it" (121). For Wharton, the menace was more defined and concrete—the German army—but metaphorically the same, for the "love had gone" from the mountain scenes "to which the mind ha[d] always turned for rest" (*Fighting France* 200). Yet there is love in *Summer;* its bittersweet tone is far different from the questioning, and sometimes romantically questing, tones of *Fighting France,* the contorted questioning of genre and morals in "Coming Home," or the martial blasts Wharton would sound in *The Marne* and *French Ways and Their Meaning.*

III. Romance and Realism: *The Marne*

In her story "Coming Home," Wharton had expressed through Macy Greer the possibility that the war would "teach us not to be afraid of the obvious" in the stories we tell (244). In *The Marne,* Wharton seems to have decided to embrace "the obvious." Doing so allowed her to handle topics she previously might have avoided; it also meant that *The Marne* adhered to the principle behind England's Defense of the Realm Act: "art should be good for war, or it should not exist" (Hynes 80).

The Marne must have been composed hastily, probably between mid-July 1918—when the second Battle of the Marne occurred—and November 1918, as the novel was published in December of that year. Wharton had described *Summer* as being "as remote as possible . . . from the scenes about" her; it was precisely those scenes on which she focused in *The*

Marne, writing (sometimes heavy-handedly) of the wartime experiences of a teenage American boy, Troy Belknap. Much of the novel focuses on Troy's frustration with his mother and her society friends, who see war primarily as a personal inconvenience. Troy's love of France is encouraged by his French tutor, Paul Gantier, whose family is fragmented early in the war; Paul himself is killed in the first Battle of the Marne. Troy, whose fifteenth birthday was on the day the Archduke Ferdinand was shot at Sarajevo, waits impatiently to be old enough to join the action. In the novel's climax Troy, finally a driver for the American Ambulance, is swept up by a passing truckload of American soldiers after his ambulance breaks down. They are going to fight in the second Battle of the Marne (July 15–17, 1918), and Troy joins them. He volunteers for a scouting party, is shot, and is later carried to a hospital where he is told that he was rescued by a mysteriously disappearing soldier—and recalls hearing the voice of Paul Gantier.

It has been said that *French Ways and Their Meaning* "enlightens us more on what Edith Wharton came to find in France than it does about the French" (de Margerie vii);[5] *The Marne,* written almost simultaneously,[6] is its fictional counterpart, and like *French Ways* reveals almost transparently Wharton's wartime emotions and beliefs. As even a very favorable early review of the novel noted, "Troy Belknap . . . never becomes entirely real to us. Moreover, we are in truth shown it [France at war], not as it would or could appear to a boy in his teens, no matter how sympathetic and highly gifted, but as it has been seen by an experienced woman of the world" (Tuttleton et al. 267). Troy Belknap's opinions correspond almost precisely with Wharton's. Wharton praised the Norman countryside in *A Motor-Flight Through France;* Troy adores it. Wharton, deeply disturbed by the U.S. reluctance to enter the war, came to accept Henry James's change of citizenship (*Letters* 373), declaring "As to our own country, I prefer silence, because I really don't understand any longer" (*Letters* 387). As we saw in chapter one, Wharton expressed both relief and enthusiasm when the United States at last broke off diplomatic relations with Germany in February 1917. In the same way, Troy is impatient to fight for France and irritated with a senator who tells him that "'This isn't our war'" (37); when one of his uncles comments that Troy is merely at an age at which "'every fellow wants to go out and kill something'" (38), Troy chafes: "*To save France*—that was the clear duty of the world, as he saw it" (38). Wharton expressed frustration at "the silly idiot women who have turned their drawing-rooms into hospitals . . . [and who] are robbing the poor stranded ouvrières of their only means of living" (*Letters* 334) as well as the "fluffy fuzzy people" who, mercifully in her opinion, left France as soon as they could after mobilization (*Letters* 341). Troy too is irritated by the wealthy American expatriate crowd: "Troy could not bear to listen to their endlessly reiterated tales of flight from Nauheim or Baden or Brussels, their difficulties in drawing money, hiring motors, bribing hotel-porters, battling for seats in trains . . . and their general tendency to regard the war as a mere background to their personal grievances" (14–15).

Finally, Wharton bestows her profound admiration of France on Troy. She wrote to Sally Norton in June 1916 that "France continues to be magnificent" (*Letters* 380), and to another friend in January 1917 that "France is greater than ever" (*Letters* 386). Troy adores France from his childhood, and his French tutor, Paul Gantier, instructs him in tones predictive of *French Ways and Their Meaning* about the best reasons for loving France:

he had shown Troy how France had always been alive in every fibre, and how her inexhaustible vitality had been perpetually nourished on criticism, analysis and dissatisfaction.

"Self-satisfaction is death," he had said; "France is the phoenix-country, always rising from the ashes of her recognized mistakes." (39)

Perhaps more than any other character in her fiction, Troy *is* Wharton. That she imagined herself as a teenage boy is, in the context of her other war works, not surprising; as we have seen in "Coming Home" and will see in more detail later, Wharton reflected her own frustrated inability to act in a series of incapacitated male characters: Jean de Réchamp in "Coming Home," Charlie Durand in "The Refugees," and finally John Campton in *A Son at the Front*. Troy is the youngest of these characters, the one young enough to express in unguarded and enthusiastic terms what the more reserved Wharton felt.

Wharton's choice of a male focalizer is, moreover, consistent with the gender issues that haunted her throughout the war. Troy, once old enough, is at least of the correct sex to enter "the real business" of war; moreover, his attitude conforms to Wharton's belief, expressed in *French Ways and Their Meaning*, that men are "closer to reality" than women (103). Indeed, although *The Marne* contains a few brief sympathetic portraits of women, the novel's portraits of men are generally far more flattering. Women are usually portrayed as self-satisfied and self-concerned. The novel begins before the outbreak of war, but in this part of the novel as well, Wharton portrays women as less in touch with the "real" things in life than men. Troy's mother, like an older (and only slightly more maternal) Undine Spragg, hurries Paul through the lush countryside of Normandy so that she can reach Paris in time for her appointment with her dressmakers; it is Paul who manages to catch a glimpse of the real, wandering off into Norman villages during his mother's protracted lunches: "Troy had time . . . to slip away alone, and climb to the height where the cathedral stood, or at least to loiter and gaze in the narrow crooked streets, between gabled cross-beamed houses, each more picture-bookishly quaint than its neighbors" (4). Even Troy's effaced and inarticulate father seems to understand the allure of France better than Troy's mother. Though the annual July tour "invariably ended in the Swiss Alps"—a measure of Mr. and Mrs. Belknap's ultimate failure in taste, if one judges them by Wharton's low opinion of Switzerland as expressed in *Italian Backgrounds*—it is always Mr. Belknap who finds "ways lovelier, more winding, more wonderful" of reaching the Alps (6).

Men's relative perspicacity, their capacity to deal with the "real" that Wharton would praise in *French Ways and Their Meaning*, also prevails in *The Marne* after mobilization. Not only are American women in Paris portrayed as the primary culprits in the selfish grasping for staterooms and complaints about inconvenience; even in the scenes set in the United States they fail to see the war properly in the terms of the novel—which are also Wharton's terms. In some cases women's tangential war-related experience becomes merely another form of social activity and social competition. Mrs. Belknap, sure she is "not strong enough for nursing" (22), ponders "tak[ing] convalescent officers for drives in the Bois in the noiseless motor"; she finally "donned a nurse's garb [and] poured tea once or twice at a fashionable hospital" (23). Wharton's portrait of Mrs. Belknap suggests someone lazy, elitist, and unrealistic: her refusal even to consider nursing suggests only her own lack of concern; her interest in driving officers and pouring tea (perhaps only once) at a "fashionable hospital" indicates that the war is, for Mrs. Belknap, mainly a social event. Even when she uses this small amount of experience as a lever for "obtain[ing] permission to carry supplies (in her own motor) to the devastated regions" (23)—an activity similar to Wharton's experience—Mrs. Belknap misses the point. Accompanied by a staff officer to the site of the Battle of the Marne, she pays little attention to his narration of the high points of that battle, making "vague comments" while her eyes "wander" (26). It is Troy who is gripped by the officer's narration. Yet when she returns to the States, Mrs. Belknap capitalizes on her meager experiences: "'The tragedy of it—the tragedy—no one can tell who hasn't seen it, and been through it,' Mrs. Belknap would begin, looking down her long dinner table between the orchids and the candelabra" (34). But soon Mrs. Belknap "find[s] herself hopelessly outstoried, out-adventured, out-charitied" (35): others too have discovered the newest coin of social exchange. Her shift to a "calmer and more distant view of the war" (35) suggests neither maturity nor political indifference so much as the realization that having opinions about the war will not gain her any further social advantage.

Other women in the novel, though they may not share Mrs. Belknap's particular weaknesses, are generally depicted as mistaken in their attitudes as well. Sophy Wicks, Troy's contemporary, affects an "airy indifference" to the war (41). Other girls, "Troy's age, or younger," borrow specious glory from their brothers' enlistment, and treat Troy with condescension (47). Once the United States enters the war, some young women are even criticized for their overenthusiasm, Wharton labeling them "war-mad" (45). Prominent among irritating females in this novel is a character with a satiric name of Dickensian proportions, Hinda Warlick. Anyone familiar with numerous other works by Wharton will immediately recognize her type of callow fatuity, the awkward, ill-informed Midwesterner: "she was singing in a suburban church choir while waiting for a vaudeville engagement. Her studies had probably been curtailed by the need of preparing a repertory, for she appeared to think that Joan of Arc was a Revolutionary hero, who had been guillotined with Marie Antoinette for blowing up the Bastille; and her notions of French history did not extend beyond this striking episode. But she was ready and eager to explain France to Troy" (60–61).

Even worse than Hinda's education is her sense of mission—which she shares with many of the Americans with whom she and Troy are traveling to France. While men are implicated here too, Wharton specifies that "The women were even more sure of their mission" (59). "'We must carry America right into the heart of France. . . . We must teach her to love children and home and the outdoor life; and you American boys must teach the young Frenchmen to love their mothers,'" Hinda smugly preaches (61). This attitude of American moral superiority and condescension— along with Hinda's naive assertion that "'we mustn't despair of teaching even the Germans!'" (62) and her mispronunciation of French place names

("'Eep and Leal and Rams'" [61–62])—exemplifies the ways in which most American women, in Wharton's estimation, failed to grasp the war's real meaning.

The Marne implicitly criticizes a wide range of attitudes. The "pretty women and prosperous men" who "listen for a moment, half-absently" to talk of the war are clearly wrong (34); so are those who "used the war as an opportunity to have fun" (43). Those who have "the odd belief that life-in-itself—just the mere raw fact of being alive—was the one thing that mattered, and getting killed the one thing to be avoided" (44) are as wrong as the German-American boys who are "full of open brag about the Fatherland" (31), or the "flat-faced professor with lank hair, [who] having announced that 'there were two sides to every case,' immediately raised up a following of unnoticed ladies who 'couldn't believe all that was said of the Germans' and hoped that America would never be 'drawn in'" (31–32). Lest there be any doubt that these attitudes are mistaken, Wharton contrasts this group with the "right-minded" in the remainder of the sentence: "while, even among the right-minded, there subsisted a vague feeling that war was an avoidable thing which one had only to reprobate enough to prevent its recurrence" (32). For Wharton, who had insisted to her friend Sally Norton that "the 'atrocities' one hears of *are true*" (*Letters* 335), any questions about the villainy of Germany or the necessity of the war were naive and unacceptable. The impatience Wharton expressed in many letters to her friends inserts itself—uncharacteristically—into *The Marne* and onto her characters.

Men—while not universally portrayed as right-thinking—seem to stand a better chance than women of adhering to what Wharton strongly suggests are the proper attitudes. Troy's father, though not engaged in the war effort, is from the outbreak of war someone "with whom [Troy] might have talked . . . ; and Troy could not talk to his mother" (14). Later Wharton relates that "Mr. Belknap had always been less eloquent about the war than his wife; but somehow Troy had fancied he felt it more deeply" (36). And when Troy, on his eighteenth birthday, asks to go to France to drive an ambulance, his mother protests, but his father finally "blurt[s] out" to his wife, "'*I understand Troy*'" (56).

Troy's desire to serve in the American Ambulance and Mr. Belknap's support of that view reflect again Wharton's belief that the real business of war was at the front—a place women could not go. Although her portrayal of American soldiers in *The Marne* is mixed, it is ultimately admiring as the men head toward battle. Before their engagement, American soldiers and officers discourage the more cosmopolitan Troy with their provincial wondering "where in the blasted place you could get fried hominy and a real porter-house steak for breakfast" (78). But he finds them transformed as they head toward the front, much like the transfigured soldiers Wharton described in *Fighting France:* "now he seemed to see a different race of men. The faces leaning from the windows of the train glowed with youthful resolution. The soldiers were out on their real business at last" (79).

Men heading to battle are "out on their real business," a business that, moreover, confirms their manhood. *The Marne* clearly links masculinity and frontline duties through a quotation from Shakespeare:

Troy suddenly remembered a bit of Henry the Fifth that M. Gantier had been fond of quoting:
And gentlemen in England now a-bed
Shall think themselves accursed they were not here,
And hold their manhoods cheap whiles any speaks
That fought with us. (28)

In conferring "manhood," war necessarily excludes women. In the all-male zone of combat and the ambulance corps (there seem to be no women ambulance drivers in Wharton's France), a man even replaces, at least symbolically, the uniquely female function of maternity. When Troy recalls his rescue from the lines, he also recalls the face of Paul Gantier hovering over him, "bending low and whispering: '*Mon petit—mon pauvre petit gars . . .*' [My little boy—my poor little boy]. Troy heard the words distinctly, he knew the voice as well as he knew his mother's" (127). Women exist only on the fringes of this world, as problems and irritants—or, very occasionally, as with Sophy Wicks later in the novel, as helpmeets—but unrealized ones. Here, as elsewhere, it is the frontline experience that defines the real experience of war for Wharton.

This definition again leads to the anomalous position of Wharton's war writings in the canon of Great War literature. Wharton accepts the proposition that the experience of soldiers is both unique and exclusive. Her writing, as the previous examples also illustrate, is full of the disillusionment that has come to be a hallmark of World War I work: disillusionment with American soldiers, American charities, American expatriates in general. But her disillusionment is, finally (and not surprisingly) limited to the territory with which Wharton herself was most familiar, the world behind the lines. Her exclusion from the world of combat, though she simultaneously accepted it and chafed at it, allowed her to continue to romanticize the world of the front—at least to some extent.

For Wharton did not wholly romanticize that world. As we have seen, the "flush and shiver of romance" were gone for Wharton by the time she composed *The Marne;* the fascination of the war's early days had been superseded by horror and fatigue. In spite of the extent to which she gives her beliefs and enthusiasms to young Troy, she also steps back from him occasionally, reflecting the knowledge of someone who had lived through the war. When Troy rails against the self-centeredness of his mother's friends trapped in Paris by mobilization, the narrator intervenes and tells readers that "The choristers were all good and kindly persons, shaken out of the rut of right feeling by the first real fright of their lives. But Troy was too young to understand this, and to foresee that . . . they would become the passionate advocates of France" (18). When Troy first sees a landscape ravaged by battle, his reaction is one of outrage at once realistic and melodramatic: "This was what war did! It emptied towns of their inhabitants as it emptied veins of their blood; it killed houses and lands as well as men. Out there . . . men were dying at that very moment by hundreds, by thousands— . . . War meant Death, Death, Death—Death everywhere, and to everything" (25). Within a matter of hours, however, Troy has returned to a view more purely idealistic: "Ah yes—ah, yes—to have been in the battle of the Marne!" (28). It is the narrator who remarks that Troy "forgot the horror of war, and thought only of its splendours" (27). Wharton, older, more experienced, and more disillusioned than her creation, has a skepticism he has not.

Yet her very creation of Troy, her decision to portray battle (however briefly), and her choice of the Marne rather than of any other battle, suggest how deeply she still believed in a fundamentally, if not wholly, romantic view of war. The name *Troy* itself recalls a war both epic and heroic, a war which has entered the annals not only of history but of mythology. Troy's experience in the ambulance corps is different from that of better-known fictional figures who have undergone the same experience: unlike Martin Howe in John Dos Passos' *One Man's Initiation: 1917,* e.e. cummings in *The Enormous Room,* and Frederick Henry in Hemingway's *A Farewell to Arms,* Troy is not profoundly disillusioned by his months in the ambulance service. Moreover, Wharton's choice to focus on the battles of the Marne suggests that the idea of war had not lost all its glory for her. Both the first and second battles of the Marne were relatively quick and decisive—unlike the Battle of the Somme or Passchendaele, virtual stalemates that dragged on for months, resulting in thousands of unheroic deaths in the trenches. Both battles along the Marne were fought in a few days rather than over months; both pushed the Germans back and resulted in decisive victories for the French. This type of warfare was also more typical of war as Wharton would have thought of it; it allowed her to maintain an optimistic, heroic, and somewhat romantic view of war.

Although Wharton respected frontline combat as a male province, she took the risk of portraying it—briefly—in *The Marne*. This choice may in part account for the novel's eventual fall into oblivion: Wharton had crossed the invisible line by portraying an experience she as a woman could not have had, the same mistake made by Willa Cather in *One of Ours*.[7] Further, Wharton had made the error of romanticizing that experience, at least partially. To some extent, Troy's experience adheres to the Myth of the War as defined by Paul Fussell and Samuel Hynes. His encounter starts out badly: his ambulance breaks down, and he is uncertain whether to stay with it or leave it. Far from being swept into a battle frenzy or overcome with a sense of heroism, he is acutely aware of his own lack of knowledge; he is afraid not of war but of "doing something stupid, inopportune, idiotic" (113). But at this point Wharton's depiction runs into trouble. Troy's actions are probably meant to seem heroic, but read in the context of other World War I writings, they seem hapless at best and foolish at worst. He volunteers for a mission before he knows what that mission is; when a shell falls near his scouting party and a man near him is wounded, his "year's experience in ambulance work" (122) makes him realize that if he cannot pick up the man and carry him to safety, the man will die on the field. Although he realizes that the sky is beginning to lighten and his standing will expose him to German soldiers, Troy picks up the wounded soldier, stands, and is shot.

However foolish this action may seem to others—Fussell discusses the danger of the lightening sky, against which a standing soldier was an easy target, and Ford Madox Ford chose his title *A Man Could Stand Up* with that danger in mind—it is likely that Wharton meant her readers to see Troy's rescue of the wounded soldier as a heroic act. She makes it clear that Troy, though ignorant of other soldierly functions, is aware of the danger of what he does. Further, his wounding is reminiscent of the description of Jean du Breuil's death: "'It was in a superb gesture that he was struck, wanting to look for one of his wounded men close to the Germans. He went straight ahead, without the slightest hesitation and the least worry of danger, and he was spotted by some Prussians lying in ambush . . .'" (*Uncollected Critical Writings* 203). Wharton saw du Breuil's death as heroic; in partially recreating it in Troy's injury, she must have meant it to convey the same heroism.

Moreover, the novel as a whole reads heroically, not ironically. Although Wharton allows Troy to have the "real" experience of war, the experience she could not have, he nevertheless feels haunted by Wharton's sense of the unreality of war. "If it had not been for his pumping heart and his aching bursting feet Troy at moments would have thought it was a dream . . . " (114). "'We're going toward a battle,' Troy sang to himself . . . But the words meant no more to him than the doggerel the soldier was chanting at his elbow . . . " (114–15). Even after Troy has been wounded and brought back to a hospital he has a hard time believing he has been in the real war itself. It is Jacks, his fellow ambulance driver (whose own authority may be questionable: he was absent from the field during the battle), who tells him of "all the great things in which he had played an unconscious part" (125), and who reassures him "'Battle of the Marne? Sure you were in it—in it up to the hilt, you lucky kid!'" (125).

It might be argued from this passage that Wharton is undermining not only Troy's experience but, perhaps, the very mythos of war. But *The Marne* is not a skeptical book; the passage immediately following Jacks's reassuring words proclaims excitedly, "And what a battle it had been! The Americans had taken Vaux and driven the Germans back across the bridge at Château-Thierry" (125). Far from doubting the reality of his own experience, Troy accepts it once Jacks has confirmed it, just as he accepts his belief that the ghost of Paul Gantier has saved him. The novel concludes with Troy dedicating his life to serving the spirit of France, represented by Gantier: "—he would do it on the battle-fields of France" (128).

The romanticism of the conclusion is consistent with Wharton's language throughout much of the novel. As we have seen, Wharton's writing does not follow a simple pattern of being more idealistic at the outset of the war and more cynical as it went on. While *Fighting France* has elements of romanticism, it is, overall, too eerie to be romantic; but *The Marne* contains little that is eerie (even the "ghost story" of Paul Gantier fails to send shivers down the spine) and much that is prescriptive. Samuel Hynes has noted that "official art" is official—approved by war offices—precisely because it is "not *strange*" (160). Wharton had caught the strangeness of war in *Fighting France* in a way she did not in *The Marne*. By such a definition, *Fighting France* is not official art; *The Marne* is. The tone of *The*

Marne is more didactic, more strident than that of *Fighting France;* the Germans are even worse and the French are even better than in that earlier work. Correspondingly, romantic language is common (and generally unchallenged) in *The Marne.* The Germans are described as "the hosts of evil" (14); devastated landscapes are described in metaphors of disease: "The great stretch of desolation spreading and spreading like a leprosy" (17); war is an "adventure" (21)[8] or heroic quest that confers manhood. French soil is "sacred" and French troops are "valiant" (83). Even in defeat they are glorified and admired as "the tragic and magnificent armies" (17). Viewing the battlefield of the Marne, Troy senses that "A name of glory and woe was attached to every copse and hollow, and to each gray steeple above the village roofs" (27). More than in *Fighting France,* Wharton chose in *The Marne* to use the "'raised,' essentially feudal language" (Fussell 21) of the prewar world.

Another way in which *The Marne* violates the principles of the Great War canon is in its expression of Wharton's ongoing faith in the war's ability to transform those who participated in it. The war years change Troy from a boy into a man with battle experience; they transform hapless, selfish American expatriates into men and women who help France's cause. If Troy's father looks "older and fatter" in his Red Cross uniform, he also looks "more important and impressive" (72). Perhaps most significantly, Wharton pays homage to the power of France itself in creating a transformed Hinda Warlick, who admits the error of her former belief in U.S. cultural superiority. Late in the novel Hinda remarks, "'Since I came to Europe, nearly a year ago, I've got to know the country they're dying for—and I understand why they mean to go on and on dying—if they have to—till there isn't one of them left. Boys—I know France now—and she's worth it! ... I have to laugh now when I remember what I thought of France when I landed'" (97–98). The terms in which Hinda thinks have not altered; it is only that she is pleasantly relieved to find that every French soldier seems to have "'a photograph of a baby stowed away somewhere in his dirty uniform'" (99). She asserts with a crudely admiring racism, "'I tell you, they're *white!*'" and concludes by cheering "'Veever la France!'" and bursting into "'the Marsellaze!'" (99–100). Hinda's pronunciation is still bad and her sentiments crude: she comes to admire the French not, as Wharton will suggest in *French Ways,* because of their differences from Americans, but because of what she sees as their similarities. Nevertheless, Hinda is improved and almost redeemed by her change in sentiment: she has accepted what Wharton would have liked all Americans to appreciate, the value of France—and the importance of fighting and even dying for France.

Another mark of Wharton's nonconformity to the standard Myth of the War is her use in *The Marne* of Horace's "Dulce et decorum." As she would again in *A Son at the Front*, she quotes it sincerely, admiringly: "[Troy] remembered the anguish of regret with which he had seen M. Gantier leave St. Moritz to join his regiment, and thought now with passionate envy of his tutor's fate. 'Dulce et decorum est . . .' The old hackneyed phrase had taken on a beauty that filled his eyes with tears" (52). That belief in the worth of ideals above the worth of life itself governs *The Marne*, accounting for its romanticism and for the value Wharton would continue to see in war: its power to alter and transform, its power to ennoble.

While such a belief seems specious to most readers today, it is important to recall that a belief in the futility of the war was not, after all, de rigueur in 1918: "in 1920 the war was still a political issue. . . . There was still a war party and an anti-war party" (Hynes 287). Most of the books that would create the myth of the war did not begin to be published until 1926 (Hynes 424–25). It was not until about 1930 that fiction and film had established an "essential Myth: each told a war story that was individual, violent, and mortal—a story not of battles won, but of lives lost. . . .[T]here was only one story, in which young men went to war, fought there, and died" (Hynes 447). Even then, not everyone agreed that the Myth was also history. The 1930 "War Books Controversy" in England raised points that confirm much of Wharton's perspective in *The Marne* and engendered speeches with which Edith Wharton must have agreed. Brigadier General John Carteris maintained that "Many men went through the War and came back ennobled by the fact that they had taken part in it and had put into actual practice towards their fellow men some of the finest instincts in human nature" (qtd. in Hynes 450). General Sir Ian Hamilton was reported as saying that "surely it was extra queer that these elaborate attempts to exclude virtue, nobility and even valour from war should choose this time to begin to flourish like toadstools on the tombs of our dead heroes" (qtd. in Hynes 451). Wharton was not alone in her abiding belief in "dulce et decorum."

Any view of literary history and the notion of realism is inevitably limited, and when *The Marne* is dismissed as slight or "bloodthirst[y]" (Cooperman 41), the implication is also that it is an unrealistic novel—that Wharton did not really know her topic. While there may be elements of truth in this assumption, it is also full of fallacies. Wharton's knowledge of battle was necessarily secondhand, but she does not make gross errors in her brief fictional foray to the front; on the contrary, the chaos the novel describes is consistent with other accounts of the war. Certainly her own extensive knowledge of American expatriate behavior in wartime is reflected in the novel. And, although Wharton was probably too credulous in believing that "the atrocities one hears of *are true*," as many of these were, as history has shown, fabricated by British propagandists,[9] the atrocity mentioned in this book—the execution of old M. Gantier—echoes fact. Early in the war a newspaper informs Troy of the devastation of Gantier's village:

> And he read: "Not a house is standing. The curé has been shot. A number of old people were burnt in the hospice. The mayor and five of the principal inhabitants have been taken to Germany as hostages."
>
> The year before the war, he remembered, old M. Gantier was mayor! (13)

This fictional event reflects historical actuality. On September 2, 1914, German troops traveling through the French town of Senlis "took the Mayor . . . and six other citizens hostage. They were taken to a field outside the town and shot" (M. Gilbert 66).

Even the scene in which the ghost of Paul Gantier rescues the wounded Troy is not entirely fanciful, but rather reflects many stories circulating among the soldiers in what Paul Fussell has called "an approximation of the popular psychological atmosphere of the Middle Ages" (115). Legends were common: for example, the Angel of Mons was "reputed to have appeared in the sky during the British retreat from Mons in August, 1914, and to have safeguarded the withdrawal" (Fussell 115–16). Among other popular tales is one that might have served as the basis for Paul Gantier's ghost: "the legend of the ghostly German officer-spy who appears in the British trenches just before an attack. . . . No one sees him come or go" (Fussell 121–22). The tutor's ghost seems to be a benevolent version of this ghost—one who does his job and vanishes. He becomes, as one early reviewer said, "a consummating symbol for [Wharton's] conviction of the immortality of the French spirit and the French civilization" (Tuttleton et al. 269). But this spirit is based not only on Wharton's adulation of the French; it also derives from and reflects stories that had emerged from the trenches.

The Marne also illustrates that Wharton was beginning to shape the war to her uses. She had dedicated the novel to Ronald Simmons; if Troy has much of Wharton in him, he also has much of Simmons's youthful energy. Wharton had planned a different ending for the novel, one in which Troy "is killed in the fight for Neuilly-le-Pont" (manuscript of *The Marne, Wharton Collection* Yale). As we have seen, her actual ending for the novel softens this considerably; Troy is only wounded. She could not bring Simmons back, but in her fiction she took the author's prerogative of mitigating the fates of characters who bore characteristics of people she loved—a prerogative she would exercise again, once more on Simmons's behalf, in *A Son at the Front.*[10]

IV. The Loss of Ambiguity: *French Ways and Their Meaning*

Wharton would write in her memoir that a psychological escape from the war "was possible only to real workers, as it is possible for a nurse on a hard case to bear the sight of the patient's sufferings because she is doing all she can to relieve them" (*Backward Glance* 356). While much of her "real work" was in the form of the various charities she administered and for which she raised funds, her writing was a significant part of that work as well. Troy Belknap served as a nearly transparent—certainly a translucent—version of Wharton in *The Marne*. In *French Ways and Their Meaning*, she abandoned her mouthpiece to say, in her own strong voice, what she believed needed to be said about the war—and about the supreme importance of French culture. *French Ways* is the culmination of Wharton's movement away from the ambiguous and ironic toward "the obvious" that her Macy Greer had praised.[11]

French Ways and Their Meaning is generally known as the book Wharton addressed to American soldiers.[12] This book began not as a manuscript per se, but rather as a talk Wharton was asked to give to the Soldiers' and Sailors' Club in Paris. Her "Talk to American Soldiers," as she named it (see Appendix B), called on her to address an audience unfamiliar with French culture and to serve unofficially as a kind of ambassador—to "talk to you [the soldiers] about French ways and their meaning," as she put it on the third page of her speech. Most U.S. soldiers were coming to France for the first time—usually, from Wharton's perspective, with the best and noblest intentions, but with the attitude she had re-created in Hinda Warlick: the woefully mistaken assumption that American culture was far superior to French culture. For Wharton, of course, just the opposite was true; she used this speech as an opportunity to provide American sailors and soldiers with elementary instruction in French culture and French etiquette.

The issues that pervade Wharton's war work are also addressed in her "Talk." Her concern with gender roles is reflected as she begins her talk with amusing self-deprecation based in part on her gender: "I never expected to speak in public. I consider it a man's job and not a woman's[.]" But Wharton promptly turns this disadvantage into an advantage, charmingly—and perhaps rather disingenuously—asking her male audience for their indulgence:

> and I never *did* speak in public till last February, when I was asked to try to explain to a French audience some of the reasons why America has come into this war.
>
> That occasion was "positively my first appearance"; but it went off very well . . . and I wasn't the least nervous, because I spoke in French, and was sustained by the thought that my audience probably didn't understand more than half of what I was saying.
>
> Now, on the contrary, I am to talk in my own language to my own country-people, and if I don't interest you I can't say afterward that it was because you missed all my best things; so you must make allowances for my timidity, and encourage me by laughing at all my jokes. ("Talk to American Soldiers," *Wharton Collection* Yale)

After this ingratiating introduction, however, Wharton asserts her authority as a longtime resident of France. That and her devotion to France override her sense that speaking is a "man's job" as she says self-confidently, "if I were dead, and anybody asked me to come back and witness for France, I should get up out of my grave to do it" ("Talk," *Wharton Collection* Yale).

Wharton's profound admiration for the French is the keynote of both the "Talk to American Soldiers" and *French Ways and Their Meaning*. One paragraph of her talk begins by suggesting that most Americans admire France: "I had always admired the country and the people, as we Americans *usually* do" (*Wharton Collection* Yale; emphasis added). But by the end of the same paragraph she is suggesting that admiration is the only reasonable attitude for Americans. After listing "the beauty of the cities . . . the scientific care of the great forests . . . the eloquence and beauty of the magnificent French literature" among other assets, she says, "I had admired and enjoyed these great national treasures of France as *all* thoughtful Americans do" (*Wharton Collection* Yale; emphasis added). Any American soldier who wanted to consider himself "thoughtful" had best "admire and enjoy" France too.

Much of the "Talk" is an exercise in removing ambiguity and insisting on the simple black-and-white of the war. Wharton knew that the French and the Americans did not always make the best initial impression on each other, and she attempts to remedy this situation by constructing a rhetoric that insists that American soldiers side not only actually but psychologically with the French—and against the Germans. This concern in the "Talk" influenced the shape of *French Ways:* its opening chapter was taken directly from Wharton's speech. Entitled "First Impressions," it urges American soldiers not to trust their initial reactions to the French. She tells soldiers that "the newcomer must perpetually remind himself that almost all that is best in France is in the trenches" and not in the leisure-spots he is most likely to have seen. Again, combat emerges as the site of real experience: "I have no fear of what the American will think of the Frenchman after the two have fraternized at the front" (*French Ways* 8).

Concerned that American soldiers' first impression of the French would be negative, Wharton also worried that their impression of the Germans might be positive. She encourages Americans to mistrust this first reaction as well: "Some of [our soldiers] may even, in their first moment of reaction, have said to themselves 'Well, after all, the Germans we knew at home were easier people to get on with'" (*French Ways* 10). Wharton launches herself into combating this error, decoding the mysteries of cultural difference for soldiers—and her reading public—and in doing so further emphasizing her "us/them" dichotomy: "The answer is not far to seek. For one thing, the critics in question knew the Germans at home, *in our home,* where they had to talk our language or not get on, where they had to be what we wanted them to be—or get out" (*French Ways* 10). Wharton's attitude here is decidedly monocultural: "*in our home*" implies a unified American culture, as does her emphasis on "our language" and the apparently absolute demands of the dominant culture: "they had to be what we wanted them to be—or get out." Despite her many friends in France and England, and despite her adulation of everything French, Wharton was frequently uneasy about immigrants and foreigners in the United States—particularly lower-class immigrants and foreigners. This fear is reflected in more muted tones in her fictional works,[13] but emerges as blatant xenophobia in this passage. She does concede that German-Americans are not all bad: "as we all know in America, no people on earth, when they settle in a new country, are more eager than the Germans to adopt its ways, and to be taken for native-born citizens" (*French Ways* 10). This concession, however, serves primarily as a stepping-stone to reemphasize the villainy of Germans: "The Germans in Germany are very different" from those in America, she insists (*French Ways* 10).

Nor is Wharton content to let the matter rest there. She opens *French Ways* by warning her readers that "Hasty generalizations are always tempting. . . . But nine times out of ten they hit wild"(3). Yet in her first chapter she uses anecdotal evidence—the insistence of a guard at the Berlin Opera House that she take off her cloak—to reach a sweeping conclusion: "The German does not care to be free as long as he is well fed, well amused and making money. The Frenchman, like the American, wants to be free first of all, and free anyhow—free even when he might be better off, materially, if he lived under a benevolent autocracy" (14–15). Contrary to American first impressions, Wharton argues, the French are fundamentally like the Americans—and the Germans, who "differ from us totally in all of the important things" (16), are fundamentally despicable. There is no gray middle ground.

Wharton had parodied attitudes of American superiority in the fictional Hinda Warlick; in *French Ways* she returned to this topic, urging soldiers to set aside their own provincialism. She put her concern into the most direct language in her "Talk": "I hear a good deal in these days of the phrase: 'what America can teach France.' My idea is that we'd better leave it to the French to discover that, and apply ourselves to finding out what France can teach us" (*Wharton Collection* Yale). A certain provincialism may have had a degree of charm in Charity Royall, if only because it points up her naiveté. But Wharton did not see it as charming in American soldiers. She occasionally criticizes the French, generally for minor failings like their refusal to eat blackberries (*French Ways* 20–21). But all her criticisms—even her faulting the French for refusing to give generously to war charities (*French Ways* 89)—are inconsequential in comparison to the praise she heaps on the vast majority of the habits, beliefs, towns, arts, and institutions of her beloved, adopted, and threatened country. She concludes *French Ways* with a burst of patriotism (perhaps it might better be called expatriotism): "the best answer to every criticism of French weakness or French shortcomings is the conclusive one: *Look at the results!* Read her history, study her art, follow up the current of her ideas; then look about you, and you will see that the whole world is full of her spilt glory" (*French Ways* 149).

French Ways and Their Meaning is a very different book from what would seem to be its counterpart, *Fighting France;* the war had seen to that. *Fighting France* is full of questions, wonders, horrors, and ambiguity. *French Ways* is the most propagandistic of Wharton's wartime writing. This is not to suggest that it is consciously propagandistic, that is, full of statements Wharton knew to be exaggerated or untrue. On the contrary, her letters from the war suggest that *French Ways* reflects her views about France and the war quite accurately. But those views had shifted between the composition of *Fighting France* and the composition of *French Ways;* the war had become a daily reality that Wharton had accepted, as she may also have accepted—after a final plunge into literary ambiguity in *Summer*—that writing about the war could be, and perhaps ought to be, simple and straightforward. Wharton's view of France had changed as well. Although Wharton had from the outset been a strong partisan of France, she had come to see her adopted country as increasingly heroic and "good," and to see Germany—which she had visited before the war, but would never visit again after it (Lewis, *Edith Wharton* 394)—as increasingly villainous and "bad." As Fussell has written, the war encouraged "The modern *versus* habit: one thing opposed to another, not with some Hegelian hope of synthesis involving a dissolution of both extremes, . . . but with a sense that one of the poles embodies so wicked a deficiency or flaw or perversion that its total submission is called for" (79). This "habit of simple distinction, simplification, and opposition" (Fussell 79) pervades *French Ways:* the Germans are bad, the French are good; provincial unenlightened Americans are bad (though not as bad as the Germans), while enlightened Francophile Americans are good (though not, probably, quite so good as the French).

Wharton's tendency toward simplification in *French Ways* (and her corresponding shift away from the more complex view of *Fighting France*) is exemplified in the differences between two parallel passages. In *Fighting France* Wharton had written, "There have been mothers and widows for whom a single grave, or the appearance of one name on the missing list, has turned the whole conflict into an idiot's tale" (224). Although this passage turns toward accolades of the stoic Frenchwoman, it acknowledges that for some, at least, the cost was "too bitter to be borne." In *French Ways* Wharton allows for no such weakness. She writes of "the millions of brave, uncomplaining, self-denying mothers and wives and sisters who sent them forth smiling [husbands, sons, and brothers], who waited for them patiently and courageously, or who are mourning them silently and unflinchingly, and *not one of whom*, at the end of the most awful struggle in history, is ever heard to say that the cost has been too great or the trial too bitter to be borne" (121; emphasis added). In *French Ways*, Wharton portrays the French as universally stoical, unequivocally unified in their dedication to the war, whatever its cost.

The shift in tone from the relative realism of *Fighting France* to the heroic in *French Ways* reflects not only Wharton's buckling down to the task of writing for France, but also her growing conservatism. While some critics and historians have argued that the war had a liberating effect on women, others have pointed out that the end of war often causes political backlash and neoconservatism. As one historian has put it, "Did millions of veterans return from the front having thrown off their traditional prejudices? . . . Is it not a more probable human reaction, after so great a tragedy, to seek to revive the status quo ante bellum—to 'return to normalcy,' in the language of the 1920s?" (Hause 102) Wharton wrote in *French Ways* that "There is nothing like a Revolution for making people conservative" (34). The Great War seems to have had the same effect on her. She praises not French willingness to change but the French "instinct to preserve," citing as an example their preservation of their cathedrals even "when they ceased to feel the beauty of Gothic architecture, as the French had ceased to feel it in the seventeenth century" (31). She names this instinct as another reason for French self-defense in the war, arguing that "The French have nearly two thousand years of history and art and industry and social and political life to 'conserve'" (35).

French Ways reflects two types of conservatism: the conservatism contained in "the instinct to preserve" and the political conservatism that is latent in what Wharton has to say about France. Wharton presents France in wartime as both unified and heroic: "Look at her [France] as she has stood before the world for the last four years and a half, uncomplaining, undiscouraged, undaunted, holding up the banner of liberty. . . . [L]ook at her, as the world has beheld her since August, 1914, fearless, tearless, indestructible, in [the] face of the most ruthless and formidable enemy the world has ever known, determined to fight on to the end for the principles she has always lived for" (120–21). In Wharton's portrait, France stands "fearless, tearless, indestructible," and united. But history suggests that France was not as unified as Wharton portrays it. The universal harmony Wharton describes was not universal; in the town of Creusot, for instance, families whose men had been sent home from the front to work at metalwork jobs deemed essential "'tended to make perhaps too frank a show of their delight at a time when others were learning of the death of those who had remained at the front,' with the result that there was some jealousy and envy" (Becker 27). A wartime antiwar movement and some workers' refusal of the notion of *Union sacrée* also indicates that the French were not completely united (Becker 80). Wharton can portray France as united only because she fails to mention any of the strikes occurring in France in the spring of 1917, when "many workers ignored the imperative that the least they could do while others were sacrificing their lives at the front was to work as hard as they could" (Becker 211); in May 1918 a "major wave of strikes hit munitions factories in the Paris region" (Becker 260). *French Ways* contains not the smallest hint of these important events.

Wharton's sense of "eternal France" pervades *French Ways* in another way as well. Her emphasis on continuity in France's "two thousand years of history" elides the political changes, especially for women, that occurred in the years immediately preceding the war. As we have seen, Wharton was like many English writers in remembering the summer of 1914 as exceptionally long, sunny, and pleasant, and in recalling the prewar years—erroneously—as free of political turmoil and struggle. In fact, France was changing in the years before the war, not only artistically but also in the area of women's rights. By 1914 France had "several hundred 'women doctors,'" and "ten or more women practiced law"; increasing numbers of women were pursuing the *baccalauréat* degree, previously obtained almost exclusively by men; legal changes were making divorces somewhat easier to obtain, and "the number of divorce procedures instigated by women" was rising (Perrot 53). Many women were agitating for the vote, and five thousand women marched through Paris in support of women's suffrage in 1914 (Hause 101). The French equivalent of the "New Woman"—referred to as "American women"—were a conspicuous minority, and "their attractive image, diffused by fashion magazines, had cultural prestige" (Perrot 52).

Before the war and even into its early months, Wharton seems to have shared, in at least a minor way, the prewar expansion of attitudes toward women, a shift that carried into her writings from the early months of the war. Her portrait of Yvonne Malo, a musician who lives alone, is, as we have seen, a flattering one. Her eulogy for Jean du Breuil provides a rare moment of liberalism for Wharton, one in which she writes that her friend "opened my eyes to a question of which—I admit it to my shame—I had not until then understood the immense social implications," that of the enfranchisement of women (*Uncollected Critical Writings* 200). She concludes that on this topic, du Breuil "made me see that the only thing that matters, in the feminist movement, is the fate of those women 'whom the brutal economic law of big-city life waits to devour,' of those poor hard-working women who accept their long misery with an animal fatalism because they do not know that they have a right to a more humane existence. In short, one would be tempted to say that women who argue for the right to vote could very well do without it, but it is necessary for those women, so much more numerous, who do not even know what it is, or why others are demanding it in their name!" (*Uncollected Critical Writings* 200–201).

Thus in May 1915. But by the time she was writing "The New French-woman," originally published in *Ladies' Home Journal* in April 1917 (Garrison 457), she had been affected by the neoconservatism sweeping the country and declared emphatically, "There is no new Frenchwoman" (*French Ways* 98). Wharton concedes that "It would be easy enough to palm her off as a 'new' Frenchwoman because the war has caused her to live a new life and do unfamiliar jobs" (99) and acknowledges that "one of the few benefits of the war" will be that "the French young girl . . . will never again be the prisoner she has been in the past" (116). Such concessions, however, only feed Wharton's central point. Of young girls as "prisoner[s]" she goes on to remark, "But this is relatively unimportant" (116). Similarly, she admits that Frenchwomen have fewer legal rights than English or American women, but adds that this "technical situation" is unrelated to the "practical fact"—that Frenchwomen are in closer touch with reality than American women (105–106). The issue that haunted her throughout the war—women's exclusion from battle, and hence from the real war, from real experience—returns again in *French Ways*. Asserting that Frenchwomen are "grown up"—unlike American women, and superior to them—Wharton describes them as men's "partners."

But a close examination of the terms of the partnership suggests that even Frenchwomen aren't quite as "real" as their male counterparts. In the following passage it is implied that the Frenchman is still the head of the family business: "It is not only because she saves him a salesman's salary, or a book-keeper'[s] salary, or both, that the French tradesman associates his wife with his business; it is because he has the sense to see that no hired assistant will have so keen a perception of his interests, that none will receive his customers so pleasantly, and that none will so patiently and willingly work over hours when it is necessary to do so" (106). In business as in war, men's experience is primary, women's secondary; women become "real" only through their contact with men. If Frenchwomen were superior to American women for Wharton, it is because of their closer contact with men and what they represent: daily business, including the business of war. Frenchwomen, as Wharton saw them, were closer to the war's reality because of the sacrifice they made through their husbands and sons: women are described as "self-denying mothers and wives and sisters" (*French Ways* 121) and are valued for their sacrifice to the cause of the war, as Wharton honors French wives for their participation in their husbands' businesses. Wharton's remarks are illuminated by Margaret Higonnet's observations on sacrifice and changing gender roles during wartime: the appeals for women to take on new kinds of work "were contained within a nationalist and militarist discourse that reinforced patriarchal, organicist notions of gender relations. It stipulated that women's new roles were 'only for the duration' and that wives and mothers must make heroic sacrifices 'for the nation in its time of need'" ("Introduction" 7).

Wharton's remarks on French marriage in *French Ways and Their Meaning* also reveal her growing conservatism. They may have startled American readers with their implication of acceptable love relationships outside marriage: the French "have decided that love is too grave a matter for boys and girls, and not grave enough to form the basis of marriage. . . . [T]hey allow it, frankly and amply, the part it furtively and shabbily, but no less ubiquitously, plays in Puritan societies" (131–32). At the same time Wharton asserts that—despite legal changes—"in the deepest consciousness of the French, marriage still remains indissoluble" (131–32). Such a view might have seemed radical to many American readers of the time, both those who adhered to ideas of companionate marriage and to those who advocated "free love." Yet Wharton's view is, from the perspective of French culture and history, conservative. She staunchly argues that marriage is for procreation and the perpetuation of the family (128), thus ignoring the fact of political change and shifting social mores. Not only was divorce somewhat easier to obtain, but companionate marriage was increasingly accepted. From the mid-nineteenth century up until the war, marriage was gradually being seen as "'no longer exclusively dedicated to procreation but . . . to the blossoming of sentiment and sensuality for the couple'" (Schnapper, qtd. in Perrot 53). For Wharton, the old order had more appeal than the new one, and it is the old—and frequently idealized—order that she celebrates in *French Ways*.[14]

V. Shifting Tones

Wharton published a final work of note in 1918: an elegy for Ronald Simmons. As we have seen, the death of this young man upset her deeply; her
elegy for him expresses a mixture of stances and emotions: shock, loyal
affection, refusal to be mollified by stock sentiments, and—as in "Beaumetz," her elegy for Jean du Breuil—belief in an afterlife created in human
memory. She begins with a conundrum, a statement of fact paired with the
inability to accept it: "He is dead that was alive. / How shall friendship
understand?" The poem thus opens with a bald statement; later lines re-
verberate with the prewar tones of chivalry, remnants of the romanticism
of *Fighting France:* "He, with so much left to do, / Such a gallant race to
run. . . ." But far from presenting the war as under God's divine gover-
nance, as one might expect from such diction, Wharton presents God as
inscrutable: "What concern had he with you, / Silent Keeper of things
done?" Similarly, she refuses facile visions of an afterlife: "Tell us not that,
wise and young, / Elsewhere he lives out his plan." Yet she concludes by
describing a hopeful Elysium in human memory:

> Long and long shall we remember,
> In our breasts his grave be made.
> It shall never be December
> Where so warm a heart is laid,
> But in our saddest selves a sweet voice sing,
> Recalling him, and Spring.

Despite its grief and bafflement, the poem ends on a note of hope.

Although this poem is an elegy for Simmons, Wharton does not emphasize it as such. Her title is "'On Active Service': American Expeditionary Force," and only under this title are Simmons's initials and the date of
his death published. Wharton saw her public expression of grief as representative: her poem speaks for others as well as herself, and of others as
well as of Simmons. Similarly, the poem makes no mention of the circumstances of Simmons's death: a hospital death caused by double pneumonia.
Certainly his loss was as sad as any other, but—unlike the death of Jean du
Breuil—it was not one that lent itself to descriptions of wartime heroism.
Wharton's 1915 words about Henri's death are implicitly echoed in this
poem: "Oh, this long horror! It comes home with a special pang when an
obscure soldier drops out of the lines, & one happens to know what an
eager spirit beat in him" (*Letters* 361). The "long horror" returned with

Simmons's death; he, like Henri, was unlikely to go down in the annals of history, yet like Henri possessed "an eager spirit." Amidst the strong pro-French expressions of *The Marne* and *French Ways* stands this quiet, questioning, but ultimately reassuring elegy, a harbinger of the elegies she would write in 1919.

Wharton wrote a great deal, and often hastily, between 1916 and 1918. While *Summer* is rarely thought of as a war work, it bears traces of the war, not only in the description of fireworks that echo Wharton's descriptions of bombs and in the way the deprivations of the Mountain people draw on Wharton's experience with refugees, but also in minor details: in Charity's dinner at a "a little open-air place . . . that called itself a French restaurant" in Nettleton (89); in her vague wondering what "North Dormer look[ed] like to people from other parts of the world" (2); and perhaps in Wharton's evocation of rural American places at a time when she was seeing so many rural French towns devastated by the German army. For all Charity's traumas, there is a deep sense of safety in *Summer* that must have been part of the refuge the novel provided not only for its author but for readers like Joseph Conrad. And, despite the apparently abrupt shift between *Summer* and the two works that followed it, there are threads of continuity. North Dormer's thin but sometimes moving Old Home Week reappears parodically in *The Marne*, as Hinda Warlick proposes to "'organize an Old Home Week just like ours, all over France, from Harver right down to Marseilles. And all through the devastated regions too . . . right up at the front . . . So that even the Germans would see us and hear us, and perhaps learn from us too'" (61–62). Both Charity and Troy are juvenile focalizers who mature in the course of their respective novels, and in ways traditionally associated with their gender: Charity through love, pregnancy, and marriage, Troy through war. Charity even exemplifies Wharton's ideas about marriage as expounded in *French Ways:* her love and preference for Lucius Harney prove the passing fancy of girlhood, and her marriage to Mr. Royall is founded not on love but "to secure their permanent well-being as associates in the foundation of a home and the procreation of a family" (*French Ways* 128). Even though the first child born in this marriage will not be Lawyer Royall's child, he or she will probably be publicly known as such. "The French marriage," Wharton tells us approvingly, "is built on parenthood, not on passion" (*French Ways* 128).

It may be somewhat paradoxical, then, that what seems to unite these three works, composed in such close juxtaposition, is passion itself, a passion that the deeply affecting war years moved Wharton to express. In

Summer, it is sexual passion to which she gives voice, as well as a longing for order and stability; in *The Marne* and *French Ways* it is passion for a country and a set of ideals. There can be little doubt that *Summer* is a work superior to the other two in literary terms—at least judging by aesthetic criteria that are not dictated by war. In *Summer,* Wharton's success was in the communication of complexity, ambivalence, ambiguity, and nuance, qualities largely absent from *The Marne* and *French Ways and Their Meaning.* Though readers today see the loss of those qualities in *The Marne* and *French Ways* as a failing, in another way their very absence from these works constituted a success in wartime. *French Ways* instructs its readers clearly and cogently in some essential aspects of French culture; Wharton's goal in these essays was didactic, and ambivalence and ambiguity would have defeated her own purpose. In late 1918, Wharton's enthusiasm and use of "the obvious" are probably what caused the great initial success of *The Marne.* The reviewer for the *New York Times* remarked that the novel was "beautifully written. Never, perhaps, has Mrs. Wharton's style been of a more pellucid clearness" (Tuttleton et al. 268); in *Publisher's Weekly,* Frederic Taber Cooper praised it as "one of the very few clear-cut, pure-water, almost flawless gems of war fiction" (Tuttleton et al. 269). As Shari Benstock has written, *The Marne* "captures the high-flying sentiments" of the summer of 1918 (*No Gifts* 346), the same sentiments that infused *French Ways and Their Meaning.*

The composition of *Summer* in 1916 provided Wharton with a much-needed psychological refuge from the war, even as it reflected, in subtle ways, the war itself. In 1917 and 1918 Wharton turned her pen as well as her volunteer activities to the war effort in her unabashedly pro-French works, *The Marne* and *French Ways.* "'On Active Service'" suggests a more complex view of the deaths caused by the war, but not until the war's end would she articulate more fully this more ambivalent view. The two war-related stories Wharton would publish in 1919, "The Refugees" and "Writing a War Story," are wry and satirical, a far cry from the strong political opinions that sustained *The Marne* and *French Ways.* Only her final, major war work, the novel *A Son at the Front,* would combine Wharton's idealism and her skepticism in its portrayal of American expatriate civilian life in wartime France.

4

Elegies and Satires

Works from the War's End (1919)

Every one of you won the war,
You and you and you—
You that carry an unscathed head,
You that halt with a broken tread,
And oh, most of all, you Dead, you Dead!
Wharton, "You and You" (January 1919)

[C]onsider the case of Philip Gibbs. . . . [W]hile the war went on he
had served the war cause well. As the official correspondent for the
Daily Chronicle on the Western Front, Gibbs was probably the most
widely read, and most influential, of English journalists. His dis-
patches were vivid, but they were also consistently positive. . . . But
once the war had ended, Gibbs's view of it changed; or rather, the
view that he felt free to express changed[.]
Samuel Hynes, *A War Imagined* (283–84)

I.

The end of the war was a huge relief for Edith Wharton, as it was to millions of others. In *A Backward Glance* she recalled how church bells rang
out all over Paris "till all their voices met and mingled in a crash of triumph" (359). The moment was overwhelming: "We had fared so long on
the thin diet of hope deferred that for a moment or two our hearts wavered
and doubted. Then, like the bells, they swelled to bursting, and we knew
the war was over" (*Backward Glance* 360).

The works written immediately after the war—the poems "You and
You," an elegy for Theodore Roosevelt entitled "With the Tide," and a
short essay called "How Paris Welcomed the King"—reflect the thrill of
the war's end tempered with a deep sense of grief for the deaths caused by

the war. The idealized and "the obvious" that Wharton had accepted as a mode of wartime writing in works like *The Marne* and *French Ways and Their Meaning* may have begun to wear on an author so capable of subtler things. While Wharton admired "the illuminating incident," as we have seen, she mistrusted the "tremolo note" in which she had written some of her wartime nonfiction. By November 1918 she was writing to Minnie Jones that the *Saturday Evening Post* had accepted "The Refugees" and rejected an article entitled "How Victory Came to Paris": "Both these facts caused me to rejoice, but chiefly their refusing the article, for I am more bored and depressed by having to write that kind of thing than any other form of literary 'output'" (29 Nov. 1918, *Wharton Collection* Yale). The majority of Wharton's wartime writing, and all of the composition of "that kind of thing," was behind her.

The end of the war allowed Wharton to write differently and more critically. Her case parallels that of the English journalist Philip Gibbs, who had "served the war cause well" during the war; but the war's end allowed a "change of tone . . . Gibbs found a new ironic voice for new kinds of stories that in wartime he had not told" (Hynes 285). The works Wharton published in 1919 employ new tones, including both an ironic voice in her short stories and a voice both celebratory and elegiac in her poetry.

II. The Elegies

Scholars of World War I literature have noted that one immediate postwar impulse was to create monuments to the dead. In some cases these monuments were physical: cenotaphs and formally arranged cemeteries created a sense of order out of the chaos of the war; in others they were verbal: voluminous official histories of the Great War proliferated in its wake (Hynes 278). Such monuments, as Hynes has written, "affirmed . . . that it was a good war, a just war, a *great* war. . . . The stories have their dark moments and their tragic losses, but they swell with emotion and pride at the end, and the Big Words [that is, capitalized ideals] sound out again, as though they had never been doubted" (278). "[S]well[ing] with emotion and pride" was certainly Wharton's reaction as she heard the bells pealing the end of the war. It was, moreover, an emotion that expressed itself in one of her first postwar works, the poem "You and You."

Wharton wrote to Minnie Jones that she had composed "a piece I think fairly good in a 'popular' way. . . . [T]he splendid fighting of our soldiers . . . wrung it out of me suddenly a few days ago" (29 Nov. 1918, *Wharton*

Collection Yale), surely a reference to the poem "You and You," which was published in both *Scribner's Magazine* and the *Pittsburgh Chronicle Telegraph* in January 1919. As its title implies, the poem is addressed directly to American soldiers—a carryover from her "Talk to American Soldiers" at the Soldiers' and Sailors' Club. Moving with a strong martial rhythm, the poem reflects both its author's admiration of American soldiers and her sense of the cost of the war:

> Every one of you won the war—
> You and you and you—
> Pressing and pouring forth, more and more,
> Tolling and straining from shore to shore
> To reach the flaming edge of the dark
> Where man in his millions went up like a spark;
> . . . .
> And now, when the last of them all are by,
> Be the Gates lifted up on high,
> To let those Others in,
> Those Others, their brothers, that softly tread,
> That come so thick, yet take no ground,
> That are so many, yet make no sound.
> Our Dead, our Dead, our Dead!
>
> O silent and secretly-moving throng,
> In your fifty thousand strong,
> Coming at dusk when the wreaths have dropt,
> And streets are empty, and music stopt,
> Silently coming to hearts that wait
> Dumb in the door and dumb at the gate,
> And hear your step and fly to your call—
> Every one of you won the war,
> But you, you Dead, most of all!

In its enthusiasm for the soldiers, and with its assumption that the war was worth fighting and dying in, the poem is one of the verbal monuments that both memorialized and justified the war. Further, it restores glory to a war that had sunk from idealism into horror. The "Big Words" are here, announced by capital letters: not only for "the Dead," but in everything associated with them: "Where's the Arch high enough, / Lads, to receive you"; "Lift up the Gates for these that are last, / That are last in the great Procession."

Wharton's elegy for Ronald Simmons opened with a conundrum ("He is dead that was alive. / How shall friendship understand?"); "You and You" relies on a similar trope: paradox. After the procession of returning soldiers, Wharton writes, will come another procession of "Those Others, their brothers, that softly tread, / That come so thick, yet take no ground, / That are so many, yet make no sound[.]" The dead are both absent and present, both sorely missed and eagerly reclaimed. In a further paradox implied by the poem, the dead are both victims of the war and victors over it: "Every one of you won the war, / But you, you Dead, most of all!" Like "'On Active Service'" and her elegy for Jean du Breuil, "You and You" both mourns the dead and asserts their afterlife among those who loved them best. And like both those earlier poems, this one is a monument, reasserting the value of the war. Although the loss is great and deep, there is no fundamental questioning here, no challenging the necessity of the war itself: the Dead died victorious in a worthy cause and are rewarded not only with written public tributes, but with a significant afterlife in the memories of those they loved.

A number of Wharton's works from the end of the war reaffirm the idealism that supposedly died after the first year of the war, suggesting that from a great cost came a great victory. This is certainly true of Wharton's short essay "How Paris Welcomed the King"—probably a re-titled version of "How Victory Came to Paris," the piece whose rejection by *The Saturday Evening Post* she claimed to have "rejoice[d]" at. The latter part of the essay reworks material from *French Ways* as it urges the British, Americans, and French to get along (369). But the opening paragraphs describe and analyze new material, with Wharton finding a redemptive symbolic meaning in the rain that poured on Paris on November 28, 1918, the day King George arrived to celebrate the Allies' victory. Certainly a major share of Wharton's job in writing this article was to find meaning, or to create meaning, in the actual events of the day; if the sun had shone gloriously on November 28, she doubtless would have managed to find an appropriate symbolic meaning in that too. Contriving to find symbolic meaning in any given event was, perhaps, a part of what made Wharton "bored and depressed" by "writ[ing] that kind of thing[.]" Nevertheless she takes her job seriously, and there is nothing insincere in the meanings she attributes to this occasion; her tone is consistent with that elsewhere in her war writings. Wharton finds some symbolism in the weather, using it to fashion a semihumorous (if somewhat facile) revenge against the German army: the rain, she relates, stopped just as the parade started, "and to see it sneaking away just as the show began added to the general hilarity by reminding the lookers-on of a certain 'strategical retreat' which had set it the example not so many weeks ago" (367). Her tone in this passage echoes that in several passages in *Fighting France*, those in which she wanted to convince American soldiers that the German soldiers are less admirable than they might think. The German army, from having been the monstrous Hun, has, in defeat, been reduced to providing harmless comic behavior.

More profoundly, Wharton finds meaning in the "thousands and thousands of dripping but rejoicing people[,]" remarking that "one began to be actually glad of the rain, glad of the wet flags, the demoralized wreaths, the wrecked decorations; for they left no semblance of a stage-setting between Paris and the guest she was greeting, no possibility of an idea that the public was 'out for the fun,' and not for the event that occasioned it" (368). In *Fighting France* Wharton had been intrigued by the way in which the war transformed a "lifeless little town into a romantic stage-setting" (146), but four years of war had left her with little patience for events or people who were merely stagy; her criticism of such superficial ostentation permeates her portrayal of characters like Mrs. Belknap in *The Marne*, as it would several portrayals in *A Son at the Front*. The rain had obviated the possibility of mere staginess on November 28th. What remained was the authentic:

> It was a magnificent and mighty show, that short quiet-coloured line of victorias and landaus driving slowly down between two walls of shouting spectators; a plain unadorned show, symbolic rather than pictorial, as democratic shows tend to be; but all the better for that.
> . . .
> It was a magnificent and mighty show. (368)

Wharton's description of this procession calls to mind her description in *Fighting France* of French soldiers "rid[ing] straight into glory" (140). Yet the language in "How Paris Welcomed the King" is far more subdued. Wharton continued to believe that the war had been a necessary war, one, moreover, which conferred glory upon its participants. But four years of war had stripped away the need for superficial ostentation. The procession described in *Fighting France,* with its emphasis on visual details— "Through the dust, the sun picked out the flash of lances and the gloss of chargers' flanks"—differs significantly from the "short quiet-coloured line of victorias and landaus," the "plain unadorned show, symbolic rather than pictorial." If, in 1914, a parade of soldiers and horses created a glorious picture, in late 1918 this "line of victorias and landaus"—the vehicles of royalty, but of royalty in peacetime rather than of soldiers in wartime— constituted "a magnificent and mighty show."

Not long after the events Wharton described in "How Paris Welcomed the King," the death of Theodore Roosevelt, a long-time friend of hers, caused her to turn her hand once again to elegy. "With the Tide," the poem she wrote on this occasion, in some ways resembles her earlier elegies. But to those elegies she adds a strong element of myth, while also incorporating, as she had in "How Paris Welcomed the King," descriptions derived from the war. Like "You and You," the work was written rapidly. To Roosevelt's sister she wrote that "My lines on your brother were written in a rush, out of a heart wrung with sorrow, sorrow for the lost friend & for the great leader gone when he was most needed" (*Letters* 422). Indeed they were "written in a rush": Roosevelt died on January 6, 1919, and Wharton's poem is dated January 7. The blank verse poem that she composed, drawing on *The Golden Bough* and echoing Arthurian legend, emphasizes the mythic.[1]

> Somewhere I read, in an old book whose name
> Is gone from me, I read that when the days
> Of a man are counted, and his business done,
> There comes up the shore at evening, with the tide,
> To the place where he sits, a boat—
> And in the boat, from the place where he sits, he sees,
> Dim in the dusk, dim and yet so familiar,
> The faces of his friends long dead. . . .

Though a postwar poem, this elegy includes few direct references to the war; it emphasizes the mythic and refers to an undefined but protracted time span, evident in the speaker's very vagueness in the opening lines ("Somewhere I read, in an old book whose name / Is gone from me"), as well as in its references to myth. Yet much of the poem is permeated by the war. Its readers in 1919 would have felt the war as part of the poem's context; the war dead are doubtless a part of this poem. Wharton implies that Roosevelt will be one of those who joyously welcome the boat that comes to ferry them to the land of the dead:

> . . . others, rising as they see the sail
> Increase upon the sunset, hasten down,
> Hands out and eyes elated; for they see
> Head over head, crowding from bow to stern,
> Repeopling their long loneliness with smiles,
> The faces of their friends; and such go forth
> Content upon the ebb tide, with safe hearts.

The war dead—including Roosevelt's youngest son, Quentin, who was killed in action—are not explicitly named, but are strongly implied in lines that shortly follow those just quoted:

> Softly they came, and beached the boat, and gathered
> In the still cove under the icy stars,
> Your last-born, and the dear loves of your heart,
> And all men that have loved right more than ease,
> And honor above honors; all who gave
> Free-handed of their best for other men,
> And thought their giving taking: they who knew
> Man's natural state is effort, up and up—

Such lines echo, in slightly muted tones, the cry for American involvement that Wharton had articulated in "The Great Blue Tent": "'Where did you learn that men are bred / Where hucksters bargain and gorge, / And where, that down makes a softer bed / Than the snows of Valley Forge?'" It echoes as well the frustration of Troy Belknap with men who, to reverse the formulation in "With the Tide," loved ease more than right. And, in its reference to the death of Quentin Roosevelt, it echoes the elegies Wharton had written for her own friends, for "the dear loves" of her heart. She knew what it meant to sacrifice to the war—and she knew what the loss of Quentin meant to Roosevelt. In a typed letter to Wharton (apparently a response to a letter of condolence from her), Roosevelt had written, "I value your letter, and naturally I am pleased at what you say about Quentin." In a handwritten postscript Roosevelt adds, "There is no use of my writing about Quentin, for I should break down if I tried. His death is heartbreaking. But it would have been far worse if he had lived at the cost of the slightest failure to perform his duty" (15 Aug. 1918, *Wharton Col-*

lection Yale). Wharton could envision what a reunion with the war dead—and particularly his son—might mean to her old friend.

Only in the final lines of the poem does Wharton introduce a specific wartime image, that of the transport:

> And there you saw that the huge hull that waited
> Was not as are the boats of the other dead,
> Frail craft for a brief passage; no, for this
> Was first of a long line of towering transports,
> Storm-worn and ocean-weary every one,
> The ships you launched, the ships you manned, the ships
> That now, returning from their sacred quest
> With the thrice-sacred burden of their dead,
> Lay waiting there to take you forth with them,
> Out with the ebb tide, on some farther quest.

Though the image resonates with mythic overtones, Roosevelt's passage is on a "towering transport"—not a "frail craft"; moreover, this transport is "storm-worn and ocean-weary." This image, however startling, is immediately reincorporated into the mythic context. Its dead, among them those of the Great War, are not simply sacred but "thrice-sacred." The mythic is further evoked in the final line. In language reminiscent of prewar and early war imagery of war's nobility, the transports are carrying Roosevelt not to rest but "on some farther quest." Roosevelt, like Arthur, is the once and future leader in a noble and unending quest. With this elegy, Wharton had created yet another monument not only to a public figure—she addresses Roosevelt as "O great American" in the poem—but to the war as well. "With the Tide" brought readers back to a world in which "Everyone knew what Glory was, and what Honor meant" (Fussell 21).

III. Satires

But the world could not go back, and neither could Edith Wharton; Roosevelt, like Arthur, was in truth dead and buried. Early in the war Wharton had been torn between fascination and horror; now her writing moved between elegy and satire. Along with the elegies—"You and You" in January 1919 and "With the Tide" in March 1919—came satirical stories: "The Refugees" in January 1919 and "Writing a War Story" in September 1919. With the war over, it was no longer a concern that "art be good for war," and "The Refugees" and "Writing a War Story" are a distinct departure both from the elegiac and from the strong political opinions that impelled *The Marne* and *French Ways and Their Meaning*.

As early as June 1915 Wharton had declared her intent to write a number of stories, "not precisely war stories, but on subjects suggested by the war" (*Letters* 357). In the postwar period she finally had time to turn her attention to creating some of these stories, though their tone might have surprised some of the readers who had read her wartime articles, *The Marne*, or her elegies of early 1919. As one of her postwar impulses was toward elegy, it may seem inconsistent that her other—and nearly simultaneous—impulse was toward satire. Similarly, anyone who had read Wharton's depictions of refugees in articles in *Scribner's Magazine*—of the sights they had seen that "one dare not picture," of the pathos and tragedy of their homeless condition—might well have been surprised to read a story by Wharton entitled "The Refugees" in which actual refugees make only a brief appearance, and in which the tone is not tragic but wry. Wharton seemed to be turning her back, or at least her pen, on the cultural and political issues that had absorbed so much of her attention for more than four years.

But Wharton, devoted though she was to managing and fund-raising for a remarkable number of wartime charities, never saw herself as one of the women who had "found their vocation in nursing the wounded, or in other philanthropic activities" (*Backward Glance* 356). She had found her "inexorable calling"—writing—long before the war began (*Backward Glance* 356), and she recounted with glee Percy Lubbock's quip that he could forgive her for her philanthropic goodness "only because I so visibly hate what I am doing" (*Letters* 343). "As soon as peace is declared I shall renounce good works forever!" she had announced as early as the end of September 1914 (*Letters* 341). Although many of Wharton's charities still needed attention in the aftermath of the war, a part of her huge relief at the war's end must have derived from her being able, at last, to return to her "inexorable calling."

In this context, it is perhaps less surprising that her first efforts at fiction should be satires—relatively light treatments of topics that Wharton had treated so seriously for so long. Significantly, too, both "The Refugees" and "Writing a War Story," while "suggested by the war," are stories about the home front, not about the fighting that Wharton respected and, in some ways, even revered. The end of the war allowed her, like others, to find "a new ironic voice for new kinds of stories that in wartime [they] had not told" (Hynes 285). Yet, inevitably, even these bagatelles reflect Wharton's wartime experiences: her shaken sense of reality, her fear of missing out on the real adventure in war. Moreover, they allowed Wharton to portray topics she had not touched during the war: first, the sordid social competition that sometimes existed in the proffering of charity; and second, her own somewhat threatened sense as a woman writer handling that most masculine of topics, war.

"The Refugees" is not about literal refugees, but rather about two elderly people, each misplaced in a different way, each mistaking the other for a refugee. The story's central character is Charlie Durand, a "Professor of Romance Languages in a western University" (570). On sabbatical in Europe, he is in Louvain when German soldiers attack. After fleeing to Normandy he takes a boat to England, encountering on board many Belgian refugees. When he lands in England he is seized upon by Miss Audrey Rushworth, an elderly woman whom he mistakes for a refugee. It gradually dawns on him, however, that she has made the exact same error. Though he attempts to enlighten her about his real status, she repeatedly interrupts and misinterprets him, hardly giving him a chance to correct her mistake. She carries him off to Lingerfield, her family's ancestral home; having a sense of curiosity and adventure he suffers her to remain under her misconception. Only one of Miss Rushworth's family, a niece named Clio, discerns that Charlie is not an actual refugee, but even she urges him not to enlighten her aunt. The very end of the story finds Charlie back in Boulogne with a position at the YMCA library for U.S. soldiers—and finally encountering Audrey Rushworth as a Colonel in charge of the placement of real refugees.

As such a plot summary suggests, this is one of Wharton's lighter stories, an amusing comedy of errors. Occasionally Wharton's language suggests that she is parodying her own concerns, her own earlier work: "Professor Durand had read 'L'Abbesse de Jouarre' and knew that, in moments of extreme social peril, superior persons often felt themselves justified in casting conventional morality to the winds. He had no thought of proceeding to such extremes; but he did wonder if, at the hour when civilization was shaken to its base, he, Charlie Durand, might not at last permit himself forty-eight hours of romance..." (580). L'Abbesse de Jouarre, an 1886 play by Ernest Renan, suggests that in times of crisis—particularly in the face of imminent and untimely death—sexual union is not only morally acceptable, but even laudable. Over tea with Miss Rushworth, Charlie Durand has already imagined that she might be pursuing him sexually: "With these foreign women you could never tell: his brief continental experiences had taught him that. After all, he was not a monster, and several ladies had already attempted to prove it to him" (576). He has refused such opportunities, however, and knows that "romance" is the best he can hope for.

The issue of illicit sexuality is reminiscent of Wharton's earlier story, "Coming Home," in which she suggested the necessity of "casting conventional morality to the winds": a woman may have granted sexual favors to save her fiancé's home; a man may have quietly and guiltlessly murdered a political and personal enemy. For Charlie Durand, "casting conventional morality to the winds" is something much smaller: allowing Audrey Rushworth to continue to think he is a refugee so that he might see one of England's aristocratic manors. Wharton's reintroduction of the issue of casting off morality may suggest that life behind the lines was different from life at the front: what was truly necessary for Yvonne Malo in Réchamp would be merely an excuse for misconduct in London. It may also suggest that Wharton had rethought "Coming Home," and now found such a story too heavy-handed or too radical in its apparent approval of profoundly unconventional behavior.

In this passage, Wharton also reuses, in a gently mocking fashion, some of her own phrases from early in the war. Durand, like Wharton, felt that "civilization was shaken to its base." But the tone here is light; through Charlie, who overreacts to a number of events, Wharton might be suggesting, with postwar wryness, that a phrase that she herself had used ("Hasn't it shaken all the foundations of reality for you?" [Letters 333]) might be melodramatic rather than accurate. "The Refugees" does nothing to undermine the essential gravity of the war, but for once Wharton allows herself to suggest that perhaps, on the home front fringes of the war, some rather comical things were going on.

Nevertheless, Wharton strikes some deeper notes as well in "The Refugees." The story's central plot reflects Wharton's concern with missing out on the real war; its conclusion suggests her lingering frustration with her exclusion from the front lines. And like so many of her other characters, Charlie Durand represents a number of her own reactions to the war. After his arrival in Normandy, for instance, Charlie tries "to think the war would soon be over" (570). Wharton immediately notes that such wishful thinking was not the result of Durand's being "hard or aloof," but rather the result of his own inability—so much like her own and her contemporaries'—to grasp the reality of the war: "the whole business was so contrary to his conception of the universe, and his fagged mind, at the moment, was so incapable of prompt readjustment, that he needed time to steady himself" (570). Though he does not become an organizer of charities as Wharton did, she creates him as a person of whom she would have approved: in particular, he donates generously "to the various appeals for funds" (570). Further, his contact with genuine refugees on shipboard results in a sense of closer humanity: "It was impossible to sit for three mortal hours with an unclaimed little boy on one's lap, opposite a stony-faced woman holding a baby that never stopped crying, and not give them something more than what remained of one's chocolate and buns" (571). He is touched, as Wharton was, by the human disasters surrounding him.

Durand also shares Wharton's sense of irony as well as her alertness to the unexpectedly nasty turns of human nature. He sees the besieging mass of the helpful English as "the light battalions of the benevolent" (572) and satirizes their ill-pronounced French: "wee, wee" (572). He also sees—or at least imagines—the darker side of the human soul in the Englishwomen swarming to help the refugees, reflecting that "Affliction was supposed to soften, but apparently in such monstrous doses it had the opposite effect" (574).

Perhaps most significantly, Durand reflects Wharton's longing for romance. The narrator relates that "[Durand's] sister Mabel . . . had once taken one of his cards and run a pen through the word 'Languages,' leaving simply 'Professor of Romance'; and in his secret soul Charlie Durand knew that she was right" (579). As the story develops, Charlie comes to see that his being mistaken for a refugee will give him an entrée to one site of the romantic—the world of the English aristocracy—and certainly the little adventure he has at Lingerfield is far better than no adventure at all. But it is not enough. *Fighting France* suggested Wharton's fear that she was missing out on the real business of war; this is exactly what Charlie Durand fears as well. Though he is thrilled to see the Rushworths' ancestral home, Charlie's deepest sense of romance is tied into the war raging in Europe. Because he is forty-five years old and has the "slight congenital lameness" common to so many of Wharton's wartime males, he is unable to take part in combat. Near the story's conclusion he is wearing the uniform of the YMCA, contentedly working at a YMCA canteen library. But this occupation, though it is far closer to war than his excursion to Lingerfield, is not enough either: "he could never quite console himself for the accident of having been born a few years too soon to be wearing the real uniform of his country" (590). He has missed the real experience of war, just as he has missed the "real uniform."

Paradoxically, Wharton immediately links the real with the romantic, suggesting Charlie's deep devotion to the war: enlisting in the army "would indeed have been Romance beyond his dreams" (590). But like Wharton, Charlie has had to settle for work behind the lines: "he had long ago discovered that he was never to get beyond the second-best in such matters. None of his adventures would ever be written with a capital" (590). Yet he has learned to be "content," especially once the United States has entered the war—again reflecting both Wharton's attitude and her strong belief in U.S. involvement.

Charlie's achievement of resignation-with-contentment would be a logical conclusion for the story: Charlie Durand has learned, as Wharton did, to accept the role he can play without undue pining for the role he cannot. This is not, however, the story's end. In its course Wharton satirized the British socialites who see the housing and entertaining of refugees as the newest form of social competition, a social competition as intense and pointless as that between Bertha Dorset and Judy Trenor in *The House of Mirth* and as fraught with pretension as that depicted in her short story "Xingu." Wharton also portrayed sympathetically, if archly, the woman whom Charlie had mistaken for a refugee, Audrey Rushworth. Durand becomes, her niece Clio insists, Miss Rushworth's one "great Adventure" (592); Audrey Rushworth has both longed for and missed the same sense of Adventure or Romance as Charlie Durand. Both are refugees not from the German army, but from life; each supplies, satisfactorily if fraudulently, romance or adventure for the other. Classic Whartonian symmetry and irony are here, elements that would reappear perfected in the postwar story "After Holbein" (1928), in which two elderly people unknowingly use each other to the satisfaction of both. Yet Wharton settles for neither the social satire of "Xingu" nor the sad, if aesthetically satisfying, misunderstandings of "After Holbein." Instead, "The Refugees" works on through another three pages that make it one of those stories Wharton had identified in "Coming Home"—a story that defies classification, a story whose conclusion leaves one not quite knowing how to react.

On his return to Boulogne, Charlie encounters Clio Rushworth, who takes him to see Audrey. Yet now, instead of the timid, misplaced woman who was so excited to nab Charlie as her personal refugee, Audrey Rushworth has become an important administrator in the placement of actual refugees. Moreover, she has been transformed from timid to intimidating. From fighting with her relatives to secure a single refugee in England, she now has more than enough, saying "'Not another refugee, Clio—not *one*! I absolutely refuse'" (592). Colonel Audrey Rushworth has a "resolute and almost forbidding eye" and bends "sternly to her writing" (592). She fails to recognize Charlie, though she still mistakes him for a refugee. Charlie is relieved that the fraudulence of his earlier role goes undetected, but he is also "aware of a distinct humiliation" (593): only a couple of years earlier, she had been almost abjectly grateful for his acquaintance, murmuring, "I can't tell you. . . I can't tell you how happy I am. . . I thought no one would ever want me[,]" as if he had proposed to her (576). Now, in Boulogne, Clio apologizes for her aunt, explaining that "it's she who does the forgetting now"—she who had been so often overlooked in earlier days. The story concludes with Clio's remark, "I'm sorry—but you must excuse her. She's just been promoted again, and she's going to marry the Bishop of the Macaroon Islands next month" (593).

The reader is thus left hanging. Wharton gives no record of Charlie's reaction, no resolution of the issues raised. What we have instead is confusion and conundrum; how *is* one to react? Should we be pleased that Audrey Rushworth has, like the title character in Radclyffe Hall's 1926 story "Miss Ogilvy Finds Herself," found her true worth in the war? Yet, unlike Hall's Miss Ogilvy, Audrey Rushworth is unsympathetic: she is portrayed as tyrannical and ruthlessly ambitious—a more military version of her socially competitive relatives. Her forthcoming marriage to the "Bishop of the Macaroon Islands" suggests that despite her stern exterior, she is one of the "fluffy fuzzy people" Wharton disliked: it is hard to think of a cookie less substantial than a macaroon. Should we be pleased that Charlie Durand, who has not found real romance or adventure, has at least found his niche? Yet we—and he—seem robbed of this comfort by his sense of humiliation at the story's end. Clio, named after the muse of history, knows who he is, but she realizes that he is at most a very minor character in the history of the war; even her pathetic Aunt Audrey, whatever her real value, has come to seem more important than little Charlie Durand in his YMCA uniform. Wharton's story concludes with a strong sense of inconclusiveness, suggesting that the war genre is exactly that which leaves readers wondering "how [one] ought to classify" such a story.

Wharton's final war-related short story, "Writing a War Story," is, like "The Refugees," satirical in tone while also suggesting serious topics. While the story cannot be read as strictly autobiographical, it suggests the difficulties Wharton had writing about the masculine topic of war. As we saw earlier, Wharton eschewed typically feminine approaches to war writing; her fiction does not center on love stories or animals, nor does it chronicle, as Mary King Waddington had in *Scribner's*, a woman's retreat to the countryside when Paris was threatened. Yet she could not claim the frontline experience that is usually associated with the phrase "war writing"; she could not rival Richard Harding Davis's adventures behind the German lines nor deliver the inside story, as did "Captain X—of the French Staff" in the October 1915 *Scribner's*. Barbara White notes Wharton's discomfort with the concept of authorship in "Writing a War Story," remarking that "Wharton must have been anxious about resuming her career after the war. . . . As a short-story writer she seems to have returned in a sense to her early years and started anew" (88). Indeed, "Writing a War Story" displays an anxiety of authorship that hearkens back to Wharton's 1900 story, "April Showers," in which another young woman learns that writing is primarily the province of men.[2] Yet in this it reflects perhaps not so much Wharton's anxiety about "resuming her career" as the anxiety she underwent writing about war. One point is made utterly clear in this story: pitfalls await those who, not having been on the front lines, attempt to portray the experience of those who had.

The central figure in the story, a young woman named Ivy Spang, is pouring tea weekly at an Anglo-American hospital in Paris during the war when she is requested to write a short story for a special edition of a magazine for enlisted men, *The Man-at-Arms*. Wharton parodies—though not without sympathy—Ivy's groping for an appropriate subject and an appropriate approach to that subject. The plot or "subject" Ivy finally settles on derives from the frontline experiences of an actual French soldier, Chasseur Alpin Emile Durand, who while wounded had told his experiences to Ivy's former governess, who had served as a nurse. Ivy and her governess work on the story together; Ivy finds the writing of it so difficult that she almost backs out of her commitment, but she finally sends in the story when she sees the publicity photo of herself in her nurse's uniform, "exceedingly long, narrow and sinuous" (364), that is to accompany her tale. When the magazine comes out, she decides that her story is a success after all. Through a series of comic misunderstandings she believes that her hospital patients are complimenting her on the accuracy with which her story has captured the reality of the war experience—only to find that they are complimenting her on the accuracy of the lovely photograph of her in her nurse's uniform. None of them has the first word to say about her endeavors as an author; in fact, "It was evident that not one of them had read her story" (368). By chance, a prominent soldier-novelist has also been assigned to her ward, and she turns to him for a more professional opinion—an opinion that, in the end, differs very little from that of the less literary soldiers.

The story is, to some extent, a parody of novice writers; it also has much to say about what Wharton had learned about war writing, and particularly the position of women vis-à-vis war writing. Even in its satirical moments "Writing a War Story" is not always critical of Ivy; as with Charlie Durand in "The Refugees," Wharton creates a character who is both laughable and sympathetic, and Wharton simultaneously mocks Ivy and elicits sympathy for her as she describes Ivy's attempts to begin her first work of fiction.

Increasing the reader's sympathy for Ivy is the fact that she may be set up for failure from the outset. The editor of *The Man-at-Arms* invites her to contribute a story simply because he wants "an American contributor," and "that pretty Miss Spang" happens to be nearby when the editor is visiting the hospital (360). The editor himself is inept. He is satisfied with a doctor's remark that Ivy "writes"; he exaggerates the amount (and kind) of "hospital experience" she has had; his attitude toward his own magazine, which he implies will "bring joy to the wounded and disabled," surely overrates his achievement: the publication might bring wounded soldiers distraction or even momentary cheer, but something as significant as "joy" seems unlikely. Paradoxically, his purposes jibe with the established expectations for World War I writing; he tells Ivy that "We want . . . all the articles written by people who've done the thing themselves, or seen it done" (360). But apparently his definition of "do[ing] the thing" one's self is rather flexible: he is amateurishly impressed that she has been "As far as Rheims, once[,]" equating this with being "at the front" (360).

Further, the editor's genre expectations may doom Ivy's efforts. He outlines a set of requirements that would be difficult for the most skilled author to fulfill with integrity: "[a] good rousing story" with "a dash of sentiment, of course, but nothing to depress or discourage"—a tale that would, in effect, conform to England's Defense of the Realm Act, which stipulated that "art be good for war." As the editor rambles on, he ignorantly asks for the impossible: "A tragedy with a happy ending" (360). This phrase is one that Wharton echoed from William Dean Howells, who remarked to her that the dramatized version of *The House of Mirth* failed because "What the American public always wants is a tragedy with a happy ending" (Lewis, *Edith Wharton* 172). The editor further expects that fiction can be made to order, telling Ivy to "Give us a good stirring trench story, with a Coming-Home scene to close with . . . a Christmas scene, if you can manage it" (360). Although Ivy is the main object of Wharton's satire, the editor is undoubtedly an object of scorn as well, a man who, despite his profession, has very little idea what literature is about.

Ivy, however, takes his instructions seriously; she doesn't realize that "a tragedy with a happy ending" is a contradiction in terms, and so, attempting to fulfill his request, she comes in for her own share of parody. She secludes herself in Brittany and attempts to write. The passage that follows is replete with mockery, humor, and (paradoxically) shreds of truth:

> [Her old governess] promised to defend at all costs the sacredness of her mornings—for Ivy knew that the morning hours of great authors were always "sacred."
>
> She shut herself up in her room with a ream of mauve paper and began to think.
>
> At first the process was less exhilarating than she had expected. She knew so much about the war that she hardly knew where to begin; she found herself suffering from a plethora of impressions.
>
> Moreover, the more she thought of the matter, the less she seemed to understand how a war story—or any story, for that matter—was written. Why did stories ever begin, and why did they ever leave off? Life didn't—it just went on and on. (360–61)

The predominant tone here is satirical: the young would-be author has vague and romanticized notions of how "great authors" work; she selects "mauve paper" to write on, a choice reminiscent of Undine Spragg's ill-advised choice of "pigeon-blood" paper when she needs to respond to a dinner invitation early in *The Custom of the Country* (13). Yet Ivy is not totally misguided. Many great authors (Wharton among them) have devoted their morning hours to writing. Even Ivy's naive questioning about where stories begin and end is valid: Henry James, like many authors both before and after him, addressed it in his notebook entries on *Portrait of a Lady*, writing that "the *whole* of anything is never told; you can only take what groups together" (Edel and Powers, 15). Moreover, the question of how to structure a narrative—Ivy's sense that life "just went on and on"— was a pressing question for writers during and after the war. As Hynes explains, one of the distinctive qualities of war writing is its structure: "there is no order in war except chronology, event followed by event without evident reason" (Hynes 95). Ivy is naive and unskilled, but her instincts are not necessarily wrong.

As the passage continues, Ivy, wandering along the beach, picks up a magazine called *Fact and Fiction* and consults story openings. Again, her instincts are not wrong; studying other authors' works is certainly a time-honored approach to the craft of fiction. But Ivy's judgment, at least in this case, is faulty, as Wharton shows us when Ivy rejects the quiet opening by "one of the most famous names of the past generation of novelists" (361), instead admiring—and later plagiarizing—the hackneyed "'A shot rang out'" (362). Ivy further reveals her lack of experience as a writer in her instant adherence to whatever writing advice she happens to encounter. Earlier in her brief writing career, she had been immediately influenced by an obscure editor who told her about "not allowing one's self to be 'influenced'"[3] (361); having come to believe that "'People don't bother with plots nowadays'" (362), she respects this notion as a principle, declaring that "'[T]he subject's nothing!'" (363). Only at the urging of her governess does Ivy settle on any subject at all—the soldier's tale recorded by her governess. Convinced that "it's only the treatment that really matters" (363), Ivy sets about "transform[ing]" the true story of Emile Durand "into Literature" (364).

It is this transformation that proves Ivy's undoing. Pouring tea once a week at a hospital does not supply much war experience at all, even by home front standards; her very limited experience makes it impossible for her to grasp either the reality of war or the factual, unsentimental, stripped-down prose that was becoming characteristic of war writing. The reader is never told what Durand's story is; much as in "Coming Home," the central box is empty: the war experience goes unrelated. But a further comparison of the original story—that recorded by the governess—with Ivy's "Literature" suggests that it is the governess, not Ivy, who ought to be telling the story: she had copied Durand's story verbatim, much as Macy Greer tells Jean de Réchamp's story without embellishment. In this way both the governess and Greer are reporters or journalists, sticking to the facts of their story much as Wharton had done in *Fighting France*. Ivy's authorial error occurs when she fails to recognize that, at least in this war, facts were beginning to be treated as speaking for themselves. Reading over her governess's unadorned account of Durand's experiences, she condescendingly thinks that Mademoiselle's narrative "poured on and on without a paragraph—a good deal like life. Decidedly, poor Mademoiselle did not even know the rudiments of literature!" (364). Her decision to "transform" Durand's tale into "Literature" by giving it what she believes is the right "treatment" (363–64) could not be more mistaken. Even the governess, who initially had the good judgment simply to record the story, falls into the error of "carefully revis[ing] and polish[ing] the rustic speech in which she had originally transcribed the tale, so that it finally issued forth in the language that a young lady writing a composition on the Battle of Hastings would have used in Mademoiselle's school days" (364) In other words, she commits the grave error of using language that romanticizes war: language that the war had made not only obsolete but ridiculous.

Wharton continues both her parody and her appeal to the reader's sympathy as she records the ups and downs of Ivy's writerly confidence. After completing her story, Ivy's confidence wanes; as we have seen, she sends it to the editor only because the accompanying photograph of herself in her nurse's uniform is "really too charming to be wasted" (364). Yet when she receives a copy of the finished magazine, her confidence rebounds. She judges others' contributions (and even their photographs) harshly, and feels that her story "loom[s] up rather large" in comparison (365). "Bewilder[ed]" that none of her acquaintances comment on her story, she buys "a dozen copies" and brings them to her hospital (366).

Ivy's overconfidence contributes further to her undoing. Her elation when she believes that the soldiers admire her story is replaced by "mortification" (368) when she realizes that they are admiring her photograph— and each wants a copy to "take away with us," suitably framed by one of their number, who "makes rather jolly frames out of Vichy corks" (367). In an attempt to soothe her authorial ego, she reassures herself that the soldiers are poor literary critics: "it was absurd to have imagined that the inmates of the ward, dear, gallant young fellows, would feel the subtle meaning of a story like 'His Letter Home'" (368). Such a thought is, first, condescending; Ivy assumes that, though the soldiers may be "dear, gallant" men, they are unable to grasp the "subtle meaning" of her story. Second, Ivy's analysis assumes a divide between life and literature: she believes that, although the soldiers have experienced the war, they have no qualifications for judging writing about the war. "Writing a War Story" had earlier introduced the question of the link between life and literature: Ivy wonders how to isolate a story when life itself just goes "on and on," yet looks down on Mademoiselle's transcription of Durand's story because it is too simply a copy of "life." Ivy believes that the soldiers understand "life," but not "literature," even literature about their own lives. Only from Captain Harold Harbard, a wounded army officer and famous novelist, does she expect a fair verdict: "Now, indeed, she was to be face to face with a critic" (368). He alone of all the characters in the story knows both the life of a soldier and the standards a writer must meet.

In the end, however, Harbard's response is much the same as the soldiers'; apparently "those dear, gallant young fellows" do have the one qualification that counts when it comes to judging war stories: experience at the front. And yet, however lampooned Ivy has been by her own ineptitude earlier in the story, it is hard for the reader not to feel sympathy for her in the story's final paragraphs. The successful Harbard shatters all her fragile confidence when he explains to her why he has been laughing at her supposedly "subtle" and moving story:

"You've got hold of a wonderfully good subject; and that's the main thing, of course—" [he began.]
Ivy interrupted him eagerly. "The subject is the main thing?"
"Why, naturally; it's only the people without invention who tell you it isn't." (369)

Ivy is left "gasp[ing]" from this revelation; when Harbard adds that she has "rather mauled" her otherwise good subject, she is reduced to tears, though she attempts to speak with "stony gaiety" (369). Harbard completes his abasement of her by asking "for one of these photographs" the soldiers had been demanding (369), and the story concludes with his words: "You were angry just now because I didn't admire your story; and now you're angrier still because I do admire your photograph. Do you wonder that we novelists find such an inexhaustible field in Woman?" (370). Harbard's very name suggests his fitness for writing about war: his name not only incorporates "bard" but echoes "halberd," a spike-like weapon of the Renaissance. He is clearly the man in the know in the two fields in which Ivy feels she will never be competent—war and writing—and both by virtue of his sex. Women cannot fight in the war; women cannot write; even two women collaborating, Ivy and her governess, cannot write. For Captain Harbard, "Woman" remains the object of fiction, not its source: his phrase "we novelists" clearly implies an all-male group. Women, Harbard implies, are valued only for their lovely appearance and their illogical, but intriguing, behavior. The story ends with his humiliating words.

The conclusion of "Writing a War Story" strongly resembles that of "The Refugees" in both its method—the reader is left hanging—and in its closing tableau: the final word is given to a military authority figure, and the civilian is humiliated. Just as Charlie Durand's peace with himself is shattered by the disregard of Colonel Audrey Rushworth, so Ivy Spang's confidence is broken by Captain Harbard. In Ivy's case, however, some of Harbard's criticisms may be deserved. Her story is hackneyed, sentimental, and written in antiquated language, far from the "bare, direct, exact, and unmetaphorical" style that was coming to be seen as the only appropriate choice for war writing (Hynes 95). Yet Ivy's female anxiety of authorship surely deserves gentler handling than Harbard gives it. His judgment is, moreover, based not only on Ivy's story but on his assumptions about the author's sex. Women cannot write—and they particularly cannot write war stories.

Of course, Wharton "is" both Ivy and Captain Harbard, remembering her own fledgling talent (her first publication, like Ivy's, was a collection of verse) and her limited exposure to the front (she, too, had been "as far as Rheims"), and serving as her own harshest critic. At age fourteen Wharton wrote a novella, *Fast and Loose;* to accompany it she also completed mock reviews, which make Harbard's commentary on "His Letter Home" pale in comparison. In one she wrote: "in such a case, it is false charity to reader & writer to mince matters. The English of it is that every character is a failure, the plot a vacuum, the style spiritless, the dialogue vague, the sentiments weak, & the whole thing a fiasco" (*"Fast and Loose" and "The Buccaneers"* 117). From the infancy of her career Wharton was tough on her own work; though a famous and respected author by the time she penned "Writing a War Story," she seems to re-create in Ivy Spang the misgivings and fears of deserved failure that haunted her early in her career. "Writing a War Story" suggests that such fears were revived by Wharton's experience of encroaching on the male province of war writing. Her misgivings were sufficient that she almost never ventured into the front lines in fiction. Her one brief excursion there, as we have seen, was at the end of *The Marne;* the fact that "Writing a War Story" was published after *The Marne* may suggest that Wharton saw that excursion as a not-to-be-repeated mistake. Wharton's final war fiction, *A Son at the Front,* stays well away from the front lines. Ivy Spang may give up writing altogether; Wharton would never be discouraged as easily as her clinging Ivy, but she avoided the mistakes Ivy made. As the war continued Wharton adhered to a simpler, less romantic prose style; perhaps even more important, she sedulously avoided the front in her fiction.

Wharton's failure to include "Writing a War Story" in any of her collections of short fiction may suggest that she felt it was like some of her early stories, which, she said, were "written 'at the top of my voice'"; she added that one such story, "The Fullness of Life," was "one long shriek" (*Letters* 36). "The Fullness of Life" is the story of an unhappily married woman who, in heaven, finds her perfect soulmate—only to decide that she must wait for her husband instead; the "long shriek" Wharton heard in it was undoubtedly the sound of her own unhappy marriage. "Writing a War Story" as well may have struck her as too much "'at the top of [her] voice'": too autobiographical, a story that put insufficient distance between the author and her main character as it reflected her feminine discomfort with the masculine topic of war—and, to some extent, her bitterness about that fundamental sense of exclusion.

Wharton's 1919 satires seem a sharp departure from her writing during the war, and in some ways appear, at least initially, to repudiate both her wartime writing and her wartime activities. "The Refugees" seems to parody Wharton's own worthwhile war work administering care for thousands of displaced people during the war. Similarly, the special edition of *The Man-at-Arms* to which Ivy Spang contributes in "Writing a War Story," "to which Queens and Archbishops and Field Marshals were to contribute poetry and photographs and patriotic sentiment in autograph" (360), is reminiscent of *The Book of the Homeless*. But looked at more closely, these stories do not undermine either her war efforts or her work as author and editor. "The Refugees" satirizes neither her own charitable efforts nor the thousands of refugees she helped, but rather those who were involved in charitable work only for their own social advancement or even their entertainment—an issue she would return to more seriously in *A Son at the Front*. Similarly, *The Man-at-Arms* in "Writing a War Story" is not a parody of her own *Book of the Homeless* but, possibly, of some of its competitors. Wharton wrote proudly that *The Book of the Homeless* was "considered by far the best of the war-books, & of course artistically there is no comparison" (*Letters* 373). The two stories are based on the war activities Wharton knew best—the life she observed behind the lines. With the war over, she could begin to tell some of the more comical, even quirkier, tales of civilian life in wartime.

Although Wharton's true summing up of her war experiences would come in *A Son at the Front,* her writings from the end of the war began the process of summarizing and shaping her war experiences. The elegies sounded the note of mourning and mythical glorification that had been Wharton's since the war's beginning, though they are also sobered by the experience of more than four years of living in a state of war. The satires sound a different note of relief, but also echo earlier works as well as each other: the central tragedy—the story of Emile Durand—is missing from "Writing a War Story" as it is from "Coming Home"; in all three stories, readers are left hanging, left to work out conclusions as best they can. Wharton's war works were beginning to echo each other: the editor of *The Man-at-Arms* asks Ivy Spang for a "Coming-Home" scene, and Ivy entitles her story "His Letter Home": both are sly references to Wharton's earlier war story. Charlie Durand, so afraid of missing out on the adventure of war in "The Refugees," is transformed into Emile Durand, one of the legendary Chasseurs Alpins, in "Writing a War Story"; the soldier Jean de Réchamp of "Coming Home" would be anglicized and transformed into John Campton, civilian painter, in *A Son at the Front.*[4] All three of Wharton's war-related stories imply her fear of missing out: the unnamed opening narrator in "Coming Home" is a bystander; Macy Greer works only behind the lines, and even Jean de Réchamp is disabled early in the war; Charlie Durand and Audrey Rushworth both miss out on the war's adventure, and Ivy Spang's errors stem from her exclusion from battle. These short stories reconfirm the importance of gender, exclusion, the "real" meaning of war, and the wartime role of civilians—including women writers—in Wharton's thinking about the war.

IV. Coda

Wharton devoted her energies to one more war-related poem, entitled simply "Elegy." First published in Wharton's 1926 volume *Twelve Poems,* the poem is preceded by a full page listing its title and—in brackets below it—the date 1918, suggesting that the poem was written in that year. If so, it must surely have been after the war's end: this poem differs significantly in emphasis and tone from her previous war-related elegies.

As we have seen, Wharton's earlier elegies, even while acknowledging the deaths caused by the war, confirm the importance of the war. "You and You" stresses noble abstractions and praises the soldiers for their sacrifice: "Every one of you won the war, / But you, you Dead, most of all!" "'On Active Service'" concludes with the reassurance that "a sweet voice"

will "sing" in the hearts of the grieving, "Recalling him [the dead], and
Spring"; similarly, "Beaumetz," the elegy for Jean du Breuil, reassures its
readers that "he shall burst" the grave's limits, "And come to us with shining eyes." "With the Tide" restores romance and heroism to the war, implicitly comparing Roosevelt to King Arthur and presenting his death as
the beginning of "some farther quest."

Such reassurances are missing from "Elegy." The poem begins with a
brief reminder of the sacrifice of the young soldiers who have died: "Ah,
how I pity the young dead who gave / All that they were, and might become, that we / With tired eyes should watch this perfect sea[.]" The soldiers' sacrifice is stated simply, and without romantic flourish, in these
lines. Further, these lines convey the speaker's appreciation that the
"young dead" gave up their lives for her and those like her. The "tired
eyes" suggest the fatigue and gloom of the war years, introducing the
possibility that such a loss was purposeless: why sacrifice for people who
are tired? Even more solemnly, the speaker evinces some sense of guilt, or
at least of questioning: why should the young and energetic have sacrificed
themselves for the older and less vital? The poem moves from this briefly-
stated sense of sacrifice toward the speaker's haunted sense that the very
landscape, with its plants and flowers, will remind her perpetually of those
who died:

No more shall any rose along the way,
The myrtled way that wanders to the shore,
Nor jonquil-twinkling meadow any more,
Nor the warm lavender that takes the spray,
Smell only of the sea-salt and the sun,

But, through recurring seasons, every one
Shall speak to us with lips the darkness closes,
Shall look at us with eyes that missed the roses,
Clutch us with hands whose work was just begun[.]

Wharton's love of landscape and gardening is reflected in her naming of
specific flowering plants—the rose, the myrtle, and so on; her sense of the
magnitude of the lives lost in the war is reflected in her prediction that all
of these plants will become anthropomorphized reminders of those losses,
"speak[ing]" and "look[ing]" with the eyes of the dead, and—alarmingly—even "Clutch[ing] us with hands whose work was just begun[.]"

Finally, Wharton emphasizes loss, the loss of the "young dead" themselves who will never know again the beauties, and indeed the perfection, of the natural world:

Ah, how I pity the young dead, whose eyes
Strain through the sod to see these perfect skies,
Who feel the new wheat springing in their stead,
And the lark singing for them overhead!

Wharton does not suggest the dead are "on some farther quest" here, nor that their rest is complete. Instead she suggests that the dead maintain a certain residual consciousness, just enough consciousness to be aware of what they have lost. In the same way they retain just enough energy to "Strain" their eyes "through the sod to see these perfect skies," to envy "the new wheat springing in their stead," and to feel "the lark singing for them overhead!" The lark may offer a memorial song—it sings, after all, "for them." But the emphasis in the last three lines of "Elegy" is on all that the "young dead" have lost, and which they can never regain.

The end of the war brought change for Wharton, some of it welcome and some of it unwelcome. She came to find her beloved Paris too crowded with Americans as the war drew to a close; even before the war's end, she had initiated plans to leave Paris, beginning negotiations to buy Pavillon Colombe, a small chateau north of Paris. She had also become acquainted with the French Riviera town of Hyères, where, in 1920, she would buy a second small chateau to live in during the winter months (Benstock, *No Gifts* 352–53). The end of the war evoked ambivalent reactions in her— grief and celebration, reverence and mockery—which reflected themselves in the variety of her writings in this period. She also began writing *A Son at the Front*, but would not be able to finish it until 1922—a contrast to the breakneck speed at which she composed some of her wartime writings, such as *The Marne*, written in a matter of months, and "With the Tide," apparently written in a single day. Only in *A Son at the Front* would Wharton be able to reflect, more fully than in any other work, the complex nature of what it had meant to be part of the home front during the Great War.

Monument Building

A Son at the Front

I have just received your letter of Sept. 21ˢᵗ, and am much touched by
your praise of "A Son at the Front." I wanted to do something about
the war that would help a little to keep it alive in people's memories.
Edith Wharton to Robert Grant (1 Oct. 1923,
Wharton Collection **Yale)**

I.

The general neglect of Wharton's war-related writings is perhaps made
most conspicuous by the lack of critical commentary on *A Son at the Front*.
Published in 1923, this full-length novel was clearly of great importance to
Wharton: though she started it in 1918, her composition of it was interrupted by work on *In Morocco* (1920), *The Age of Innocence* (1920), and
Glimpses of the Moon (1922). She persevered, however, finally completing
it in 1922, and when Appleton—her publisher for the latter part of her
career—was unable to accept it, she returned to Scribner's, her earlier publisher, to get *Son* into print. She had a strong personal stake in the novel;
she wanted to "keep [the war] alive in people's memories" as she wrote to
Robert Grant, reiterating that sentiment on the same day to her friend
Daisy Chanler: "it's a sort of 'lest we forget,' & I'm glad I've done it" (*Letters* 471). Yet the novel received a plethora of negative reviews when it was
released; until 1995 it was out of print; and even since its reprinting it has
received little critical attention.

The troubled history of this novel may have been prognosticated by
Wharton's difficulties finding it a publisher. After the end of the war the
American public had an aversion to war-related works, and publishers
were unwilling to risk sales by printing war-related fiction. Joseph Sears of

Appleton, who was trying to sell serial rights to *A Son at the Front*, had no luck: "editors who would pay [\$15,000] for something by Edith Wharton did not want a war story"; later, Appleton stipulated that it "would have to withdraw" the advance it had agreed to pay her on her next novel if Wharton met the agreement with *Son* (Benstock, *No Gifts* 355–56). Scribner's, "eager to have [Wharton] on their list again" after her defection to Appleton, finally agreed to publish the novel, which came out in September 1923 (Benstock, *No Gifts* 361, 372).

The American aversion to war works was frequently a factor in the negative reviews the novel received. A number of reviewers criticized Wharton for publishing a war novel so long after the war had ended; in the *Nation*, John Macy asserted that "Her story is out of date. She evidently began it five years ago and laid it aside until last year. It need never have been finished" (Tuttleton et al. 340). An anonymous English reviewer agreed, calling it "a belated essay in propaganda" (Tuttleton et al. 344). Reviews, however, were not uniformly negative. On September 9, 1923, Maurice Francis Egan claimed in the *New York Times Book Review* that "So far [Wharton] has done nothing that equals it. She sounds the finest depths of sentiment without becoming sentimental. . . . Only the production of a masterpiece could reconcile us to the treatment of that terrible epoch by a writer of fiction" (Tuttleton et al. 325). But on the same date Burton Rascoe, writing in the *New York Tribune,* wrote:

> One wonders, after reading *A Son at the Front*, where in the world Mrs. Wharton has been all this time. Certainly she cannot have been remotely in touch with French, English and American fiction since 1914. . . .
>
> Mrs. Wharton has been wholly oblivious of the war inspired fiction of the Messrs. Wells, Bennett, George, Cannan, Hankey, Hay, Mackenzie, McKenna, Barbusse, Latzko, Duhamel, Geraldy, Dos Passos, Cummings and Boyd, to say nothing of the work of the Misses Sinclair, West, Stern, Macaulay and Cather. (Tuttleton et al. 329)

Rascoe struck the note that would serve to dismiss Wharton's war-related writings in general and *A Son at the Front* in particular: she was simply out of touch. Recent scholarship on Wharton's work generally passes over *Son* quickly.[1] The 1995 reissue of *Son* attempts to market the novel by presenting it as an "antiwar masterpiece"—a description unlikely to be accepted by anyone who reads the novel attentively.[2] The novel is neither "antiwar" nor, most readers would agree, is it a "masterpiece."

A Son at the Front focuses on John Campton, an expatriate American painter nearing sixty who is living and working in Paris when the war breaks out. Divorced, he has one son—George—now in his early 20s, who is coming to Paris to take a vacation with his father. As George, however, happened to have been born in France, he is a French citizen, and their trip is canceled when George is mobilized along with all other French men of military age. George is wounded once, but returns to the front. Wounded a second time, he is recuperating in a hospital, but dies shortly after hearing from friends and relatives that the United States has declared war on Germany. The novel concludes after John Campton witnesses the parade of American soldiers down the Champs Elysées on July 4, 1917 and after he finally agrees—under pressure from his ex-wife, her husband, and his son's friend—to design a monument for his son's grave.

Written from John Campton's point of view, the novel focuses on the Parisian expatriate community in wartime. Wharton here followed, even more strictly than in her earlier works, the dictum that noncombatants not portray scenes at the front: Campton visits his son at a hospital near the front, but does not witness combat; though frequently arrogant, he never assumes that he understands soldiers' experience and is grateful for rare "glimpses" into his son's life at the front. In spite of its title, *A Son at the Front* is really about John Campton, the painter, rather than about his son. The novel follows the artist as he lives in wartime Paris, becomes involved with a war charity and, in doing so, becomes close to Boylston, a friend of his son; he also expends considerable energy conniving—along with his ex-wife, Julia, and her husband, Anderson Brant—to keep George at a safe desk job during the war. He and Brant, though generally at odds with each other, come together to support George when they find out he has secretly moved to a position at the front; they travel together, thanks largely to Brant's resources, to see George at a frontline hospital when he is wounded.

The novel chronicles the years from the war's outset through, and slightly beyond, the United States' entry into the war in 1917. Its scope is panoramic: it documents the social scene among expatriate Americans and the changes in attitudes toward the war within that community; the bitter and pointless bickering over the administration of one wartime charity; the effects of the war on art and character; the competition between parents and step-parents as each strives to protect or possess a son who, in differing ways, belongs to all of them; the gradually increasing understanding on the part of those at home that life on the front was wretchedly miserable, far from the heroics they had initially pictured. It may be the very scope of the novel that leads to its aesthetic weaknesses; the novel sags, or perhaps wanders, under the weight of its burden. As Cynthia Griffin Wolff has written, "*A Son at the Front* is a vexing novel: one feels that it should have been better" (336). Perhaps most vexing is Wharton's portrayal of John Campton, which, while complex, does not always seem to be fully under her control. Yet in spite of its weaknesses, the novel is complex and engaging. Examining it in the light of the war and in the context of Wharton's other war-related writings reveals its richness, regardless of its flaws. As the reviewer for the *Times Literary Supplement* put it, the novel has "permanent value among the minor documents of the war" (Tuttleton et al. 334). Further, it has permanent value in Wharton's oeuvre, serving as a crucial pivot between the wartime and postwar writings. *A Son at the Front* is Wharton's culminating portrayal of the war. Into it she poured the accumulated experiences of the war years; in it, she also revised, refined, and extended her earlier war writings. Finally, the novel reflects Wharton's complex attitude toward the war, suggesting that, for her, realism about the war—a comprehension of its terrible conditions, its terrible cost—was not inconsistent with a tempered idealism and a firm belief that the war was necessary.

II. Biographical Sources

Samuel Hynes has written that Robert Graves composed *Goodbye to All That* in order "to exorcize the war by mythologizing it. If you could turn your war into a story, you might quiet its uproar, might give it some order, perhaps even some significance. And then maybe you could turn away from it and get on with life" (Hynes 429). Graves fought in the war; Wharton, who did not, was spared its direst circumstances. Nevertheless, there was sufficient material to be "exorcized," sufficient reason to turn her own war "into a story." As Wharton wrote in *A Backward Glance*, "My spirit was heavy with these losses, but I could not sit still and brood over them. I wanted to put them into words" (368). Wharton drew wide and deep on her wartime experiences in creating *Son*; the result is a work that is far more complex than any of her previous war-related writings.

The fundamental situation of the novel—an artist father with a soldier son—was probably suggested to Wharton by at least three examples. The first was Pierre-Auguste Renoir's contribution to *The Book of the Homeless*, a sketch of his son, who had just returned from the front (fig. 2);[3]

Fig. 2. Sketch of his son by Pierre-Auguste Renoir, from *The Book of the Homeless.*

Wharton referred to it in a letter as a "thrilling" contribution (12 Oct. 1915, *Wharton Collection* Yale). Renoir's son is astonishingly youthful in this sketch, seeming little more than a boy. In this the sketch is like the photograph of Newbold Rhinelander preserved in Wharton's papers, in which, for all his uniform, Newbold looks, if anything, younger than his twenty-one years (fig. 3).

Another contributor to *The Book of the Homeless,* Joseph Conrad, presented a similar father-son scenario in a letter he sent to Wharton. As discussed in chapter three, Wharton had sent Conrad a copy of her novel *Summer.* In his thank-you letter he wrote her that "On the very morning the book arrived our eldest boy went away after the usual 10 days' leave from the front. C'est un très brave garçon [he is a very brave boy] who tho' he's only nineteen understands his father in a heart-ensnaring way. Some-

Fig. 3. Photograph of Newbold
Rhinelander (Wharton's cousin)
in uniform. Yale Collection of
American Literature, Beinecke
Rare Book and Manuscript Li-
brary.

how the parting was even harder than the times before" (1 Oct. 1917,
Wharton Collection Yale). The "heart-ensnaring way" in which young
Conrad understands his father, the father's difficulty at seeing, yet again,
his son go off to the front—both are elements of the relationship between
George and his father in *Son*.

Another letter Wharton received, this one from Henry James, suggests
yet more clearly the way in which George divines his father's wish that his
son fight at the front. James wrote to Wharton that "My own small domestic plot here rocks beneath my feet, since yesterday afternoon, with the

decision at once to volunteer of my valuable and irreplaceable little [servant] Burgess! I had been much expecting and even hoping for it, but definitely shrinking from the responsibility of administering the push with my own hand: I wanted the impulse to play up of itself" (Powers 297). In his quasi-paternal role, James is pleased when Burgess enlists—just as Campton is pleased when he finds out that, despite George's pretense of writing from a desk job, he has been at the front a good long while (309–10). The son divines the father's wish and acts on it. And on the part of both son and father there is a sense of purpose, of nobility—a sense that despite the risk, this action must be taken: the son must go to the front.

James's reluctance to "push" Burgess to enlist may have stemmed from a feeling he described in an earlier letter to Wharton: a sense that those unable to take part in combat had no right to push the able-bodied into it, a sense that the "Old Men" ought not to send a generation of young men off to the slaughter. Writing to Wharton on August 19, 1914, he said, "Life goes on after a fashion, but I find it a nightmare from which there is no waking save by sleep. I *go* to sleep, as if I were dog-tired with action—yet feel like the chilled vieillards [old men] in the old epics, infirm and helpless at home with the women while the plains are ringing with battle" (Powers 293). Similarly, John Campton tells a friend that "As soon as I open my lips to blame or praise I see myself in white petticoats, with a long beard held on by an elastic, goading on the combatants in a cracked voice from a safe corner of the ramparts" (190). Noncombatant older men ran the risk of feeling feminized by their nonparticipation—as well as feeling guilty over the risk of death that younger men faced.

In addition to working from the artist-father/soldier-son configurations she saw around her, Wharton re-created some of the circumstances affecting her and other artists during the war. In particular, she portrayed the war's power to distract, disorient, and mentally disable artists. Campton finds it difficult to paint during the war for a number of reasons. The first is practical: having recently established himself as Paris's most sought-after portrait painter, he is frustrated to find his market—and his income—drying up as the war begins. More profoundly, he also finds that "his artist's vision had been strangely unsettled. Sometimes . . . he saw nothing: the material world, which had always tugged at him with a thousand hands, vanished and left him in the void. Then again, as at present, he saw everything, saw it too clearly, in all its superfluous and negligible reality, instead of instinctively selecting, and disregarding what was not to his purpose" (95). Later in the novel, Campton comes to feel, at least temporarily, that the artist has no role in wartime. His eye for the beautiful "made him feel more than ever unfitted for a life in which such things"— that is, his sense of the artistic—"were no longer of account[.]" Worse, "it seemed a disloyalty even to think" of aesthetic questions in time of war (221).

Campton's artistic dilemma may have been partly suggested to Wharton early in the war by a letter she received from Max Beerbohm. She had asked him to contribute to *The Book of the Homeless*, and in reply he wrote, "In times of peace I am by way of being a cartoonist—a dealer in symbolic groups with reference to current events. But now there is only one current event; and it, the war, is so impossible a theme for comedy that one cannot (unless one is on the staff of a comic paper, and *has* to) do a cartoon touching the remotest fringe of it. My cartooning days are thus over, for the present" (11 Aug. 1915, *Wharton Collection* Yale). Beerbohm wrote yet more succinctly to John Singer Sargent, "The Comic Muse, who helps me in time of peace, sits nowadays with ashes on her head, wailing, and having nothing to say to me" (11 Aug. 1915, *Wharton Collection* Yale). Art did not fare well in time of war.

James, too, found himself incapable of concentrating on his art. In a letter to Wharton he mockingly depicted Mrs. Humphry Ward's heartless-ness in being able to go on with her work. Her explanation to James was that she was writing for a U.S. market, "where[,]" as she told him, "they mind the War so much less." James concludes sardonically, "I am going really, I think, to try that precious solution of our friend's: I mean making it, and thinking of it as, so preponderantly for America, where they don't care, that their belle insouciance [beautiful carelessness] will infect my condition and perhaps even my style" (Powers 313–14).

Three weeks later he wrote again, more darkly, that the war cast a shadow not just over the present and the future but over the past as well. In retrospect, he told Wharton, he saw the previous few decades as having led toward the war. He found himself almost completely unable to write, saying that he was "try[ing] to get back to work—but it's of a stiffness of uphill—a sheer perpendicular. I crawl like a fly—a more or less frozen fly—on a most blank wall." He understood this not as a personal writing block, but rather as an effect of the war: "It's impossible to 'locate anything in our time.' Our time has been *this* time for the last 50 years, & if it was ignorantly and fatuously so the only light in which to show it is now the light of that tragic delusion. And that's too awful a subject. It all makes Walter Scott, him only, readable again" (Powers 316). When James did return to writing, it was to rework his ideas for *The Sense of the Past*—a novel that, as Lyall Powers has pointed out, allowed James an "escape" from his own time (291). This was one possible solution to the problem of how an artist writes in light of the war—a solution, as we will see in chapter six, that Wharton would turn to herself in postwar works like *The Age of Innocence* and *Old New York*.

Campton, the artist-father, was thus suggested by a number of men Wharton knew; so too was George, the soldier-son. The sons of Renoir and Conrad were not boys she knew, nor did she know James's Burgess well. But she had met a number of young American soldiers, and her impressions were almost exclusively positive; in none of them did she encounter the demoralization recorded by numerous English authors, as well as American authors like Hemingway, Dos Passos, and e.e. cummings. Her defense of the way her fictional soldiers speak emphasizes that her cheerful soldiers were drawn from life. Writing to her friend Daisy Chanler, she implied that the speech of her soldiers was realistic, while that of some authors credited as realists was based on fabrications: "—No, I'm afraid my young Americans don't talk the language as spoken by the Scott Fitzgerald & Sinclair Lewis jeunesse; but I saw dozens of young Americans from all parts of America during the war, & none of them talked it, any more than your sons-in-law do! I believe it's a colossal literary convention, invented by the delightful Sinclair Lewis, & adopted by the throng of lesser ones" (*Letters* 471).

Some of Wharton's contact with American soldiers was brief. She was impressed by the young men she had met when she delivered her talk to the Soldiers' and Sailors' Club in spring 1918; she had accepted that invitation to speak, as she wrote to a friend, specifically "in order to see the men, & was so glad I had done so. They were delightful[.]" She continued, "You may imagine what the popularity of our army here is, from Genl Pershing down. And it is genuine too, & not merely borne of gratitude. The men of all ranks have made themselves popular" (2 Sept. 1918, *Wharton Collection* Yale). To Sally Norton she wrote, "I wish you could hear all the splendid things that are said of our troops on all sides" (5 Oct. 1918, *Wharton Collection* Yale). But her main sources for characters like George Campton and Boylston (as well as Troy Belknap in *The Marne*) were two young men she knew: her young friend Ronald Simmons, and her young aviator cousin, Newbold Rhinelander.

Wharton's notes confirm the notion that she drew Boylston on the model of Ronald Simmons. Her notation in a notebook entry on *Son* states, "Upsher is not Simmons—but 'Boylston' may be—" (Notebook 1918–23, *Wharton Collection* Yale).[4] Further, the letters of Simmons to Wharton, as well as the letters of Newbold Rhinelander to his family (copies of which were given to Wharton) provide the basis for the cheerful soldier characters she portrays in *A Son at the Front*. Simmons, for instance, expressed the eagerness to go to the front that Wharton would re-create in Boylston: "Even you can never know how I envy those men who have the nerves, health and qualities to go to the Front[,]" he wrote her (7 July 1918, *Wharton Collection* Yale). Similarly, Newbold Rhinelander wrote home to remark that he was "truly ashamed to say that since I have been here I haven't been over the lines yet. Two of the teams have been over on reconnaissance and I'm hoping my turn will come very soon" (18 Sept. 1918, *Wharton Collection* Yale). He notes cheerfully that "It's such fun being here more like a small happy family than a post" [*sic*] (18 Sept. 1918, *Wharton Collection* Yale). In another letter to his mother he writes—evidently in response to his mother's request for birthday wishes—that while he thinks it would be nice if she could bring the war to a close, "have you reflected on how you and I would feel if I didn't get a good crack at the Hun?" (4 Sept. 1918, *Wharton Collection* Yale).

The image of the happy soldier was confirmed by Newbold's close friend in the squadron, W. Clarkson Potter. After Newbold was shot down in September 1918, Potter wrote to Newbold's father that "Bo's loss to this squadron is irretrievable, he was the very life and soul of it, always cheerful and perpetually singing ragtime and playing the mandolin day in and day out; besides being a 'finished pilot,' one of the *very best* the Air Service had" (29 Sept. 1918, *Wharton Collection* Yale). After Newbold's death, his father—Wharton's cousin—sent her some extracts from Newbold's diary. Wharton wrote back that "there is a delightful gaiety & freshness about these impressions that are the very essence of youth" (18 Jan. 1919, *Wharton Collection* Yale). It was this sense of "gaiety & freshness," as well as devotion to duty, that Wharton re-created, even memorialized, in characters like Boylston and George Campton.

It is tempting to see Boylston as a portrait of Simmons and George Campton as a portrait of Newbold: the fictional characters' relationships to Campton imitate the historical characters' relationship to Wharton. Campton, though related to George, sees little of him, and seems not to know him particularly well; George is the golden boy who is sacrificed to the cause. Boylston, though no blood relation to Campton, knows him well; Campton sees him frequently. Wharton, though related to Newbold, apparently met him only a few times; Newbold, like George, was the golden boy who died of wounds sustained in combat. Wharton, though unrelated to Simmons, was closer to him than to her cousin. *A Son at the Front*, like *The Marne*, is dedicated to the memory of Simmons, and in both memorials Wharton takes the author's prerogative, reversing death: Troy Belknap, though wounded, survives; Boylston, like Simmons, is given a noncombat position that allows him significant involvement in the war— but unlike Simmons he does not die of double pneumonia, and is alive, healthy, and active at the novel's end. Wharton could not change history, but in her fiction she allowed herself to imagine a happier fate for characters based on people she knew.

III. Revising the Earlier War Writings

In broader ways as well, Wharton drew on her wartime experience in *A Son at the Front;* in doing so she also revisited issues she had treated earlier in her war-related writings. In some cases she expanded on themes she had already touched; in others, she allowed herself to portray with greater depth the difficulties, irritations, and disillusionment of the war years—as well as her abiding sense of respect, even awe, for the men with frontline experience. The length of the novel, and the freedom of expression available in the postwar period, gave her the latitude to portray more fully than she had before both her admiration for human ability and her frustration with human flaws.

Wharton's extensive involvement with administering and fund-raising for charities gave her a wealth of experience—including much frustration—from which to work. Among many other activities, she had organized two fund-raising concerts; though these were financially successful, she found the work exhausting, remarking to a friend, "for ten days I was never at peace for a quarter of a second" (*Letters* 346). She also discovered that such events could lend themselves to the ridiculous. From across the Channel, Henry James wrote to Wharton of a wartime recital he planned to attend. He described himself as working up the strength "to face the privilege" of attending "a vocal recital by a Belgian baritone . . . ; which performance narrates with premeditated art, and an effect guaranteed by Réjane [a French actress] to drown us all in tears, the manner in which he *sang* himself out of captivity in Germany, bribing his captors by the beauty of his gift, and from one acute danger of being hung or shot for a spy to another, to get on, to go free, a little further and further, till he at last escaped altogether. He has arranged the story as a musical monologue, I believe" (Powers 333). James, for all his belief in the war, seems to find the prospect of this performance rather daunting and mildly risible. Wharton depicted a similarly strange combination of horror and entertainment in one scene from "The Refugees," in which an aristocratic lady remarks, "The Committee has given us a prima donna from the Brussels Opera to sing the Marseillaise, and the what d'ye-call-it Belgian anthem, but there are lots of people coming just for the Atrocities" (587). Atrocities as entertainment would be further satirized in *A Son at the Front*.

In *Son*, Harvey Mayhew is a cousin of Campton's who comes to Europe as a delegate to a peace conference. En route to The Hague, however, he is detained by German soldiers, and though he is only restricted to his hotel for a week, the experience turns him from a proponent of peace into a vehement enemy of the Germans. His decision to "devote himself to Atrocities" (141) is risible and made even more so when this devotion takes on a musical character. One day Campton finds him rehearsing for a fund-raiser at Mrs. Brant's, his "oratorical accents accompanied by faint chords on the piano[.]" Mayhew has "a perfect pearl in his tie and a perfect crease in his trousers," and in his oration (which is, like the Belgian baritone's described by James, decidedly "premeditated art") he describes himself as "one of the first Victims of [German] barbarism" (202–3). Wharton did not neglect to use the "tremolo note" on occasion, but it is clear that Mayhew uses it constantly, enjoying "the prestige it was bringing him in French social and governmental circles" (230). Though posing as a one-time victim now devoted to the war effort, Mayhew is out to improve his social standing and his opinion of himself—an attitude with which Wharton had no patience. Wharton extends her parody by implying that the American public is undiscriminating, as they respond enthusiastically to Mayhew's overdramatized performance: "Mr. Mayhew's harrowing appeals were beginning to bring from America immense sums for the Victims" (230).

Even more irritating than such posing, however, was the fact that such misguided behavior could have a deleterious effect on the recipients of wartime charities—something Wharton saw in the charities she herself supervised. As Alan Price has illustrated, Wharton was frustrated when, in 1917, the American Red Cross began to take over a number of her charities.[5] She wrote that "I am sick to think of the mischief they [the Red Cross] have done, & the impression they are giving everywhere of incompetence and arrogance combined" (qtd. in Price 137). In *A Son at the Front* the representative charity is the "Friends of French Art," no doubt based on a charity, le Comité des Etudiants Américains des Beaux-Arts, in which Ronald Simmons had been involved. Wharton described the work of this committee in a letter; like the fictional "Friends of French Art," it sought to help the families of art students fighting on the front, not by making gifts of money but by organizing concerts and securing orders for work (171).[6] As the novel progresses, the initial hard work of Boylston and others, including Campton and his friend Adele Anthony, is undermined when fashionable people like Mme. de Dolmetsch first show an interest in, and then gradually begin to take over, the charity. Wharton describes a fund-raiser in which the four organizers—Campton, Adele Anthony, Mlle. Davril (sister of a deceased soldier-artist), and Boylston—are marginalized by their guests: "They seemed, all four, more like unauthorized intruders on the brilliant scene than its laborious organizers. The entertainment, escaping from their control, had speedily reverted to its true purpose of feeding and amusing a crowd of bored and restless people" (329). The "fluffy fuzzy people" Wharton had been relieved to see leaving Paris early in the war were, after all, still a part of the scene; further, they were a counterproductive force in the war.

The rivalry within "Friends of French Art" comes to a head over social issues thinly disguised as financial ones: "Mr. Mayhew was attending all their meetings now, finding fault, criticizing, asking to have the accounts investigated . . . ; and all this zeal originated in the desire to put Mme. de Dolmetsch in Miss Anthony's place, on the plea that her greater social experience, her gift of attracting and interesting, would bring in immense sums of money" (332–33). Such an attempted coup echoes the fashionable Mabel Boardman's takeover of the Red Cross from the plain Clara Barton (see Price 118–19); further, Wharton's general criticism of the Red Cross as "incompetence and arrogance combined" is much implied in her portrait of Mme. de Dolmetsch's and Harvey Mayhew's takeover of the "Friends of French Art." Ultimately Campton resigns, Adele Anthony and Boylston decline merely "ornamental posts," and "Paris drawing-rooms echoed with the usual rumours of committee wrangles and dark discoveries" (371). There was deep disillusionment among soldiers on the front; though no lives were at stake at the rear, there was, in some instances, also much disillusionment as good works by the competent were commandeered and mismanaged by misguided and self-important social climbers.

In characters like *The Marne*'s Mrs. Belknap, Wharton had portrayed hypocrisy earlier in the war; in *A Son at the Front* she repeatedly draws attention to hypocrites. Julia Brant, for instance, insists on using every connection she and her husband have in order to be sure that George will be given a safe staff job, yet she criticizes others for doing exactly what she herself has done: "'it seems there are no end of officers always intriguing to get staff-jobs: strong able-bodied young men who ought to be in the trenches'" (179). Further, she displays George's portrait in uniform prominently, and includes herself in the phrase "'We mothers with sons at the front'" while believing that George is actually at a staff job (219). She is fully aware of the social prestige to be derived from her son's military position—or what she falsely presents as his position. Campton, though he objects to Julia's prominent display of George's military portrait, can be faulted for the exact same hypocrisy. He objects to Mme. de Dolmetsch's attempt to get her lover, Ladislaw Isador, a safe position, but still firmly believes in his right to shield his son George: "His gorge rose at the thought that people should associate in their minds cases as different as those of his son and Mme. de Dolmetsch's lover" (179). To the reader it is perfectly clear that George's case is identical to Isador's. On a larger scale, Wharton satirizes pleasure-loving expatriates who, while enjoying luxuries, persuade themselves they are being heroic: "hundreds and thousands of lads like [Benny Upsher] . . . were thus groping and agonizing and stretching out vain hands, while in Mrs. Talkett's drawing-room well-fed men and expensive women heroically 'forgot the war'" (254).

In many other ways as well, *A Son at the Front* extends the issues inherent in Wharton's earlier war writings. As we have seen, Wharton's own impatience with doing nothing and her need to be active during the war were reflected in Jean de Réchamp's need to be up and doing in "Coming Home"; *Son* reiterates Wharton's perception of work, however draining, as a blessing. In *A Backward Glance* she would compare the efforts of war workers to those of "a nurse on a hard case" (356); she uses the same medical analogy to describe the activity of Campton's friend Paul Dastrey: "He had done his utmost, and knew it; and the fact gave him the professional calm which keeps surgeons and nurses steady through all the horrors they are compelled to live among" (187). The metaphor is realized in the doctor Fortin-Lescluze, who returns to his frontline hospital immediately after the funeral of his only son, saying "'Thank God. If it were not for [my work]—'" (121). Campton's concierge, Mme. Lebel, echoes Fortin-Lescluze's gratitude for work. After receiving bad news of her son and his family, she remarks to Campton, "'Oh, Monsieur, thank God for the work! If it were not for that—'" (126–27). Even Campton begins to grasp that perhaps "a real job"—which he defines as work at or near the front—would "shut [the war] out" for a time (188).

Wharton also re-creates in *Son* one of the hallmarks of *Fighting France:* the sense of unreality that affected her during the early months of the war. Campton, like Wharton, is repeatedly overcome by a sense of unreality. When France is mobilized, Campton "was overcome by a sense of such dizzy unreality that he had to grasp the arms of his ponderous leather armchair to assure himself that he was really in the flesh and in the world" (75). Later, when driving with Brant to see George at a field hospital near Doullens, Campton is seized anew with a sense of unreality: "It was he, John Campton, who sat in that car" (263)—an echo of Wharton's experience at Châlons ("I stood there in the pitch-black night, suddenly unable to believe that I was I, or Châlons Châlons" [*Fighting France* 88]). When Campton and George have left the Doullens hospital behind for a quieter hospital at the rear, the scene near the front lines becomes "as a nightmare to a wakened sleeper" (291), strange and insubstantial in spite of its very reality. And when George is wounded for the second time, "the old sense of unreality enveloped [Campton] again, and he struggled vainly to clutch at something tangible amid the swimming mists" (402).

Campton's struggles to hang on to reality also align him with Charity Royall; George's hospitalization echoes Charity's struggle to obtain the most basic necessities. Coming down from the Mountain, Charity appreciates anew "the pleasant animal sensations of warmth and rest" (179); she needs to "return to life" (179). This reduction to necessities is infantilizing: she follows Royall "as passively as a tired child" (183). Wounded, George goes through a similar regression. When Campton sees George at the frontline hospital, his son is "as hard to get at as a baby; he looked at his father with eyes as void of experience, or at least of any means of conveying it" (292), even though his experiences in the war have made him look older. George is remote from "everything but the things which count in an infant's world: food, warmth, sleep" (292). In some ways Campton's presence at the hospital allows him to make up for his absence as a father during George's early years; not only does he assure that George receives the "food, warmth, sleep" that he needs, but he is present at George's "first steps in the wards" (312) as George recovers from his wounds. In this world Campton's prewar priorities are reversed; art is irrelevant, and his parental role, securing his son's simple survival, becomes his all-absorbing concern.

A Son at the Front also extends Wharton's concern, reflected in "Coming Home," with the ways in which war was altering behavior and even morality. To some extent the war broke down social codes; Julia tells Campton about the aristocratic Mme. de Tranlay opening a conversation with Mme. de Dolmetsch: "'Only fancy—the last person she would have spoken to in ordinary times!'" (242). Similarly, Campton is surprised to find Julia Brant "on terms of playful friendliness" with the banker Jorgenstein, whom she used to mistrust: "Of all strange war promiscuities, Campton thought this the strangest" (237).

More significantly, the war affected sexual mores. Wharton touched on this topic in passing in "The Refugees": Charlie Durand momentarily fears that Audrey Rushworth may be planning a sexual conquest of him. In *Son*, Wharton's implied stance is more conservative, suggesting that the war's alteration of sexual mores was merely temporary and primarily frivolous. Madge Talkett resists a sexual liaison with George Campton before the war, though she believes that her holding back was caused not by any moral misgiving, but by "timidity, vanity, the phantom barriers of old terrors and traditions" (340). After the war begins, however, the situation is reversed, and George tells his father that Madge Talkett "'has come to care for me awfully; if we'd gone all the lengths she wanted, and then I'd got killed, there would have been nothing on earth left for her'" (383). It is she who is willing to "go all lengths," and he who resists on principle: "'I hadn't the right, don't you see? We chaps haven't any futures to dispose of till this job we're in is finished'" (383). As in "The Refugees," this situation reverses traditional sex role typing, with the female pursuing the male. In neither case is this presented as a moment of sexual liberation or true intimacy; it is merely one of strange reversal. Further, Madge seems dismayed by George's insistence that she divorce her husband, Roger, and marry him before they begin a sexual relationship. At the same time she defends the idea of divorcing Roger as the only moral position. When John Campton urges her to stay with her husband and "'give up my son,'" she replies, "'Oh, but you don't understand—not in the least! It's not possible—it's not moral——. You know I'm all for the new morality. First of all, we must be true to self'" (343).

From Wharton's perspective, the "new morality" was deeply flawed. Mrs. Talkett rivals Julia Brant in vapidness and in her inability to think logically; as with Polonius in *Hamlet* (whom she echoes), any ideas she espouses are instantly suspect. Readers of Wharton's *The House of Mirth*, moreover, will recognize "old terrors and traditions" as being, in fact, positive values: what keeps Gus Trenor from raping Lily Bart are "Old habits, old restraints, the hand of inherited order" (147). In *French Ways and Their Meaning* Wharton had emphasized that marriage ought not to be about "mak[ing] two people individually happy for a longer or shorter time" (128). This is precisely the flaw in Madge Talkett's reasoning: marriage, and indeed morality in general, ought not to be interpreted as being "true to self" when doing so is interpreted as merely pursuing one's individual happiness. In "Coming Home" most of the moral changes presented seemed to be if not positive, at least justified as necessary; the same cannot be said of the shifting morality in *A Son at the Front.*

The gender issues that emerged in *The Marne* also surface in *Son.* As we have seen, most of the female figures in *The Marne* are figures of ridicule: they fail to understand the need to fight; they are involved in nonproductive social positioning; some even suffer from too much enthusiasm, with Wharton labeling them "war-mad"; others, most conspicuously Hinda Warlick, are so completely provincial that they fail to understand the principles behind French culture even when they begin to appreciate France. Much the same can be said of the women in *A Son at the Front.* Some of this negative cast is due to Campton's frequently misogynistic viewpoint, but certainly not all of it. For instance, women are portrayed as overprotective mothers: Julia Brant, like Troy Belknap's mother, only wants to protect her son, failing to realize the importance of sending him to the front. Similarly, the mother of Benny Upsher, a young relative of Campton who comes to France to volunteer in the war effort, is presented as hysterical, telegraphing Campton frantically (and somewhat incoherently): "'please do all you can to facilitate his immediate return to America dreadfully anxious your cousin Madeline Upsher'" (108). Further, women are presented as uncomprehending or hysterical: Julia never comes to understand that "in the matter of human life, victories may be as ruinous as defeats" (392); even the levelheaded Adele Anthony is occasionally presented as an "elderly virgin on the war-path" (85). Of the women in the novel, only the matronly French concierge, Mme. Lebel, emerges as completely admirable; her moment of despair upon hearing of the death of her grandson—"'I don't understand any more, do you?'" (376)—is forgivable under the circumstances, an illustration of Wharton's remark in *Fighting France* that some women despaired under the strain of the war. But Mme. Lebel returns doggedly to the war effort, an example of the determination Wharton praised in *Fighting France:* "of this company of blinded baffled sufferers, almost all have had the strength to hide their despair and to say of the great national effort which has lost most of its meaning to them: 'Though it slay me, yet will I trust in it'" (225).

Wharton does not automatically confer credibility on males, however. Harvey Mayhew, whether as a peace delegate or as the orator of Atrocities, is generally ridiculous, as are intellectuals like Ladislaw Isador and Roger Talkett, who refuse to enter the war on the grounds that war was no business of theirs. Bloomsbury's Clive Bell had made the same argument, believing that "the artist's only duty to his country in wartime was to go on being an artist. Indeed, the existence of a war made that duty even more imperative, for 'a nation that would defend the cause of civilization must remain civilized'" (Hynes 85). Wharton, who admired the French army and emphasized that it included men from "the universities" as well as those who had left "the plough" behind ("Talk to American Soldiers," *Wharton Collection* Yale), found such arguments specious at best, and both Isador and Talkett are mocked and their manhood questioned by her portrayal of them in the novel. In this, *Son* continues the tacit challenging of capable men who avoid the war, an attitude reflected in *The Marne* through its quotation from *Henry V* ("And gentlemen in England now a-bed") and its ridicule of the "flat-faced professor with lank hair, [who] . . . announced that 'there were two sides to every case'" (31). Indeed, Wharton believed that as many American men as possible should enlist. She was thrilled when her cousin Newbold Rhinelander joined first the ambulance corps and later the air corps, and asked her cousin Tom Rhinelander, Newbold's father, why more of Newbold's "able-bodied young cousins" weren't volunteering (6 Oct. 1916, *Wharton Collection* Yale). The only excuses she seemed to find legitimate were advanced age—the case of John Campton, to whom she also gives a severe limp—or other disabilities, such as Boylston's "bad heart and . . . blind eyes" (323). These two are exempt from the novel's scorn, as Jean de Réchamp and Charlie Durand are sympathetic figures not to be criticized in her earlier stories. But they are exempted only because of their genuine disabilities—and their energetic war efforts.

Nevertheless, the male characters in *Son* seem to stand a better chance than the women of achieving a real understanding of the war. Mayhew (despite his weakness in other areas) approves of Benny Upsher's enlistment in the army, stating "'Benny's a man, and must act as a man. That boy . . . saw things as they were from the first'" (143). George writes to his father about his mother in a way that suggests that men, unlike women, are able to deal with the essential things: "'Sorry mother is bothering about things again; as you've often reminded me, they always have a way of "being as they will be," and even war doesn't seem to change it. Nothing to worry her in my case—but you can't expect her to believe that, can you?'" (196). Campton and Brant, despite their frequent disputes, come to agree long before Julia does that George should take his place at the front—an echo of an earlier scene in *The Marne* in which Mr. Belknap blurts out to the protesting Mrs. Belknap that he understands why Troy wants to be involved in the war. Further, Wharton confers on the men who fight at the front—those who were willing to take on "the real business of the nation"—a semisacred status.

The satire and the disillusionment of *A Son at the Front* are, in fact, balanced by the novel's expression of the power of war to ennoble both soldiers and civilians, and by its implication that the front is a place where, however awful the circumstances, the near-mystical occurs. In *Fighting France* Wharton had written that mobilization had instantly transformed the nation's young men: "The youngest of them looked suddenly grown up and responsible" (12). Civilians changed as well: "the Parisian face, after six months of trial, has acquired a new character . . . as though the long ordeal had hardened the poor human clay into some dense commemorative substance" (38). In *Son*, Wharton re-created such transformations in detail. As with so much else in this postwar novel, however, Wharton's belief in ennobling transformations is tempered. Some changes, like Julia Brant's, are suspect. Campton notes that "She had made herself a nurse's face; not a theatrical imitation of it . . . , nor yet the face of a nurse on a war-poster" (202), but he also observes skeptically that "her nails were as beautifully polished as ever" (203). Julia Brant may have more in common, after all, with Mrs. Belknap pouring tea "once or twice at a fashionable hospital," or with Ivy Spang, who cannot resist her own portrait as a nurse, than she does with professional nursing; Julia Brant's "gift of adaptation" (202) suggests more Undine Spragg's manipulative alterations than any significant improvement in her character. Other transformations may be temporary: Harvey Mayhew goes from fierce peace delegate to fierce propagandist, but collapses when he receives news of the death of his nephew, Benny Upsher. Campton's own transformation—particularly his acceptance of Anderson Brant as his son George's other (and equally important) father—waxes and wanes with the situation and his mood.

But there can be no doubt of the permanently ennobling effects of the war on other characters in the novel. Adele Anthony matures: from being an "eternal schoolgirl" she "grow[s] into a woman" (175). Boylston is altered by his engagement with charity work, as Adele Anthony notes: "'He *was* a pottering boy before—now he's a man, with a man's sense of things'" (217). His transformation is completed with his entry into a military role: "fagged as he was . . . , his blinking eyes had at last lost their unsatisfied look, and his whole busy person radiated hope and encouragement" (413). Of course the most important transformation is that of George, who changes from an apathetic political observer to a fighter on the front lines, articulating on his visits home the new vision that war has given him: "'War makes a lot of things look differently,'" he writes his father (196), and Madge Talkett later confirms that "'the war has changed him. He says he wants only things that last—that are permanent'" (343).

Although much of the home front scene is satirized, some characters are ennobled; although the front provided "horrors," *Son* assumes that much of what went on there was still noble, even mystical, in nature, though incomprehensible to civilians. Wharton's epigraph from Whitman's *Specimen Days*—"Something veil'd and abstracted is often a part of the manners of these beings" (738)—suggests the semimystical unknowableness of the soldiers, represented by Campton's son George. Wharton's language reflects this belief, particularly in Campton's occasional "glimpses," as he thinks of them, into George's life on the front. When George insists on returning to the war after his first injury, Campton sees a "mysterious look" in George's eyes: "It was Benny Upsher's look . . . inaccessible to reason, beyond reason, belonging to other spaces, other weights and measures, over the edge, somehow, of the tangible calculable world . . ." (359). Wharton uses quasi-religious language to describe John Campton's moment of intuiting the camaraderie of the front: "Once again Campton was vouchsafed a glimpse of that secret George" when his son encounters a fellow soldier. Again, the sense of the front as a place that cannot be fully comprehended by noncombatants emerges: "Campton saw the look the two exchanged: it lasted only for the taking of a breath; a moment later officer and soldier were laughing like boys. . . . But again the glance was an illumination; it came straight from that far country" (377), the country of nearly unlimited devotion to the war and one's fellow soldiers. The mystical is emphasized yet again in Campton's intermittent sense of his son as "that beautiful distant apparition, the wingèd sentry guarding the Unknown" (394). And both the tragedy of the many deaths and their semisacred nobility is reflected in Campton's sense of "this great headlong outpouring of life on the altar of conviction" (397). In this last and most disillusioned of Wharton's war fictions, she continued to believe in the potential nobility, even the possible transcendence, of experience on the front.

IV. *A Son at the Front* and the History of the War

R.W.B. Lewis has written that "The enduring effect of the war upon Edith Wharton . . . was to give her an entirely new consciousness of history" (*Edith Wharton* 423). Wharton's historical consciousness might not have been "entirely new"; her first novel, *The Valley of Decision*, was a thoroughly researched historical novel. But with *The House of Mirth* she had turned almost exclusively to contemporary settings, and the war caused her to begin looking back, to begin naming specific places and dates more precisely than in her previous writings. First with *The Marne*, and now in *Son*, she turned again to the historical novel as a central genre—a trend that would continue in several postwar works as well.

It may sound strange to call *The Marne* a historical novel, as it was written immediately after the events it narrates. But Wharton emphasizes history in the novel: Troy's fifteenth birthday is on June 28, 1914, "'the very day that odious Archduke was assassinated,'" as his mother puts it (41), and Troy follows the succeeding years with mounting excitement as he approaches the age at which he will be allowed to enlist. To no other character in her fiction does Wharton assign such a specific or significant date of birth.

Wharton employs a similar, but less obvious, technique in *Son*. In Wharton's notebook entries about *Son*, she mentions specific dates for a number of chapters, though many of these did not find their way into the finished novel; she seems to have preferred implying, rather than specifying, dates in most of the novel. For instance, though the novel does not specify the date, it mentions the sinking of the *Lusitania* on May 7, 1915 (254); "Preparedness" becomes Boylston's battle cry in book III, chapter 28 (313), implicitly establishing the time as early 1917. Similarly, Campton notes the coming of spring each year, with its inappropriate symbolism of rebirth and renewal. Yet Wharton does not specify the year each time spring returns; she may have been expecting readers to track this themselves or implying that most of the springs of the war years were strangely blurred together. As a whole the novel is deeply shaped by the war's chronology: it begins on July 30, 1914, the last real day of peace; it reaches its climax—George's death—on April 6, 1917, when the United States enters the war; it describes the parade of American soldiers down the Champs-Elysées on July 4, 1917; and its final scene takes place some five months after George's death (414), setting it in September 1917.

In addition to having obvious historical significance, these dates were personally important to Wharton as well as to her fictional Campton. July 30, 1914, was the day on which Campton anticipated a trip with his son George; on that date, Wharton was returning from a motoring trip, making her final stop at Chartres, where "the serenity of the scene smiled away the war rumours which had hung on us since morning" (*Fighting France* 4). Her visit to the cathedral constituted a "perfect hour," yet her description of the great stained glass windows seems shaped by a retrospective knowledge of the war, as some of the windows "glittered and menaced like the shields of fighting angels" (*Fighting France* 5). April 6, 1917, the day on which the United States declared war, was the day on which, as we have seen, Wharton felt that Americans could "hold up [their] heads" again (5 May 1917, *Wharton Collection* Yale); it is one of the few dates Wharton specifies in the novel, suggesting just how important the U.S. declaration of war was to her. George dies peacefully after his parents, stepfather, and friends all crowd around his hospital bed, telling him the good news of American involvement. His final words are to his father: "everything all right" (408). George has been the representative American soldier: now that others are coming in to fulfill his nation's obligations, George can die in peace. Finally, the parade of American soldiers on July 4, 1917, resonates with Wharton's experience. Campton watches the new recruits, thinking, "'How badly they march—there hasn't even been time to drill them properly!'" (412). Yet he is deeply moved: "he felt a choking in his throat" (412). A year later Wharton watched the Fourth of July parade from the Place de la Concorde—just as Campton does. She saw better-trained troops, but was, like Campton, moved, calling it "the greatest 'Fourth' in history . . . really a great show, only slightly unreal from its sheer beauty, & the extraordinary weight of associations, historic, symbolic, & all the rest, added to the aesthetic perfection of the setting" (*Letters* 406). The novel's emphasis on dates relevant to American involvement reminds us that Wharton, though happily residing in France, was still an American, and one very much focused on the need for U.S. involvement in the war.

As a "lest we forget" novel, *Son* not only emphasizes key dates and events but re-creates many aspects of the war and several of its phases, the noble and the ignoble, the transformative and the disillusioning. Despite accusations in contemporary reviews that the novel seemed "a belated essay in propaganda" (Tuttleton et al. 344), the novel displays hindsight—a reminder that *Son*, unlike *The Marne*, was written in retrospect. For instance, Wharton re-creates the mood of jubilation and the ignorance that prevailed early in the war. At the novel's outset, George breezily embraces an internationalism that allies him with others of his generation regardless of their national origin. This view was profoundly affected by Norman Angell's argument, stated in the influential *The Great Illusion*, that modern nations were too economically interconnected to make the mistake of going to war. George articulates this widely-held view to his father: "'*Our* whole view is different: we're internationals. . . I meant 'we' in the sense of my generation, of whatever nationality. I know French chaps who feel as I do—Louis Dastrey, Paul's nephew, for one; and lots of English ones. They don't believe the world will ever stand for another war. It's too stupidly uneconomic, to begin with: I suppose you've read Angell? Then life's worth too much, and nowadays too many millions of people know it'" (32).

Wharton re-creates other beliefs that were widespread early in the war. Louis Dastrey, later killed in the fighting, embraces war once it begins to seem inevitable. "'War's rot; but to get rid of war forever we've got to fight this one first,'" he says (76), echoing popular sentiment as well as the title of H.G. Wells's 1914 book, *The War That Will End War*. Louis Dastrey also believes, as so many others did, that the war would be brief: "'If only England is with us we're safe—it's a matter of weeks[,]'" he remarks (77), a view that Wharton, in 1922, knew was not only erroneous but also naive. George, initially incredulous at the prospect of war, reflects the galvanizing of public opinion that took place after Germany invaded Belgium: "For the first time the boy's feelings were visibly engaged; his voice shook as he burst out: 'Louis Dastrey's right: this kind of thing has got to stop. We shall go straight back to cannibalism if it doesn't.—God, what hounds!'" (91). Though Wharton's intent here may well have been historical—to re-create the powerful feelings of the early days of the war—such language likely contributed to some reviewers' sense of the novel as belated propaganda. Some passages in *Son* are strongly reminiscent of *The Marne*'s unlimited enthusiasm for war: "Yes; France was saved if England could put her army into the field at once. But could she? Oh, for the Channel tunnel at this hour! Would this lesson at last cure England of her obstinate insularity? Belgium had announced her intention of resisting; but what was that gallant declaration worth in face of Germany's brutal assault? A poor little country pledged to a guaranteed neutrality could hardly be expected to hold her frontiers more than forty-eight hours against the most power-ful army in Europe. And what a narrow strip Belgium was, viewed as an outpost of France!" (91). Wharton quickly locates this outburst in "Camp-ton's mind" (91), as she locates some of the more impassioned outbursts in *The Marne* in Troy Belknap's consciousness; it seems that Wharton is try-ing both to re-create the strong emotions of wartime and to suggest that such emotions were perhaps overwrought.

Wharton's description of the composition of *A Son at the Front* epito-mizes the tension between postwar objectivity and the re-creation of the strong emotions of wartime. She acknowledged that, in creating *Son*, she had to give herself time to "deal objectively with the stored-up emotions of those years," but also notes that after completing both *The Age of Inno-cence* and *Glimpses of the Moon*, "I settled down to 'A Son at the Front'; and although I had waited so long to begin it, the book was written in a white heat of emotion" (*Backward Glance* 369). A passage like the one quoted above—with its emphasis on "sav[ing]" France, "cur[ing]" En-gland," and on "little" Belgium's "gallant declaration"—employs the ro-mantic rhetoric of the early war years, recapturing the strong emotions of that time. But Wharton knew, and surely expected her readers to know, that those strong emotions were, while heroic, also the beginning of a se-ries of long and awful events. Further, she portrays the process by which the war became, however strangely, a normal part of life: "By virtue of some gift of adaptation which seemed forever to discredit human sensibil-ity, people were already beginning to live into the monstrous idea of it, acquire its ways, speak its language, regard it as a thinkable, endurable, arrangeable fact" (111).

In *Son*, Wharton also depicts the ways in which people were beginning to "speak its language," the language of war—in which it was becoming impossible to say certain words or express certain ideas. The simple word "gone" changes, for instance, coming to mean "mobilised" (64). In one scene, Campton discusses with his friend Paul Dastrey the possibility of his keeping George out of the fighting. The conversation soon centers on the meaning of the word "honourable," foreshadowing Hemingway's fa-mous dispensing with abstractions:

"I see[," Dastrey said. "]Your idea is that ... you've no right *not* to try to keep your boy out of it if you can?"

"Well—by any honourable means."

Dastrey laughed faintly, and Campton reddened. "The word's not happy, I admit."

"I wasn't thinking of that: I was considering how the meaning had evaporated out of lots of our old words, as if the general smash-up had broken their stoppers. So many of them, you see," said Dastrey smiling, "we'd taken good care not to uncork for centuries. Since I've been on the edge of what's going on fifty miles from here a good many of my own words have lost their meaning, and I'm not pre-pared to say where honour lies in a case like yours." (187–88)

James compared words in wartime to car tires that had gone flat; Whar-ton's image suggests words as fragile glass tubes, their meanings held in by stoppers and left closed up—unexamined—"for centuries." This passage suggests that it might, in fact, be good to reexamine language and its as-sumptions—but that suddenly having to do so in wartime was a jarring and inconclusive experience. Neither Dastrey nor Campton comes to any firm conclusion about "'where honour lies in a case'" like George's, nor to any firm definition of "honor" itself. But such abstractions, while not be-ing jettisoned, as they would be by Hemingway, were being profoundly questioned. Later in the novel Wharton mocks mindlessly idealistic rheto-ric through Harvey Mayhew's ready-made phrases: "'All that I have to give, yes, all that is most precious to me, I am ready to surrender, to offer up, to lay down in the Great Struggle which is to save the world from barbarism'" (203) But Mayhew's willingness to "'offer up'" is proven empty as he collapses in "large invertebrate distress" when he hears that his nephew may be dead (204). His romanticized rhetoric is proved mean-ingless; as he goes off to write a telegram, even the most basic of words seem to have abandoned him: "Campton heard him say timidly to the clerk: 'No doubt you speak French, sir? The words I want don't seem to come to me'" (207). War was indeed smashing the stoppers of language.

Similarly, Wharton re-creates the disillusionment that the home front population experienced. Some of this was the shock caused in the civilian population by the high number of deaths of French and English soldiers; it was also, as in England, caused by the gradually increasing comprehension that some of the deaths were caused by mismanagement from the top. Despite Wharton's continued efforts to promote U.S. involvement and support the French, she was aware of military mismanagement as early as March 1915. To Henry James she wrote that she had heard from their mutual friend, Robert Norton, "what a ghastly blunder [the battle at] Neuve Chapelle was. One rather understands why the French think that the English are heroes, but not professional 'militaires.' The Dardanelles attack looks a good deal like another muddle, & I heard it criticized as such here on the first day, when we all thought they were going to week-end at Byzantium!" (Powers 335).

During the war, Wharton had not published a word that questioned in any way the doings of the military. After the war, however, she felt free to reflect what she knew about the conditions of war. She articulates this awareness through Campton:

> Wherever he went he was pursued by visions of that land of doom: visions of fathomless mud, rat-haunted trenches, freezing nights under the sleety sky, men dying in the barbed wire between the lines or crawling out to save a comrade and being shattered to death on the return.... Some of [the soldiers'] histories were so heroically simple that the sense of pain was lost in beauty, as though one were looking at suffering transmuted into poetry. But others were abominable, unendurable, in their long-drawn useless horror: stories of cold and filth and hunger, of ineffectual effort, of hideous mutilation, of men perishing of thirst in a shell-hole, and half-dismembered bodies dragging themselves back to shelter only to die as they reached it. Worst of all were the perpetually recurring reports of military blunders, medical neglect, carelessness in high places[.] (192)

The idea of mismanagement, of "the lives that might have been saved" (192), is indeed "Worst of all" for Campton, as it was for Wharton. But such disillusionment did not become the sole lens through which either saw the war. As in this passage, the war also yielded stories that were "heroically simple" and thus beautiful; moreover, Campton—like Wharton—refused to be disillusioned to the point of giving in, nor does he see those around him collapsing under disillusionment: "the 'had to be' of the first day was still on every lip. The German menace must be met" (193). Indeed, the French persevered.

V. The "Permanent Value" of *A Son at the Front*

Of all Wharton's war-related writings, *A Son at the Front* is the one that most exemplifies the remark about war stories made by the opening narrator in "Coming Home": that "Some of [the] tales are dark and dreadful, some are unutterably sad, and some end in a huge laugh of irony. I am not sure how I ought to classify the one I have written down here" (230). *A Son at the Front* defies classification. Despite its devotion to the French, it is not the pro-French, semipropagandistic material Wharton offered the American public, however sincerely, in *The Marne* and *French Ways and Their Meaning;* despite its important vein of satire, it is not primarily satirical, like "The Refugees" and "Writing a War Story"; despite its admiration for and grief over soldiers like Louis Dastrey and George Campton, it is not primarily elegiac, like Wharton's poems "Beaumetz," "You and You," and "'On Active Service'"; despite its acknowledgment of military mismanagement and the horrible conditions of war, it is not solely ironic or despairing, like most of the works included in the canon of Great War writing. With its lack of frontline action, it is hard to categorize as a "war novel," but it would seem foolhardy to ignore the novel's setting and argue that it is not really a war novel at all. The very difficulty in knowing how to classify the novel has made it difficult for critics to respond to it.

Wharton's remarks about the novel as well as some of her remarks about the war suggest that the novel's complexity, its resistance to categorization, very much reflect her own complex views about the war. For Wharton, an understanding of the high costs of the war did not exclude a sense that the war was worth fighting. She had found the war "thrillingly interesting" at its outset; by March 1915 she was already aware of military mismanagement on a large scale, and by October 1915 she was reduced to a cry of "Oh, this long horror!" Yet in October 1917 she still saw the war, especially the U.S. entry into the war, as exciting, writing to a friend that "You must be having thrilling times, with both of the boys in the war already" (15 Oct. 1917, *Wharton Collection* Yale). A full year later, she wrote a letter to her friend and fellow novelist Robert Grant that demonstrates how she could both find the war "glorious" and recall it as "darkness and chaos":

> I am glad your son Bob still sticks to his job. It is useless for every one to rush to the front—but I understand how he must want to! Our entry into the war was so glorious that of course every young man from Maine to San Francisco wants to be there. . . .
>
> [Earlier in the war] the news grew blacker every day, our quarter was shelled three or four days a week, & we were raided every night that there was a moon!
>
> All this—& especially the anxiety about the future—made sleep difficult, & convalescence slow; but now that events have turned almost 'full circle' there is no use in dwelling on that period of darkness & chaos. (2 Oct. 1918, *Wharton Collection* Yale)

Wharton's attitude is pragmatic: the "darkness and chaos" are over, so why "dwell" on them? Such a sentiment recalls Yvonne Malo's question in "Coming Home": "Why brood on other horrors—horrors we were powerless to help?" (251). Yet in writing her memoir nearly twenty years later, Wharton did not oversimplify the war years; she did not recall only the "glorious" parts of the war while ignoring its horrors. As she looked back to planning *A Son at the Front*, her vision remained complex: "I saw the years of the war, as I had lived them in Paris, with a new intensity of vision, in all their fantastic heights and depths of self-devotion and ardour, of pessimism, triviality and selfishness" (*Backward Glance* 368). If anything, the balance in this passage is negative: there is "ardour" and there are "heights," but these are accompanied by "self-devotion . . . pessimism, triviality and selfishness."

The "ardour" in *Son* is indeed a tempered one. Boylston and George are admirable; as we have seen, other characters also have moments of ennobling transformation. Acknowledging military mismanagement, Campton—and Wharton—still see the war as something that "had to be." And a tempered idealism remains. In *The Marne*, as we have seen, Wharton quotes Horace's famous "dulce et decorum est pro patria mori." She quotes it unironically in *Son* as well, but in an abbreviated and somewhat tentative way. Boylston quotes it to explain George's return to his regiment to Campton: "'It's the thought of their men that pulls them all back. . . . There's something in all their eyes: I don't know what. *Dulce et decorum*, perhaps—'"; to this explanation Campton simply agrees, "'Yes'" (391). The men agree on this point, yet neither elaborates on the sentiment, nor completes the phrase; no one quotes Shakespeare, as Troy's tutor had in *The Marne*. Similarly, the concept of a glorious death is downplayed in *Son*. Troy's near-death in *The Marne* was probably based on the heroic death of Jean du Breuil, so admired by Wharton and James; in *Son* readers learn indirectly that George received his first wound "in circumstances which appeared to have given George great glory in the eyes of his men" (302). But what these circumstances are we never learn. George's eventual death occurs not gloriously in the field (or even ingloriously in a trench), but quietly in a hospital bed. Dying for one's country is still acknowledged in the novel as a noble sacrifice, but it has been stripped of its fanfare.

Wharton's deep ambivalence about the war and her tempered idealism are both embodied in her central character, John Campton. If most readers feel, as Cynthia Griffin Wolff does, that *A Son at the Front* "should have been better" (336), it is probably Campton himself who triggers that response. Although a keen, articulate, and frequently thoughtful observer, he is also irascible, misogynistic, hypocritical, and, at times, cruel. At some points in the novel, readers may question whether Wharton has entire artistic control over Campton, or whether he affects readers significantly differently than she had intended. She left little commentary on Campton's character or his behavior; what little there is focuses on his role as father. Wharton had written Rutger Jewett at Appleton that her novel was "never intended to be a 'war novel.'. . . The original title 'A Son at the Front' is purely ironic and represents the state of mind of three Americans, father, mother, and the mother's second husband, all of whom are trying to keep the son in question away from the front" (24 July 1920, *Wharton Collection* Yale). While this argument may have been somewhat disingenuous— Wharton knew that war novels were hard to place and was trying to convince Jewett that *Son* wasn't a war novel—there is also much truth to it. As she wrote to Daisy Chanler, "the thing that interested me was the love of the ill-assorted quartette for their boy, & the gradual understanding between the two men" (*Letters* 471). Thinking of *Son* as a novel about parents and children—particularly fathers and sons—helps to bring the irascible Campton into better focus.

A Son at the Front is in some ways a pivotal novel in Wharton's career. It bridges the war and the postwar years in her work; one central support in this bridge is its focus on parent-child relationships, which, particularly in postwar works like *The Mother's Recompense* and *The Children*, are frequently troubled. In *Son*, Campton abandoned his wife for the sight of a Spanish beauty; his wife gives birth to George and quickly acquires a second husband, the wealthy banker Anderson Brant. Although Brant has been a central presence in George's life—George has grown up in the home of his mother and his stepfather—Campton has a hard time grasping the idea that Brant has played a significant role in his son's life, becoming in effect a second father to him. Adele Anthony (who shadows Julia as George's second mother) points out to Campton that Brant's role in George's life has benefited him as well: "'Well, poor Anderson really *was* a dry-nurse to the boy. Who else was there to look after him? You were painting Spanish beauties at the time. . . . I see perfectly that if you'd let everything else go to keep George you'd never have become the great John Campton: the *real* John Campton you were meant to be. And it wouldn't have been half as satisfactory for you—or for George either. Only, in the meanwhile, somebody had to blow the child's nose, and pay his dentist and doctor; and you ought to be grateful to Anderson for doing it'" (117).

Although Adele's argument never makes much impression on Campton, it is cogent. To the reader it is obvious that his artistic success could not have been achieved if he had not been able to fall back on Brant to support his son; yet he resents the very fact that Brant has been the one to "pay [George's] dentist and doctor." Indeed, money becomes the actual as well as symbolic form of combat between the two fathers. John Campton repeatedly refuses or resents Brant's offers to do anything involving money, even though he has moments of appreciating that Brant's wealth does open some doors—including finding George a safe staff job. But Campton gloats when Brant's money cannot accomplish some things. When George is running a high fever after his first injury, Campton rudely tells Brant what Brant must already know: "'there are times when your money and your influence and your knowing everybody are no more use than so much sawdust——'" (289). Money remains the focus of contest between the two men through the novel's final pages.

Part and parcel of Campton's competition with Brant is Campton's possessiveness toward his son. At the novel's opening, Campton's possessiveness of George is not apparent: he is simply a middle-aged father looking forward to a trip abroad with his son. But as the novel continues, his possessiveness becomes alarmingly apparent, dictating his behavior not only toward George, but toward Julia, Brant, and others. When Campton and Brant travel to visit the wounded George in a hospital near the front, Campton thinks impatiently, "'I shan't even have my boy to myself on his death-bed'" (273). Events prove him wrong, but this is, indeed, a strong, selfish, even bizarre form of possessiveness. Campton's obsession with owning George blinds him to Brant's genuine love for the boy, and he thinks pityingly of Brant, "How ghastly to sit all day in that squalid hotel . . . with nothing to do but to wonder and wonder about the temperature of another man's son!" (283). On one occasion his possessiveness may blind him even to his son's physical welfare. When George receives the wound that will eventually kill him, Campton argues against bringing him to a Paris hospital "partly perhaps because he felt that in the quiet provincial hospital near the front he would be able to have his son to himself"— despite the fact that a Paris location would mean "more possibilities of surgical aid" (401).

Campton's attempt to regain, or perhaps simply to gain, possession of his son is one of the central themes of the novel and, as in other Wharton novels—*The House of Mirth* and *The Custom of the Country* most conspicuously—possession is (mistakenly) allied with money.[7] Gus Trenor believes that, because he has given Lily Bart money, he is entitled to her body; Undine Spragg sells her beauty to the highest bidder. Here George is the object to be owned, or so his father perceives him. The effaced Anderson Brant, who has spent uncountable hours with George since the boy's infancy, repeatedly demonstrates his genuine love for his stepson. Though readers are never privy to Brant's consciousness, every indication is that he loves George as a son—not because he has paid George's way or because George has grown up under his roof, but simply because, having filled so many of a father's roles, that love is his natural (or even generous) response. Campton has visited his son periodically, but seems to have played only a small role in the boy's development, as he has paid little toward George's support and education. Now that he is, at last, becoming affluent—his portraits have suddenly mushroomed in popularity, and he can ask any price he wants—he plans to take back his son.

The financial nature of the competition between Brant and Campton (or, more accurately, of Campton's competition with the noncompetitive Brant) evinces itself repeatedly in Campton's refusal to let Brant purchase some of his portraits of "their" son. Campton has not only turned down Brant's offers, but has done so vindictively. In the first case he donated the portrait in question to the Luxembourg Museum, not from public-spirited motives, but "with the object of inflicting the most cruel slight he could think of on the banker" (58); his donation of the painting assures him that Brant will never possess it, for John worries that if he kept the picture himself, and "if his will were mislaid[,]" the picture "might fall into Brant's hands after his death" (59). Campton later worries that a sketch of George he is donating to benefit "Friends of French Art" might end up as Brant's possession (158, 162). After George's death Brant and Julia wish Campton to make a monument for George's grave. Campton initially refuses, speaking of George as if he had produced the boy parthenogenetically (Julia is not even mentioned): "'I don't want my son to have a monument . . . He's my son—my son. He isn't Brant's'" (414). He finally agrees to create the monument, but only after Boylston has strategically flattered him, telling him that "'You've had him; you have him still. . . . But they've never had anything, those two others, Mr. Brant and Miss Anthony'" (415). Campton mentally extends Boylston's argument even to Julia: "They had never—no, not even George's mother—had anything, in the close inextricable sense in which Campton had had his son" (421). Paradoxically, it is only once he has convinced himself of his sole possession of his now-dead son that Campton agrees to accept Brant's money to pay for the monument—the symbolic equivalent of accepting that Brant has played at least a minor role in his son's life. And even Campton's acceptance is made utterly gracelessly, as he tells Boylston, "'it's going to cost a lot—everything of the sort does nowadays, especially in marble. . . . And prices have about tripled, you know'" (424-25). He then adds, "'That's just what Brant'll like though, isn't it?' . . . with an irrepressible sneer in his voice" (425). Boylston reddens at Campton's "irrepressible sneer," and Campton himself feels a shred of regret as he remembers Brant's devotion to George. Yet his final comment on the matter is only slightly more neutral in tone: "'tell Brant—that I'll design the thing; I'll design it, and he shall pay for it. He'll want to—I understand that. Only, for God's sake, don't let him come here and thank me—at least not for a long time!'" (425).

Campton has undergone a series of war-engendered transformations in the novel: from thinking the war was not "his business" as an American to believing in America's necessary involvement in the war; from being an idle expatriate to playing an active role in a war charity. He has gone from skepticism to grasping the war's necessity, even at the tremendous cost the war was exacting; from hoping his son would be exempted from military service to wanting him to play an active role on the front; from bitter competition for name of "father" to some comprehension that another man has a legitimate claim to some part of that title. In the end, regardless of his vindictiveness, Campton's acceptance of Brant's money symbolizes his grudging acceptance of Brant's role in his—their—son's life. But this is far from a pure transformation; it is also distant from the ending Wharton had originally planned for this novel.

In Wharton's draft of *Son*, Campton finally comes to terms with Julia and Brant, asking himself "'Why should I be so savage to them, when [crossed out] now that we're all in the same boat?'" (holograph ms., *Wharton Collection* Yale). But Wharton has struck out the entire passage in the draft, and no similar statement appears in the final version of the novel. In notes for the novel, Wharton also envisioned a final reconciliation: "The sketch Campton has made of George lying asleep on his bed at the Crillon on the night of July 31 is advanced enough for him to use it for his statue of a recumbent figure for his boy's grave. Brant pays the expenses— *Campton somehow wants him to.*" From this last sentence a line leads to the upper right hand corner of the page, where Wharton has written in ink, "He sees it is Brant's only means of expression." Scribbled in pencil after this and underlined: *"This is good."* Wharton's plan continues, "The book ends with the setting up of the statue on the grave. They are all there—Mr. and Mrs. Brant, Adele Anthony, Campton, 'Madge.' Benny Upsher [crossed out]—Boylston. Queer group." (Notebook 1918–23, *Wharton Collection* Yale). "Queer group" indeed, but one that suggests reconciliation, not continued bitterness. Furthermore, such a tableau would suggest that Campton, like his son, has been changed and ennobled by the war. It would also be a fitting elegy for the fictional George, as well as for the actual Newbold Rhinelander and Ronald Simmons.

It is impossible to know why Wharton altered the ending for the final version of the novel. Perhaps the original plan came to seem too pat, too contrived—too much of a "happy ending" for a sad and bitter story, the reflection of a sad and bitter war. Perhaps she wanted to leave readers with an image of Campton—art his central passion—alone in his studio, starting what will be, despite his acrimoniousness toward Brant, a fitting tribute to the son he still sees as primarily his own—or, rather, a tribute to the memory of that son.

The ending of the novel is not what one would have expected of the author of *The Marne*, which ends in a burst of glory as Troy vows to "devote the rest of [his] life to trying to find" the symbolic ghost of Paul Gantier "on the battle-fields of France"(128). But, though somber in tone, the conclusion of *A Son at the Front* is consistent with the attitude toward death Wharton described in her wartime elegies. By its very existence, an elegy suggests the crucial role of memory, which Wharton had emphasized in "'On Active Service'":

Long and long shall we remember,
In our breasts his grave be made.
It shall never be December
Where so warm a heart is laid,
But in our saddest selves a sweet voice sing,
Recalling him, and Spring.

So, too, Campton begins to find moments in which he feels close to his dead son:

George had been; George was; as long as his father's consciousness lasted, George would be as much a part of it as the closest, most actual of his immediate sensations. He had missed nothing of George, and here was his harvest, his golden harvest.

Such states of mind were not constant with Campton; but more and more often, when they came, they swept him on eagle wings over the next desert to the next oasis; and so, gradually, the meaningless days became linked to each other in some kind of intelligible sequence. (423–24)

Campton was a solitary figure at the novel's beginning; he remains one at its end. At the beginning he anticipated his son's arrival and a long-awaited trip with him; at the end he is also in the presence of the absent George, as he "pull[s] out all the sketches of his son from the old portfolio" and begins his work on a clay model for the monument to George (426). As Wharton suggested in her notes for the novel, the final monument will be based on the sketch of the sleeping George he made on the night before mobilization, the sketch that, even to his horrified parent's mind, suggested his son's death: "the effigy of a young knight." Such a monument suggests— as does the name "Troy" in *The Marne*—that, despite Wharton's understanding of the war's cost, some notion of nobility remains. George Campton sculpted in a pose reminiscent of a young knight will remind the visitors to his monument—family, friends, and strangers alike—of noble ideals, of a beautiful young man sacrificed, of the romantic past of warfare.

This final moment is reminiscent of the end of *The House of Mirth*, in which Lawrence Selden gazes on Lily Bart's body and, readers are told, "there passed between them the word which made all clear" (329). For some readers this ending is consoling: however belatedly, Selden and Lily finally come to some kind of understanding. For most readers recently, the ending only confirms Selden's fundamental fraudulence: alive and well, he fails to see the ways in which he has disappointed the dead Lily, and, moreover, consoles himself with the sentimental illusion that they have achieved a kind of understanding. As more readers study *A Son at the Front*, a similar debate is likely to emerge. For some readers, Campton will have come to a final acceptance of Brant's role in George's life and will be finding what consolation he can in creating a monument to his—their— much-loved son; he will be continuing George's life in his consciousness. For others, the ending will only reinforce their reading of Campton as self-deceiving, an artist who "rob[s] from everyday actuality to feed his art" (Wolff 339), a narcissist who is so used to his son's absence that he takes the same kind of pleasure from contemplating his drawings of his dead son as, at the novel's outset, he did in contemplating a forthcoming voyage with George.

In any case, there can be no doubt that *Son* is, and will remain, a vexing novel. Its flaws may be, in part, aesthetic; Wharton's scope may be simply too broad for one novel to carry. According to Blake Nevius, *The Marne* "abused the medium of the long tale by compelling it to absorb [too] many issues" (163); similarly, Cynthia Griffin Wolff chalks up the weaknesses of Wharton's 1906 novel *The Fruit of the Tree* to its lack of focus: "What is the 'problem' of the novel? Euthanasia, the need for industrial reform, the old problem of idealized expectations coming up against the harsh realities of real-world existence, marriage, the role of women" (Wolff 135). In the same way, *A Son at the Front* may tackle too many questions, ponder too many issues: the pointless and counterproductive lives of "fluffy fuzzy" American expatriates; the bitter political bickering of these people even when they are engaged in charitable activities; the plight, and the beauty, of Paris in wartime; the horrors of war and its ability to transfigure; the dangers of parents trying too hard to direct their adult children's lives; the dangers of possessiveness, even the potential vampirism of artists; the need to create, amidst the horrors of war, a kind of memorial for the dead who, as Wharton still firmly believed, had fought to save civilization. *A Son at the Front* was Wharton's last and largest effort to recapture the complex war years and refine the issues she had had to write about all too quickly during those years. It was perhaps inevitable that the novel would wobble under its own weight.

Paradoxically, however, it may be the novel's lack of unity, its refusal to adhere to a monomythic view of the war, that gives it its greatest biographical interest and its greatest historical authenticity—its "permanent value among the minor documents of the war" (Tuttleton et al. 334). *A Son at the Front* insists on the profound complexity of the Great War, implicitly suggesting that the war could not be reduced to a unified artistic vision. This is the exact problem John Campton experiences in the novel as he "saw everything, saw it too clearly, in all its superfluous and negligible reality, instead of instinctively selecting, and disregarding what was not to his purpose" (95); the novel's limitations suggest that Wharton's artistic vision too was blurred by the war years. The canonized writings of World War I insist on the irony of the war; some feminist interpreters of women's World War I literature insist on the war as a liberating experience for women. *A Son at the Front* adheres to neither of these models, nor does it create its own monomythic view. It accepts the horrible cost of World War I while preserving a belief in the war's transformative power. It describes women and men, including noncombatant men, whose lives are ennobled by the war; even moments of despair end quietly in a reassertion of the absolute necessity of the war:

> When Campton met Paul Dastrey for the first time after the death of the latter's nephew, the two men exchanged a long hand-clasp and then sat silent. As Campton had felt from the first, there was nothing left for them to say to each other. If young men like Louis Dastrey must continue to be sacrificed by hundreds of thousands to save their country, for whom was the country being saved? Was it for the wasp-waisted youths in sham uniforms . . . ? Or for the elderly men like Dastrey and Campton, who could only sit facing each other with the spectre of the lost between them? . . . And not even a child left by most of them, to carry on the faith they had died for . . .
>
> "If we're giving all we care for so that those little worms can reopen their dance-halls on the ruins, what in God's name *is* left?" Campton questioned.
>
> Dastrey sat looking at the ground, his grey head bent between his hands. "France," he said.
>
> "What's France, with no men left?"
>
> "Well—I suppose, an Idea."
>
> "Yes, I suppose so." Campton stood up heavily.
>
> An Idea: they must cling to that. (365–66)

Campton is not perfectly satisfied by this conversation; he wishes it would "help [him] more" (366). But he acknowledges its validity, thinking of France as "a luminous point about which striving visions and purposes could rally" and as a "second country" to "thinkers, artists, to all creators" (366). The very language of this passage emphasizes that, however great the loss, it is a noble one: soldiers are not "going to the slaughter," as Wharton wrote early in the war, but are described in quasi-religious terms as being "sacrificed" to "save" their country. Ideas, and ideals, may have lost the romantic glory they had possessed when Wharton watched a "magnificent river of war" in the early months of the conflict, but they nevertheless retained a significant place in Wharton's final statement on the war.

VI. Monuments

Writing to her cousin Tom Rhinelander in January 1919, only a few short months after Newbold's death, Wharton remarked that she was sending him a copy of a volume of war-related poetry by the English author Laurence Binyon. In particular she recommended one "on the young in England which is most beautiful, & which expresses exactly the spirit in which Newbold lived & died" (18 Jan. 1919, *Wharton Collection* Yale). This is probably "The English Youth," which voices many of Wharton's own views on the war: its cost, but also its necessity, which in turn confers nobility on those who died. It runs in part:

> There was wrong
> Done, and the world shamed. Honour blew the call;
> And each one's answer was as natural
> And quiet as the needle's to the pole.
> Who gave must give himself entire and whole . . .
> So, books were shut; and young dreams shaken out
> In cold air; dear ambitions done without,
> And a stark duty shouldered. . . .
> . . . It was the world's debt,
> Claiming all: but they knew, and would not wince
> From that exaction on their flesh; and since
> They did not seek for glory, our hearts add
> A more than glory to that hope they had
> And gloriously and terribly achieved.

Earlier in the war, Binyon had been more insistent on romantic imagery of war, on the simple, noble sacrifice of lives. His 1917 poem "For the Fallen" idealizes war: "Solemn the drums thrill: Death august and royal / Sings sorrow up into immortal spheres"; "They went with songs to the battle, they were young, / Straight of limb, true of eye, steady and aglow. / They were staunch to the end against odds uncounted[.]" "The English Youth," published in 1918, still expresses a belief that the war was not in vain, but it represents a sobered view. The emphasis is not on "Death august and royal" but on a vague hope "gloriously *and terribly* achieved" (emphasis added). The romance of history is not forgotten, but "There is a dimness fallen on old fames"; the "histories of old time" are only "half-believed." The poem's conclusion reasserts that there is "Romance . . . About the heads of heroes dead and bright." But this romance is tempered by the realities of more than four years of high casualties:

> We are accompanied with light
> Because of youth among us; and the name
> Of man is touched with an ethereal flame;

There is a newness in the world begun,
A difference in the setting of the sun.
Oh, though we stumble in blinding tears, and though
The beating of our hearts may never know
Absence in pangs more desolately keen,
Yet blessed are our eyes because they have seen.

Wharton's recommendation of this poem is of a piece with *A Son at the Front*. Dastrey, his eyes downcast, asserts the importance of the survival of "France," even if it is only as an idea—an echoing of Wharton's sentiments articulated throughout the war. Further, Binyon's poem, like *Son*, describes the war as unavoidable. It depicts soldiers as quietly stalwart, but also surrounded in a kind of glory: Binyon's description of soldiers with "Romance" halo-like "About the heads of heroes" is reminiscent of John Campton's "glimpses" into the semisacred realm of soldiery and of Boylston's belief that it is sweet and fitting to die for one's country. Moving toward its conclusion, the poem documents the "blinding tears" and the "pangs"—with the war over, the horrible levels of grief could at last be acknowledged. But it closes on the note of transformation and elegy: "Yet blessed are our eyes because they have seen." It is hard to imagine a poem about the war that Wharton would have recommended more strongly.

When Campton is asked to create a monument to George, his first reaction is one of consternation: "A monument—they wanted a monument! Wanted him to decide about it, plan it, perhaps design it—good Lord, he didn't know!" (415) He also begins to acknowledge to himself that such a monument would force him to recognize fully that George is dead: "the making of it had struck him as . . . building up a marble wall between" himself and George (416). As Campton learns, the war demanded monuments: or, more precisely, those who had survived the war demanded monuments to those who had not survived it.

Samuel Hynes's definition of official war monuments and monumental histories—those that "affirmed . . . it was a good war, a just war, a *great* war," those stories that "have their dark moments and their tragic losses, but . . . swell with emotion and pride at the end, and the Big Words sound out again" (278)—suggests that *Son* is not quite an official monument: the "Big Words" are called into question, and "tragic losses" loom over the novel's end. But neither does it fit into the category of "anti-monuments," works that "rendered the war without the value-bearing abstractions"; it is not among the "conscious, aggressive rejections of the monument-making principles" (Hynes 283). And yet, like many antimonuments, it "turn[s] away from celebration, in search of war's reality" (283).

Wharton took on a huge task in creating *A Son at the Front*. It is her written monument to the war, but what a complex monument it is: one that simultaneously honors the deaths of the soldiers and acknowledges the grim conditions under which they fought; one that respectfully keeps its distance from soldiers' work—the "real business" of war—while portraying both the valid and the futile efforts made on the home front. It is a work that is both satirical and elegiac: satirical of social life on the expatriate home front, but elegiac for soldiers like George Campton. The novel's closing scene attempts to capture the satire and the elegy in a final tableau, as the flawed Campton begins to sculpt what will be a fitting memorial to George and those like him. Campton's monument, like Wharton's, is not to the Harvey Mayhews and Mme. de Dolmetsches of the war, nor is it to the "Old Men" like himself who both benefited from the protection the young soldiers afforded them and felt guilty about their own survival. It is, rather, a monument to the young men who died, gloriously or not, in the war.

6

Writing in the Wake of the War

After "A Son at the Front" I intended to take a long holiday—perhaps to cease from writing altogether. It was growing more and more evident that the world I had grown up in and been formed by had been destroyed in 1914, and I felt myself incapable of transmuting the raw material of the after-war world into a work of art. Gardening, reading and travel seemed the only solace left . . .
Wharton, *A Backward Glance* (369–70)

Civilization was what the war had been fought for . . . Now, with the war over, many writers took up that claim, to question it. . . . What was civilization? Had it been destroyed by the war, as some said? . . .
Hynes, *A War Imagined* (311)

I.

The Great War changed the world in which Wharton lived and worked. Yet this was not wholly apparent even to her at first; in *A Backward Glance* she wrote, "The war was over, and we thought we were returning to the world we had so abruptly passed out of four years earlier. Perhaps it was as well that, at first, we were sustained by that illusion" (362). The illusion, however, did not last long: "The blissful thought: 'now there will be no more killing!'—soon gave way to a growing sense of the waste and loss wrought by those irreparable years" (363–64). Wharton's sense of loss was deepened by her perception that "the world I had grown up in and been formed by had been destroyed in 1914" (369–70). Indeed, to Wharton, all was "changed, changed utterly."

The effects of the war did not end with the Armistice. In large and small ways, political and personal ways, the war remained with Wharton for months, even years, after its ostensible conclusion. Some of the problems, like the ongoing plight of the refugees, were large-scale, public problems that, paradoxically, ran the risk of being invisible to the American donors who had helped fund Wharton's charities during the war. As Wharton wrote to Minnie Jones, "The real difficulty will be to make people realize that the situation of the refugees is worse than ever, as the Germans have stripped literally *everything* from the towns that are still standing & destroyed all possibility of reviving industrial life by wrecking the machinery in all the factories. People have literally died of hunger in some places, & the government will not allow any one to return to the liberated districts for months to come, because it is impossible to feed, clothe & employ them there" (29 Nov. 1918, *Wharton Collection* Yale). Nor were other war-related charities a thing of the past. An April 1919 letter describes the problem at one of Wharton's tuberculosis facilities: "the long waiting-list at the Dispensary of women & children waiting to be received at Groslay is really heart-breaking" (23 April 1919, *Wharton Collection* Yale). As others have written, Wharton's war-related charity work lasted long after the war's end.[1]

In many other ways as well the war continued to haunt Wharton. The deaths of those close to her remained very much in her mind; in April 1919 she wrote to her cousin Tom Rhinelander, Newbold's father:

I am so thankful that Newbold went so straight & swiftly out of life, & found such pity & kindness among those who live about his quiet resting-place.

I went to see poor Ronald Simmons' pathetic grave, crowded into a narrow corner of a huge cemetery at Marseilles, & was so glad that Newbold is in a country grave-yard where there are birds and flowers. (23 April 1919, *Wharton Collection* Yale)

Wharton had written that the dead were at rest, but even the expression "his quiet resting-place" suggests a certain residual consciousness; for Wharton, it is better to be buried "where there are birds and flowers" than "crowded into a huge cemetery[.]" In her poem "Battle Sleep" she had contrasted the "flame-seared lids" of soldiers with "the cooling vision" of the ocean; similarly, a soothing sense of the pastoral pervades her description of Newbold's grave.

As 1919 led into 1920, Wharton noted distinct and generally negative changes in the postwar world. Some of these were practical, even domestic, in nature. In a letter to her niece Beatrix Farrand in June, 1920, she noted that "The old type of quiet lady's maid ... has vanished from the post-war world, & one had best cling on to the survivors with hooks of steel" (30 June 1920, *Wharton Collection* Yale). On a larger scale, Wharton felt that the war had ruined Paris for her. Though she had thrilled at the sight of U.S. soldiers in the city, the influx of other Americans after the war—and the increased motor traffic—were overwhelming: "Paris is simply awful—a kind of continuous earthquake of motor busses, trams, lorries, taxis & other howling & swooping & colliding engines, with hundreds of thousands of U.S. citizens rushing about in them & tumbling out of them at one's door" (*Letters* 432).

In other ways as well the war continued to affect Wharton's life. She was aware that the war had exhausted her. To her friend Mildred Bliss she described herself in April 1920—a year and a half after the war's end—as being "in a state of abrutissement [stupefaction], almost of anéantissement [prostration], that seems to have become chronic with me since the Armistice!" (10 April 1920, *Wharton Collection* Yale). As late as July 1923, following her trip to the United States to receive her honorary doctorate from Yale, Wharton wrote, "Then I motored a lot, saw a good many people, . . . & altogether shook off (I hope) the physical apathy which had been creeping over me since the war" (*Letters* 468). She also continued to be aware of the injustices in the ways war workers were—or were not—rewarded. Frustrated when her own candidates for the Medaille de la Reconnaissance Française were overlooked, she observed, "Meanwhile I see the medal showered on ladies who have poured tea at Paris hospitals, or begun their war-work in 1918—but every appeal is vain to obtain recognition of the faithful workers who have toiled with me in Paris & America since Sept. 1914" (4 May 1920, *Wharton Collection* Yale). The war had exhausted Wharton physically, emotionally, and psychologically—and the Ivy Spangs and Mrs. Brants still irked her.

All in all, however, Wharton was gradually able to turn back to writing, the "inexorable calling" that had claimed her years before the war (*Backward Glance* 356). But resuming her normal course of writing was more complicated than she had anticipated. "[W]hen I am in full (literary) blast, especially after 4 years' abstinence, there are queer lapses in my mind," she wrote to Tom Rhinelander (23 April 1919, *Wharton Collection* Yale). Further, the literary ground had shifted under her feet. To some extent she must have foreseen this; she had almost immediately grasped that the war would provide writers with "extraordinary and dramatic situations" (*Letters* 357). She had also been concerned about literary quality, joking with Henry James in March 1915 that their letters were nearly the only "good literature . . . that the war has produced" (Powers 335). As early as April 1916, her awareness of the war as material and her concern about literary quality merged in a letter to Robert Grant: "One wonders what the novelists will do, in the next years, with all the superabundance of incredible romance that is coming out of this world-upheaval? After the first cheap harvest, some great slow fruit will no doubt ripen" (17 April 1916, *Wharton Collection* Yale).

But the "ripen[ing]" of the "great slow fruit" proved difficult, at least in her own case. Her frustration is audible in her September 1919 letter to Charles Scribner:

> In the first relief from war anxieties I thought it might be possible to shake off the question which is tormenting all novelists at present: "Did the adventures related in this book happen before the war or did they happen since?" with the resulting difficulty that, if they happened before the war, I seem to have forgotten how people felt and what their point of view was. I should feel ashamed of these hesitations if I did not find that all novelists I know are in much the same predicament. Perhaps it will not last much longer & we shall be able to get back some sort of perspective; but at present, between the objection of the public to so called war-stories and the difficulty of the author to send his imagination backward, the situation is a bewildering one. (*Letters* 425)

There is irritation with the reading public here, but there is a personal and professional lament as well: the sense that her own memory and imagination have, in the wake of the war, failed her. Wharton was suffering—at least temporarily—from the debilitating sense that her occupation was gone. Beerbohm had lamented in 1915 that "The Comic Muse . . . sits nowadays with ashes on her head, wailing, and having nothing to say to me" (11 Aug. 1915, *Wharton Collection* Yale). Wharton, perhaps simply too busy during the war years to notice such a sense of deprivation, felt it in the war's wake. Even while mourning, however, Wharton was writing. *In Morocco* and *The Age of Innocence* appeared in 1920, *The Glimpses of the Moon* in 1922, *A Son at the Front* in 1923, *Old New York* in 1924, *The Mother's Recompense* and *The Writing of Fiction* in 1925; and from 1926 until the end of her life in 1937 she published steadily, producing at least one book—whether novel, short story collection, poem collection, or memoir—almost every year.[2]

The war's effect on her postwar writing, while elusive in some ways, is clear in others. Some have argued that Wharton experimented with literary modernism in the prewar period, but it is clear that she rejected it in the years following the war. Though she admired a few modernists—Joseph Conrad and Marcel Proust, for instance—what she valued in their work was their creation of vivid and memorable characters; in both her 1925 book *The Writing of Fiction* and her 1934 essay "Permanent Values in Fiction" she argues that such characters are one of the hallmarks (indeed, perhaps the most important hallmark) of accomplished fiction. Similarly, Wharton praised Proust not for his innovations, but for his continuation of the French tradition in the novel, remarking in an essay entitled "A Reconsideration of Proust" that "it is truer to say of him . . . that he ends the long and magnificent line of nineteenth century novelists, than that he opens a new era" (*Uncollected Critical Writings* 182); in *The Writing of Fiction* she argued similarly that he was not an "innovator" but a "renovator" of the novel (109).

The war had shaken up genre for Wharton, but in the postwar period her literary preferences, like her politics, became more conservative. *The Writing of Fiction*, published six years after T. S. Eliot's important essay "Tradition and the Individual Talent" and four before Virginia Woolf's landmark work *A Room of One's Own*, is occasionally antimodernistic on its surface. Wharton seems particularly disturbed by the sexual frankness of some modernist work, protesting the "'now-that-it-can-be-told school' (as someone has named it)" and what she saw as "dirt-for-dirt's sake, from which no real work of art has ever sprung"; she was concerned that "laborious monuments of schoolboy pornography"—a reference to James Joyce's *Ulysses* (see *Letters*, 461–62)—"are now mistaken for works of genius" (50). In general, however, Wharton's point of view in *The Writing of Fiction* is so far from that of the modernists that she did not need to decry modernism. She pays great attention to matters of the author's selection of a subject and to technique (hearkening back to Ivy Spang's misinformed disregard of such matters in "Writing a War Story"); she also devotes several pages distinguishing between novels of character and novels of situation. Genre classifications, which had been muddied during the war, had in Wharton's mind reemerged and risen to prominence once again. The matters that interest Wharton in this book are not at all those that interested the modernists.

Wharton asserts in *The Writing of Fiction* that contemporary novelists' "distrust of technique and the fear of being unoriginal . . . are in truth leading to pure anarchy in fiction" (15), fears to which she would turn in more clearly antimodernistic tones in her 1934 essays "Tendencies in Modern Fiction" and "Permanent Values in Fiction." In the first of these essays she explicitly linked the effect of the war with shifts in fiction-writing: "The moral and intellectual destruction caused by the war, and by its far-reaching consequences, was shattering to traditional culture; and so far as the new novelists may be said to have any theory of their art, it seems to be that every new creation can issue only from the annihilation of what preceded it" (170). Wharton emphasizes that the contrary is true: "the accumulated leaf-mould of tradition is essential to the nurture of new growths of art, whether or not those who cultivate them are aware of it" (170). Her analysis of "modern fiction" is general; she avoids discussing the work of any particular modernists.

In "Permanent Values in Fiction," however, her criticism is more focused. She argues, for instance, that to an older generation, the novel was "a work of fiction containing a good story about well-drawn characters[,]" but that "To a generation nurtured on Mr. Joyce and Mrs. Woolf such a definition would seem not only pitifully simple, but far from comprehensive" (175). She chastises the modernists for creating characters who are little more than mouthpieces for their views, citing D. H. Lawrence as an example (175)—and perhaps forgetting the extent to which she had done the same thing in *The Marne*. As in *The Writing of Fiction*, she argues in this essay that the creation of memorable characters who contribute to the reader's understanding of "the general law of human experience" are the hallmarks of accomplished fiction; the implication, of course, is that the work of the modernists does not measure up to this standard. In some surprising ways, however, Wharton's views coincided with those of the modernists. Little as Virginia Woolf had in common with Wharton, they objected to James Joyce's *Ulysses* in strikingly similar terms, as Shari Benstock has pointed out: Wharton, as we have seen, referred to it obliquely in print as "schoolboy pornography"; in a letter she was even more emphatic, calling it "a turgid welter of pornography (the rudest schoolboy kind)" (*Letters* 461). Woolf commented on it in her diary, saying that the novel "is diffuse. It is brackish. It is pretentious. It is underbred. . . . I'm reminded all the time of some callow bored school boy" (qtd. in Benstock, "Landscapes of Desire" 33). Wharton further dismissed Joyce's work by saying that "until the raw ingredients of a pudding *make* a pudding, I shall never believe that the raw material of sensation & thought make a work of art without the cook's intervening." From Joyce she moved to Eliot, whose "Waste Land" had recently been published: "The same applies to Eliot" (*Letters* 461). Yet she and Eliot shared some important views, not only on the fragmentation of culture in the postwar period, but on the role of tradition in literature. In "Tradition and the Individual Talent," for instance, T. S. Eliot argued that critics over-valued originality and underestimated the importance of a poet's relation to tradition; further, he claimed that "the most individual parts of [a poet's] work may be those in which the dead poets, his ancestors, assert their immortality most vigorously" (1202). He also remarked that tradition "cannot be inherited, and if you want it you must obtain it by great labour" (1202). In these remarks his view is identical to Wharton's. Despite such significant similarities in their views—similarities of which she was probably unaware—Wharton thoroughly dismisses the modernists.

But there is more than one kind of literary change, and Wharton's own definition of style in *The Writing of Fiction* provides a useful framework for reflecting on the ways in which her fiction changed in the postwar period. She writes that "Form might perhaps . . . be defined as the order, in time and importance, in which the incidents of the narrative are grouped; and style as the way in which they are presented, not only in the narrower sense of language, but also, and rather, as they are grasped and coloured by their medium, the narrator's mind, and given back in his words" (21). Wharton's relationship to the postwar world differed from her relationship to the prewar world. As Dale Bauer has noted, Wharton "anticipat[ed]" Theodor Adorno's observation that "'one must have tradition in oneself to hate it properly'" (6). Wharton objected to the "suggestion" that she had "'stripped' New York society" in *The House of Mirth*, adding that "New York society is still amply clad, & the little corner of its garment that I lifted was meant to show only that little atrophied organ—the group of idle & dull people—that exists in any big & wealthy social body" (*Letters* 96–97). Her remarks, while defending "New York society," also acknowledge that it was a part of her own social class that she was criticizing in her 1905 novel; in Adorno's terms, her tradition was sufficiently "in" her for her to criticize it, if not hate it. *The House of Mirth* implies the need for adjustments in the social system, not the need to overturn, revolutionize, or annihilate it.

As Wharton wrote in *A Backward Glance*, she felt that the war had destroyed the world into which she had been born. Before the war she had written as an insider, critiquing her own society; after the war she wrote as an outsider, a critic of the fast-and-furious upcoming generation of which she was not a part and which, perhaps, she did not wholly understand—though she perceived exactly what she did not like about this society: its rush, its superficiality, its heedlessness of everything that seemed most important to her; and, as Dale Bauer has argued, its refusal to cultivate, or even to acknowledge, the inner life. In Wharton's postwar novels, Bauer writes, "the new objects and status of culture in and of themselves—film, psychoanalysis, drugs like twilight sleep, even celebrityhood, among others—symptomized how culture operated upon the individual to erase the 'inner life.' Substituted in its place was the outer life, the life of standardized and commodified beauty, taste, culture" (6). In the postwar fictions, the only sympathetic characters are, like Wharton, all uncertain of their place in, or their relationship to, modern society: Kate Clephane in *The Mother's Recompense*, Martin Boyne in *The Children*, and Nona Manford in *Twilight Sleep*, for instance, are all people who, at least at times, long for the stability and clearer moral delineations of an older society—even when, like Nona, they are part of the postwar generation. After the war, Wharton's subjects changed; so, too, did her style, as she defined it: in the way a novel's incidents "are grasped and coloured by their medium, the narrator's mind." Her postwar narrators dwell in a moral uncertainty that would have been foreign even to Lily Bart, despite her many temptations.

Wharton's first response in the postwar years, however, was to turn to the past, finding in it—as Henry James had—an "escape" from the present (Powers 291), a strategy that led her to *The Age of Innocence*, the first novel she completed after the war, and *Old New York*, a set of novellas with clearly defined historical settings. While her letters and nonfiction writings, particularly *A Backward Glance*, indicate nostalgia for the prewar world, which, for Wharton as for so many other authors, became bathed in a golden glow in comparison to the war and postwar years, these historical fictions are complex in tone, revealing a profound ambivalence toward the past. As the war receded into the past, Wharton began to treat the war differently than she had in her wartime writings. Instead of using it as a setting, she mentions the war to establish dates or to suggest historical change, and uses some characters' war histories to indicate their integrity—or lack thereof. In Wharton's 1925 novel, *The Mother's Recompense*, the war, though it has been reduced to the status of backdrop, plays a crucial role in shaping character and society. Wharton was adapting her literary strategies and her wartime musings to the postwar world.

II. The War, the Past, and *The Age of Innocence*

The Great War acted as a sharp divide that made the past seem more past, more irretrievably remote than it otherwise would have. As R.W.B. Lewis has pointed out, "it was ... only in the wake of the First World War that the New York society [Wharton] had been born into and in which she had passed her adolescence and early married years became, in her view, *old New York*" ("Introduction" v). Although Wharton had to struggle to regain her grasp on "how people felt and what their point of view was" in the years immediately preceding the war (*Letters* 425), she found herself fully able to turn back to a more distant past—the past of her childhood.

It was a world she re-created in great detail in *The Age of Innocence*. In writing *Summer*, she had remarked that the "inner scene" of the novel appeared to her with a rare intensity (*Backward Glance* 356); the vision of rural Massachusetts provided her a psychological respite from the war around her. So, too, the writing of *Age* seems to have evoked a powerful "inner scene," one allowing her to re-create from memory a world that was distant in time, place, and culture. It also allowed her a respite from both the present, with its ubiquitous Americans and motorcars, and the memory of the immediate past, which she was inevitably reliving as she wrote *A Son at the Front*. "I found a momentary escape in going back to my childish memories of a long-vanished America, and wrote 'The Age of Innocence[,]'" she explained in *A Backward Glance* (369). Only after completing *Age*—and after a "still further flight from the last grim years" in creating *The Glimpses of the Moon* (*Backward Glance* 369)—was she able to complete *A Son at the Front*. In one important way, *Age* and *Son* are the result of the same impulse. Wharton had written that *Son* was "a sort of 'lest we forget'" (*Letters* 471); so was *The Age of Innocence*. The notion that the war, so recently concluded, could be so quickly forgotten must have led her to be concerned about how rapidly the world of her childhood was evaporating.

Wharton's vision of the past in *Age* is remarkably detailed—an indication that she thought of the novel as a historical novel and her work as that of the chronicler of a long-lost world, a role she had also assumed in writing her first novel, *The Valley of Decision*. When Wharton tells her readers that "The persons of [May's and Newland's] world lived in an atmosphere of faint implications and pale delicacies" (17), she is not just describing; rather, she is both preserving the social code of the 1870s for posterity and implying that this is, indeed, a lost era. Although there were, in fact, many people in 1920 who could have recalled New York of the 1870s, she described herself as nearly alone in her memory of that era, quoting her friend Walter Berry's remark that he and she were "the last people left who can remember New York and Newport as they were then" (*Backward*

Glance 369). In innumerable scenes Wharton describes the physical appearance of a world with which, she assumes, her readers are unfamiliar, specifying, for instance, details of interior decoration ("the Gothic library with glazed black-walnut bookcases and finial-topped chairs" [4]); food (describing a number of meals course by course); and jewelry (for example, May's engagement ring, "a large thick sapphire set in invisible claws" [29]), as well as details of architecture, city layout, fashion, specific book titles, and prominent public figures of the day. From the first sentence of the novel—"On a January evening of the early seventies, Christine Nilsson was singing in *Faust* at the Academy of Music in New York" (3)— Wharton makes it clear to the reader that this is a historical novel. Setting the scene immediately in this fashion was one way of dealing with the annoying but, as Wharton had observed, necessary question of whether "the adventures related in this book happen before the war" or after it.

For all its wealth of detail, however, *Age* is not simply—as Wharton wrote to a friend—a "'costume piece'" (*Letters* 433); it is a novel of manners and mores. Wharton's main character, Newland Archer, is engaged to marry the beautiful and socially appropriate May Welland. May's long-lost cousin, the Countess Ellen Olenska, returns to New York on the eve of the announcement of May's and Newland's engagement. A refugee from a failed marriage with a Polish aristocrat, Ellen calls forth both Newland's sense of chivalry and his sense of loyalty to the Welland family: he feels it his duty to defend Ellen's reputation. In doing so, however, he gradually begins to find Ellen fascinating, May vapid and conventional; in short, he ends up falling in love with Ellen. But—at Ellen's urging—he honors his engagement to May. Two years after their marriage Newland is still thinking of Ellen Olenska; May's family, which has quietly (and erroneously) assumed that Newland and Ellen are lovers, contrives to send Ellen back to Europe. As Newland is about to announce to May one evening that he is planning an extended trip—a screen for following Ellen—May interrupts and announces that she is pregnant. Newland never takes, or even mentions, his projected trip. He remains in New York as May's husband; they have three children and lead the conventional lives of New Yorkers of their generation and social station. Only in the final chapter of the book—an epilogue set nearly thirty years later—does Newland reflect on his life and his choice to remain with May, who has since died. He also gives up his last chance to renew his acquaintance with Ellen Olenska.

Though *Age* is much more than a "costume piece" as Wharton averred, in this work more than in any other she had written, the details of daily life—the clothing, the jewelry, the socially crafted choices of what to say or avoid saying—are intrinsically bound to the story; manners and mores are inextricably linked. Wharton wrote to a friend that *Age* was "a 'simple & grave' story of two people trying to live up to something that was still 'felt in the blood' at that time" (*Letters* 433), and the novel's copious details insist on "that time" as well as on what "was still 'felt in the blood.'" On the one hand Wharton insisted that some minor anachronisms in her 1870s setting were of "small importance" (*Letters* 440).[3] On the other, however, the details were crucially important to her. When she learned that Zoe Akins was planning to dramatize *Age*, she wrote excitedly to Minnie Jones, "I am very anxious about the staging & dressing. I could do every stick of furniture & every rag of clothing myself, for every detail of that far-off scene was indelibly stamped on my infant brain. I am so much afraid that the young actors will be 'Summit Collar' athletes, with stern jaws & shaven lips, instead of gentlemen. Of course they ought all to have moustaches, & not tooth brush ones, but curved & slightly twisted at the ends" (*Letters* 439). This letter goes on to specify the type of flowers gentlemen of the day would wear, their shoes, the manner of "a N.Y. drawing-room of my childhood[,]" and the language: "Above all, beg her to avoid slang & Americanisms, & tell her that English was then the language spoken by American ladies & gentlemen[.]" The details were important, she emphasized, to create "the right atmosphere."

The details mattered because of their significance: only in "the right atmosphere" could this particular story occur in this particular way. Some details—like May's sapphire set in the "invisible claws" that will eventually keep Newland from straying—are symbolic, as well as historically accurate; others are metonymic, the physical manifestations of social and psychological restrictions. In earlier novels Wharton had generally trusted her readers to grasp the importance of details for themselves—for instance, to understand that Undine Spragg's choice of "pigeon-blood" notepaper in *The Custom of the Country* (13) reveals her newness to the upper strata of society as well as a rather vulgar running after superficial and passing trends. But in *Age* Wharton not only describes details, but interprets them, making sure that readers understand the significance of particular details in a world that, she implies, belongs to a far-distant past.

In some cases Wharton archly allows details to pass unremarked, but is, in effect, exchanging a sly wink with her 1920s reader. When Newland Archer, Ellen Olenska, and Julius Beaufort relieve a moment of social awkwardness by discussing the rumors of strange innovations like the tele-phone (137), or when Wharton refers to the "inaccessible wilderness near the Central Park" (13), she trusts her readers to see, with her, the quaint-ness of an age in which such things were remarkable. In such passages (as in the "pigeon-blood notepaper" from *The Custom of the Country* men-tioned above), she follows the principle she delineated in her preface to *Ghosts:* "I was conscious of a common medium between myself and my readers, of their meeting me halfway among the primeval shadows, and filling in the gaps in my narrative with sensations and divinations akin to my own" (*Collected Short Stories* 2:876).

In many passages in *Age,* however, Wharton does not rely on her reader to "fill in the gaps." During the war years Wharton often wrote for audi-ences who needed to be swayed; though understatement is among the most elegant of literary strategies, it is not a reliable one for audiences who might not share an author's background or views. In *The Marne* and *French Ways and Their Meaning* Wharton had disciplined herself to spell out her lesson for readers who might otherwise misinterpret her; while Wharton trusted the readers of *Age* to understand the quaintness of a time in which the telephone, electric lights, and quick transatlantic travel were seen as marvelous innovations, she did not trust them to interpret prop-erly the hieroglyphic ways of 1870s New York. *French Ways* was a guide to French culture for Americans; *Age* is a guide to the past for readers of the 1920s and beyond, and Wharton takes pains to make sure readers will understand that culture—a culture made foreign by the gap created by the war—and that they will understand it correctly.

Wharton's cultural interpretations are sometimes arch, particularly early in the novel; but even in these cases, they are generally interpretive. In the opening chapter, Wharton both describes and interprets Newland's intentionally late arrival at the opera: "There was no reason why the young man should not have come earlier. . . . But . . . New York was a metropolis, and perfectly aware that in metropolises it was 'not the thing' to arrive early at the Opera; and what was or was not 'the thing' played a part as important in Newland Archer's New York as the inscrutable totem terrors that had ruled the destinies of his forefathers thousands of years ago" (4).

Similarly, Wharton both records and mocks the conventions of opera performance and translation, extending this criticism to the convention-ity of New York society: Marguerite in *Faust* "sang, of course, 'M'ama!'

and not 'He loves me,' since an unalterable and unquestioned law of the musical world required that the German text of French operas sung by Swedish artists should be translated into Italian for the clearer understanding of English-speaking audiences. This seemed as natural to Newland Archer as all the other conventions on which his life was moulded: such as the duty of using two silver-backed brushes with his monogram in blue enamel to part his hair" (5).

As the novel continues, however, the level of interpretation increases and its tone becomes more serious. In a famous passage, Wharton explains that "In reality they all lived in a kind of hieroglyphic world, where the real thing was never said or done or even thought, but only represented by a set of arbitrary signs" (45). Wharton is the Champollion of this ancient world with its nearly lost codes. One notable example of Wharton's interpretative role occurs when Newland is telling May about a trip he is to take to Washington, ostensibly on business but, as they both know, really to see Ellen—though Newland has not so much as mentioned Ellen's name. May simply remarks that he "must be sure to go and see Ellen" (266). Wharton elaborates the coded subtext of this message:

> It was the only word that passed between them on the subject; but in the code in which they had both been trained it meant: "Of course you understand that I know all that people have been saying about Ellen, and heartily sympathize with my family in their effort to get her to return to her husband. I also know that . . . you have advised her against this course . . .; and that it is owing to your encouragement that Ellen defies us all. . . . Hints have indeed not been wanting; but since you appear unwilling to take them from others, I offer you this one myself . . . : by letting you understand that I know you mean to see Ellen when you are in Washington, and are perhaps going there expressly for that purpose; and that, since you are sure to see her, I wish you to do so with my full and explicit approval—and to take the opportunity of letting her know what the course of conduct you have encouraged her in is likely to lead to." (266)

As the ellipses here indicate, the decoded message is, in fact, even more detailed than it appears in this abridged form; Wharton wants to be sure that her readers understand exactly what is being communicated through the coded conversation of the 1870s. Moreover, her novel illustrates that even the frankest relationships of this period are governed by this code. Although Ellen and Newland are, on the whole, far more open and frank in their conversations than are May and Newland, they too speak in code. When Ellen and Newland share their emotionally passionate but physically chaste lunch in Boston, Wharton gives her readers the subtext as well as the text of their dialogue:

> There they were, close together and safe and shut in; yet so chained to their separate destinies that they might as well have been half the world apart.
>
> "What's the use—when you will go back?" he broke out, a great hopeless *How on earth can I keep you?* crying out to her beneath his words.
>
> She sat motionless, with lowered lids. "Oh—I shan't go yet!"
>
> "Not yet? Some time, then? Some time that you already foresee?"
>
> At that she raised her clearest eyes. "I promise you: not as long as you hold out. Not as long as we can look straight at each other like this."
>
> He dropped into his chair. What her answer really said was: "If you lift a finger you'll drive me back: back to all the abominations you know of, and all the temptations you half guess." He understood it as clearly as if she had uttered the words. . . . (243)

It is not what Newland and Ellen say, but what they do not say, that is most significant: the questions "beneath his words," the difference between the words she speaks and "what her answer really said[.]" For all their obliqueness, these messages seem clear to their recipients: "He understood it as clearly as if she had uttered the words[.]"

Wharton's interpretive narration in *The Age of Innocence* assumes the pastness of the past and the need to tutor the reader in proper interpretation. Yet—like all historical fiction—this novel, though set in the 1870s, bears myriad traces of the period in which it was written, the immediate postwar period. Wharton's emphasis on "the hieroglyphic world" would not have been so strong without her wartime experiences; the need to write in franker, less ambiguous terms during the war, as well as the general influence of the more explicit writing emerging from the war, must have brought home to her the extreme obliqueness of the prewar social and verbal codes of her class. Prewar novels like *The House of Mirth* and *The Custom of the Country* illustrated the gap between open speaking and socially acceptable remarks and comments; but in *Age*, that gap is depicted as a chasm. Like the war-influenced description of Charity's dead mother in *Summer*, *Age* is subtly but profoundly shaped by the war years.

Age echoes Wharton's wartime writings in many ways. Anyone who reads *French Ways and Their Meanings* or *Fighting France* before coming to *Age* hears Wharton's adulatory tones when M. Rivière, Count Olenski's secretary, praises conversation as the highest pleasure in life, or when Newland sees the dome of the Invalides as "drawing up into itself all the rays of afternoon light . . . like the visible symbol of the race's glory" (358). *Age* echoes the war works in more somber ways as well. The grimmer passages of *Fighting France* are echoed in *Age;* "eyes that have seen what one dare not picture"(*Fighting France* 50), a phrase Wharton uses to describe the faces of the emotionally and physically exhausted refugees flooding Paris, return in a different guise. After the Beaufort financial scandal, for instance, May's mother—the perennially cheerful Mrs. Welland, who never acknowledges actual or potential problems—is "blanched and demolished by the unwonted obligation of having at last to fix her eyes on the unpleasant and the discreditable" (272). Mrs. Welland is, characteristically, trying to shield her dyspeptic husband from the worst of the news; May's response to her mother's concerns both demonstrates the extent to which she is her mother's daughter and emphasizes the importance of seeing—or rather, of avoiding seeing—horrors: "'After all, Mamma, he won't have *seen* them[,]'" she reassures her mother (272). In *Age,* as in *Fighting France,* Wharton refers repeatedly to the difference between merely hearing of "horrors" and actually seeing them: if one has not actually seen them, it is easier to continue denying their existence.

The society in which May and Newland live has a very high resistance to "the unpleasant." Not only do Ellen's family members refuse to listen to the details of her marriage to, or her escape from, her tyrannical and degenerate husband, they also manage to convince themselves that inconvenient or unpleasant details simply don't exist. Mrs. Mingott suffers a stroke after Regina Beaufort comes to ask for her backing during her husband's financial crisis; within a day or two, however, Mrs. Mingott has managed to transform her stroke into "an attack of indigestion" brought on by eating chicken salad too late in the day (278). In "Coming Home" Macy Greer had expressed his belief that the war would "teach us not to be afraid of the obvious" (244). The prewar world Wharton depicts in *Age* is deeply "afraid of the obvious"; the inhabitants of Old New York are the opposite of the French Wharton so admired, with their "[i]ntellectual honesty, the courage to look at things as they are" (*French Ways and Their Meaning* 58). A society that refuses even to acknowledge anything unpleasant is not so much innocent as self-willed and culpably ignorant; or, in the terms of *French Ways*, a society "still in its childhood. . . . Till a society ceases to be afraid of the truth in the domain of ideas it is in leading-strings, morally and mentally" (58–59).

Reading *Age* in the light of *French Ways* implies a powerful criticism of 1870s New York. As we have seen, Henry James had written to Wharton in 1914 that "Our time has been *this* time for the last 50 years, & if it was ignorantly & fatuously so the only light in which to show it is now the light of that tragic delusion" (Powers 316). Henry Seidel Canby, in his 1920 review of *Age*, expressed the same view, making a crucial link between social mores and political perceptions. He commented that "America is the land of cherished illusions. Americans prefer to believe that they are innocent. . . . Americans do not like to admit the existence (in the family) of passion, of unscrupulousness, of temperament. They have made a code for what is to be done, and what is not to be done, and whatever differs is un-American. If their right hands offend them they cut them off rather than admit possession. They believed in international morality when none existed, and when they were made to face the disagreeable fact of war, cast off the nations of the earth, and continued to believe in national morality" (Tuttleton et al. 287–88). France is the land of adults, unafraid to look at the truth; America is the land of children, avoiding unpleasantness at all costs—even "fatuously so" when it came to war: for the Wellands are the ancestors of those who, so culpably from Wharton's perspective, refused for so long to involve the United States in the Great War.

In its attention to details, its language, and its implied criticisms of Old New York the novel is shaped by the war; so too are its central characters—Newland Archer, Ellen Olenska, and May Welland. In particular, Ellen's stoicism and her emotional maturity build on Wharton's praise for Frenchwomen as described in *Fighting France* and *French Ways and Their Meaning*. May Welland and others of her ilk fear unpleasantness and avert their eyes to avoid seeing anything that might disturb them; Ellen will look at anything unblinkingly. Early in the novel Newland is "frightened . . . to think what must have gone to the making of her eyes" (63); his reluctance to "think" of what made those eyes echoes Wharton's comments about the eyes of refugees: "it is a grim sight . . . to meet with the dazed stare of eyes that have seen what one dare not picture" (*Fighting France* 50). Ellen, on the contrary, approaches anything with eyes wide open. When Newland admiringly tells her "'you look at things as they are,'" she replies, "'Ah—I've had to. I've had to look at the Gorgon.'" She adds further that the Gorgon "'doesn't blind one; but she dries up one's tears'" (288).

Ellen's "look at the Gorgon" in context refers to her marriage with the Count, a man whom Wharton described in her plans for the novel as a "charming gambler, drug-taker & debauché" (Price, "Composition" 25). Yet the Countess's terms could easily be seen as outsize, disproportionate to her experience: as terms that reflect not only the Countess's personal experience, but Wharton's experience in the war years as well. In *Fighting France* Wharton wrote of "pass[ing] in the street women whose faces look like memorial medals—idealized images of what they were in the flesh" (38–39); she adds that "the masks of some of the men . . . look like the bronzes of the Naples Museum, burnt and twisted from their baptism of fire" (39). Ellen's experience with the Count seems to have been a similar "baptism of fire"; like the soldiers and the involved civilians Wharton admired, Ellen has been transformed and ennobled by suffering.

Ellen also embodies the ideal of French womanhood Wharton came increasingly to appreciate during the war, and which she praised in *French Ways and Their Meaning*. When Newland scans the faces of his fellow diners at the van der Luydens' home, he notes that Ellen is "the only young woman" present; yet the faces of the older women "struck him as curiously immature compared with hers" (62–63). Like the American women Wharton criticizes in *French Ways*, these women are "still in the kindergarten" (101); Ellen, with her more varied European experience, is, like the Frenchwomen Wharton praises, "*grown up*" (*French Ways* 100). Not yet thirty (61), Ellen has achieved a kind of maturity that neither May nor the older women in the novel—Mrs. Welland, Mrs. Archer, or even Mrs. Mingott—will ever achieve.[4]

Indeed, Ellen's family's inability—or refusal—to perceive the bleak reality of her marriage to the Count is the basis on which they press her to return to her marriage. They refuse to listen to the details of the marriage because such details must be "unpleasant"—a refusal, which, at one point, drives even the dry-eyed Countess Olenska to tears. As she tells Archer, her family "'want[s] to help'" her—"'But on condition that they don't hear anything unpleasant. . . . Does no one want to know the truth here, Mr. Archer? The real loneliness is living among all these kind people who only ask one to pretend!'" (78). When M. Rivière, the Count's secretary, privately asks Newland not to urge Ellen to return to her husband, he remarks, "'If Madame Olenska's relations understood what these things were, their opposition to her returning would no doubt be as unconditional

Fig. 4. "A French palisade." Edith Wharton at the front.
Frontispiece from Wharton's *Fighting France.*

as her own'" (253–54). Like the unmentioned atrocities at the heart of
"Coming Home," exactly what "these things" are is never mentioned.
Wharton may be demonstrating the vestiges of her own Old New York
character by refusing here to describe "the unpleasant"; as in *Fighting
France* and "Coming Home," Wharton seems to shy away from a detailed
listing of atrocities or other horrors. But her Ellen—who, like Jean de

Réchamp or Yvonne Malo, knows what these unnamed horrors are—faces them in a way that no other character in the novel, including Newland, does.

Ellen is, in fact, far more able to deal with realities than Newland; she has had the "baptism of fire," which he has not. While Newland declares to her in a carriage that "'the only reality is this,'" his "reality" is merely an insubstantial romance. Ellen detects the irony of his making this declaration to her in May's carriage, but Newland reverts to impractical romanticism, asking her to "'just quietly trust to'" his "'vision'" of the two of them together "'to come true'" (289). It is Ellen who insists that they "'look, not at visions, but at realities,'" and finally asks, "'Is it your idea, then, that I should live with you as your mistress—since I can't be your wife?'" (289). Newland's reaction to this question as "crude" (289) shows how far he is from accepting reality, despite his stated desire for the real. Similarly, it is Ellen, not Newland, who takes the initiative in crucial scenes, creating the possibilities that might turn his imagined affair with her into a reality: it is she who kisses him in the carriage (288) and who asks, "'Shall I—once come to you; and then go home?'" (312). It is also Ellen who wordlessly withdraws from their planned tryst, returning the hotel key Newland had given her once May has told her that she is pregnant. In fact, one might argue that Ellen's only character weakness is her love for Newland. She is the novel's model of firm self-control and intellectual honesty, the embodiment of the accomplishments and character Wharton so admired in French women.

If Ellen reflects much that Wharton came to admire in French women during the war years, Newland also represents some of her experience during those years. In particular she re-creates in him the almost vertiginous loss of a sense of reality that she experienced at some moments during the war. May is entirely sure of herself and the reality of her domestic expectations, while Ellen is equally sure of her artistic and aristocratic milieus. But Newland has profound moments of uncertainty, of not knowing what is real and what is unreal. Early in his engagement to May, Ellen seems unreal; but when he is with Ellen, all of Old New York—including May—recedes to a huge distance, and Newland feels as if he were looking at his normal life "through the wrong end of a telescope" (77). After he and May return from their European wedding-tour to settle in New York, he finds his new life "fairly real and inevitable" (206). Yet he finds life at the Wellands' house in Newport eerily "unreal" (206). An important passage establishes the extent to which the imaginary has become the real, and the real—that is, the "actual"—has become unreal to Archer: "he had built up within himself a kind of sanctuary in which [Ellen] throned among his secret thoughts and longings. Little by little it became the scene of his real life, of his only rational activities. . . . Outside it, in the scene of his actual life, he moved with a growing sense of unreality and insufficiency. . . . Absent—that was what he was: so absent from everything most densely real and near to those about him that it sometimes startled him to find they still imagined he was there" (262).

Archer confuses and sometimes even reverses the real and the unreal, the absent and the present, the actual and the imagined—as when he thinks of the others as "imagin[ing]" he was still present when, in terms of physical reality, he *is* present. The fluctuation of the "real" and "unreal" continues throughout the novel. Newland counts his imagined life with Ellen his "real" life, and tells Ellen when they are alone in May's carriage that "'The only reality to me is this'" (289). At the farewell dinner for Ellen he has, like Charity after her intent observation of the unaware Lucius Harney, a sense of profound unreality: he "seemed to be assisting at the scene in a state of odd imponderability, as if he floated somewhere between chandelier and ceiling" (335). This feeling is much like Charity's sense of "floating high over life, on a great cloud of misery beneath which everyday realities had dwindled to mere specks in space" (*Summer* 70). In these ways, Newland seems to associate the "real" with his largely imagined life with Ellen, and the "unreal" with his actual life with May. But in the novel's final chapter, Newland looks around the library that has been his for nearly thirty years and thinks of it as "the room in which most of the real things of his life had happened" (344). And these "real things" are the major points of his domestic life in New York: his marriage to May, their three children, and his work for the public good.

Even on the novel's final page Wharton is questioning which life is real and which unreal for Newland. A few years after May's death, Newland is sitting on a bench outside Ellen's Paris apartment. Although Ellen is expecting him, and although his twentyish son has already gone up to see her, Newland remains in his place. Again the real and the imagined are conflated: "'It's more real to me here than if I went up,' he suddenly heard himself say; and the fear lest that last shadow of reality should lose its edge kept him rooted to his seat" (361). What he imagines—Ellen in her apartment—is real. Yet Archer prefers to keep that reality in the realm of his imagination, to keep Ellen a mere "shadow of reality." More deeply than any other novel, *The Age of Innocence* reproduces the sense of an altered and protean reality that Wharton had felt so keenly during the war.

Like Wharton's, Newland Archer's sense of the real—and his sense that the real is going on somewhere else, to someone else—is part of his fear of missing out on some crucial, some essential experience. Waiting at the front of the church for May to arrive for their wedding, for instance, he recalls the family argument over whether to display their wedding gifts: "it seemed inconceivable to Archer that grown-up people should work themselves into a state of agitation over such trifles. . . . 'And all the while, I suppose,' he thought, 'real people were living somewhere, and real things happening to them . . .'" (182). In this way, Newland Archer is the unlikely heir of Charlie Durand of "The Refugees." Through Charlie, Wharton most clearly figured forth her fear of missing out on the real war, the real adventure, the real things in life. Charlie has to settle for wearing the YMCA uniform rather than "the real uniform of his country" (590). In a civilian setting, Newland is haunted by the same fear—a fear that would surface again in Martin Boyne, the main character of Wharton's 1928 novel *The Children*, who "would have loved adventure," but who finds that "adventure worthy of the name perpetually eluded him" (2). When Newland looks at Ellen, he sees her as a figure "to whom things were bound to happen" (116). One of Archer's greatest fears is articulated when he misses seeing Ellen at the Blenkers': "his whole future seemed suddenly to be unrolled before him; and passing down its endless emptiness he saw the dwindling figure of a man to whom nothing was ever to happen" (227).

Wharton's notebook entries for the novel emphasize the grimness of such a fate. In an earlier plan for the novel, Ellen is "very poor, & very lonely, but she has a real life"; May "marries some one else"; Archer's fate is that "nothing ever happens to him again" (Price, "Composition" 24). In the completed work, Wharton tempers his fate; he leads a productive life, and yet this is not quite enough for him: "Something he knew he had missed: the flower of life" (347). Like Charlie Durand before him, like Martin Boyne after him, and like his creator in wartime, Newland Archer worries incessantly—and correctly—that he is missing out on some central experience, an experience that has much to do with the nature of reality, and hence with the power to lead a full and rich life.

In a number of other ways as well, *The Age of Innocence* incorporates Wharton's wartime musings. In particular, her statements in the final chapter of *French Ways* suggest that, to some extent, she might condone an affair between Ellen and Newland. As was discussed in chapter three, Wharton wrote approvingly that the French "have decided that love is too grave a matter for boys and girls, and not grave enough to form the basis of marriage; but in the relations between grown people, apart from their permanent ties (and in the deepest consciousness of the French, marriage still remains indissoluble), they allow it, frankly and amply, the part it furtively and shabbily, but no less ubiquitously, plays in Puritan societies" (131–32). *Age's* example of shabby furtiveness under the guise of Puritanism is, of course, Larry Lefferts, who covers up his miscellaneous affairs with lies and moralistic speeches. In contrast, Ellen's straightforward question about whether she ought to become Newland's mistress is a breath of fresh air—though one too chilling for Archer, pride himself how he might on his advanced views about the equality of women. Read in the context of *French Ways,* even Ellen's suggestion does not undermine Newland's marriage with May. "Marriage, in France, is regarded as founded for the family and not for the husband and wife. It is designed not to make two people individually happy for a longer or shorter time, but to secure their permanent well-being as associates in the foundation of a home and the procreation of a family" (128). *A Son at the Front* gives a brief portrait of such a family; the physician Fortin-Lescluze is someone Campton has usually seen in a "studio with amusing talk, hot-house flowers, and ladies lolling on black velvet divans" (66). But when the doctor's son is about to leave for the front, Campton is shown into the more sedate family dining room, where he is introduced to Fortin-Lescluze's wife and mother: "the family . . . seemed as happily united . . . as if no musical studio-parties and exotic dancers had ever absorbed the master of the house" (68). The doctor's extramarital interests seem not to threaten family harmony; for Wharton, apparently, it was not impossible to imagine a scenario in which a happily married man could also have a satisfactory relationship with a mistress.

But, although *The Age of Innocence* is influenced by Wharton's wartime experiences, it is after all a historical novel—one set in New York of the 1870s, not in turn-of-the-century France. If at some level Wharton felt that Newland's and Ellen's problems could be solved by a discreet long-term affair, at another level she did not. In none of her projected plans for the novel do Newland and Ellen achieve a lasting union.[5] Further, and in keeping with an unironic reading of her novel's title, Wharton seems to have approved the abstinence of Ellen and Newland. As we have seen, she wanted the novel to be taken "as a 'simple & grave' story of two people trying to live up to something that was still 'felt in the blood' at that time"

(*Letters* 433), something that treasures chastity and fidelity over the grati-
fication of desire—even at the cost of "the flower of life." In the end, Newland's and May's marriage may comprehend both the Puritanical sexual
mores Wharton claimed to dislike and the stability she praised in French
marriages. The cost of the stability is May's close-mindedness and Newland's sacrifice of "adventure," something Wharton claims most Frenchmen abandon in favor of stability (*French Ways* 87–88). But their marriage accomplishes what Wharton most admired in French marriages: it
may not ensure their happiness as individuals, but it establishes them "as
associates in the foundation of a home and the procreation of a family"
(*French Ways* 128). Toward the end of the novel Newland implicitly corroborates this view, reflecting with some satisfaction that "Their long
years together had shown him that it did not so much matter if marriage
was a dull duty, as long as it kept the dignity of a duty: lapsing from that, it
became a mere battle of ugly appetites" (347).[6]

Even more than the satisfaction of having "the dignity of a duty," the
fact that his marriage to May results in the "procreation of a family" compensates Newland for his decision to stay with her. Newland and his son
Dallas—his first child, and therefore the child for whom he gave up
Ellen—are "born comrades" (350). At the end of Wharton's 1934 story
"Roman Fever," Grace Ansley remarks vengefully to her friend and social
rival, Alida Slade, that "I had Barbara"—the perfect, if secretly illegitimate, daughter Mrs. Slade covets, and the child who compensates Mrs.
Ansley for her lackluster marriage. Newland is not interested in vengeance, but the fact that he "had Dallas" is a great compensation; had he
left May, he would never have known this child, this "born comrade"—a
situation Wharton explores with a mother and daughter in *The Mother's
Recompense.* Newland's fidelity to May, an American version of the
French marriages so admired by Wharton, has had its rewards—significant ones.

The tone of *Age* is complex, as complex as that of any novel Wharton
wrote. The age of innocence is also an age of ignorance, an ignorance that is
self-willed and culpable. From a postwar perspective, moreover, the issues
on which this society expends so much energy could be seen either as the
central issues of civilization—for civilized behavior is surely at the heart of
the very concept of civilization—or as remarkably trivial, trivial to the
point of mere quaintness. For, from the perspective of people who had just
been through a terrible war, what is, after all, the novel's great tragedy?
Even Newland Archer acknowledges that on balance his days have been

"filled decently" (347). If the Welland family and its allies have had the temerity to cast out Ellen Olenska "'without effusion of blood'" (335), one may nevertheless ask whether being exiled to an apartment in a fashionable Paris quarter is such a terrible fate. In light of the tragedies of the war, the fates of Newland Archer, May Welland, and Ellen Olenska—like the problems of Charity Royall in *Summer*—may have seemed relatively minor, normal, or even attractive. Compared with the bloody deaths of World War I, the bloodless fate of Ellen Olenska is appealing indeed. And yet *Age* is, if not a tragic novel, a sad one. Newland's coming so close to winning Ellen, the "only prize" among the "hundred million tickets in *his* lottery" (347), but failing to do so, lends the novel's conclusion a powerful poignancy.

The novel's concluding chapter is a masterpiece of ambivalence. Critics have seen it as both a negative and an affirmative ending, and have seen Newland's decision not to climb the stairs to Ellen Olenska's apartment in particular as both admirable and foolish.[7] The novel has also been described more simply as "shrewdly ambivalent" (Lewis, "Introduction" v), a description that particularly fits the final chapter, in which Newland Archer reflects that "There was good in the old ways" (347) and that "There was good in the new order too" (349). Like the conclusion of *Summer*, the ending of *The Age of Innocence* hangs with a certain precise ambivalence, its tone at once nostalgic and skeptical, ironic and sincere.

This ambivalence is captured in the apparent golden age Wharton presents in this novel's final chapter. If there is a true golden age in this novel, a true age of innocence, it exists in the depiction of Newland's New York and Paris, circa 1905. In this chapter, set about thirty years after the main action of the novel, change has finally occurred. Newland reflects that although his daughter Mary is "no less conventional, and no more intelligent" than her mother was, she "yet led a larger life and held more tolerant views" (349). Similarly, without being by any stretch of the imagination a radical or a nonconformist, Dallas leads the life his father had meant to lead: he is about to marry a woman he deeply loves, one who seems to share his interests and tastes, and one who would have been a socially unacceptable choice in Newland's prime. Dallas is active and cheerful; he has a real profession; he is self-assured in a way that Newland never was. As Newland imagines his son going up to Madame Olenska's apartment in the lift, "He pictured Dallas entering that room with his quick assured step and his delightful smile, and wondered if the people were right who said that his boy 'took after him'" (361). While describing himself as "old-fashioned" (360), Newland sees his son Dallas as his own second chance, the self he would have been in the new world after the turn of the century. The period presented in the final chapter is also presented imagistically as a golden age, one bathed in sunlight. As Newland strolls through Paris he wanders through the Louvre, moving "from gallery to gallery through the dazzle of afternoon light" (357). He and Dallas admire the dome of the Invalides, "drawing up into itself all the rays of afternoon light" (358); even the awnings of Ellen's apartment are "still lowered, as though the sun had just left it" (360). Newland is engulfed by the "thickening dusk" (361) as he sits on a bench outside Ellen's building, but Paris, the city of light, has been bathed in a golden glow.

Yet Wharton never really succumbs to nostalgia in this novel, not even nostalgia for prewar Paris. The first age of innocence—New York in the 1870s—believed in its own rectitude and dignity, but Newland is always aware, for instance, that "most of the other marriages about him" were "a dull association of material and social interests held together by ignorance on the one side and hypocrisy on the other" (44–45). His own son Dallas criticizes the coded social exchanges of the seventies. When his father relates that May never "asked" him to give up Ellen, Dallas replies, "'You never did ask each other anything, did you? And you never told each other anything. You just sat and watched each other, and guessed at what was going on underneath. A deaf-and-dumb asylum, in fact'" (356). But even the golden era in the novel's final chapter has its drawbacks. After criticizing the "deaf-and-dumb" marriage of his parents, Dallas also concedes, "'Well, I back your generation for knowing more about each other's private thoughts than we ever have time to find out about our own'" (356): the new era lacks time for deep knowledge of another, or even for self-knowledge.

Other shadows as well may be part of the "thickening dusk" in which Newland sits. Wharton and her readers of the 1920s who were paying attention to the novel's chronology knew that the golden age of the final chapter would be, at best, a short one—one that would be interrupted within a few years by the outbreak of the Great War. At worst, the society portrayed as close to ideal in the final chapter—Newland so proud of his son, Dallas so occupied with his work and love life, and even Fanny Beaufort so occupied with the latest musical scores—could also be seen as part of the self-satisfied, overly idealistic world depicted at the beginning of *A Son at the Front*, a world that congratulated itself on its sophistication even as war hung just over the horizon.

Apart from treating the end of the novel as part of a realistic chronology exterior to the fiction itself, Wharton harbored skepticism about the golden future of Dallas Archer and Fanny Beaufort. In a 1921 letter, Wharton described a projected sequel. The novel, "to be called 'Homo Sapiens,' . . . would be about the son of Newland Archer, who marries Beaufort's illegitimate daughter at the end of 'The Age.' Newland Archer and the Countess Olenska would reappear, and Homo Sapiens would of course be the omniscient youth of the present date, who has settled in advance all social, religious and moral problems, and yet comes to grief over the same old human difficulties" (9 Nov. 1921, *Wharton Collection* Yale). As this brief description suggests, Wharton did not believe in golden ages: if war had not disrupted the world depicted at the end of *The Age of Innocence*, human frailty would nevertheless have interrupted its happiness.[8]

Wharton's composition of *The Age of Innocence* seems to have triggered an avalanche of reflection about the past—or, rather, about multiple pasts. The main action of *Age* is set in the 1870s, but the epilogue is set in the first decade of the twentieth century; various references in the novel allude to other points in history as well. Wharton links the 1870s to a long past, referring back not just to the youth of Newland's mother but to the time of her grandparents and great-grandparents (49), to Newland's "forefathers thousands of years ago" (4), and even to "the dawn of history" (179). In short, the novel spans almost all of history—from its "dawn" until the novel's end—a period shortly before the outbreak of the Great War. Further, Wharton plays with ideas of past and present throughout the novel. When Mrs. Welland, May, and Newland Archer visit the formidable Mrs. Mingott after the engagement of May and Newland, Mrs. Welland remarks to Mrs. Mingott a bit apologetically that May's engagement ring "'looks a little bare to old-fashioned eyes'" (29). Mrs. Mingott denies her advancing years, responding, "'Old-fashioned eyes? I hope you don't mean mine[.]'" But she later adds, "'In my time a cameo set in pearls was thought sufficient'" (30). A sense of the real can fluctuate; so, throughout this novel, does the definition of the past, the present, of history.

Wharton's concern with the past spilled over into the composition of the four novellas that constitute *Old New York*, the work she completed after *Age*. As with *Age*, Wharton's readers could not escape the fact that they were reading historical fiction, as each novella has a decade appended to its title: "False Dawn (The 'Forties)"; "The Old Maid (The 'Fifties)"; "The Spark (The 'Sixties)"; and "New Year's Day (The 'Seventies)." *Age* is set primarily in the 1870s but refers to a number of other eras; each of the novellas in *Old New York* does the same, regardless of the decade to which each story is assigned. Wharton extended the "lest we forget" of *A Son at the Front* into *Age;* from *Age* she extended it yet further, into *Old New York.* If the war could be forgotten, so could the past of her youth–or perhaps the past altogether. Even more than *Age, Old New York* abounds in details of menu, costume, furniture, customs; readers learn what constituted a feast in upper-class society in the 1840s ("False Dawn"), of proper room decor for young married ladies in the 1850s ("The Old Maid"), and so on. Wharton was not simply recalling her past; she was recording it (as well as the two decades preceding her birth), preserving that past for a generation to whom it was not only unfamiliar but, she believed, foreign.

Moreover, the narration routinely draws attention to these details, to their social significance, and to history itself. The novellas comprising *Old New York* include in passing characters Wharton had created in *The Age of Innocence*—such as the Van der Luydens, Mrs. Manson Mingott, and Sillerton Jackson—and actual historical figures such as Edgar Allan Poe, Charles Dickens, John Ruskin, Walt Whitman, and Jenny Lind. The first of these novellas to be published, "The Old Maid," was a direct outgrowth of *The Age of Innocence.* "Clementina," the illegitimate daughter of Charlotte (the "old maid" of the title) was the original name for Ellen Olenska (Price, "Composition" 22); Charlotte's consummated affair with Clem Spender dates from Wharton's original plan for Ellen and Newland to "go to the South together—some little place in Florida. Arrange somehow that all this is done *very secretly*" (qtd. in Price, "Composition" 26). This affair never occurs in *Age,* but it does—albeit on a smaller scale—in "The Old Maid."

Unlike *Age,* however, *Old New York* employs, in three of its four novellas, a narrator who frequently draws attention to the fluctuations of history—a man who, speaking from the early twenties when the stories were published, reflects on the present, the past, and the social changes that had occurred over time.[9] Wharton's choice of this device, as well as her use of details in the stories themselves, allow her to emphasize the multiple pasts depicted in these stories. Not only a sense of the past but a sense of mutability emerges as the narrator reflects on his own youth, his maturity, and the changes he, his elders, and his juniors have seen and are likely to see. Even the term "Old New York" is mutable: the grouping of the novellas set in four different decades suggests that "Old New York" itself stretched over a number of periods. Elderly characters in "The Spark," for instance, in a scene set in the 1890s, discuss "the vanished 'Old New York' of their youth" (202), while the 1890s themselves are called "archaic" by the narrator (177). If the war years had made the past seem irretrievably distant for Wharton, they also prompted her to preserve that past—and to meditate on the innate flexibility of the concept of the past itself. In *Walden*, Henry David Thoreau describes "the present moment" as "the meeting of two eternities, the past and the future" (16), a phrase that suggests the steady forward movement of the present: the movement that transforms the future into the present and, a split-second later, the present into the past, making the past—whether a few moments, a few days, or a few years ago—part of a different eternity. In *Old New York*, Wharton quietly illustrates the way in which the present constantly and irretrievably moves from currency and novelty into the quaint, the distant, the archaic, and then the lost—or nearly lost—past.

III. Reconsidering Literature and War: "The Spark"

The novella that most reflects on Wharton's work during the war years is the third in the collection, "The Spark (The 'Sixties)." This story, related by an unnamed younger man, focuses on Hayley Delane, a man several years his senior who, to the narrator, seems both inexplicably dominated by a misbehaving wife and to possess a kind of character that far surpasses the requirements of his polo-playing, dining-out, essentially frivolous life. It is only after the narrator stumbles across the fact that Delane served as a very young man in the Civil War that he begins to make sense of Delane's character. This story has all the hallmarks of *Age* and the other stories in *Old New York*: multiple references to multiple pasts, the sense that the past will be lost if it is not recorded, and the sense that a part of the narrator's job is to interpret that world for readers too young to understand his story without proper guidance. When Mrs. Delane publicly chastises her husband for thrashing her lover, for instance, the narrator, who is standing close by, "could not hear what she said; people did not speak loud in those days, or 'make scenes,' and the two or three words which issued from Mrs. Delane's lips must have been inaudible to everyone but her husband" (187). Similarly, when Mrs. Delane leaves her husband for a number of months, the narrator tells his audience that "Such events were not, in those days, the matters of course they have since become" (217), as if in the decadent 1920s leaving one's husband were a step taken as casually and regularly as a trip to the seaside. And when Mrs. Delane's troublesome father finally relieves her and Hayley Delane by dying, the narrator remarks that her "crape veil was of exactly the right length—a matter of great importance in those days" (220). L. P. Hartley observed in *The Go-Between* that "the past is a foreign country: they do things differently there" (7). It is a sentence Wharton might have used as an epigraph to *Old New York*. As the narrator portrays it, the past is both superior to and inferior to his own time: an era in which domestic difficulties were kept within the domesticity of the home (at least as far as possible); a time in which marriage meant something; but also a time in which something as trivial as the length of a woman's veil was seen as vitally important. In this ambivalence "The Spark," and indeed the other novellas of *Old New York*, reveal the same profound ambivalence about the past as *Age*.

More clearly than *Age*, however, and indeed more clearly than any other work after *A Son at the Front*, "The Spark" suggests Wharton's further reflections on the war. After her difficulty finding a publisher for *Son*, Wharton knew that the American public was tired of "war stories"; "The Spark" cleverly disguises the fact that it is, at a remove, a war story—or rather, a story in which a war is the catalyst for later events. The war in this case is not the Great War, but a war in which Wharton assumed (apparently correctly) that the American public was still interested: its own great war, the Civil War. Although the main action of the story itself is clearly set in the 1890s, the story's designated decade is "The 'Sixties": without Hayley Delane's involvement in the Civil War, his character never would have been transformed in the ways that so fascinate the story's unnamed narrator.

As we have seen, Wharton described war as a great transformer of character, a force that could elevate ordinary men (and even ordinary women, in some instances) into heroic, fully mature individuals. Such is decidedly the case with Hayley Delane as well, who, the narrator learns, ran off as a mere "school boy" to fight in the Civil War. He was wounded at Bull Run and recovered slowly at a hospital near Washington where he was cared for by a man he describes variously as "'that queer fellow in Washington'" (207), "'a sort of big backwoodsman who was awfully good to me when I was in hospital'" (207), and "'an old heathen'" (212)—a man the narrator later identifies as Walt Whitman. Delane's character is shaped by this experience to such an extent that it precludes all later development: the narrator remarks that "People . . . all stopped living at one time or another, however many years longer they continued to be alive; and I suspected that Delane had stopped at about nineteen. That date would roughly coin-

cide with the end of the Civil War, and with his return to the commonplace existence from which he had never since deviated" (199–200). While
Delane has a mind of "monumental simplicity" (186)—a mind some assess
even as "stupid" (188)—he also has the power to act with utter probity
under circumstances others find daunting: he thrashes his wife's lover not
from jealousy but because the man has beaten his polo pony, behavior that
Delane finds inexcusable because of its cruelty; he takes in his wife's scape-
grace father, Bill Gracy, when everyone else—including his wife—advises
him to turn Gracy away, a decision that is eventually justified; in matters
of civic interest he acts not to improve his own social standing, as other
men do, but simply to "'get the business done'" (204). The war—including
both Delane's combat experience and his exposure to "'that queer fellow in
Washington'"—has given him a moral integrity others in his social set
lack.

"The Spark" suggests, however, that Wharton had tempered her claims
about the transformative power of war in the years since 1918. Even *A Son
at the Front*, which generally emphasizes the ennobling power of war, allows that some characters—such as Harvey Mayhew—only reveal their
weaknesses under war's pressure, a possibility for which the rhetoric of a
wartime document like *Fighting France* had made scant allowance. In "The
Spark," Hayley Delane is incontestably improved by the war, but the story
establishes that such is not the case of every soldier who fought. Through
sketches of other characters, Wharton presents a range of possible
"wrong" reactions to the war. Dining with a number of Civil War veterans
one evening, the narrator observes that "Hayley Delane had felt the war,
had been made different by it" (200). But the three other veterans present
"had fought all through the war, had participated in horrors and agonies
untold, endured all manner of hardships and privations . . . ; and it had all
faded like an indigestion comfortably slept off, leaving them perfectly
commonplace and happy" (202). The three other veterans had not "felt" it
as Delane had: one uses "as a preface to almost everything" the phrase
"'When a fellow's been through the war,'" thus rendering the expression
meaningless (201); another exhibits perfect manners to distract people
from his complete wordlessness (201); a third specializes in outmoded descriptions and attitudes toward the war, speaking of "'the blue and the
grey,' the rescue of lovely Southern girls, anecdotes about Old Glory, and
the carrying of vital despatches through the enemy lines" (203). This
man's attitude—like the language of pre–World War I writings—is hope-

lessly romantic and utterly divorced from the realities of "horrors and agonies . . . hardships and privations"—generalizations that Wharton here, as in her World War I writings, avoids describing in any detail.

Hayley Delane, however, is clearly an example of the "real" soldier. He rarely speaks of the war and never speaks of combat; yet the wound he received at Bull Run symbolizes for the narrator (and implicitly for Wharton's reader) his heroic involvement in the "real" war, that is, in combat. Moreover, his character and even his physical presence display a certain transhistorical quality; Wharton felt strongly the appeal of war, perhaps best demonstrated in her description in *Fighting France* about the French army advancing "as smoothly as if in holiday order . . . as if, under the arch of the sunset, we had been watching the whole French army ride straight into glory" (*Fighting France* 139–40). The narrator reflects this fascination. Even before he knows that Delane fought in the Civil War, he feels that Delane "belonged elsewhere, not so much in another society as in another age" (177), an age in which "there might have been outlets for other faculties, now dormant, perhaps even atrophied, but which must . . . have had something to do with the building of that big friendly forehead, the monumental nose, and the rich dimple which now and then furrowed his cheek with light" (178). When the narrator looks at Hayley Delane on his polo pony, heavy as Delane is and trivial as his occupation may be, the narrator "recalled the figure of Guidoriccio da Foligno, the famous mercenary, riding at a slow powerful pace across the fortressed fresco of the Town Hall of Siena" (184). Constantly reminding the narrator "of times and scenes and people greater than he could know" (184), Hayley Delane is an example of what Wharton found redemptive in war: the forging of solid, responsible citizens who not only serve their country heroically but who carry that sense of probity throughout their lives after the war.

Therein, however, is the rub of the story. For, in several complex ways, "The Spark" treats the same issue as "Writing a War Story": the relationship of the true soldier to the literature of war. In "Writing a War Story," as we have seen, Ivy Spang's efforts to write a war story fail. As noncombatants and women, neither she nor her governess can grasp the subject of war nor the treatment of it that had become mandatory. Ivy insists on adding a "love interest" while her governess rewrites the story in "language appropriate to the Battle of Hastings"—efforts to turn the material of war into old-fashioned, indeed obsolete, "Literature." The soldiers want only Ivy's photo—they want her to be an object, not an author—and the acclaimed author Harold Harbard finds even her distress over his merci-

less criticism of her story both surprising and amusing, ending by reminding her of her place as object, not subject, in the literary firmament: "You
were angry just now because I didn't admire your story; and now you're
angrier still because I do admire your photograph. Do you wonder that we
novelists find such an inexhaustible field in Woman?" (370). Wharton
elicits sympathy for Ivy, but also criticizes her: from everything we are
told about her story, it is not only contrary to the rapidly-jelling "rules"
for writing about the Great War, but unworthy in itself: a pastiche of cliché
and plagiarism. As a woman whose greatest contact with the war has been
pouring tea for not-too-badly wounded soldiers in a suburban hospital,
Ivy Spang is excluded from the real world of war—and, consequently,
from valid writing about the war. As combatants, those who have had the
real experience of the war, the soldiers in her ward—from the least important to the great novelist—have the authority to judge what does and does
not count as authentic writing about the war.

In "The Spark" Wharton returned to the issues of soldiers and the literature of war, but in this story the implications about the relationship
between the two are grimmer. "Writing a War Story" is about gender,
demonstrating the inability of women to write the real literature of war as
well as the ability of male combatants to identify intuitively what qualifies
as valid war-writing. "The Spark" acknowledges, even admires, the existence of real soldiers; it acknowledges the existence of valid war-literature;
but it suggests the disturbing possibility that there may be no genuine
communion between real soldiers and real war writing, valid as each may
be. Wharton removes the variable of gender in this story. While Mrs.
Delane is an important figure, she is not part of the all-masculine triangle
central to the story: Hayley Delane, Walt Whitman, and the narrator.
Similarly, there can be no questioning the authenticity of the other characters involved. As we have seen above, Hayley Delane occupies the position
of the real soldier, of the man whose life has been shaped by war and by the
fellow he met in the war, "Old Walt" (226). Similarly, Whitman's experience as a nurse in the war has generally been accepted as valid war experience, that is, experience sufficient to qualify his poetry as the authentic
poetry of war.

When the narrator reads Whitman's poetry to Delane, however, telling
him reassuringly (and a little condescendingly) that Whitman wrote
"'Things for you'" (223), Delane is not impressed. His face is "painfully
attentive" (223), but as the narrator continues through a number of poems
"His face was still a blank" (225); "No spark had been struck from him"

(224). The narrator persists, sure that he will read a poem that will strike the spark of communion between the true soldier and the true poet of the war. But this never happens. Delane, whose literary taste was, like his character, formed early in his life, and who still idolizes Edward Gibbon in prose and Thomas Gray in poetry, cannot even identify the genre of Whitman's work. The story itself—much like "Writing a War Story"—ends with a magnificent anticlimax:

> [O]n the threshold he paused to ask: "What was his name, by the way?"
> When I told him he repeated it with a smile of slow relish. "Yes; that's it. Old Walt—that was what all the fellows used to call him. He was a great chap: I'll never forget him.—I rather wish, though," he added, in his mildest tone of reproach, "you hadn't told me that he wrote all that rubbish." (226)

In "Coming Home," the opening narrator expresses the opinion that some of Macy Greer's war stories "are dark and dreadful, some are unutterably sad, and some end in a huge laugh of irony. I am not sure how I ought to classify the one I have written down here" (230). The war destabilized genre for Wharton, and a reader of "The Spark" has exactly the problem articulated by the narrator of "Coming Home": is this a comic story? a sad one? an ironic tale? The narrator of "The Spark" expresses similar misgivings about the genre of his own story:

> This is not a story-teller's story; it is not even the kind of episode capable of being shaped into one. . . .
> It is not a story, or anything in the semblance of a story. (193)

The one thing the narrator asserts is that it is a character study, "an attempt to depict for you . . . the aspect and character of a man whom I loved, perplexedly but faithfully, for many years" (193). To a reader of Wharton's war-related writings, however, another thing is clear: this is also a story about the relationship, or rather the startling lack of relationship, between a true soldier and the true literature of the war. At the end of "Writing a War Story," the reader has at least the consolation of assuming that soldiers can judge whether literature really captures war; "The Spark" progresses on the same assumption—only to undermine it in its final pages. Having just achieved a significant insight—that the key to the character of Hayley Delane is the influence of Walt Whitman—the reader, like the narrator, has it snatched away again (or at least considerably reduced in value) by Delane's reaction to Whitman's poetry. Delane's lack of interest, his confusion, his "mildest tone of reproach," all suggest that he, too, has been let down: the man he idolized for so many years, the man on whose principles he modeled his own moral behavior, is, from his perspective, only a third-rate poet. Like Ivy Spang and Charlie Durand, the reader, the narrator of "The Spark," and Hayley Delane himself have their moments of revelation spoiled by belittlement.

IV. War as Backdrop: *The Mother's Recompense*

A Son at the Front was Wharton's final work set in the war years; in "The Spark" she had found that she could handle war-related themes by transferring the questions raised by the Great War in Europe to the Civil War in the United States. With *The Mother's Recompense,* published in 1925, she employed another new strategy for incorporating the war and its influences—or, more precisely, its aftermath—into her fiction. Wharton set *The Mother's Recompense* in the postwar period in southern France and New York; her main character, Kate Clephane, lived in France during the war years. While this novel both mentions the war and echoes the themes of several wartime works, in it Wharton de-emphasizes the war, using it as a historical backdrop. Yet the importance of the war as backdrop should not be overlooked: as she presents it in *Recompense,* the Great War shapes the novel's central characters and their lives both during and after the war. Further, Wharton's use of the war in the novel—and particularly her portrait of the war's influence on its central characters—suggests that Wharton's stance toward the war, slightly moderated in *Son* and further in "The Spark," had shifted yet further by the time she wrote *Recompense.*

The *Mother's Recompense* shows Wharton merging her wartime concerns with the usual focus of her work, social and psychological concerns. Most criticism of this novel has focused on the novel's social and psychological aspects, and in particular on the quasi-incestuous triangle at its heart:[10] Kate Clephane returns to New York about 1919, rejoined at last to the daughter lost to her years earlier when she left her husband with another man; her attempts to visit, and even to communicate with, her toddler Anne were repeatedly blocked by her mother-in-law. After a joyous reunion with Anne, now about twenty, Kate finds that her daughter has fallen in love with a man named Chris Fenno—a man who was Kate's own lover in France for two or three years, ending in 1916. Kate tries repeatedly to break off the match, but fails because she fears that revealing her own liaison with Chris to Anne would cause her daughter to break off their renewed relationship. Anne and Chris marry; Kate considers the marriage offer of an old friend, Fred Landers, who persists in his desire to marry her even when she finally tells him about her affair with Chris. In the end, however, she prefers to return to France with only her maid. Because Kate is a sympathetic figure, most critics have taken a kind view of her situation, coming down accordingly hard on Chris. Reading *The Mother's Recompense* in the context of Wharton's war writings, however, complicates our understanding of both Kate and Chris.

After Wharton's difficulty placing *A Son at the Front* and with her awareness of readers' concerns about whether "the adventures related in this book happen[ed] before the war" or "since" (*Letters* 425), Wharton adopted different techniques for handling war-related material in *The Mother's Recompense*. *Son*, despite its insistently home-front setting, was clearly a novel about the war years; *Recompense*, despite its references to the war, is decidedly a novel about society. Wharton had taught herself to allude to the war without dwelling on it, allowing her readers to focus on the social aspects of the novel.[11] The novel's opening pages, for instance, deftly but clearly establish the novel as "since" the war: Kate Clephane justifies her choice of a "cheap hotel" on the Riviera by reflecting that "One couldn't afford everything, especially since the war" (5–6). Similarly, on the verge of opening a telegram that she hopes is from Chris Fenno, she is aware that "Since Armistice Day her heart had not beat so hard" (10).

Wharton also calls up home-front scenes of the war in ways reminiscent of earlier war-related works. But in each case, the description is briefer, more compressed, and generally less vitriolic than in earlier works; the critic who had called *A Son at the Front* "a belated essay in propaganda" (Tuttleton et al. 344) would probably have been pleased by these changes. In "The Refugees" and *Son*, Wharton had targeted those who saw in the war only the newest form of social competition; the same concern emerges briefly in *Recompense* as Kate Clephane plans to attend "a Ladies' Guild meeting about the Devastated Regions' Fancy Fair" (12) and in her awareness of others' social obsession with questions like "whether it would 'do' to ask Mrs. Schlachtburger to take a stall at the Fair in spite of her unfortunate name" (12). The members of the Ladies' Guild are very concerned about Mrs. Schlachtburger's conspicuously German name, but wholly unaware of the ironic juxtaposition of "Devastated Regions" and "Fancy Fair" in the name of their own event. Through Kate, who remains slightly aloof from her own social circle, Wharton ridicules other minor characters who seem to have stepped out of the pages of *Son* and into this novel, such as "the Consul's sister, who dressed like a flapper, and had been engaged during the war to a series of American officers, all of whom seemed to have given her celluloid bangles; . . . [and] Mrs. Fred Langly of Albany, whose husband was 'wanted' at home for misappropriation of funds, and who . . . had now blossomed into a 'prominent war worker,' while Mr. Langly devoted himself to the composition of patriotic poems, which he read (flanked by the civil and military authorities) at all the allied Inaugurations and Commemorations; so that by the close of the war he had become its recognized bard, and his 'Lafayette, can we forget?' was quoted with tears by the very widows and orphans he had defrauded" (22).

Wharton's satire here is relatively brief and mild; neither the sister nor the Langlys come in for extended parody. As in *The Marne*, however, Wharton saves a few bitter barbs for Americans who deny the war entirely, or who see it simply as an unjustified expense. Mr. Langly may, as the title of his poem implies, write bad patriotic poetry; the widows and orphans he has defrauded may be fools for being swayed by his conveniently patriotic fervor. But they are not as bad as the ironically named Betterlys. Mrs. Betterly refuses the "retrospective piety about the war" embraced by the others in Kate's social set, instead remarking loudly "'Oh, the *war*? *What war*? Is there another one on? What, that old one? Why I thought *that* one was over long ago . . . You can't get anybody I know to talk about it even!'" (26) Her equally obtuse husband chimes in with "'Guess we've got our work cut out paying for it'" as he "stretch[es] a begemmed and bloated hand toward the wine-list" (26). Such characters seem lifted straight from the pages of *The Marne*, in which Mrs. Belknap tells her dinner guests about "the tragedy" of the war while "looking down her long dinner table between the orchids and the candelabra" (34), or from the draft of an unfinished story in which prominent American businessmen discuss the relationship between war and profit over wine and roses, endorsing the government's decision not to enter the war.[12] Wharton still retained some bitterness about the war and about the United States' belated and sometimes begrudging involvement, but minimized her expression of that bitterness in the pages of *The Mother's Recompense*.

Overall, then, the tone of even the satirical passages is milder in *The*

Mother's Recompense than in its predecessors, and in general Wharton's attitude toward the frivolous people she satirized so harshly during the war years and in *A Son at the Front* had moderated. Her treatment of Kate Clephane illustrates this tendency. Kate is precisely the sort of woman Wharton scorned repeatedly in both stories and letters. Kate's status as one of the "fluffy fuzzy people" is indicated by her inability to calculate her own age, her daughter's age, or the current age of her former lover—an inability created by her unwillingness to acknowledge that she is forty-five (9). It is confirmed by her pointless wandering through the day, with its schedule of trying on hats and dresses, mollifying people she despises, and dining with "dull noisy" people (12). But what we might expect to be most damning from Wharton's perspective—the perspective of the avid supporter of the war effort and administrator of many war charities—is that Kate sees the war almost wholly as an event that has affected her personal life. In fact, her personal life remained her paramount concern even *during* the war years, as the following description implies: "She had her 'set' now in the big Riviera town where she had taken refuge in 1916, after the final break with Chris, and where, after two years of war-work and a 'Reconnaissance Française' medal, she could carry her head fairly high, and even condescend a little to certain newcomers" (12). For Kate Clephane, 1916 is not a war-related date, but rather a personal date, that of "the final break with Chris"(12). When readers are told that the arrival of a telegram—a telegram Kate hopes is from Chris—makes her heart beat as fast as on Armistice Day, they have the key to Kate. The end of the war was deeply exciting for her—but no more so than the thought that she might be reunited with her regretted lover. Similarly, Kate's war work seems not the result of benevolent impulses, but of her wish to achieve social rehabilitation. Even her "Reconnaissance Française" may have stood—at least for Wharton privately—as a mark of Kate's frivolity: as we have seen, Wharton had complained that this award was being "showered on ladies who have poured tea at Paris hospitals, or begun their war-work in 1918— but every appeal is vain to obtain recognition of the faithful workers who have toiled with me in Paris & America since Sept. 1914" (4 May 1920, *Wharton Collection* Yale). One of the main functions of the war in Kate's life is that it served admirably as a cover-up: the final months of her affair with Chris, "the most reckless and fervid, had been overshadowed, blotted out of everybody's sight," in the "universal eclipse" of the war (43). In Kate's solipsistic universe "the war had begun only when Chris left her" (43).

Surprisingly, however, given Wharton's general disdain for the kind of woman she portrays in Kate, her presentation of Kate is deeply sympathetic. If in some ways Kate is frivolous, she is also the self-aware, socially sensitive center of consciousness through whom Wharton tells her story. Further, Kate extends into the twenties the portraits of women trapped by marriage and its constraints in earlier works like "Souls Belated." Lydia, the main character in that 1899 story, gradually comes to realize that marriage is such a powerful social force that she must marry Gannett, her lover, in order to have any social life at all; while she despises the social codes of that world, she is unable to exist without it. Kate Clephane, after leaving her marriage in much the same way and for much the same reason as Lydia, marries neither the man who escorted her out of her marriage nor the man who, a number of years later, became both her lover and her one true love; but it takes a war to complete her social rehabilitation. Far from satirizing Kate for using the war as an instrument to help herself, Wharton seems simply to accept in this novel that the war, for many, did serve an important social function. That function becomes the backdrop against which the novel is played out, an essential part of the world through which her main character moves: "Then the war came; the war which, in those bland southern places and to those uprooted drifting women, was chiefly a healing and amalgamating influence. It was awful, of course, to admit even to one's self that it could be that; but, in light of her own deliverance, Kate Clephane knew that she and all the others had so viewed it" (24). Wharton, like Kate, seems to have accepted that although the war was a terrible episode, it would be foolish to deny—however "awful" the admission might be—that the war had some positive effects. It is as if Wharton had taken to heart her narrator's intrusive comment in *The Marne* that expatriates upset by the war were, at heart, "all good and kindly persons" (18)—or, failing that, at least not the demons she had sometimes represented them as being in earlier works. The social dimensions of the home front were simply another interesting and valid topic for the writer's pen, one of the "great slow fruit" to come out of the "world-upheaval" of the war (17 April 1916, *Wharton Collection* Yale).

In this context, Chris Fenno, like Kate, becomes a more complex character than he is usually perceived as being. A short summary of the novel's plot initially suggests he is a villain, almost in the melodramatic sense: he is the lover who wakes Kate to her true self only to leave her suddenly and, soon after, to woo her daughter. But Chris appears less villainous when examined through the lens of Wharton's war writing. Given Wharton's oft-repeated admiration for soldiers in *Fighting France* (and for American soldiers in particular in a number of her letters, as well as the poem "You and You"), and given her insistence in works like *Fighting France, The Marne*, and *A Son at the Front* that war could transform and ennoble character, it is possible that Wharton intended Chris Fenno—now Major Fenno—to be seen as a changed man, one who would make an admirable husband for Anne, regardless of his failings before the war.

Several details in *The Mother's Recompense* suggest that this might be the case. The contrast between Kate's superficial experience of the war and Chris's deep involvement reiterates the contrast Wharton had drawn in works like *The Marne* and *A Son at the Front* between women's inauthentic participation in the war and men's participation in the real war for which Wharton to some extent yearned. Kate sees the war almost wholly in personal terms and is only one of a number of women who "were creeping slowly back into the once impregnable stronghold of Social Position" (24) while men like Chris were fighting. In the war's earlier months, Chris and Kate, much like the more frivolous Americans portrayed in *A Son at the Front*, traveled and amused themselves, rationalizing their noninvolvement in the war: "Around them they found only the like-minded; the cheerful, who refused to be 'worried,' or the argumentative and paradoxical, like Chris himself, who thought it their duty as 'artists' or 'thinkers' to ignore the barbarian commotion" (43). But Chris eventually experiences an enlightenment much like that of George Campton: "It was only in 1915, when Chris's own attitude was mysteriously altered, and she found him muttering that after all a fellow couldn't stand aside when all his friends and the chaps of his own age were getting killed—only then did the artificial defences fall, and the reality stream in on her. Was his change of mind genuine? He often said that his opinions hadn't altered, but that there were times when opinions didn't count . . . when a fellow just had to *act*" (43). Chris's decision to "*act*" suggests not just his commitment to the war effort, but his incipient transformation from dilettante playboy to serious adult. His decision to enlist causes Kate to come into closer contact with "the reality" of the war. Further, his act gratifies Kate exactly as George Campton's decision to move away from a safe desk job gratifies his father: Chris's decision to enlist "was [Kate's] own secret thought" (43). Yet more significantly, once he has enlisted, Chris distinguishes himself. Kate learns from Anne that Chris was wounded "'[a]t Belleau Wood . . . He has the Legion of Honour and the D.S.M.[,]'" the Distinguished Service Medal (103).

Chris's medals of honor and his exceptional service at Belleau Wood, a crucial battle in which Americans played a central role,[13] speak for his admirable performance in the war—and for his probable transformation through the vehicle of the war. Nollie Tresselton, a level-headed friend of Anne, tells Kate reassuringly that "'the war transformed him; made a man of him'" (116). When Chris was Kate's lover he was an aspiring painter; after the war he is an aspiring writer. This might argue his fundamental dilettantishness, but Nollie suggests that the change is genuine. "'[N]ow he believes he's really found his vocation'" (116–17) she tells Kate at one point, and at another reiterates, "'He's "made good," you see. It's not only his war record, but everything since. He's worked so hard—done so well at his various jobs—and Anne's sure that if he had the chance he would make himself a name in the literary world'" (170). From Wharton's portraits of characters like George Campton and Adele Anthony in *A Son at the Front*, and from her words of praise for transformed soldiers in *Fighting France*, judging even by an improved Hinda Warlick in *The Marne*, everything would seem to suggest that Chris Fenno, Legion d'Honneur, D.S.M., is an ennobled man—and, whatever his past faults, he may make a respectful son-in-law for Kate and an admirable husband for Anne. The war allowed Kate to put her past behind her; in all fairness, readers should allow it to do the same for Chris.

Wharton's moderated stance toward Kate herself, her acceptance of someone she would earlier have categorized as a "fluffy fuzzy" person, may also suggest, however, that her belief in the war as a great transformer of character had also moderated. If Kate, despite her frivolity, is sympathetic, so Chris may not be automatically admirable simply because of his service, however distinguished, in the war. If Chris's war wound and honors, like his spontaneous decision to fight in the war itself, speak in his favor, other elements are less encouraging. Like the true soldier, Chris "'never talks of'" the war or his honors (104); but he is not without self-praise. When Nollie reassures Kate that the war "'transformed'" Chris and "'made a man of him[,]'" she adds, "'he says so himself'" (116). And Nollie's reassurance that Anne thinks Chris can "'make himself a name in the literary world'" is hardly objective evidence of a profound change of character: Chris's record of "various jobs" since the war—even if he has done well at them—may indicate that he is the same charming, dilettantish drifter he was when Kate knew him before the war. Further, Wharton's portraits of Civil War veterans in "The Spark" indicate that she had ceased to think that all soldiers were necessarily transformed by their war experience; Hayley Delane may have been, but the other veterans described have not "felt the war" as Delane did; they have merely gone through great events "unaware" (200).

In the end, it is impossible for readers to judge Chris conclusively. The story, told entirely from Kate's perspective, does not give us multiple angles from which to judge Chris. Wharton's sense of ambiguity, always profound and perhaps made even deeper by the war, leaves Chris a cipher. Chris is a war hero; Chris is a man who marries the daughter of his former lover. Kate is allowed to achieve social rehabilitation through her war efforts, a superficial but personally important transformation of her reputation. Might Chris have achieved a deeper transformation of his entire character through his far deeper involvement in the war? Wharton ends the novel shortly after the wedding of Chris and Anne; readers are not able to judge Chris's transformation (or lack thereof) by any information about his behavior after this time. Kate, however, has regained her poise and her social adroitness: having refused Fred Landers's offer of marriage, she is now spending considerable time with an English lord and enjoying the increased social prestige that results from having a "beautiful daughter married to a War Hero" (263).

The Mother's Recompense, like "The Spark," suggests that Wharton was reevaluating her wartime assessments of various kinds of people. So, too, she continued her analysis of the changes in prewar and postwar mores. In both *The Age of Innocence* and *Old New York* Wharton revealed profound ambivalence toward both the new and the old orders, suggesting optimistically in *Age* that "There was good in the old ways" (347) and "good in the new order too" (349). Wharton revisits this statement less optimistically in *Recompense*. With regard to the new, less demanding routine surrounding Anne's engagement, Kate reflects that "All this fitted in with the new times. The old days of introspections and explanations were over; the era of taking things for granted was the only one that Anne's generation knew" (206). This statement echoes pessimistically Dallas Archer's observation to his father that "'I back your generation for knowing more about each other's private thoughts than we ever have time to find out about our own'" (*Age* 356). The age of introspection was over; the age of taking-for-granted and rushing had arrived.

Of course the "old" and the "new" eras in *Age* and *Recompense* are not the same: in *Age* the "old" is the 1870s and the "new" is the decade of 1900–1910. In *Recompense* the "old" is the era right around 1900 and the "new" occurs about 1920—in short, the "old" is prewar and the "new" is postwar. Notably, the golden age implied at the end of *Age*—even if it is a golden age on which the sun is already setting—is less than a decade later than the period in which Kate Clephane met and married her husband and entered the marriage that she found so stultifying. Yet in *Recompense* Kate comes to prefer the era of older mores, despite their harshness, simply because that period did have standards—something she sees lacking in her daughter's generation, which can condone the moral, sexual, and personal laxities of a character like Lilla Gates, whose friends and family repeatedly cover up her indiscretions. Kate's preference for the old mores reflects Wharton's own growing preference for the stricter moral order that preceded the war, as well as her growing distaste for the social and moral climate of the 1920s—a climate she would further criticize in *Twilight Sleep* (1927) and *The Children* (1928). Kate's decision to decline marriage to Fred Landers and live on her own on the Riviera imitates Newland Archer's decision not to renew his acquaintance with Ellen Olenska. But while Newland's decision is left profoundly ambivalent in *Age*, in *The Mother's Recompense* Wharton leaves no doubt that readers are meant to admire Kate's choice:

> And this afternoon, when she returned home and found [Fred Landers's] weekly letter . . . she would bless him again, bless him both for writing the letter, and for giving her the strength to hold out against its pleadings.
> Perhaps no one else would ever understand; assuredly he would never understand himself. But there it was. Nothing on earth would ever again help her—help to blot out the old horrors and the new loneliness—as much as the fact of being able to take her stand on that resolve, of being able to say to herself, whenever she began to drift toward new uncertainties and fresh concessions, that once at least she had stood fast, shutting away in a little space of peace and light the best thing that had ever happened to her. (272)

The last phrase refers to Fred Landers's acceptance of her confession about her affair with Chris, not only for itself but for the glaring light that confession turned on her reaction to the engagement between Chris and Anne. Fred had not only accepted that confession but sympathized with Kate, grasping that the experience of the engagement had put her "'through hell'" (257). This conversation had left Kate exhausted but relieved, so that "It seemed to her that for the first time in her life she had been picked up out of the dust and weariness, and set down in a quiet place where no harm could come" (259). Yet, like Newland Archer acknowledging his "old-fashioned" marriage to May by choosing not to renew his acquaintance with Ellen Olenska, Kate Clephane chooses to place this near-perfect moment with Fred Landers in semisacred isolation. The marriages and remarriages of her daughter and her daughters' friends had not been matches Kate either understood or condoned; her own decision not to remarry implies the value she places on an older order, harsh as that order's standards might sometimes be. In this lies her connection to Wharton. Insubstantial as Kate's role in the war may have been, Kate values what Wharton, after the war, increasingly valued: a certain stability and continuity that had become increasingly rare in the postwar years.

The Mother's Recompense, published only two years after A Son at the Front, has strong thematic ties to the earlier novel. Most important, both are novels about parents who have of their own volition separated themselves from their children when their children were still quite young; both Kate Clephane and John Campton return when their children have reached adulthood, and expect—or at least hope for—a kind of ideal companion in their adult child. And in both cases the perfect companionship, while it seems possible for a short while, falters. In John Campton's case it is because his son George dies in the war, though his own possessiveness of his son also interferes with his ability to see his son as a separate person. In Kate Clephane's it is because her brief, perfect companionship with her daughter Anne is interrupted by Anne's plans to marry a man who happens to be Kate's own former lover; but even before Kate knows of Anne's engagement, she dreads the time when, almost inevitably, her daughter would turn her central loyalty from her mother to a husband. During the war years, Summer and The Marne formed a pair of coming-of-age stories, each based on traditional beliefs about women and men: Charity Royall comes to adulthood through a difficult encounter with love, sex, pregnancy, and marriage, while Troy Belknap achieves adulthood through his experience, however brief, on the battlefield. A Son at the Front and The Mother's Recompense form a similar gender-related diptych: war pulls George away from his father, while love pulls Anne away from her mother.

Further, both Son and Recompense reveal Wharton's deepened understanding of love and loss, understanding that came during the war years through both direct and vicarious experiences. As Shari Benstock has written, "The lessons 1918 held for Edith concerned parents and children—a mother watching her daughter's slow death; a father searching for his missing son; a woman nearing sixty who had never had a child but who, in her grief for her young cousin and for the pathetic Simmons, came to know something of the special sorrow reserved for those who are asked to bury their children" (342–43). During the war years, Wharton had assumed legal responsibility for four boys whose mother had deserted them and whose father seemed incapable of providing for them; the death of one in 1921 deepened her sense of what it must be to lose a child (Benstock 343, 374). The losses caused by the war—the deaths of Ronald Simmons and Newbold Rhinelander among others—and those that occurred during and after the war years seem also to have made Wharton wonder what a comfort it might be to have had a child herself. Her work in both *A Son at the Front* and *The Mother's Recompense* reflects that longing and suggests that, at a deep level, Wharton feared that finding such a child—or, in her case, a substitute child—was impossible. The experiences of John Campton and Kate Clephane imply that any parent who suddenly finds an adult child who is also a perfect companion is fated to lose that child—both to jealousy and to distance, whether the distance of death, as with George Campton, or geographical and emotional distance. At the end of *The Mother's Recompense*, Anne is married to Chris, of all men the one who will most surely act as a barrier between Kate and her daughter. This psychological distance is symbolized by geographic distance: Anne is "halfway across the Red Sea, on her way to India, and there would be no news of her for several weeks to come" (264). The perfect companionship of the aging and lonely parent and the adult child, in this work as in *Son*, is temporary at best, a joyous anomaly that cannot become a permanent state.

V. Echoes of the War: Four Late Stories

The Mother's Recompense is the last novel in which Wharton used the war as a significant backdrop; in her writing as in her life, the war had begun to recede into the background. Nevertheless, war-related issues haunt a number of postwar works. For instance, the narrator of Wharton's 1927 novel *Twilight Sleep* comments on the difference between the prewar and the postwar generations, noting that two central characters, Nona Manford and Lita Wyant, "belonged to another generation: to the bewildered disenchanted young people who had grown up since the Great War, whose energies were more spasmodic and less definitely directed, and who, above all, wanted a more personal outlet for them" (6–7). Later in the same novel

Wharton's choice of metaphor is decidedly influenced by her trips to the front lines in France. Nona Manford, the single level-headed member of a complex family, is described as feeling

> more and more like one of the trench-watchers pictured in the wartime papers. There she sat in the darkness on her narrow perch, her eyes glued to the observation-slit which looked out over seeming emptiness. She had often wondered what those men thought about during the endless hours of watching, the days and weeks when nothing happened, when no faintest shadow of a skulking enemy crossed their span of no-man's land. What kept them from falling asleep, or from losing themselves in waking dreams, and failing to give warning when the attack impended? She could imagine a man led out to be shot in the Flanders mud because, at such a moment, he had believed himself to be dozing on a daisy bank at home... (280–81)

The length and detail of this passage suggest the powerful influence of Wharton's visits to the front as well as her sympathy for the soldiers who had been given a job that required extraordinary vigilance despite great tedium. The war informed a number of Wharton's postwar stories as well. "Miss Mary Pask" (1925), like "Elegy," blurs the line between the living and the dead, with the narrator recounting an evening in Brittany on which he met what he believed was the ghost of an old acquaintance—only to find later that she was, in fact, still alive. "'There's a shady corner down at the bottom [of the garden] where the sun never bothers one. Sometimes I sleep there till the stars come out'" (380), Miss Mary Pask tells the narrator; understandably, he interprets her words as the description of a peaceful grave, reflecting Wharton's concern over the burial sites of Newbold Rhinelander and Ronald Simmons. The haunting sense of the instability of the real and the unreal emerges in a number of stories, including "The Day of the Funeral" and "Joy in the House," while many characters—for instance, John Kilvert in "A Glimpse," Christine Ansley in "Joy in the House," and Paul Dorrance in "Diagnosis"—are haunted by the fear of missing out on real life or their real selves. In four postwar stories, however, Wharton refers to the war years explicitly. As she had in *The Mother's Recompense*, she employs the war years as a background for the central action.

"Velvet Ear Pads" (1925) describes the unsought adventures of Professor Loring G. Hibbart, who, much against his own best intentions, becomes involved with a beautiful young woman who describes herself as a Russian refugee—an involvement triggered by his donation of a copy of his book, *The Elimination of Phenomena*, to a Y.M.C.A. refugee center during the war. Hibbart is much like Charlie Durand in "The Refugees": he is unaccustomed to what he thinks of as "exciting situations"; he suffers a moment of sexual panic when he suspects that the "refugee" may be propositioning him; and soon after this misperceived proposition, he concludes that she must be a lunatic (479). Yet he is also the antithesis of Charlie Durand: Durand hoped for adventure, while Hibbart does all he can to avoid it. Wharton also allowed herself an outlet for one of her wartime irritations in this story. In a 1916 letter to Minnie Jones, she had complained of donors who asked for official acknowledgment: "Then the demand of Miss Robinson Smith for official recognition by the War Office gave me a good deal of trouble & involved great fatigue. People in America don't seem to understand that at the most critical period of a terrible war it is hard to get the attention of the War Office for any matter outside the real business of the nation" (*Letters* 366). A situation of this sort triggers the refugee's involvement with Professor Hibbart: a note in the book he donated states that "'A word of appreciation'" for the donation of the book "'sent by any reader to the above address, would greatly gratify Loring G. Hibbart'" (477).

Though the well-dressed refugee is sincere in her remarks, her comments on this note continue Wharton's parody of American self-absorption: "'Almost all the things sent from America to the refugee camp came with little labels like that. You all seemed to think we were sitting before perfectly appointed desks, with fountain pens and stamp cases from Bond Street in our pockets. I remember once getting a lipstick and a Bernard Shaw calendar labeled: "If the refugee who receives these would write a line of thanks to little Sadie Burt of Meropee Junction, Ga., who bought them out of her own savings by giving up chewing gum for a whole month, it would make a little American girl very happy"'" (477–78). In this parodic passage, Wharton allowed herself to express her long-standing irritation with many Americans' failure to understand the conditions of war. And yet this situation has an aspect of the irony frequently used by Wharton: Hibbart himself is not at fault—someone else had written that catalytic sentence into a copy of his book. But it is he who pays the price.

Parody and sincerity are intermixed in this tale, and the demarcations between them are often hard to detect—somewhat like the blurred definition between the living and the dead in "Miss Mary Pask." The refugee explains to Professor Hibbart that, in spite of her frustration with Americans' need for acknowledgment, she really had wanted to thank him for his book. When she read it, she tells him, "'I had quite discarded philosophy. I was living in the Actual—with a young officer of Preobrajensky—when the war broke out. And of course in our camp at Odessa the Actual was the very thing one wanted to get away from'" (478). While she is an entertaining figure, the refugee is also an object of satire: a woman who received her Ph.D. in philosophy at the age of sixteen, who "'gave up philosophy the year after for sculpture; the next year I gave up sculpture for mathematics and love. For a year I loved. After that I married Prince Balalatinsky'" (477). Like the Princess Buondelmonte in *The Children*, the refugee is a character Wharton develops, in part, to mock higher education for women. The young woman further confirms the reader's sense of her intellectual ineptness when she tells Professor Hibbart that his book led to her "'two first Eliminations'"—namely, "'giv[ing] up my lover and divorc[ing] my husband'" (477). From the little we know of Hibbart, it seems likely that his book, *The Elimination of Phenomena*, is a work of scientific philosophy; she seems rather to have taken the "phenomena" of its title to refer to the men in her life. Yet there is poignancy in her remark about the need for refugees to avoid "the Actual." It was, after all, just such an escape from reality Wharton found in the creation of *Summer* and just such a refuge which that novel created for Joseph Conrad. The refugee is simultaneously an outlet for Wharton's frustration, a target of her satire, and a reminder of the difficult conditions under which civilians displaced by war lived.

The "Russian refugee" of "Velvet Ear Pads" may or may not be a refugee, a princess, a shop assistant, a con artist, or some combination of these; the reader, like Professor Hibbart, is never really sure. What is clear, however, is that she is part of the group Wharton would nickname "wardrift" in her 1934 story "Charm Incorporated," one of the many whom the war had cast adrift—and, conceivably, one of those people who may have taken advantage of others' sympathies for their own personal profit. Similar characters are portrayed in "Her Son" (1932). While the story's central figure, Mrs. Stephen Glenn, never knows that she is the victim of an elaborate scheme, both the reader and the story's narrator, Mr. Norcutt, gradually realize the situation: three con artists are exploiting a mother's grief to support themselves for years on her income. In her 1915 letter to Charles Scribner, Wharton had written that "So many extraordinary and dramatic situations are springing out of the huge conflict that the temptation to use a few of them is irresistible" (*Letters* 357). More than fifteen years later, Wharton was still finding "dramatic situations . . . springing out of the huge conflict" and its aftermath. Not only does "Her Son" focus on "war-drift": the catalyst for its action is the death of Mrs. Glenn's son in the Great War. While the story's primary interest is psychological—Wharton had returned to one of her great subjects—it takes the war as its starting-point. A decade and a half after the war, Wharton had added it to the reper-toire of subjects, the range of history, which she could employ in her work.

Philip Glenn, the son of Mr. and Mrs. Stephen Glenn, dies in aerial com-bat in World War I, "the first American aviator to fall" (623). Mr. Glenn dies not long after; Mrs. Glenn becomes consumed by the drive to locate a son she and Mr. Glenn had had before their marriage, whom she had borne in secret and immediately given up for adoption. After searching Europe, she finally locates her lost son—or believes she has. The young man is in poor health; the man and woman who claim to be his adoptive parents, Mr. and Mrs. Brown, rarely leave his side. Mrs. Glenn joyously acknowledges "her son," but also feels gratitude to the boy's putative parents, particu-larly his mother—despite Chrissy Brown's irritating and possessive be-havior. Wharton pursues the premise of this story to its logical, if pathetic, conclusion: "Stephen," the supposed son, finally reveals to Mr. Norcutt, the friend of Mrs. Glenn who narrates the story, that he is not Mrs. Glenn's son, but only one member of a trio of con artists. Norcutt makes Stephen promise not to tell Mrs. Glenn the truth because he believes that the truth will destroy her fragile peace of mind. Stephen eventually dies; but Mrs. Glenn, rather than shaking off the irritating Mrs. Brown, continues to live with and support her and her husband. After a number of years pass, Mr. Norcutt relocates Mrs. Glenn and the Browns, only to find all three of them living together in relative poverty: the Browns have managed to run through Mrs. Glenn's entire income, though they insist on believing that she must be hiding money somewhere. In bitterness, Mrs. Brown insists on confronting Mrs. Glenn with the truth: she was not Stephen's adoptive mother but his lover. But this crushing news comes too late. Mrs. Glenn's precarious mental health will not allow her to grasp this revelation, and she returns with a social barb about Mrs. Brown's crooked hat.

The story, which appeared in the appropriately entitled volume *Human Nature*, is a complex study in human psychology; further, it has strong links to a number of works Wharton had written since the war. The compe-tition between mothers—Mrs. Glenn and Mrs. Brown—is strongly remi-niscent of the conflict between fathers in *A Son at the Front*. The story also reiterates a motive from "New Year's Day," the final novella in *Old New York*. When Mrs. Brown finally confronts Mrs. Glenn with the news that she was Stephen's lover, she justifies her actions by explaining that "'he was desperately ill, and down and out, and we hadn't a penny, the three of us, and I had to have money for him, and didn't care how I got it, didn't care for anything on earth but seeing him well again, and happy'" (668). This avowal parallels Mrs. Hazeldean's explanation in "New Year's Day" for her years-long affair with Henry Prest: the money he gave her allowed her to support her much-loved husband through his years of illness in a comfort the couple could never have otherwise afforded. Similarly, Mrs. Glenn's heartache over Stephen's loss is reminiscent of Charlotte's loss of relationship with her daughter in "The Old Maid": both women suffer for their very success in giving up their infants.

The main interest of "Her Son" may be psychological, but the story nevertheless has a number of significant references to the war. As in *The Mother's Recompense,* "The Refugees," and portions of *A Son at the Front,* the social scene of "Her Son" is strongly influenced by the Great War. The Glenns, for instance, who had come "to be regarded as wooden, pompous and slightly absurd[,]" become socially "interesting" again only after Philip's death (623). People see them differently, assuming simply because of the son's death that behind the Glenns' cool facades "were a passionate father and mother, crushed, rebellious, agonizing, but determined to face their loss dauntlessly, though they should die of it" (623). Wharton's irony is at work here. As she showed in *The Mother's Recompense,* social prestige was conferred not only on combatants but on their home-front relatives. Kate Clephane basks in the social glory of having her "beautiful daughter" marry a "War Hero" (263); so the Glenns regain their lost social prominence when their son dies, "attacked alone in midsky by a German air squadron" (623).

In other ways as well Wharton quietly but tellingly reflects the experience of the war years. Certainly the death of her young cousin Newbold Rhinelander is revisited in the death of Philip Glenn, though Wharton revises that reality in creating her fiction. In Boylston she had portrayed Ronald Simmons, but exercised her authorial license in refusing to kill him off: Simmons died, but Boylston does not. She similarly, though less dramatically, revises the death of her cousin in the fate of Philip Glenn. Newbold was shot down, reported missing, and finally presumed dead; his body was eventually recovered and buried in the town where he had died, but his parents could not attend his funeral (Benstock 342). Like Newbold, Philip is shot down; but it is known immediately that he has died a hero's death instantaneously. There is none of the agonizing waiting that

Newbold's parents suffered through. Wharton also fulfills in her fiction what must have been the wish of her cousin Tom and his wife Kitty: Philip's parents, unlike Newbold's, are able to attend their son's funeral. The service itself is meaningful: Mrs. Glenn relates that "'One of our army chaplains read the service. The people from the village were there—they were so kind to us'" (620). This fictional and, as it were, improved funeral still has its limitations: because of travel restrictions, none of the Glenns' friends can attend. It is, nevertheless, a clearer, more significant, and more conclusive event than the funeral of Newbold Rhinelander could have been. Even in dealing with such grim topics, Wharton both re-created some of the realities of the war and softened, at least slightly, their harshest aspects.

Mr. Norcutt, Wharton's narrator, also reflects her memories of the war in his practical outlook, wondering "why it had not occurred to [Mrs. Glenn] that her oldest son had probably joined the American forces and might have remained on the field with his junior" (630). Norcutt's attitude, like Wharton's, is that any right-minded able-bodied young American man should have enlisted; accordingly, although he likes young Stephen, he is troubled by the fact that Stephen did not participate in the war. He is relieved when Stephen (whose authenticity as Mrs. Glenn's son he has not yet, at this point, questioned) explains that he "had tried to pass himself off as a Canadian volunteer in 1915, and in 1917 to enlist in the American army" (634)—only to be rejected each time because of his overall poor health. Readers have no reason to question Stephen's veracity in reporting this; even Norcutt comments that "with his narrow shoulders and hectic cheekbones, [Stephen] could never have been wanted for active service" (630). His death at an early age serves, if nothing else, to confirm the fact of his ill health. Although Stephen is the bait who draws Mrs. Glenn into the trap set by the trio of con artists, his attempts to serve in the war—like Chris Fenno's distinguished service in the Battle of Belleau Wood—speak well for at least some aspects of his character.

In *A Son at the Front* Wharton had commented on many French families' sacrifice of their sons—whether families had a single son or many. The concern about losing an only son in the war is an essential part of "Her Son" as well. When Mr. Glenn dies two years after Philip is killed, his friends believe that "'It was the loss of the boy'" that killed the father, "and added: 'It's terrible to have only one child'" (623). It is, after all, the death of this "only" child that drives Catherine Glenn to search for the son she bore first.

Oddly, however, Mrs. Glenn's belief that she has found her lost son seems to allow her to forget Philip's death: "She seemed to have forgotten that there had ever been a war, and that a son of her own, with thousands of young Americans of his generation, had lost his life in it" (630), the narrator explains. As this aspect of the tale suggests, "Her Son" is a profoundly postwar work for Wharton. In *Fighting France* and *French Ways and Their Meaning* she had insisted on mothers' willing sacrifice of their sons; in *French Ways* she goes so far as to claim that of the "millions of brave, uncomplaining, self-denying mothers" who sent their sons off to the front, "not one . . . is ever heard to say that the cost has been too great or the trial too bitter to be borne" (121). Of course, these are French mothers, and in "Her Son" Wharton depicts a merely American mother; nevertheless this long story marks the distance that separates Wharton from the extreme sentiments of the war years. Catherine Glenn, far from being one of the staunch and stable mothers whom Wharton praises, is emotionally and perhaps mentally destabilized by the death of her son in the war; yet the mere belief, on the scantiest of evidence, that a young man supposedly named "Stephen Brown" is her biological son not only provides her sufficient proof of his identity, but allows her to forget her other son. The noble and sometimes romantic vision of war expressed in *Fighting France* is nowhere represented in "Her Son"; the deaths of young men in *A Son at the Front*—viewed as necessary but tragic—have no emotional parallel in this tale. Wharton was able to use the war as a catalytic event without fear that doing so would reflect badly on, or negatively affect, the war effort. As in her other fictions written after the war, Wharton's more extreme wartime statements and implications have moderated, and the instability of Catherine Glenn may indicate a tacit admission that for some mothers the losses engendered by the war were, in fact, "too bitter to be borne."

In other ways as well, "Her Son" reflects the distance that Wharton had traveled emotionally since the war. As we have seen, "The Spark" revised the discussion about the relationship between soldiers and war writing that Wharton had initiated in "Writing a War Story," suggesting emptiness at the heart of that relationship: there are true soldiers and true war writing, but perhaps no significant connection between them. A similar emptiness haunts "Her Son." As mentioned earlier, the conflict between Catherine Glenn and Chrissy Brown echoes the competition between the two fathers in *A Son at the Front*. Yet the competition in *Son* is legitimate: both men have strong claims to fatherhood, John Campton a biological claim and Anderson Brant the claim of the adoptive father. In "Her Son," neither Mrs. Glenn nor Mrs. Brown has any legitimate claim to mother-hood. Catherine Glenn is not the young man's biological mother; Chrissy Brown is not his adoptive mother. Their claims are tenuous at best: Chrissy hangs desperately onto Stephen, who seems bored with her; the tie be-tween Stephen and Catherine is based on the fiction that he is her son—though Stephen genuinely comes to admire "Mother Kit," and Catherine derives genuine joy from the belief, however spurious, that she has recov-ered her lost son. Further, the facts at the center of the story remain un-clear. Ultimately, neither Mrs. Glenn, Mr. Norcutt, nor the reader ever learns "Stephen Brown's" real name or identity—nor is there ever any reassurance that "Chrissy Brown" and "Boy Brown," his supposed par-ents, are who they say they are. In a paradoxical return to her first war-related story, "Coming Home," Wharton has created in this profoundly postwar story another box constructed of rumor, innuendo, and story-telling—another box with nothing definite inside.

Wharton's narration in "Her Son" further marks the distance she had traveled since the war years. The story makes allusions to the war—in-deed, in the second paragraph Norcutt refers to the last time he had seen Mrs. Glenn: "toward the end of the war, in 1917 it must have been" (619). But the allusions are brief. Even the phrase "it must have been" suggests the time that had elapsed both chronologically and emotionally for Whar-ton's narrator and, possibly, for herself: Norcutt can no longer pin down exactly every date related to the war; enough time has passed since the war that absolute precision is neither possible nor necessary. As in *Old New York*, Wharton's narrator refers occasionally to social mores of the past; Catherine Glenn, for instance, had traveled the country with a troupe of actors in her early years, raising some question about her propriety. "Such a past, though it looks dove-colored now, seemed hectic in the nineties," the narrator remarks (621). Overall, however, he refrains from the ex-tended interpretations of the past that Wharton had used in both *The Age of Innocence* and *Old New York*. The story focuses far more on portraying the present than on preserving the past; given the contemporary setting of the story, she trusted her readers' ability to interpret for themselves.

"Her Son," like the stories that would shortly follow it—"The Looking Glass" and "Charm Incorporated"—suggests that Wharton had entered a new phase in her writerly relationship to the war. During the war years she was caught up in the fervor of the war itself, and much of her writing, from *Fighting France* to *The Marne*, reflected her profound belief in the importance of the war. Her postwar works, both elegies and satires, showed a certain reaction to this position; *A Son at the Front*, as we have seen, combines both elegy and satire, expressing a complex reaction to the war and her awareness of the war's huge cost—even while Wharton continued to believe (as she always would) that the war had to be fought. By the time she wrote "Her Son," however, the war and its fervor had receded. The war is a catalyst in this story, but so is Mrs. Glenn's decision, years before the war, to give up her illegitimate son for adoption. These two triggering actions are equally important to the story: without either one of them, there would be no crisis for Mrs. Glenn; there would be no story for Wharton to tell.

Further, the glory Wharton insisted on in earlier works has a minimal role in "Her Son." Philip Glenn may have been "the first American aviator to fall," but Wharton does not insist that this in itself is heroic. His celebrity seems, at least in part, to be that of chance: he merely happened to be the first shot down. Wharton does not depict his death in the heroic terms she used for Jean du Breuil's death, nor does she lend him the heroism she gave to young Troy Belknap even for his ill-judged actions. By the same token, there is no villainy attached to the German soldiers who shot Philip Glenn down; the German army is hardly mentioned in this story. The war had become a fact of history, a fact, which—like all historic events—affected many lives. But it was no longer the one fact that loomed over all other facts and demanded unswerving allegiance.

The Great War occupies a similar place in two stories that followed "Her Son": "The Looking Glass," published in 1933, and "Charm Incorporated," published in 1934 (originally under the title "Bread Upon the Waters"). Although "The Looking Glass" is set in the present in which it was published—the Depression, to which the story makes two quick references—it looks back doubly, both to the Gilded Age and to the years of the Great War. Moyra Attlee, a young woman in the thirties, listens impatiently to her grandmother Cora's stories about her career as a society masseuse, a career that "had ceased before the first symptoms of the financial depression" (845). Like Mrs. Heeney in *The Custom of the Country*, Mrs. Cora Attlee has become a repository of social history: "her tenacious memory was stored with pictures of the luxurious days of which her granddaughter's generation, even in a wider world, knew only by hearsay. Mrs. Attlee had a gift for evoking in a few words scenes of half-understood opulence and leisure, like a guide leading a stranger through the gallery of a palace in the twilight, and now and then lifting a lamp to a shimmering

Rembrandt or a jeweled Rubens; and it was particularly when she mentioned Mrs. Clingsland that Moyra caught these dazzling glimpses" (845).

As with "Her Son," "The Looking Glass" owes much of its impetus to an event that occurred during the Great War. In this case it is not the death of an only son, though it is related to women's fears about their sons and lovers in wartime. Mrs. Attlee also lifts the lamp on the war years, describing scenes reminiscent of some in *A Son at the Front:* she tells Moyra how "all the fine ladies, and the poor shabby ones too, took to running to the mediums and the clairvoyants. . . . The women had to have news of their men; and they were made to pay high enough for it" (848). In an attempt to save some of these women from "swindlers and blackmailers" (848), Cora Attlee rediscovers her gift of second sight and, like Mme. Olida, a clairvoyant in *Son,* uses this gift to help women who are worried about their husbands or sons.

It would be specious to argue that the war plays a large role in "The Looking Glass"; the sinking of the *Titanic* and the natural processes of aging play a far larger role. Nevertheless, the war's role, though small, is significant: without the renewed popularity of clairvoyants during the war, Cora Attlee might not have rediscovered her second sight (or, perhaps, persuaded herself that she had such a gift); she would not have delivered "messages" from lost or dead loved ones. Further, she would not have helped a network of others. Although Cora Attlee fabricates the messages she delivers from a dead young man to Mrs. Clingsland (with, ironically, the help of a bright young man who is dying), Mrs. Clingsland is truly comforted by them. Mrs. Clingsland's softened disposition benefits others in turn: she is kinder to her servants and her family members, she apparently gives Cora money to "keep that poor young fellow well looked after," and she even helps Cora pay for a new roof on her house (854). In fact, her generosity—not only with cash but with casual insider tips on the stock market—creates the wealth Cora's children and grandchildren will inherit.

As in "Her Son," Wharton is playing with a central paradox here: that a patent lie can create real comfort. Mrs. Glenn is cheered by rediscovering a young man whom she believes to be her son, though in fact he is not; Mrs. Clingsland dies believing that she has received a letter from beyond the grave, a letter written by a young man who truly loved her—though in fact readers know that the dying alcoholic penned the letter and that the young man who is the letter's putative author might have forgotten his glimpse of the beautiful young Mrs. Clingsland a day after his encounter with her. The war had sensitized Wharton to desperation, however fatuous: not only class differences but the different worries of peacetime and wartime are reflected in Mrs. Attlee's remark that well-off people "don't know what real trouble is; but they've manufactured something so like it that it's about as bad as the genuine thing" (857).

"The Looking Glass" also reflects Wharton's sense of history and change. In *The Mother's Recompense* Wharton had depicted, among other things, the restlessness of the younger generation of New Yorkers. This restlessness is also captured in "The Looking Glass," as Wharton contrasts the patient grandmother Cora with her impatient granddaughter Moyra, who, Cora realizes, is probably "'fidgety because there's a new movie on; or that young fellow's fixed it up to get back earlier from New York . . .'" (844). In *The Age of Innocence* Wharton had depicted May's patient attention to her grandmother, Mrs. Mingott; that 1870s patience is decidedly not a characteristic of Mrs. Attlee's granddaughter in a story set in the early 1930s, an era in which new distractions like movies contributed to the "fidgety" behavior of a young woman like Moyra. Even points of reference had changed. Attempting to convey the fading of Mrs. Clingsland's beauty to her granddaughter, Cora asks, "'Do you know how it is, sometimes when you're doing a bit of fine darning, sitting by the window in the afternoon; and one minute it's full daylight, and your needle seems to find the way of itself; and the next minute you say: "Is it my eyes?" because the work seems blurred; and presently you see it's the daylight going. . . . [I]t was that way with her . . .'" (847). Mrs. Attlee's comparison is well-chosen, but it is lost on her granddaughter who, the narrator informs us, "had never done fine darning, or strained her eyes in fading light" (847). In *The Age of Innocence* and *Old New York*, Wharton had re-created the lost world of the 1800s; in "The Looking Glass" she suggests that even the earlier part of the twentieth century—the post–Civil War, pre–World War I opulence of the Gilded Age—was being lost. It, too, had become a world remembered only by tedious grandmothers—albeit grandmothers still sometimes worth listening to.

Wharton explored in fiction one final "extraordinary and dramatic situation" (*Letters* 357) resulting from the war. "Charm Incorporated," like "The Looking Glass," "Her Son," and "Velvet Ear Pads," is set in the postwar period. It tells the story of Jim Targatt, one of Wharton's many male characters who have renounced emotional involvement; moreover, Targatt has no particular soft spot for refugees. It is to his own great surprise, then, that he suddenly finds himself married to a charming Russian refugee,

Nadeja Kouradjine, who had come "straight out of that struggling mass of indistinguishable human misery that Targatt called 'Wardrift'" (744). He soon finds himself caring not only for Nadeja but for her numerous relatives. Gradually becoming adept at placing various siblings (and people less clearly related to his wife) into jobs and marriages, he also begins to wonder what his relationship to his wife really is—whether he is not so much a husband as a target, as his name suggests. Though Wharton keeps her readers in suspense until the end of the story, that ending is undeniably comic—and comic without bitterness. Fearing that his wife might be unfaithful, Jim Targatt eventually comes to a true appreciation of her fidelity, her character, and even her physical beauty, and discovers that her greatest wish is neither to run off with a famous painter nor to place further relatives into jobs or marriages, but to settle down with him and have a child.

As discussed in chapter four, "The Refugees"—despite its title and Wharton's extensive involvement with refugees—was really a semisatirical treatment of those who pretended to aid them, as well as a portrait of two refugees of a different sort, Charlie Durand and Audrey Rushworth. Similarly, Wharton's exposure to so many whom the war affected might lead the reader familiar with her biography to expect that any treatment of "wardrift" would be a serious one. But even more than "The Refugees," "Charm Incorporated" handles a seemingly heavy topic with a deft touch. In the aftermath of a tragic war, comedy could emerge.

"Charm Incorporated" is the last and lightest of Wharton's tales that were "not precisely war stories"; it is the only true comedy among them. The framing narrator in "Coming Home" had remarked that some war stories "are dark and dreadful, some are unutterably sad, and some end in a huge laugh of irony" (230). Some, as he acknowledges, are hard to classify: the group to which so many of Wharton's war-related writings belong. The comic nature of "Charm Incorporated" suggests that—as it is neither "dark and dreadful," nor "unutterably sad," nor ironic, nor hard to classify—Wharton had truly put the war behind her.

Finally, however, it may be more accurate to say that Wharton had not so much put the war behind her as she had put it *beside* her: it had become another topic she could look at coolly, dispassionately, introducing it to initiate a plot, but not allowing the war's devastation to dictate the tale's outcome. Even a change in the story's title confirms a change in mood from the serious to the light-hearted. The title under which the story was originally published, "Bread Upon the Waters," suggests that however light its surface, this tale has a strong moral. In keeping with the Biblical injunction to "cast thy bread upon the waters: for thou shalt find it after many days" (Ecclesiastes 11:1), Jim Targatt has been more than charitable to Nadeja and her family; but he is ultimately rewarded for this generosity not only by his wife's charm but by her sincere devotion to him. The title Wharton gave the story for book publication, "Charm Incorporated," has no such moral cast. Rather it emphasizes the surprising (and sometimes inexplicable) amiability of Nadeja and her extended family, suggesting that charm itself is a family industry—and, in the end, a very successful one.[14] Moreover, the revised title suggests the high life the story depicts—movie and advertising stars, quickly-made fortunes, rapid marriages and divorces—none of which, as the title also hints, should be taken too seriously.

The very existence of "Charm Incorporated" serves as a reminder that the relationship between literature and war remained a complex one for Wharton. From reading *Fighting France*, readers might have guessed that a story like "Coming Home," a novella like *The Marne*, or a novel like *A Son at the Front* might eventually be written; less predictable are the satirical humor of "The Refugees" and "Writing a War Story," the psychologically torturous convolutions of *The Mother's Recompense*, or the comedy of "Charm Incorporated." Any reader unfamiliar with Wharton's biography would have been unlikely to guess that an author who could treat "war-drift" so lightly had herself been acquainted with and provided for thousands of refugees; yet this story exhibits a certain patience and tolerance for human frailties that were, in part, the result of Wharton's experience in the war years.

Wharton herself left little, if any, commentary on the disparity between the tragedies she witnessed and the fictions that emerged from her pen during and after the war. R.W.B. Lewis, as we have seen, remarked that "one of the fascinating themes in literary history is the impact of a great war upon the creative imagination" (393). Henry James and Max Beerbohm had pondered the war's effect on their imaginations in their letters to Wharton; the war had altered Wharton's work as well. War was hard on Art; Art, when it turned to War, may sometimes have treated it in ways that even the artist would have found difficult to predict. In her June 1915 letter to Charles Scribner, Wharton had laid out a plan of activity she was unable to follow: "May I suggest, during the next six months, giving you . . . four or five short stories, not precisely war stories, but on subjects suggested by the war?" (*Letters* 357). "Coming Home" was the only story to appear on schedule; two others appeared at the war's end. Wharton herself could not have foretold exactly how many stories, poems, and novels the war would engender in her, when they would come to fruition, or what their nature would be. Like the war itself, their pattern was unpredictable—and the effects of the war on Wharton's imagination, again like the war itself, lasted far longer than Wharton could have foreseen.

From the composition of *The Age of Innocence* through the writing of "Charm Incorporated," the relationship between the war and Wharton's writing changed profoundly—as did her literary strategies. In *Age* and *Old New York* Wharton turned to the past, emphasizing its difference from the postwar world not just through her detailed portrayal of the past but through her emphasis on interpreting a world that might, she believed, have otherwise been incomprehensible to her readers—or, perhaps worse yet, misunderstood and misinterpreted. In *The Mother's Recompense* she treated the war as backdrop: not merely as background or scenery, but as a shaping force that altered the experiences, the personalities, and the mores of Kate Clephane and Chris Fenno. In later years, the war appears less frequently in Wharton's works and, when it does appear, it plays a much more minor role; seven years passed between the donated books and Russian refugee of "Velvet Ear Pads" and the duped mother of a son shot down in "Her Son." One could hardly argue that the war was a common theme for Wharton after the completion of *A Son at the Front*. Nevertheless, even passing references to the war in stories from the 1930s are significant: the influence of the war was indeed long-lasting.

Conclusion

Glancing Back at the War

Between the point of view of my Huguenot great-great-grandfather
. . . and my own father, who died in 1882, there were fewer differences than between my father and the post–war generation of Americans.
Wharton, *A Backward Glance* **(6)**

[A soldier speaks:] "They don't know what war is back there; and if you started talking about the rear, it'd be *you* that'd talk rot."
Henri Barbusse, *Le Feu* **(180)**

I. The War Years in *A Backward Glance*

The war played a diminishing role in Wharton's work in the postwar years; it played a diminishing role in her life and her memory as well. If her historical fictions emphasized the pastness of the past, so too some of Wharton's correspondence suggests that, in its turn, the war became thoroughly "past" as well. A carbon copy of a business letter from 1920 is on the reverse of a piece of the stationery for the American Hostels for Refugees, one of Wharton's charities (box 33, folder 1033, *Wharton Collection* Yale); that letter-head, once so important, had been relegated to such second-class purposes. When Rutger Jewett wrote Wharton in 1922 requesting permission to include "Battle Sleep" in an anthology of poems, Wharton wrote back, "I am obliged to confess that my mind is a perfect blank as to the poem called 'Battle Sleep.' I don't know when I wrote it, or what it is about, or who published it: but if I really did write it, and have the disposal of it, you are more than welcome to use it in your anthology. It would interest me to see what it is about" (28 Dec. 1922, *Wharton Collection*

Yale). Despite the intensity of the war years, Wharton had completely forgotten writing this poem.

It is initially surprising, then, that her 1934 memoir, *A Backward Glance*, refers to the war extensively. While this work devotes only one chapter out of fourteen to the war, in another sense the war frames the entire memoir. Wharton refers to it repeatedly in her preface, "A First Word"; and, although the chapter starkly entitled "The War" is the thirteenth chapter, the final chapter, called "And After," is clearly an appendix to it: the memoir both begins and ends with significant references to the war.

A Backward Glance confirms that the war was not only a catalyst for certain types of writing Wharton did, but created the terms in which Wharton saw her life—including her writing—from the war years on. The changes Wharton perceived in the postwar world led her to write her memoir: "If anyone had suggested to me, before 1914, to write my reminiscences, I should have answered that my life had been too uneventful to be worth recording. . . . Not until the successive upheavals which culminated in the catastrophe of 1914 had 'cut all likeness from the name' of my old New York, did I begin to see its pathetic picturesqueness" (6). Only in the light of the postwar world could Wharton see the "pathetic picturesqueness" of old New York—the world she chronicled and re-created in *The Age of Innocence* and *Old New York*. With their abundance of detail *Age* and *Old New York*, like many passages of *A Backward Glance*, are picturesque; but the tales they tell are often pathetic: tales of lives blighted needlessly over scruples and beliefs that a later world would find trivial. And yet, for all that, their picturesqueness remains. Wharton conveys the almost peculiar value that such restrictive customs had for the inhabitants of those distant worlds: the values of stability, predictability, leisure, and social harmony—or at least the appearance of social harmony. For Wharton, and doubtless for many of her readers shaken by the upheavals created by the war, these virtues—dull and even restrictive as they might be—gained a new appeal.

Wharton's long view, her backward glance from the early thirties toward the 1870s, '80s, and '90s, also affected her view of the past.[1] The arrival in New York City of the "big money-makers from the West" and "the lords of Pittsburgh" (6) after the Civil War may have seemed cataclysmic at the time, but relative to postwar changes their effect was minor: "their infiltration did not greatly affect old manners and customs, since the dearest ambition of the newcomers was to assimilate existing traditions" (6).

From the perspective of the thirties, it was the war that brought about major change. And, Wharton emphasizes, the change *was* major. Her language suggests that the war disrupted not just "manners and customs" but history, the flow of civilization itself:

> Social life . . . went on with hardly perceptible changes till the war abruptly tore down the old frame-work, and what had seemed unalterable rules of conduct became of a sudden observances as quaintly arbitrary as the domestic rites of the Pharaohs. Between the point of view of my Huguenot great-great-grandfather . . . and my own father, who died in 1882, there were fewer differences than between my father and the postwar generation of Americans. That I was born into a world in which telephones, motors, electric light [and other devices] . . . were not only unknown but still mostly unforeseen, may seem the most striking difference between then and now; but the really vital change is that, in my youth, the Americans of the original States . . . were the heirs of an old tradition of European culture which the country has now totally rejected. (6–7)

Wharton concludes this passage by comparing her past to a lost, or nearly lost, civilization: "The compact world of my youth has receded into a past from which it can only be dug up in bits by the assiduous relic-hunter; and its smallest fragments begin to be worth collecting and putting together before the last of those who knew the live structure are swept away with it" (7). Here, as in *The Age of Innocence* and *Old New York*, Wharton emphasizes the pastness of the prewar past and its fundamental irretrievability: even if all the relics are collected and assembled, they will be of historical interest only, the remnants of a civilization now gone.

Despite the popularity of several of her postwar novels, Wharton perceived herself as part of that vanishing past, one of the "last of those who knew the live structure." As early as 1921—that is, still before her sixtieth birthday—she was expressing a sense of superannuation, articulating her relief to Sinclair Lewis that he both knew and admired her work: "It is the first sign I have ever had—literally—that 'les jeunes' at home had ever read a word of me. I had long since resigned myself to the idea that I was regarded by you all as the — say the Mrs. Humphry Ward of the Western Hemisphere" (*Letters* 445). In a 1922 letter to the young novelist William Gerhardie she similarly remarked that she was "accustomed nowadays to being regarded as a deplorable example of what people used to read in the

Dark Ages before the 'tranche de vie' had been rediscovered" (*Letters* 457). At such moments she felt herself an outdated being nearly invisible in the strange new world which succeeded the Great War.

In *A Backward Glance*, a proliferation of metaphors emphasizes the extent to which the prewar world had, in Wharton's view, vanished. "Nothing but the Atlantis-fate of old New York . . . makes that childhood worth recalling now[,]" she asserts (55); at other points the past is not a drowned city but something violently broken: "that old world of my youth has been so convulsed and shattered, that as I look back, and try to recapture the details of particular scenes and talks, they dissolve into the distance" (224). Elsewhere Wharton looks back "across the chasm of the war" (259) or sees the past as a plant that had been snapped off: "One of the loveliest flowers on the bough so soon to be broken was the dancing of Isadora Duncan" (320). Some aspects of early modernism—not only the artistry of Isadora Duncan, but the music of Igor Stravinsky and Richard Strauss—delighted her; but these too would be cut off by the war: "They were vernal hours—*es war der Lenz!* [it was spring!]. But already the sickles were sharpening for the harvest . . ." (333). This is no Keatsian reaper, "sitting careless on a granary floor, / Thy hair soft-lifted by the winnowing wind" ("To Autumn" 2.3–4), but rather the reaper who would cut down so many so prematurely.

Most frequently, Wharton figures the war as apocalyptic, the end of the world as she and her generation had known it. For most readers, Wharton writes, the "only interest" of the years of her childhood "lies in the fact of its sudden and total extinction" (7). Of prewar Faubourg St. Germain society she remarks simply but decisively, "the world we then knew has come to an end" (265). Wharton had been traveling just before war was declared in France; the shift from light-hearted travel to life on the verge of war is figured as a kind of death: "There were moments when I felt as if I had died, and waked up in an unknown world. And so I had" (338). Within the first weeks of war she knew herself and her friends as "being cut off forever from the old untroubled world we had always known" (343). All was changed, changed utterly—and, although the excitement of the war years as Wharton had expressed it in *Fighting France* and *The Marne* might have suggested that "a terrible beauty was born" of that change, *A Backward Glance* emphasizes the terrible loss the war years wrought. Her world—the civilization she so valued, and, paradoxically, the civilization that she and others claimed the war had been fought to preserve—was irretrievably destroyed. Writing of that world in *A Backward Glance*, as she had in *The Age of Innocence* and *Old New York*, was Wharton's best hope for re-creating, or at least memorializing, a portion of it.

Discussion of the Great War structures the memoir as a whole, profoundly influencing the overall impression that the work leaves with its reader. The sixteen years between the end of World War I and the publication of the book in 1934 were tremendously productive years for Wharton, years in which she bought and developed two homes (each with its own extensive garden), sustained old friendships and nurtured new ones, and published prolifically: some nineteen books in total, including novels, short story collections, nonfiction, and a volume of poems—only a little less than half of her entire literary oeuvre. Yet these years are summarized in eighteen pages. Any reader of Wharton's memoir who was not familiar with her publication record and her busy life might easily assume that Wharton's claim that her world was destroyed in 1914 was nearly a literal as well as a psychological truth. Chapter thirteen, "The War," brings Wharton's prewar life to an abrupt halt; chapter fourteen, "And After," suggests that all the busy and productive years after the war were only a sort of epilogue, or even an anticlimax, to her life.

Wharton's presentation of the war in her memoir differs in some significant ways from her portrayals of it during and immediately after the war years. In particular, her portrait of women's wartime roles is generally more positive in *A Backward Glance* than it is in either her fiction or nonfiction from the war years. In her earlier war-related writings she had resisted playing the merely domestic role accepted by women like Mary King Waddington and Mildred Aldrich in *A Hilltop on the Marne*. More pointedly, Wharton had repeatedly satirized the women who were obsessed only with their own possessions and their own safety, or whose charitable efforts extended only to pouring tea for convalescing soldiers. In *The Marne* she mocks the wealthy ladies whose main concern when war breaks out is that "they could get no money, no seats in the trains, no assurance that the Swiss border would not be closed" (10). Wharton distances herself from such women simply by criticizing them; in nonfiction works like *Fighting France*, she further emphasizes that distance by presenting herself as the exceptional woman, the one woman allowed to go to the masculine world of the front.

The strong contrast between Wharton's satire of other women's wartime roles and her presentation of her own role is markedly diminished in

A Backward Glance. In chapter thirteen of *A Backward Glance,* "The War," Wharton presents herself as having far more in common with these ladies than she would earlier have allowed; their situation was her situation as well. Like them, she cannot get funds from her bank nor even borrow from friends who are (as she was) suddenly penniless; she must wait impatiently for permits and visas to travel from Paris to England in order to carry out her plan for a summer in the English countryside; once in England, she spends hours haunting the American and French embassies, hoping to get the permits that would allow her to return to Paris (339–44). The wartime writings emphasized Wharton's close ties to the "real" war of combat, her awareness of the destruction—and the excitement—of the front; a part of associating herself with that masculine world was denigrating the feminine, domestic world of the home front. In *A Backward Glance* that denigration is gone. In particular, her presentation of women's involvement in charitable work is described far more neutrally, or even generously, than one would have guessed from the wartime fiction. Certainly there were volunteers who disappointed Wharton, though with fifteen years' perspective she is able to dismiss them humorously; but she also praises the work of Elisina Tyler and other women with whom she worked. Significantly (particularly in light of Wharton's emphatic dismissal of higher education for women elsewhere in *A Backward Glance*), she thanks "the woman doctor who sold her tiny scrap of radium because she had no other means of helping" (350). Wharton presents an even-handed view of women's work, a view that does not glorify the "real" world of war at the expense of women's efforts behind the lines.

Wharton devotes several pages to describing her charitable efforts during the war, thus granting them an importance that they otherwise seem to lack in her earlier published work. While Wharton had written various newspaper articles and brochures about her charities, such documents are by their nature transitory, lacking the literary permanence more likely to be accorded to other kinds of publications. By contrast, accounts of Wharton's trips to the front were published in *Scribner's Magazine,* giving them a kind of literary stature that the newspaper accounts of the charities lacked; such importance was further emphasized by their book publication in *Fighting France.* In her memoir, however, Wharton speaks of her charitable efforts first; only after devoting several pages to them does Wharton turn to recounting her trips to the front. Within these pages, Wharton's tendency to emphasize her exceptional quality in *Fighting France*—her accomplishment as a civilian and a woman in getting close to the front—is diminished. She acknowledges that her trips to the front were permitted so that she could write about the war: "the description of what I saw might bring home to American readers some of the dreadful realities of war" (352). While she retells a few of the episodes narrated in *Fighting France,* she keeps such accounts brief.

Moreover, her tone is more subdued than it was in much of *Fighting France.* In one passage, for instance, she recounts dining in the 1930s with a musician whom she had initially met when he was a soldier in the Vosges in 1915: "Seeing Félix Raugel again brought back to me with startling vividness the scenes of my repeated journeys to the front; the scarred torn land behind the trenches, the faces of the men who held it, the terrible and interminable epic of France's long defence. I remembered the emotion of my arrival at the posts I was permitted to visit, the speechless astonishment of officers and men at the sight of a wandering woman, their friendly greetings, the questions, the laughter, the jolly picnic lunches around boards resting on trestles, the reluctant goodbyes, the burden of messages to wives and mothers with which I returned to the rear . . ." (351–52). Wharton still enjoys having been an exception, the surprising "wandering woman" in an otherwise masculine territory. But the trajectory of this passage is complex. More than in *Fighting France,* Wharton acknowledges here the grim conditions of war, conditions affecting the land Wharton loved as well as the people and the nation she so admired. The "friendly greetings" and "the jolly picnic lunches" are reminiscent of scenes in *Fighting France;* but this mood of cheer is succeeded in turn by the more somber "reluctant goodbyes" and the haunting sense of "messages to wives and mothers"—a reminder of the women relatives waiting anxiously in the world to which Wharton too must return, the largely feminine world of the home front.

During the war, Wharton had remarked that "I felt like a deserter" when she found herself safely in England while Paris was being threatened (*Letters* 335); in *A Backward Glance,* as noted in chapter three, she observed that war workers could "create within themselves an escape from the surrounding horror[,]" but that doing so was "possible only to real workers, as it is possible for a nurse on a hard case to bear the sight of the patient's sufferings because she is doing all she can to relieve them" (356). In such remarks Wharton implicitly compares herself to figures—a soldier, a nurse—with active roles at or near the front lines. The same longing for activity revealed itself in her creation of a series of lame male figures,

Jean de Réchamp in "Coming Home," Charlie Durand in "The Refugees," and John Campton in *A Son at the Front,* each kept from an active role in the war by a chance disability, rather than the nearly insuperable barrier of gender which restricted Wharton. The war years behind her, however, any longing Wharton had felt for a more active role in the war seems to have evaporated. Wharton is content with the role she played, both behind the scenes and in her trips near the front, as her self-portrait in "The War" suggests: "I saw myself, an eager grotesque figure, bestriding a mule in the long tight skirts of 1915, and suddenly appearing, a prosaic Walkyrie laden with cigarettes, in the heart of the mountain fastness held by the famous *Chasseurs Alpins,* already among the legendary troops of the French army" (351). There is a great deal of humor here. Wharton, after all, had been able to laugh at Abel Faivre's caricature of her in *Le Rire* (fig. 1)— and glancing back Wharton can see herself (along with the fashions of the day) as amusing. But there is also heroism—coupled with practicality: Wharton presents herself as a "Walkyrie laden with cigarettes," a Walkyrie whose job it is not to accompany soldiers to Valhalla but to bring them creature comforts. Wharton's description of her visit to the camp itself combines a sense of tension, good cheer, and haunting messages; similarly, this self-portrait balances heroism, humility, and humor. Wharton had accepted her own part in the war.

Ezra Pound would describe the Great War as a senseless conflict fought "For an old bitch gone in the teeth / For a botched civilization" (1132). In expressing this view he spoke for many of the younger generation fighting in the war, those whose work has become canonized and, at least until recently, thought of as *the* literature of World War I.[2] But Wharton, like many of her generation, and in spite of her increasing understanding of the war's cost, could never take that view. For her and for many others, "Civilization was what the war had been fought for" (Hynes 311). In *A Backward Glance* she defends the war:

When I am told—as I am not infrequently—by people who were in the nursery, or not born, in that fatal year, that the world went gaily to war, or when I have served up to me the more recent legend that France and England actually wanted war, and forced it on the peace-loving and reluctant Central Empires, I recall those first days of August 1914, and am dumb with indignation.

France was paralyzed with horror. France had never wanted war, had never believed it would be forced upon her[.] (338–39)

Wharton would have concurred with Maurice Maeterlinck's statement in *Débris de la Guerre* that "It is possible that some day, when time has dulled the memory and restored the ruins, wise men will tell us that we are mistaken, that our standpoint was not lofty enough, that everything can be explained and forgiven and that we must make an effort to understand; but they will say so only because what we know has been forgotten, and what we behold has not been seen" (qtd. in Schinz 10–11). The tacit rule of war writing was that only those who had experienced the front could legitimately claim the authority to write about it; Wharton, like Maeterlinck, implies a corollary principle: only those who had lived through the war could say what the war—on the battle front and home front alike—really was.

In a large sense, most if not all of Wharton's postwar work can be seen as a meditation on the question of civilization. What constituted—or did not constitute—"civilization" was a central issue even in her works before the war; certainly one of the many questions posed by *The House of Mirth, The Custom of the Country*, and other works is what, exactly, civilization is, and how those apparently at the peak of civilization—people of wealth and some degree of culture who ought to form its flower—can behave in ways so barbaric, so fundamentally uncivilized. But the question became ever more pressing after the war years. "What was civilization? Had it been destroyed by the war, as some said?" (Hynes 311). These questions hovered over Wharton's postwar work, including both her turn to the past and her portrayal of life in the postwar years. Old New York had profound limitations—but limitations preferable, she implied in *A Backward Glance*, to the freedoms of the postwar world: "the qualities justifying the existence of our old society were social amenity and financial incorruptibility; and we have travelled far enough from both to begin to estimate their value" (22). The society she presents in works of the twenties like *The Mother's Recompense, Twilight Sleep*, and *The Children* demonstrates neither "social amenity" nor "financial incorruptibility." In *A Son at the Front* John Campton and his French friend, Paul Dastrey, had questioned why the war continued if it was only to save civilization for "wasp-waisted youths in sham uniforms . . . or for the elderly men" like themselves (365). Campton and Dastrey agree that France, or even the "Idea" of France, is worth saving, regardless of who is left to appreciate it (366). In her postwar depictions of society, Wharton seemed to be questioning whether even that "idea" had been saved.

The question of civilization hovers over *A Backward Glance* as well.

Although Wharton objected to being perceived as stuffy and outdated, in addressing the question of civilization she occasionally assumes the tone of the haughty and condescending *grande dame* in her memoir. For instance, she remarks that "I used to say that I had been taught only two things in my childhood: the modern languages and good manners. Now that I have lived to see both these branches of culture dispensed with, I perceive that there are worse systems of education" (48). In another passage she takes a similarly dismissive stance toward higher education for women. After enumerating the delicious dishes of her youth, she justifies her almost Whitmanian catalog by commenting, "I have lingered over these details because they formed a part—a most important and honourable part—of that ancient curriculum of house-keeping which, at least in Anglo-Saxon countries, was so soon to be swept aside by the 'monstrous regiment' of the emancipated: young women taught by their elders to despise the kitchen and the linen room, and to substitute the acquiring of University degrees for the more complex art of civilized living. The movement began when I was young, and now that I am old, and have watched it and noted its result, I mourn more than ever the extinction of the household arts. Cold storage, deplorable as it is, has done far less harm to the home than the Higher Education" (59–60). The war played a role in creating the condescending *grand dame* who speaks here: if the war had never occurred, the difference between generations, the shift from "young" to "old," would have been less pronounced; civilization, though it would doubtless have changed somewhat during the years between Wharton's childhood and her maturity, would not have undergone what many saw as a cataclysmic change. As this passage implies, that change was perceived as all-embracing. Wharton's sense of the lost world that existed before the war extends even to "the household arts," here described not as lost or endangered but as utterly "extinct"; "University degrees" have displaced "civilized living."

The public persona that Wharton created in such passages is far more absolute, and far more nostalgic about the prewar past, than the more reflective fictional persona she created in her postwar fictions about the prewar world. Works like *The Age of Innocence* and *Old New York* suggest a different persona, one who, while mistrusting the present of incessantly and pointlessly busy lives, is also too intelligent to bathe the past in a glow of unexamined nostalgia; as Millicent Bell has written, "Nostalgia was not an adequate standpoint for someone as intelligent and realistic as Wharton" ("Edith Wharton in France" 72). The happiest years in Wharton's life were probably those immediately preceding the war: those in which she had settled in France, found a social, cultural, and intellectual milieu in which she at last felt at home, enjoyed an affair that was rejuvenating and even illuminating, and gradually broke away from a stifling marriage—all while traveling and writing extensively. This is the period she briefly memorializes in the epilogue of *The Age of Innocence*. The years before this golden period were dampened by the conventionality of Old New York; the war years, while profoundly engaging, were exhausting and disillusioning as well; the postwar world was, strangely, no longer the civilization Wharton had done everything in her power to save. It is small wonder, then, that her postwar fiction reveals that Wharton was of two minds about the prewar world. *The Age of Innocence* and *Old New York* reveal Wharton's deep and abiding ambivalence about that world: both her admiration of its leisurely and well-regulated customs and her knowledge that such a civilization existed only at a cost to some of its most valuable members. Yet in *A Backward Glance* Wharton assumed a very specific public persona: that of "the last of those who knew the live structure" of the past and whose job it was not only to recount that lost world but, at least to some extent, to chastise the postwar world for what she perceived as its lapses.

II. Wharton's War Works in Context

Wharton was, in many ways, out of place in France in the war: woman, civilian, and citizen of another country, her role in wartime was necessarily limited. To some extent she always maintained her "'civilian wonder at distant shells bursting'" (Graves, qtd. in Hynes 199). Similarly, her repeated creation of men who cannot participate actively in the war because of a limp suggests her vulnerability to the kind of satirical attack Siegfried Sassoon mounted in his poem "Glory of Women":

> You love us when we're heroes, home on leave,
> Or wounded in a mentionable place.
> You worship decorations; you believe
> That chivalry redeems the war's disgrace.
> You make us shells. You listen with delight,
> By tales of dirt and danger fondly thrilled.
> You crown our distant ardours while we fight,
> And mourn our laurelled memories when we're killed.

You can't believe that British troops "retire"
When hell's last horror breaks them, and they run,
Trampling the terrible corpses—blind with blood.
O German mother dreaming by the fire,
While you are knitting socks to send your son
His face is trodden deeper in the mud. (132)

Sassoon would probably have charged Wharton with adhering to, even promulgating, many of what he saw as the horrifying misconceptions of war. Wharton did love, or at least admire, heroes; and all the incapacitated men she created in her fiction were "wounded in a mentionable place." Even at the war's end, Wharton believed in some degree of chivalry; her elegies (most notably "You and You") "mourn our laurelled memories when we're killed." Rarely in her work did she depict ignominies like the one Sassoon portrays at the end of this poem; one of the few atrocities she portrayed in her published writing was early in the war, in "The Tryst," in which a Belgian woman describes the Germans' execution of her husband and son. (In *A Son at the Front*, as we saw in chapter five, she acknowledges through Campton the horrors soldiers endured; but she does so in generalized terms.) One central reason for this difference of view may be that Wharton was excluded from the front, as were the other women to whom Sassoon addressed this poem; she wasn't allowed to experience what the soldiers themselves experienced. In this, she is caught in a classic double bind: she is not allowed to have the very experience that she is blamed for not having had.

Even had Wharton had that experience, however, it is likely that her viewpoint would have differed from Sassoon's—that is, from the ironically detached voice that became *the* voice of the Great War. Samuel Hynes notes "the early high-mindedness that turned in mid-war to bitterness and cynicism" as one "element" of the myth of the war; another element is "the rising resentment of . . . ignorant, patriotic women" (439). Paul Fussell, as discussed in chapter three, wrote that the Great War encouraged "the modern *versus* habit: one thing opposed to another . . . with a sense that one of its poles embodies so wicked a deficiency or flaw or perversion that its total submission is called for" (79). Pairing Sassoon's "Glory of Women" with some of Wharton's work seems to suggest that one of them—probably Wharton—must be wrong. The Great War seems to have thrived on stereotypes: if the folks at home stereotyped the French *poilu*, the English Tommy Atkins, and the American doughboy as cheerful and dogged, so too the soldiers tended to type the women at home as "ignorant" and "patriotic." In literary history at least, there seems little acknowledgment that more than one perspective on the war might be legitimate.

Yet resisting "the modern *versus* habit" may have its rewards. Wharton's voice may, in some respects, have more in common with the tone of some military historians than with that of the better-known poets and novelists of the Great War. Her belief in the French cause and in French morale is corroborated not only by Jean-Jacques Becker's account of the French people during the Great War, but by the description of French *élan* given by the military historian Barbara Tuchman. "Living in the shadow" of the 1870–71 Franco-Prussian war, France, Tuchman writes,

> grew weary of being eternally on guard. . . . She needed some weapon that Germany lacked to give herself confidence in her survival. The "idea with a sword" fulfilled the need. Expressed by [Henri] Bergson it was called *élan vital*, the all-conquering will. . . . Her will to win, her *élan*, would enable France to defeat her enemy. Her genius was in her spirit, the spirit of *la gloire.* . . .
> Belief in the fervor of France, in the *furor Gallicae*, revived France's faith in herself in the generation after 1870. (31)

Wharton's admiration of the French military and her repeated assertion in *Fighting France* that the French are a "nation guerrière" [warrior nation], are both very much in keeping with such a passage.[3] Further, Wharton—like Tuchman—understands and emphasizes the French use of abstractions, including *la gloire*. She notes in *French Ways and Their Meaning* that "the Anglo-Saxon is taught *not* to do great deeds for 'glory,' while the French, unsurpassed in great deeds, have always avowedly done them for 'la gloire'" (123–24). Wharton emphatically approves of such deeds: "The whole conception of 'la gloire' is linked with the profoundly French conviction that the lily *should* be gilded; that, however lofty and beautiful a man's act or his purpose, it gains by being performed with what the French . . . call 'elegance'" (124). Indeed, Wharton's belief in "la gloire" underlay her belief that the death of her friend Jean du Breuil was a glorious one. Tuchman corroborates Wharton's work not only in general ways, but in details as well. For instance, Tuchman emphasizes the horrendously aging effect on soldiers of the long campaigns, observing that soldiers' "eyes [were] cavernous in faces dulled by exhaustion and dark with many days' growth of beard. Twenty days of campaigning seemed to have aged the soldiers as many years" (qtd. in Keegan, *First World War* 108). Such observations make believable the scene in *A Son at the Front* in which John Campton initially fails to recognize his son in the face of "a middle-aged bearded man" with "gaunt cheeks" who is "heavily bandaged about the chest and left arm" (278). George is in his early twenties, but his experiences in battle have aged him beyond recognition.

Many passages in the recent history of the Great War by the eminent military historian John Keegan further corroborate Wharton's wartime writings. His description of the singing of the Marseillaise during the early days of the war, for instance, comes as no surprise to readers of *Fighting France*, in which Wharton documented, half-humorously, the difficulty of waiters in getting their work done in August 1914: "the intervals between the courses that so few waiters were left to serve were broken by the ever-recurring obligation to stand up for the Marseillaise, to stand up for God Save the King, to stand up for the Russian National Anthem, to stand up again for the Marseillaise" (10). In *Fighting France*, Wharton had portrayed the French and German armies, each poised and waiting along the lines: "there came over me the sense of that mute reciprocal watching from trench to trench: the interlocked stare of innumerable pairs of eyes, stretching on, mile after mile, along the whole sleepless line from Dunkerque to Belfort" (216). Keegan describes the same reciprocity: "the opposing combatants [were] equally exhausted by human loss, equally bereft of re-supplies . . . , crouched in confrontation across a narrow and empty zone of no man's land" (*First World War* 136). Keegan's observation that "French generals . . . expected large casualties, which their soldiers still seemed ready to suffer with patriotic fatalism" (*First World War* 196) explains the attitude of determination and "patriotic fatalism" Wharton portrays repeatedly in French soldiers (and Americans like George Campton) in *A Son at the Front*.

In some details, modern military historians certainly differ from Wharton. In her enthusiastic support of France, for instance, Wharton claimed it as more unwavering than it really was (or could possibly have been). As we have seen, Becker notes the fluctuations in French morale; Keegan does the same. In particular Keegan notes that in 1917 the high rate of French fatalities "had deadened the French will to fight. Defend the homeland the soldiers of France would; attack they would not" (*First World War* 332). Yet ultimately he confirms the essence of Wharton's claims about the French, observing that "Even during the worst of its troubles, at the front and at home during 1917, France continued to function as a state and an economy" (*First World War* 333). The French endured, as Wharton had said they did.

In more general terms as well Keegan's *The First World War* lends credence to Wharton's writing about the war. Though the Myth of the War delineated so well by Fussell and Hynes denied that war had any heroic elements, Keegan assumes that it did—or, at least, that some of its episodes evinced heroic qualities. He writes, for instance, that Gallipoli was "one of the Great War's most terrible battles but also its only epic" (221). Writing of that campaign, he notes that in addition to the many acknowledged acts of heroism, "There were numerous other, unrecorded, feats of courage, inexplicable to a later, more timorous age" (245). In *A Backward Glance*, Wharton implies that the postwar period had fallen off from the greatness of earlier eras; more than a half-century later, Keegan similarly sees our own age as one that cannot live up to, or even grasp, the standards of heroism that obtained during the First World War. Further, Keegan restores the semichivalrous language of adventure to the ill-fated Gallipoli campaign, noting that with the evacuation of Allied forces in January 1916, "The great adventure was over" (*First World War* 248). That "adventure," he argues, had a truly heroic quality: "Troy and Gallipoli make two separate but connected epics, as so many of the classically educated volunteer officers of the Mediterranean Expeditionary Force . . . had recognized and recorded. It is difficult to say which epic Homer might have thought the more heroic" (*First World War* 249). The literary canon that emerged from the Great War made heroism not only unfashionable but ridiculous; in such a context, works like *The Marne* and *A Son at the Front* have not fared well. Viewed not from the perspective of received literary history but from that of military history, however, Wharton's wartime writings gain an authority they have generally been denied. Reading Wharton's works in the context of military history suggests that, far from being sentimental, ignorant, or propagandistic, Wharton knew exactly what she was writing about.

Examining Wharton's works in light of military history is, in fact, a salutary reminder that authors, unlike the characters they create, are (or were) actual people living through actual historical periods; that the characters they create, though fictional, have—at least in the case of realists— much in common with real people. Marianne Moore wrote that poetry created "imaginary gardens with real toads in them" (1183), a concept that transfers well to much of Wharton's war work. In an age of literary criticism that may too far separate life and art, there is a jolt of the uncanny in recognizing that, although Siegfried Sassoon might have faulted Wharton for creating male characters who were always "wounded in a mentionable place," some men really were, and are, exempted from military service because of a bad limp. John Keegan himself, though he "grew up with men who had fought in the First World War and with women who had waited at home for news of them" (*First World War* xv), is not a veteran; like Charlie Durand or John Campton, he was exempted from military service because "a childhood illness left me lame for life in 1948. . . . I [was] classified permanently unfit for duty in any of the armed forces" (*A History of Warfare* xiii). Drawn toward the military, he had, like Wharton, James, and many others, to find his role behind the lines.

Wharton's contribution to the history and the literature of the war is a limited one—but an important one. Millicent Bell has written of *A Son at the Front*, "Wharton was too professional a novelist not to realize that she could not speak for France, only for the American witness" ("Edith Wharton in France" 71). Wharton focused on American expatriates, not on French citizens; she concentrated on civilians on the home front, not on soldiers or officers at the front or at military headquarters. In the end, however, every work of literature, like every author, has its limitations. In a passage in Henri Barbusse's *Le Feu*—one of the works credited with establishing the tone of irony that would come to dominate canonized works of Great War literature—one of the soldiers in the trenches observes that those at home cannot conceive what life at the front was like. But he goes on to observe that the reverse is also true: "They don't know what war is back there; and if you started talking about the rear, it'd be *you* that'd talk rot" (180). This is a truth that has been largely forgotten—a truth of which a reexamination of Wharton's works reminds us.

The Great War was a watershed in Wharton's life and career, affecting her in almost every possible way. It altered her daily movements around Paris, France, and Europe; it meant that for over four years she devoted considerable energy to administrative tasks that were both enormous and crucially important to the welfare of French and Belgian citizens—energy she otherwise would have put into writing and other activities. It affected her financially, emotionally, and physically, as she suffered not only through cold winters but through a series of maladies, including heart attacks. Had Wharton been less attached to France, or less invested in France's victory in the war, she might have moved back to the United

States and continued, more or less uninterrupted, her devotion to fiction, gardening, travel, and friends. Yet there is no indication whatsoever that she ever considered such a course of action.

Though Wharton had found the beginning of the war "thrillingly interesting," she had become fully aware of the war's costs as it dragged on for over four years and, at last, wound to its conclusion. She did not consider herself one of those who had found her vocation in the war; she had found her calling long before when she had discovered that she was a writer. Several characters in Wharton's war-related writings are transformed by the war; it would be an exaggeration to say that Wharton underwent anything as complete as a transformation. Yet Wharton was personally affected by the war, as both her writings and commentary by several of her friends suggests.

One of the last pieces Wharton would devote to the war years, a 1923 essay entitled "Christmas Tinsel," suggests that the war allowed her deeper insight into human failings, but also into the most basic needs of human nature. In response to an editor's request from several prominent authors for an account of their most memorable Christmas, she wrote an account of her holiday in Paris in 1916—and of her work with refugees, particularly refugee children. In the hands of another author, the account of the holiday could easily have turned toward the sentimental, as it has all the ingredients: a Christmas tree, gifts, and needy children. But in Wharton's hands it is anything but sentimental. She explains that the charity in question (probably the Acceuil Franco-Belge, or American Hostels for Refugees) had so many demands upon it, and so many difficulties to deal with—both with donors and with particularly fractious refugees—that "The result was to make us sternly utilitarian. The children must be clothed and fed before they had toys, even broken ones." Given her authoritarian tone, it is a surprise to learn that "when the second Christmas came, we had got so fond of many of [the children] that utilitarianism had to give way and everybody in the office said: 'We *must* give them a Christmas tree!'" Even at this point, however, Wharton does not give in to pretty pictures and sentimentality; rather, she seems to suggest that this plan brought to her attention the illogic of donors, as well as the greed of recipients. She notes skeptically that gifts—"futilities and inutilities," as she calls them—"poured [in] at a rate the useful gifts never reached"; when the children arrive on Christmas morning, they "swarm" into the hall, and "Every face expressed a pent-up Christmas greed that made them look like little cannibals." The effect on Wharton and her fellow workers is exhausting; attempting to meet the children's demands for gifts, Wharton's assistants become "haggard" and are reduced to stripping "stars, spangles, lanterns, tinsel and finally candle ends and tin candle-holders" from the tree itself. Wharton notes that "One child got the crowning angel and barely escaped with its life" (11).

There is certainly some humorous hyperbole in the essay, but Wharton makes it quite clear that this "most memorable" Christmas was not memorable for the reasons most people would have expected. Something approaching mayhem ensues, as the philanthropical find themselves "forming a bodyguard around our valiant but bewildered guests, . . . battling with infuriated parents, silencing rapacious howls or dashing out to snatch more toys from the fast-closing shops. These emissaries, returning, reported that the street was packed with more children and the police expostulating about obstruction. Finally, through the raging mob, we fought a way out for the ambassador and his party, double-barred the doors to the approaching army and sat down aghast amid the ruins." But the tone changes from disaster to laughter as one of Wharton's fellow workers "hysterically recalled that we had said: 'Poor souls—we'll show them what an American Christmas tree is like'" (11).

Wharton's language suggests the depravity of human nature: instead of being grateful, the recipients of the gifts are "rapacious," their parents "infuriated"; parents and children together become a "raging mob." But Wharton gives the tone a final turn in the last paragraph of the essay: "They had turned the tables on us with a vengeance and shown us what a Franco-Belgian [Christmas] is like when it is offered to people, young or old, whose lives have been uprooted, whose skies have been changed, who for two bewildered years have hung on the bitter edge of hunger, sickness and sorrow with their normal surplus of enjoyment suddenly cut off. If not a pretty sight, it was an instructive one[.]" Wharton concludes that occasionally the need for the "futilities and inutilities" has to take precedence over the "sternly utilitarian": "we felt that once a year, and even on the brink of ruin, human nature needs Christmas tinsel more than coals and blankets" (11). In *The Writing of Fiction*, Wharton had discussed "the illuminating incident" as an important device for defining character. In narrating this incident, she helped to define her own: the well-organized and rigorous administrator of charities had come to understand, at its deepest level, Lear's injunction "O, reason not the need." If Wharton could be hard on human failings, she could be equally generous in acknowledging human needs.

In commentaries written for the first biography of Wharton, Percy Lubbock's 1947 *Portrait of Edith Wharton,* her friends also attested to the ways in which different aspects of Wharton's character emerged during the intense and demanding war years. Elizabeth Norton, the sister of Wharton's good friend Sally Norton, gave a brief account of that transformation: "With the war Edith threw herself into refugee work and a side of her character which was latent but had had little chance for expression developed rapidly, and her rather starved heart expanded, and she became a warmer personality, and a larger human being. One felt it in a thousand inexpressible ways—human sympathies were no longer hidden behind a social veneer and Edith Wharton, the critic, the novelist, became the humanitarian, and I think the change rendered her more free—social values were no longer of much importance, her whole outlook widened" (n.d., Series IX, *Wharton Collection* Yale).[4]

Another of Wharton's friends attested to her demonstration of profound human sympathy during the war, focusing particularly on her visits to the sanitoria for tubercular mothers and children which she administered : "If anyone had any doubt of her sympathy and tenderness, they had but to see her at Grolay [*sic*] and Arromanches—where every face—adults and children alike—lit with pleasure when she entered the wards. The world knows of her enormous intellectual equipment, but I see her always as gay, gallant, welcoming and infinitely charming" (n.d., Series IX, *Wharton Collection* Yale).[5]

Lubbock's *Portrait of Edith Wharton* has not been renowned for its objectivity; Wharton and Lubbock, a young English friend, had a falling-out over his marriage to a woman Wharton deeply distrusted.[6] The *Portrait* nevertheless provides an intriguing picture of Wharton during the war years, emphasizing her energy and sense of purpose. Among other aspects of those years, Lubbock describes her visits to the front: "she was allowed . . . a memorable vision of life at the front, the long entrenched and immobilised front of those years, through repeated visits to posts along the whole of the French line; and it was here, in the freedom and jollity, the confident cheer, the amused give-and-take which received and welcomed her, that she enjoyed her chance. If her hosts were surprised to see her they were pleased to entertain her; for among these men, younger and older, her bearing was perfect, frank and easy and adventurous, and she was passed in good humour and good fellowship from hand to hand" (130). The legitimacy of this report is corroborated not only by Wharton's own enthusiasm about her experiences at the front, but by the existence, among her

Fig. 5. Sketch done by a French soldier, "Pour Mrs. Edith Wharton." Yale Collection of American Literature, Beinecke Rare Book and Manuscript Library.

papers at the Beinecke Library, of a postcard-size drawing of a French soldier in a blue uniform (fig. 5) inscribed "Pour Mrs. Edith Wharton en souvenir de sa visite au 41ᵉ Bataillon. (Croquis éxécuté sur le front.) 23 Mai 1915" [For Mrs. Edith Wharton as a souvenir of her visit to the 41ˢᵗ Battalion. (Sketch made at the front.)] (23 May 1915, *Wharton Collection* Yale). The soldier is tossing out copies of a frontline newspaper labeled "L'Echo du Ravin"; a copy of this soldier-written paper is also preserved in Wharton's papers. Wharton must have made an impression on the soldiers—and they upon her.

Shari Benstock has written of Wharton's profound engagement during the war years, arguing that, in some ways, her involvement in war-related work benefited her:

> For Wharton, the war was a call to arms in the face of human tragedy. Its call to social activism directed her energies, revealing the deep reserves of her physical and psychological resources. She made a profoundly vital response to the war. Perhaps for the first time, her powers of leadership, organization, persuasion, and capacity for hard work were fully engaged. . . .
>
> Exhausted much of the time, diverted for weeks on end from the renewing joys of writing and travel, she even so experienced fulfillment of a kind she had never before known. ("Landscapes of Desire" 30)

In *A Backward Glance,* Wharton admits her "secret partiality" for her great-grandfather, Major-General Ebenezer Stevens: "I like above all the abounding energy, the swift adaptability and the *joie de vivre* which hurried him from one adventure to another, with war, commerce and domesticity . . . all carried on to the same heroic tune" (14). Wharton might also have been describing herself. She, too, displayed "abounding energy," "swift adaptability" and *joie de vivre* in as wide a range of activities, including experiences in wartime.

Yet the war years were tremendously exhausting for Wharton; worse, she suffered three heart attacks during this period (Benstock, *No Gifts* 345). The conclusion of the war was nothing but a relief to Wharton. She was at last able to turn back to writing, her "inexorable calling"; though she continued her work with "Mrs. Wharton's charities" for some time after the war, she was able to return to the private life she cherished.

The war affected Wharton's character in minor but important ways; its effect on her writing was profound. In July 1914, very few people foresaw the chain of events that would lead so rapidly to the outbreak of a world war; as Keegan has written, "war came, out of a cloudless sky, to populations which knew almost nothing of it" (*First World War* 9). Wharton was not among the few who knew what was about to happen. In her memoir she recounted the disbelief with which she and her friends received the first intimations of war: "On July 30th we slept at Poitiers, and all night long I lay listening to the crowds singing the *Marseillaise* in the square in front of the hotel. 'What nonsense! It can't be war,' we said to each other the next morning" (338). The war interrupted Wharton's work on her novel *Literature;* in its place she found herself working on projects she could not have imagined before the war: *Fighting France, The Marne, French Ways and Their Meaning, A Son at the Front,* and a host of newspaper articles, poems, and short stories. Nor could she have foreseen the long-term influence the war would have on her work, shaping, as it did, not only her choice of subject matter but her focus and emphasis in short stories and in full-length works like *The Age of Innocence, Old New York,* and *The Mother's Recompense.* Still less could she have foreseen the alterations the war occasioned in social mores—or the birth of the jazz age, which Wharton would satirize in works of the twenties like *Twilight Sleep* and *The Children.* In *The House of Mirth,* Lawrence Selden tells Lily Bart that "part of [her] cleverness" is her ability "to produce premeditated effects extemporaneously" (66). Wharton had protested in *A Backward Glance* that she was "incapable of transmuting the raw material of the after-war world into a work of art" (370). Yet after the war she did just that, producing her "effects extemporaneously" with "raw material" that she could not have foreseen, but which was now the material to hand. Lily Bart's efforts, despite her cleverness, end badly; but her energetic, determined, and skilled creator adapted successfully to the requirements of the "after-war world."

"The War" is a fascinating chapter in Wharton's memoir; the Great War is a fascinating, and crucially important, chapter in her life. The author who wrote *A Son at the Front* as a "'lest we forget'" (*Letters* 471) would doubtless be pleased that scholars going to study her papers at Yale's Beinecke Library walk through a courtyard dedicated to the memory of Yale students who fought and died in the Great War. On the friezes of the neoclassical buildings around Beinecke Plaza are inscribed the names of many prominent battles: "Cambrai—Argonne—Somme—Chateau-Thierry—Ypres—St. Mihiel—Marne," and on a nearby plaque are the words "In Memory of The Men of Yale who true to Her Traditions gave THEIR LIVES that FREEDOM might not perish from the Earth[.] Anno Domini 1914 1918[.]"

From the beginning of her career, Edith Wharton was a writer with a wide range. Before the war, she had written a historical novel, novels of high society and rural destitution, social satires, and travel narratives; her accomplishments in the genre of the short story were equally varied in setting, tone, and type. The war years induced her to widen her range yet further, as she added journalism and occasional poems to her repertoire—all while continuing her production of fiction. And the war influenced her return to the historical novel in the postwar years, as the social change in those years led her to write more biting social satires than she had in the prewar years. This book opened with R.W.B. Lewis's remark that "One of the fascinating themes in literary history is the impact of a great war upon the creative imagination" (393). The Great War had an immense impact on Wharton's imagination; in turn, Wharton presented the war in fiction, nonfiction, and poetry to her reading public. The increased attention being given to women's writings about, and role in, the First World War has broadened the understanding of historians and literary scholars about what, exactly, the Great War was—and of how many different, yet equally legitimate, war experiences occurred between August 1914 and November 1918. A deepened understanding of Wharton's war-related writings increases our understanding of history, of literature—and of the profound influence the war had on the life and career of Wharton herself.

Appendix A

War-Related Poems by Edith Wharton

Poems are presented in order of composition, as nearly as can be determined.

Belgium
"La Belgique ne regrette rien." [1]

Not with her ruined silver spires,
Not with her cities shamed and rent,
Perish the imperishable fires
That shape the homestead from the tent.

Wherever men are staunch and free,
There shall she keep her fearless state,
And, homeless, to great nations be
The home of all that makes them great.

Jan. 1915
(Published in *King Albert's Book,* New York: Hearst's International Library Co., 1915.)

Beaumetz, February 23rd. 1915.
(Jean du Breuil de St. Germain)

So much of life was sudden thrust
Under this dumb disfiguring dust,
Such laughter, hopes, impatient power,
Such visions of a rounded hour,
Such ardour for things deep and great,
Such easy disregard of fate,

Such memories of strange lands remote,
Of solitudes where eagles float,
Of plains where under other stars
Strange races lock in alien wars,
And isles of spicery that sleep
Unroused on an unfurrowed deep—

All this—and then his voice, his eyes,
His eager questions, gay replies,
The warmth he put into the air—
And, oh, his step upon the stair!

Poor grave, too narrow to contain
Such store of life, in vain, in vain,
The grass-roots and the ivy-ropes
Shall pinion all those springing hopes,
In vain the ivy and the grass
Efface the sense of what he was,
Poor grave!—for he shall burst your ties,
And come to us with shining eyes,
And laughter, and a quiet jest,
Whenever we, who loved him best,
Speak of great actions simply done,
And lives not vain beneath the sun.

Edith Wharton. Easter. 1915.
(Courtesy Lilly Library, Indiana University, Bloomington, Indiana.)

The Great Blue Tent

Come unto me, said the Flag,
Ye weary and sore-opprest,
For I am no shot-riddled rag
But a great Blue Tent of Rest.

Ye heavy-laden, come
On the aching feet of dread,
From ravaged town, from murdered home,
From your tortured and your dead.

All they that beat at my crimson bars
Shall enter without demur;

Though the round earth rock with the wind of wars
Not one of my folds shall stir.

See, here is warmth and sleep,
And a table largely spread.
I give garments to them that weep,
And for grave-stones I give—bread.

But what, through my inmost fold,
Is this cry on the winds of war?
"Are you grown so old? Are you grown so cold,
O flag that was once our star?

"Where did you learn that bread is life,
And where that fire is warm,
You that took the van of a world-wide strife
As an eagle takes the storm?

"Where did you learn that men are bred
Where hucksters bargain and gorge,
And where, that down makes a softer bed
Than the snows of Valley Forge?

"Come up, come up to the stormy sky,
Where our free folds rattle and hum,
For Lexington taught us how to fly
And we dance to Concord's drum!"

O flags of freedom, said the Flag,
Brothers of wind and sky,
I too was once a tattered rag,
And I wake and shake at your cry.

I tug and tug at the anchoring-place
Where my drowsy folds are caught,
I strain to be off on the old fierce chase
Of the foe we have always fought.

O People I made, said the Flag,
And welded from sea to sea,
I am still the shot-riddled rag
That shrieks to be free, to be free!

Oh, cut my silken ties
From the roof of the Palace of Peace,
Give back my stars to the skies,
My stripes to the storm-striped seas—

Or else, if you bid me yield,
Then down with my crimson bars,
And over all my azure field
Sow poppies instead of stars. . .

August, 1915

(Published in *The New York Times,* August 25, 1915. This copy follows the punctuation and capitalization in Wharton's typescript, Yale Collection of American Literature, Beinecke Rare Book and Manuscript Library.)

The Tryst

I said to the woman: Whence do you come,
With your bundle in your hand?
She said: In the North I made my home,
Where slow streams fatten the fruitful loam,
And the endless wheat-fields run like foam
To the edge of the endless sand.

I said: What look have your houses there,
And the rivers that glass your sky?
Do the steeples that call your people to prayer
Lift fretted fronts to the silver air,
And the stones of your streets, are they washed and fair
When the Sunday folk go by?

My house is ill to find, she said,
For it has no roof but the sky;
The tongue is torn from the steeple-head,
The streets are foul with the slime of the dead,
And all the rivers run poison-red
With the bodies drifting by.

I said: Is there none to come at your call
In all this throng astray?
They shot my husband against a wall,
And my child (she said), too little to crawl,

Held up its hands to catch the ball
When the gun-muzzle turned its way.

I said: There are countries far from here
Where the friendly church-bells call,
And fields where the rivers run cool and clear,
And streets where the weary may walk without fear,
And a quiet bed, with a green tree near,
To sleep at the end of it all.

She answered: Your land is too remote,
And what if I chanced to roam
When the bells fly back to the steeples' throat,
And the sky with banners is all afloat,
And the streets of my city rock like a boat
With the tramp of her men come home?

I shall crouch by the door till the bolt is down,
And then go in to my dead.
Where my husband fell I will put a stone,
And mother a child instead of my own,
And stand and laugh on my bare hearth-stone
When the King rides by, she said.

Paris, August 27th, 1915
(Published in *The Book of the Homeless,* Jan. 1916.)

Battle Sleep

Somewhere, O sun, some corner there must be
    Thou visitest, where down the strand
Quietly, still, the waves go out to sea
    From the green fringes of a pastoral land.

Deep in the orchard-bloom the roof-trees stand,
    The brown sheep graze along the bay,
And through the apple-boughs above the sand
    The bees' hum sounds no fainter than the spray.

There through uncounted hours declines the day
    To the low arch of twilight's close,
And, just as night about the moon grows gray,
    One sail leans westward to the fading rose.

Giver of dreams, O thou with scatheless wing
    Forever moving through the fiery hail,
To flame-seared lids the cooling vision bring,
    And let some soul go seaward with that sail!
(Published in *The Century,* Sept. 1915.)

"On Active Service"
American Expeditionary Force

(R.S., August 12th, 1918)

He is dead that was alive.
How shall friendship understand?
Lavish heart and tireless hand
Bidden not to give or strive,
Eager brain and questing eye
Like a broken lens laid by.

He, with so much left to do,
Such a gallant race to run,
What concern had he with you,
Silent Keeper of things done?

Tell us not that, wise and young,
Elsewhere he lives out his plan.
Our speech was sweetest to his tongue,
And his great gift was to be man.

Long and long shall we remember,
In our breasts his grave be made.
It shall never be December
Where so warm a heart is laid,
But in our saddest selves a sweet voice sing,
Recalling him, and Spring.

August, 1918.
(Published in *Scribner's Magazine* 64, Nov. 1918.)

Elegy
Ah, how I pity the young dead who gave
All that they were, and might become, that we
With tired eyes should watch this perfect sea

Reweave its patterning of silver wave
Round scented cliffs of arbutus and bay.

No more shall any rose along the way,
The myrtled way that wanders to the shore,
Nor jonquil-twinkling meadow any more,
Nor the warm lavender that takes the spray,
Smell only of the sea-salt and the sun,

But, through recurring seasons, every one
Shall speak to us with lips the darkness closes,
Shall look at us with eyes that missed the roses,
Clutch us with hands whose work was just begun,
Laid idle now beneath the earth we tread—

And always we shall walk with the young dead—
Ah, how I pity the young dead, whose eyes
Strain through the sod to see these perfect skies,
Who feel the new wheat springing in their stead,
And the lark singing for them overhead!

(1918)
(Published in Edith Wharton, *Twelve Poems*, 1926.)

You and You
(To the American Private Soldier in the Great War)

Every one of you won the war—
You and you and you—
Pressing and pouring forth, more and more,
Toiling and straining from shore to shore
To reach the flaming edge of the dark
Where man in his millions went up like a spark;
You, in your thousands and millions coming,
All the sea ploughed with you, all the air humming,
All the land loud with you,
All our hearts proud with you,
All our souls bowed with the awe of your coming.

Where's the Arch high enough,
Lads, to receive you,
Where's the eye dry enough,
Dears, to perceive you,

When at last and at last in your glory you come
Tramping home?

Every one of you won the war,
You and you and you—
You that carry an unscathed head,
You that halt with a broken tread,
And oh, most of all, you Dead, you Dead.

Lift up the Gates for these that are last,
That are last in the great Procession.
Let the living pour in, take possession,
Flood back to the city, the ranch, the farm,
The church and the college and mill,
Back to the office, the store, the exchange,
Back to the wife with the babe on her arm,
Back to the mother that waits on the sill,
And the supper that's hot on the range.

And now, when the last of them all are by,
Be the Gates lifted up on high
To let those Others in,
Those Others, their brothers, that softly tread,
That come so thick, yet take no ground,
That are so many, yet make no sound,
Our Dead, our Dead, our Dead!

O silent and secretly-moving throng,
In your fifty thousand strong,
Coming at dusk when the wreaths have dropt,
And streets are empty, and music stopt,
Silently coming to hearts that wait
Dumb in the door and dumb at the gate.
And hear your step and fly to your call—
Every one of you won the war,
But you, you Dead, most of all!

(Published in *The Pittsburgh Chronicle Telegraph,* Jan. 1919. Too late for inclusion in this book, it came to my attention that the poem exists in a longer form. Published in the February 1919 *Scribner's Magazine* (152–53), that version is forty-two lines longer than the one reproduced here.)

With the Tide

Somewhere I read, in an old book whose name
Is gone from me, I read that when the days
Of a man are counted, and his business done,
There comes up the shore at evening, with the tide,
To the place where he sits, a boat—
And in the boat, from the place where he sits, he sees,
Dim in the dusk, dim and yet so familiar,
The faces of his friends long dead; and knows
They come for him, brought in upon the tide,
To take him where men go at set of day.
Then rising, with his hands in theirs, he goes
Between them his last steps, that are the first
Of the new life—and with the ebb they pass,
Their shaken sail grown small upon the moon.

Often I thought of this, and pictured me
How many a man who lives with throngs about him,
Yet straining through the twilight for that boat
Shall scarce make out one figure in the stern,
And that so faint its features shall perplex him
With doubtful memories—and his heart hang back.
But others, rising as they see the sail
Increase upon the sunset, hasten down,
Hands out and eyes elated; for they see
Head over head, crowding from bow to stern,
Repeopling their long loneliness with smiles,
The faces of their friends; and such go forth
Content upon the ebb tide, with safe hearts.

But never
To worker summoned when his day was done
Did mounting tide bring in such freight of friends
As stole to you up the white wintry shingle
That night while they that watched you thought you slept.
Softly they came, and beached the boat, and gathered
In the still cove under the icy stars,
Your last-born, and the dear loves of your heart,
And all men that have loved right more than ease,

And honor above honors; all who gave
Free-handed of their best for other men,
And thought their giving taking: they who knew
Man's natural state is effort, up and up—
All these were there, so great a company
Perchance you marveled, wondering what great ship
Had brought that throng unnumbered to the cove
Where the boys used to beach their light canoe
After old happy picnics—

But these, your friends and children, to whose hands
Committed, in the silent night you rose
And took your last faint steps—
These led you down, O great American,
Down to the winter night and the white beach,
And there you saw that the huge hull that waited
Was not as are the boats of the other dead,
Frail craft for a brief passage; no, for this
Was first of a long line of towering transports,
Storm-worn and ocean-weary every one,
The ships you launched, the ships you manned, the ships
That now, returning from their sacred quest
With the thrice-sacred burden of their dead,
Lay waiting there to take you forth with them,
Out with the ebb tide, on some farther quest.

Hyeres, January 7th, 1919
(Published in *The Saturday Evening Post,* March 29, 1919.)

Appendix B

Selected War-Related Prose by Edith Wharton

Materials are presented in order of publication.

My Work Among the Women Workers of Paris
Noted American Novelist Tells How Her Ouvroir Gave Support to an
Army of Women Left Without Employment by the War—How Hostels
Aid Refugees

A comprehensive study of Paris war charities should be made by a detached looker-on; any sincere report by a worker can deal only with the
particular patch of misery he or she has tried to relieve. I therefore write
without apology in the first person singular, and head my opening paragraph:

My Workroom.
When the war broke out an immense number of benevolent and unoccu-
pied women in Paris felt a violent but vague impulse to "help." This impulse found its chief expression in the traditional pursuits of making lint,
hemming towels and crocheting baby jackets. Such activities are harmless
and even commendable in days of peace, but in war time any unpaid industry encroaches on the rights of the unemployed, and this fact was so
promptly understood in France that I can claim only by a few weeks' prior-
ity the honor of having founded the first paying workroom in Paris.

My ouvroir, which started tentatively and on a small scale, was at first
meant only to supply work for a few seamstresses of my own quarter, but
with the temporary paralysis of trade such a wave of misery swept over

Paris that the most prudently circumscribed charities had to enlarge their borders and take their chance of finding the means to exist. It was impossible to confine my aid to seamstresses when typists and accountants, nursery governesses and dramatic artists, cooks and concert singers were all pleading for help, but I kept, and have continued to keep, to one of my original rules: that no one I employed should be in receipt of what is called the "military allowance." All over Paris in those early days workrooms were being opened to help the wives and mothers of soldiers; wives, widows and young girls without near relatives in the army were not unnaturally overlooked, and it was for their benefit that my workroom was started.

My first step was to appeal for help to my compatriots in Paris. In spite of the preoccupations of those first distracted days, I collected over $2,000 within a week or two, and with that sum the foundations of the work were laid. I bought a large supply of materials, made arrangements to have my women fed in a neighboring restaurant, and put over my door the sign of the Red Cross, under whose auspices the work was begun. The plan then laid down has been followed ever since. The women receive 20 cents a day and a good mid-day meal in return for six hours' work. On Thursdays they have a half-holiday with full pay, but whenever there is a sudden call for hospital supplies or any urgent order they cheerfully give up their Thursday afternoon.

When a woman applies for work she shows her papers, gives references, and is asked to prove that she is not receiving either the "military allowance" or what is called the "assistance to the unemployed"—though we give work to those in receipt of the latter stipend (from 15 to 25 cents a day) if they have children or infirm relatives to support. The woman's statements are verified by inquiries at her mairie, and if the report is favorable she is engaged for two months.

The two months over, she has to leave, but if she chooses we give her piecework at home for a month. At the end of the month, if there is a vacancy, she can return to the workroom for another two months, and so on. This system of rotation was established as soon as it became evident that the war was to last a long time, and the result has been satisfactory. The fact that the women are not engaged for more than two months stimulates them to look for regular employment, and with the gradual revival of business many have found it, especially, of course, the skilled seamstresses and the typists. Still, there are always fresh cases of want coming up, and for many months past we have given work to an average of over sixty women, sometimes to as many as ninety, and have always had a long waiting list ahead.

At first, my plan was to collect money for the purchase of materials and the payment of the women's wages and board and to give away all the garments we made. This plan is still in practice in a number of Paris workrooms, but when the hope of a speedy victory disappeared it seemed to me more sensible to sell our garments at a very moderate profit and try to make the work nearly self-supporting. We still make gifts to needy hospitals or to refugees in distress whenever materials are given us, but with the material we buy we make clothes which we sell, charging about 5 per cent. profit on the cost and the women's wages. This has enabled me to keep my workroom going for fourteen months without clamoring for donations. My refugee charities cannot be made self-supporting, and for them I must clamor, and shall keep on clamoring, till we can send back to their own land the homeless and ruined people we are sheltering, but my workroom has proved its ability to live almost entirely by its own resources, *provided we get enough orders.*

The whole point is there. If the friends of the Paris workgirl will continue to send me orders as generously as they have hitherto my ninety seamstresses are safe till the war is over and they can take up their normal work. And as the second war-winter begins I venture to remind our benefactors what every order, even of a few dollars, means to our workwomen: the chance to go on earning a little more money for a new pair of shoes, or coal for a cold room, or warm gloves for the baby, or a bottle of medicine for an invalid at home, or a bundle of cigarettes for a soldier. Nothing makes our women as happy as to send a little present to one of the friendless men at the front. When we are working for the trenches or the ambulances their fingers fly twice as fast, and I know that often their savings go to buy a little gift that is secretly slipped into our big bundles.

Last September the workroom celebrated its first birthday. In honor of the occasion we had a little teaparty, at which were present not only the friends who helped to organize the work, and still direct it with me, but the eight or ten young women—cutters and lingères—who form our permanent staff. I gave them a sketch of our financial situation, and they were much interested to learn that we were almost self-supporting. Their pride in the "business" is delightful to see. Often when I come into the workroom I am met by an excited cry: "A new order! A big order!" and there is not one of our staff who does not often work overtime to get these coveted orders "rushed through," and thus increase our popularity. All

Frenchwomen of the bourgeois class have a business instinct. It is natural to them to interest themselves in "the firm" because, when they marry, they all expect to become, in the most practical sense, the business partners of their husbands, and that fact is one of France's greatest economic assets today.

Here is the statement I read to my workwomen on our first anniversary:

An average of sixty women employed for a year, representing the equivalent of 14,733 days' work.

Number of garments made, 15,200.

Purchase of materials $6,000

General expenses 500

Wages and board 5,500

Total $12,000

Value of garments given away to hospitals or sold to purchasers, $17,000.

These figures seem to make a very satisfactory showing. There is now, however, a very little margin to carry on the work for the coming Winter, so I hope you will send me, to the "Ouvroir de Mme. Wharton, 23 bis rue de l'Université," a gift of materials, or an order for hospital garments or for fine lingerie. Donations of materials, especially cotton flannel, flannel, serge and yarns are of the greatest help, and should be addressed to the American War Relief Clearing House, 5 rue François Premier, Paris, with my name on the left-hand corner of the label. They should be shipped through the New York office of the clearing house at 15 Broad Street.

The American Hostels for Refugees.

In September, 1914, the streets of Paris were swarming with thousands of lamentable refugees from Belgium and Northern France. They came all at once, in a terrible tidal wave, and no one knew how to stem it or into what channels to divert it. Paris, then at its darkest hour, deserves credit for having been able to give help to the fugitives rather than criticism for lack of method in giving it.

But the fact remains that the first weeks of the refugees were appalling. They slept on benches in the streets, on straw in the railway stations. By day they wandered helplessly about, trying to find food and shelter. The first attempts to accommodate them were not systematic or successful, and in October a few French friends who had been trying to lend a hand in straightening out the confusion came to me for advice.

They were horrified at the misery they had seen, and they felt that the first need was for some kind of a decent shelter for the poor creatures on their arrival. After that there would be time to try to provide for their future.

In response to our appeal, generous friends put at our disposal three large houses, and the American Hostels for Refugees were founded, in connection with the already existing French committee, which had taken the name of "Le Foyer Franco-Belge." We had between us about $500 in cash and a collection of more or less infirm furniture. We begged right and left for beds and blankets, we hired linen and cutlery, and within a fortnight we had opened two houses with beds for a hundred, and a third with a restaurant for 550 and a free clinic and dispensary—the latter as necessary as the beds and food, for the poor creatures we sheltered were almost all ill from hunger, fatigue and the horrors they had undergone.

The next step was to found a clothing depot, for almost all who came to me had fled without money or clothing. We opened our depot and appealed for clothes and boots, and soon gifts in kind began to pour in from France and then from America. But we wanted more, and always more, so why not employ some of our refugee women to make garments for their less fortunate compatriots? We fitted up a big workroom in the hostel which contains the restaurant and the clinic, and here about fifty women have worked for months turning out clothes for our depot and also taking orders for hospitals. This enables us to keep down the cost of the workroom, which is run at an expense of about $150 a month.

But what was to become of the babies while the mothers were sewing? Why, they must have a day nursery, of course, and a day nursery they have in a big pleasant room opening on a court where they can play. Then there is a singing class, and a class in designing, and we hope to start a sewing class for the little girls before long. Another useful adjunct to our work is the English class for grown-ups, which is given free of charge at one of our hostels by the British Young Women's Christian Association and attended by the many young men and women among our refugees to whom English will, after the war, be a valuable business asset.

At first all we could do was to shelter, clothe and feed these poor people. But as time wore on we had to think of their future. It was not possible to let them lounge away the weeks in dreary idleness. We accordingly started an employment agency, and though at first it was not always easy to induce our bewildered and demoralized protégés to look for work, or to find the right job for them in the general disorganization of things, yet little by little we have managed to adjust the supply and demand, and can now show a list of 3,400 refugees for whom we have found employment. It is a figure to be proud of, for many of the refugees were small shopkeepers who knew no trade, others were familiar only with trades which the war has temporarily suspended, and many spoke only Flemish and were, therefore, of little use in any line.

Finally, there are immense numbers whom we have helped out by financial assistance, small sums to tide them over an emergency, or a weekly allowance to eke out the 25 cents a day the Government allows them. In many cases such timely help has enabled a man to get a job, a mother to provide proper food for a sick child, a peddler to buy the stock-in-trade for his handcart. It is hardly possible for any one who has not been in Paris for the last year to realize the utter destitution of the people we have been trying to assist. There is hardly a form of human misery that has not come our way and wrung our hearts with the longing to do more and to give more.

Last month the American hostels and Foyer Franco-Belge celebrated the first anniversary of their joint work. Here is what we have to show as the result of a year's effort:

Refugees assisted 9,229
Meals served 235,000
Refugees for whom employment has been found 3,400
Garments distributed 48,333
Refugees cared for at free clinic and dispensary 7,700
Refugees receiving permanent assistance 3,000

To do all this has cost about $82,000. Of this amount $800 has been spent on the workroom and $40,000 on assisting the refugees to pay their rent. The rest has been spent on food and clothing. Our monthly expenses now average $6,000, and we face the new year with only $10,000 in the bank: that is to say, with only six weeks of life ahead. But we do not for a moment believe that America is going to abandon the American hostels. They have done a unique work in this last tragic year, for while other Paris charities have given temporary help to the exiled victims of the war, the hostels alone have tried to provide them with permanent aid and to give them more than merely material relief. It would mean the utter abandoning of thousands of homeless and penniless people if we had to close our doors, and we beg you to help us keep them open till all these poor people can go home.

The Children of Flanders Rescue Committee
(Oeuvre des Enfants des Flandres.)

This is my prettiest and showiest and altogether most appealing charity, but I am not going to say as much about it, because now that it is on its feet it needs less help than the others, though those feet number nearly a thousand!

This is their history:

Last April the Germans suddenly began to shell the few remaining towns of uninvaded Belgium. You know the story. There was no military advantage to be gained by shattering Ypres, Poperinghe, Furnes, and the other beautiful old towns of Western Flanders. There was just so much beauty to be destroyed, there were so many more thousands of harmless civilians to be ruined or slaughtered, and so Germany did it. Some day I hope all America will go and see the results of the doing, as I have seen them. If any of you had been there I should not have to beg of you.

Well, out of those awful ruins, which no one who has looked on can forget, poured hundreds and hundreds of little children. Some were picked up in the cellars of wrecked houses, some were living on offal in the bomb-swept streets, others were gathered in from abandoned farms, from burning villages, from the very trenches, and trainload after trainload of them came streaming into Paris last Spring. When the first detachment started the Belgian Government asked me to receive sixty of them—little girls—with the good Flemish Sisters in whose care they came. I called on a few friends to help; we were given a vacant house near Paris, and forty-eight hours later the sixty pitiful little creatures had come.

That was seven months ago, and now the Children of Flanders Rescue Committee has opened five houses, and cares for nearly 900 people, including the nuns and about 200 infirm old men and women, who are "children" too, for the second time, and could not be left alone in the ruins.

The work has been very difficult and very successful: difficult because when the children arrived they were for the most part ill from privation, filth and fatigue, and because it was not easy to clean, to clothe and to build up so many poor little starvelings at once; and successful because so many hearts were moved by the sight of these piteous bands of waifs that help poured in from the first days.

We have started schools of lacemaking for the older girls, and this will give them the means to make a livelihood. But many of the children are too young to learn a trade, and as yet we cannot afford to start an industrial school for the boys. At present we have only $1,800 in hand, and that is not enough to keep the work going much longer, far less to provide for the future. So I end as I began, by saying: Help us! The children's houses need less than the hostels, and smaller sums will help them, but they must be helped, too, if our houses are to remain open till the war is over, and if our pensioners are to go back with some chance of escaping starvation. No one who has not lived for a year amid all this haunting misery can picture its extent, or understand how it clings to one's thoughts and penetrates into everything one is doing. O all you happy peaceful people at home, if I could show you what we are seeing and hearing over here every day and every hour, I say again I should not have to beg of you: I should only have to tell you what I need!

Donations in money for any of my charities should be addressed to Mrs. Wharton, 53 rue de Varenne, Paris, or to Henry W. Munroe, Treasurer, in care of my sister-in-law, Mrs. Cadwalader Jones, 21 East Eleventh Street, New York.

(Published in The New York Times Magazine, Nov. 28, 1915.)

[Wharton's Preface to *The Book of the Homeless*]

Preface

I

The Hostels

Last year, among the waifs swept to Paris by the great torrent of the flight from the North, there came to the American Hostels a little acrobat from a strolling circus. He was not much more than a boy, and he had never before been separated from his family or from his circus. All his people were mummers or contortionists, and he himself was a mere mote of the limelight, knowing life only in terms of the tent and the platform, the big drum, the dancing dogs, the tight-rope and the spangles.

In the sad preoccupied Paris of last winter it was not easy to find a corner for this little figure. But the lad could not be left in the streets, and after a while he was placed as page in a big hotel. He was given good pay, and put into a good livery, and told to be a good boy. He tried . . . he really tried . . . but the life was too lonely. Nobody knew anything about the only things *he* knew, or was particularly interested in the programme of the last performance the company had given at Liège or Maubeuge. The little acrobat could not understand. He told his friends at the Hostels how lonely and puzzled he was, and they tried to help him. But he could n't sleep at night, because he was used to being up till nearly daylight; and one night he went up to the attic of the hotel, broke open several trunks full of valuables stored there by rich lodgers, and made off with some of the contents. He was caught, of course, and the things he had stolen were produced in court. They were the spangled dresses belonging to a Turkish family, and the embroidered coats of a lady's lap-dog. . . .

I have told this poor little story to illustrate a fact which, as time passes, is beginning to be lost sight of: the fact that we workers among the refugees are trying, first and foremost, to *help a homesick people.* We are not preparing for their new life an army of voluntary colonists; we are seeking to console for the ruin of their old life a throng of bewildered fugitives. It is our business not only to feed and clothe and keep alive these people, but to reassure and guide them. And that has been, for the last year, the task of the American Hostels for Refugees.

The work was started in November, 1914, and since that time we have assisted some 9,300 refugees, given more than 235,000 meals, and distributed 48,333 garments.

But this is only the elementary part of our work. We have done many more difficult things. Our employment agency has found work for over 3,500 men. Our work-rooms occupy about 120 women, and while they sew, their babies are kept busy and happy in a cheerful day-nursery, and the older children are taught in a separate class.

The British Young Women's Christian Association of Paris has shown its interest in our work by supplying us with teachers for the grown-up students who realize the importance of learning English as a part of their business equipment; and these classes are eagerly followed.

Lastly, we have a free clinic where 3,500 sick people have received medical advice, and a dispensary where 4,500 have been given first aid and nursing care; and during the summer we sent many delicate children to the seaside in the care of various Vacation Colonies.

This is but the briefest sketch of our complicated task; a task undertaken a year ago by a small group of French and American friends moved to pity by the thousands of fugitives wandering through the streets of Paris and sleeping on straw in the railway-stations.

We thought then that the burden we were assuming would not have to be borne for more than three or four months, and we were confident of receiving the necessary financial help. We were not mistaken; and America has kept the American Hostels alive for a year. But we are now entering on our second year, with a larger number to care for, and a more delicate task to perform. The longer the exile of these poor people lasts, the more carefully and discriminatingly must we deal with them. They are not all King Alberts and Queen Elisabeths, as some idealists apparently expected them to be. Some are hard to help, others unappreciative of what is done for them. But many, many more are grateful, appreciative, and eager to help us to help them. And of all of them we must say, as Henri de Régnier says for us in the poem written for this Book:

> He who, flying from the fate of slaves
> With brow indignant and with empty hand,
> Has left his house, his country and his graves,
> Comes like a Pilgrim from a Holy Land.
> Receive him thus, if in his blood there be
> One drop of Belgium's immortality.

II

The Children

One day last August the members of the "Children of Flanders Rescue Committee" were waiting at the door of the Villa Béthanie, a large seminary near Paris which had been put at the disposal of the committee for the use of the refugee children.

The house stands in a park with fine old trees and a wide view over the lovely rolling country to the northwest of Paris. The day was beautiful, the borders of the drive were glowing with roses, the lawns were fragrant with miniature hay-cocks, and the flower-beds about the court had been edged with garlands of little Belgian flags.

Suddenly we heard a noise of motor-horns, and the gates of the park were thrown open. Down toward us, between the rose-borders, a procession was beginning to pour: first a band of crippled and infirm old men, then a dozen Sisters of Charity in their white caps, and lastly about ninety small boys, each with his little bundle on his back.

They were a lamentable collection of human beings, in pitiful contrast to the summer day and the bright flowers. The old men, for the most part, were too tired and dazed to know where they were, or what was happening to them, and the Sisters were crying from fatigue and homesickness. The boys looked grave too, but suddenly they caught sight of the flowers, the hay-cocks, and the wide house-front with all its windows smiling in the sun. They took a long look and then, of their own accord, without a hint from their elders, they all broke out together into the Belgian national hymn. The sound of that chorus repaid the friends who were waiting to welcome them for a good deal of worry and hard work.

The flight from western Flanders began last April, when Ypres, Poperinghe, and all the open towns of uninvaded Belgium were swept by a senseless and savage bombardment. Even then it took a long time to induce the inhabitants to give up the ruins of their homes; and before going away themselves they sent their children.

Train-load after train-load of Flemish children poured into Paris last spring. They were gathered in from the ruins, from the trenches, from the hospices where the Sisters of Charity had been caring for them, and where, in many cases, they had been huddled in with the soldiers quartered in the same buildings. Before each convoy started, a young lady with fair hair and very blue eyes walked through the train, distributing chocolate and sandwiches to the children and speaking to each of them in turn, very kindly; and all but the very littlest children understood that this lady was their Queen. . . .

The Belgian government, knowing that I had been working for the refugees, asked me to take charge of sixty little girls, and of the Sisters accompanying them. We found a house, fitted it up, begged for money and clothes, and started The Children of Flanders Rescue Committee. Now, after six months, we have five houses, and are caring for nearly 900 people, among whom are about 200 infirm old men and women whom the Sisters had to bring because there was no one left to look after them in the bombarded towns.

Every war-work, if it has any vitality in it, is bound to increase in this way, and is almost certain to find the help it needs to keep it growing. We have always been so confident of this that we have tried to do for our Children of Flanders what the Hostels have done for the grown-up refugees: not only to feed and clothe and shelter, but also to train and develop them. Some of the Sisters are skilled lace-makers; and we have founded lace-schools in three of our houses. There is a dearth of lace at present, owing to the ruin of the industry in Belgium and Northern France, and our little lace-makers have already received large orders for Valenciennes and other laces. The smallest children are kept busy in classes of the "Montessori" type, provided by the generosity of an American friend, and the boys, out of school-hours, are taught gardening and a little carpentry. We hope later to have the means to enlarge this attempt at industrial training.

This is what we are doing for the Children of Flanders; but, above and beyond all, we are caring for their health and their physical development. The present hope of France and Belgium is in its children, and in the hygienic education of those who have them in charge; and we have taught the good Sisters many things they did not know before concerning the physical care of the children. The results have been better than we could have hoped; and those who saw the arrival of the piteous waifs a few months ago would scarcely recognize them in the round and rosy children playing in the gardens of our Houses.

III

The Book

I said just now that when we founded our two refugee charities we were confident of getting money enough to carry them on. So we were; and so we had a right to be; for at the end of the first twelvemonth we are still alive and solvent.

But we never dreamed, at the start, that the work would last longer than a year, or that its demands would be so complex and increasing. And when we saw before us the certainty of having to carry this poor burden of humanity for another twelve months, we began to wonder how we should get the help to do it.

Then the thought of this Book occurred to me. I appealed to my friends who write and paint and compose, and they to other friends of theirs, writers, painters, composers, statesmen and dramatic artists; and so the Book gradually built itself up, page by page and picture by picture.

You will see from the names of the builders what a gallant piece of architecture it is, what delightful pictures hang on its walls, and what noble music echoes through them. But what I should have liked to show is the readiness, the kindliness, the eagerness, with which all the collaborators, from first to last, have lent a hand to the building. Perhaps you will guess it for yourselves when you read their names and see the beauty and variety of what they have given. So I efface myself from the threshold and ask you to walk in.

Edith Wharton
Paris, November, 1915
(New York: Scribner's, 1916.)

Edith Wharton Tells of German Trail of Ruin

Writer Describes Vast Field of Desolation in Path of Retreat.
Women Are Massacred.
Bridges Intact, but Orchards Laid Low and Inhabitants Left Starving.

> *No woman, probably no man not engaged in military service, has seen*
> *so much of the war as Edith Wharton, the American writer, author of*
> *"Sanctuary," "The House of Mirth," "The Reef" and "Fighting France,"*
> *the last published in 1915. She has written for* The Sun *the following*
> *article, headed "In the Land of Death."*
> By Edith Wharton.

Special Cable Despatch to The Sun.

Paris, April 5.—I am just back from a stay of two days in the region lately evacuated by the Germans between Mondidier and La Fere, the country that their own newspapers boast of having turned into a "land of death." The military authorities allowed me to visit all the ruined towns and villages within a district about fifty miles long and twenty wide. In that small fragment of ravaged France I saw woe enough to cover a kingdom with mourning.

The havoc begins soon after turning north from Compiegne, and to eyes familiar with the bombarded ruins of Flanders and the fire swept towns of the Argonne and Lorraine the sight presents no novelty, but our first halt among the ruins of an annihilated village showed us that the cruelties of the German retreat surpass those of the German invasion as greatly as the subtle tortures of Nero surpassed the cruelties of primitive warfare.

Sheer Joy in Destruction.

In the first place, it is evident that the humble villages in the plain and the isolated farmhouses in the open fields were destroyed for the mere joy of destroying. They could have been no menace to retreating armies. Then there is the manner of their destruction. I have seen Ypres, Gerbevillers, Sermaize, Badonviller—all the towns from the North Sea to the Vosges whose extermination we shuddered over in the early days of the war, but these ruins, senseless though they were, were less dreadful than the merest wrecked farmhouse in the country I have just visited.

The horror of these ruins of the retreat are that many of the houses have been blown up and not burnt, and that among all the fallen beams, splintered tiles and twisted pipes one searches in vain for any trace of furniture or domestic utensils. There is not a fragment of a chair or a bed, not a torn scrap of blanket or sheet or clothing, and the people will tell you why. It is because for a month beforehand the Germans were busy systematically packing up and carrying away every movable article which these poor peasants possessed.

Ruin is Systematic.

I visited the towns of Appilly, Chauny, Villequier, Cutts, Roye, Lassigny and many villages between. Only in one house did we see the fragment of a bed dangling through the gutted floor. Everywhere in the fields is the same systematic ruin. Near each murdered house are ruined farming utensils, choked up wells and orchards with prostrate fruit trees. Trees there was no time to cut down have had the bark stripped off or a deep ring hacked into the trunks.

Again and again this scene of vain destruction passed before us, and in one of the doomed valleys where were blackened farms, ruined orchards, flooded fields, a darkened land of death, we came on a carefully tended German graveyard, above which was inscribed in conspicuous lettering "I am the resurrection and the life." The presence everywhere of these untouched German graveyards is significant of the abyss in ideals that exists between the two races. At Chateau Goyencourt the Germans broke open and defiled a family vault. At Nesle gravestones were torn up from the cemetery to build a platform for a heavy gun.

In one village through which we passed I saw that all the graves had been uncovered and the broken slabs flung in a heap among filth and refuse, yet nowhere did I see a shrub uprooted or a stone displaced in any of the gardenlike German cemeteries along our road. The French reverence for the dead extends even to the dead of such an enemy.

Male Inhabitants Deported.

I expected to gather stories of the retreat in every village, but there was no one to tell them. All the inhabitants were driven out before their houses were destroyed. An act of mercy at last? Well, ask the people who had been gathered into the surviving towns such as Noyon and Ham. They are all women and children, the sick, the infirm old people. All others from 15 to 60 had been taken away by the Germans, nobody knows where, and not only boys and men have gone but young girls too.

Mme. Carrel, wife of the great surgeon and herself at the head of the famous hospital at Compiegne, was the first woman to reach Noyon after the retreat. Even now she can hardly control herself when she describes what she heard from the fugitives who were pouring in there. At Guiscard she saw an old woman who had attempted to rescue her granddaughter, a girl of 18, whom a German officer took off as his "orderly." The grandmother intervened and the officer broke her arm with a sabre cut.

Another woman was knocked down and her thigh was broken by a blow from an officer. One mother, whose sons are all at the front and who had no news of them since the war began, has just seen her two daughters, 15 and 16, carried off by the Germans to an unknown destination.

Even this is not worse than what we found in a small village near Guiscard. The women and children, after their boys and men had been torn from them, were told to go and stand at the eastern end of the village to greet the French troopers who were coming that way. The Germans departed, but when they were a couple of hundred yards away they turned a machine gun on the helpless creatures who were waiting to welcome their rescuers. When Mme. Carrel reached Guiscard she saw bodies of little children being brought in from the massacre.

Not only were the ravaged towns and villages stripped of everything but the towns to which the homeless fugitives were driven had been thoroughly looted before they got there. On leaving Compiegne we were told to take all our provisions with us, "for you won't find a crust of bread after leaving here," and in fact in towns like Ham and Noyon, where the outward damage was relatively slight, we beheld the uncanny spectacle of a street of absolutely empty shops. There is not a yard of material or an ounce of food in any of these towns except what the French army and the relief committees are hurrying there over rapidly mended roads.

Money Has No Value.

At Ham I handed the Mayor a sum of money which a friend in Paris had asked me to distribute. He answered: "Please take it back and buy us provisions. Money has no value here." At Noyon the clerk of the town hall, who had been slaving for the Germans for thirty months, was dressed in a nightshirt and a threadbare suit of clothes, all the plunderers had left him. Every stitch of linen, every garment, ever[y] pair of shoes had been carried off from the town, and the people have literally nothing but the garments on their backs.

This would seem a small matter if they had homes to return to, but every means of livelihood has been taken from them by the flooding of their fields, the carrying off of their live stock and the destruction of their orchards. After two years of starvation and slavery they are released at last to find their whole world in ruins.

There are two marked differences between this destruction and the savagery of the first year of the war. The latter was the sudden act of an army drunk with success, flung back from the very crest of victory, wreaking its rage on everything in its path, whereas the destruction in the track of this latest retreat is a deliberately planned attempt to murder the land as well as the people, to drain its life blood, to turn it into a shelterless desert, and this insidious deviltry has been slowly and systematically applied to a helpless people who have been living for more than two years in a state of servitude to the Germans, who have been feeding the Germans, housing them, slaving for them, for whom it might have been supposed that some feeling of compassion and humanity must have sprung up in the hearts of the oppressors.

Military Reason Lacking.

There is another difference. The Germans assert that their devastations are due to military necessity, that they had to destroy everything behind them to secure their retreat. It does not take a military expert to see that the way of securing the retreat would have been to blow up roads and bridges, yet far more time must have been given to wrecking farmhouses, smashing ploughs, hacking down fruit trees than to systematic road and bridge destruction.

It is impossible to find any military reason for what they have done. Aimless and vindictive cruelty is proclaimed in every slaughtered orchard, in every stack of shattered agricultural implements. The idea that cutting down fruit trees and breaking up ploughs can check the progress of an advancing army is senseless as long as the roads remain and supplies can be pushed forward. The damage to the roads in the region I saw is not a hundredth part of what it might have been if the well poisoners, tree hackers and furniture robbers had all been concentrated on the job.

What the Germans have done is to put fiery hate into the hearts of every one of the French peasant soldiers we saw swinging along in thousands toward the front. In every poor rooftree collapsed into its blackened farmyard the French soldier sees the image of what his own home will soon be or what might have been if it had stood in the path of the German retreat. He sees also the image of what the German homesteads will be when once he gets at them. That last point is one for the people of the Rhine provinces to ponder.

Unlike Grant's Policy.

As we sped along from one wrecked village to another over hastily mended roads, skirting shell and mine craters, crossing boat bridges across swollen rivers, with lines of splendid shade trees lying slaughtered by the roadside, orchards hewn down, fields under water, I thought of a few words exchanged in Appomattox Court House between the rival leaders in the bloodiest struggle history had known until then:

"Must our cavalry give up their horses, General?"

"No, let them keep their horses. They will need them for the spring ploughing."

At the very moment when I though[t] of these great words of Grant's, the noblest ever spoken by a victorious General, they were being reaffirmed by his successor's solemn declaration that the United States is at war with Germany.

It is impossible for any Christian nation not to be at war with Germany. With such a record as is spread here it is inevitable that whosoever is not with her is against her.

(Published in The New York Sun, April 6, 1917. Headlines, introduction, and possibly subheadings by newspaper editors.)

Talk to American Soldiers

[The following is a portion of the talk Wharton delivered to American soldiers in spring 1918. As readers familiar with *French Ways and Their Meaning* will immediately recognize, it served as the seed for what was to become that book. In fact, the typescript of the talk is not complete. At least two pages of the talk appear to be missing; some pages (possibly including parts of the missing pages) were incorporated into Wharton's hand-written draft of *French Ways*. Since some pages are missing, the following transcription has two large gaps, though a review of pp. 9–12 of *French Ways* will suggest what they must have contained.

Because the typescript is written over in some places, I have had to make editorial choices in reproducing it here. My aim has been to reproduce, as much as possible, the talk Wharton probably delivered. Some of the handwritten changes are merely corrections of typographical errors; others seem to be slight modifications in what she planned to say; still others were clearly intended for revising the speech into its written form in *French Ways and Their Meaning*. Revisions of the last sort were frequently changes from the greater informality of speech toward the more formal written word. For instance, contractions (you're, doesn't) were expanded (you are, does not); the second person "you" was dropped; tone was sometimes elevated (for instance, "But to come back to the point" in the typescript of the speech becomes "This anecdote may have seemed to take us a long way from France and French ways"). As my hope has been to re-create the text of the speech, I have, where two possibilities presented themselves, generally chosen the simpler, less formal version.]

I have been asked to come and talk to you about France, and I want to begin by telling you how proud I am that I have been chosen to talk on a such a subject to the soldiers and sailors of my country.

I never expected to speak in public. I consider it a man's job and not a woman's; and I never *did* speak in public till last February, when I was asked to try to explain to a French audience some of the reasons why America has come into this war.

That occasion was "positively my first appearance"; but it went off very well—the lecturer always knows how it's going after the first five minutes—and I wasn't in the least nervous, because I spoke in French, and was sustained by the thought that my audience probably didn't understand more than half of what I was saying.

Now, on the contrary, I am to talk in my own language to my own country-people, and if I don't interest you I can't say afterward that it was because you missed all my best things; so you must make allowances for my timidity, and encourage me by laughing at all my jokes.

But perhaps you will ask what I am doing here, if I don't know how to speak in public, and don't consider it a woman's job anyhow.

Well—I'll tell you; I've been asked to talk about France. And having lived in France for many years, and continuously since the war began, having seen what she has been, and watched what she has done, during these four terrible years—well, I believe if I were dead, and anybody asked me to come back and witness for France, I should get up out of my grave to do it.

That is the way all we Americans feel who were here in those first days; who saw this great, busy, industrious, peace-loving people, hating war, and not for a moment believing it would come—you know they had withdrawn their troops 10 miles from the German frontier, in proof of their good faith and their sincere desire for peace—when, I say, we saw how the

French behaved in face of Germany's sudden unwarrantable breach of faith, her abominable attack on defenceless and neutral Belgium; when we saw the whole youth of France leave the plough and the store and the office and the universities, and go forth gladly to the job of defending their own country, and the little countries who couldn't defend themselves; when we saw the unforgettable scenes in the streets, the young men marching along with roses on their rifles, and the fathers and mothers and wives bidding them goodbye at the stations without a tear, and without one word to weaken or dishearten them—when we saw that, all we Americans, we saw not only what France was in that first great day of challenge, but also what she was going to be in the long weary time to come; and more than one of us thought, as we watched: "If ever our country is forced into such a war, may she meet it just in that way!"—And she has.

Well—having watched those first scenes, I began to study France and the French more closely. I had always admired the country and the people, as we Americans usually do; I had admired the beauty of the cities, the wonderful pictures and sculpture in the great Museums, the splendid roads all over the country, the perfection of the vegetable and fruit-culture (I must tell you that I'm a gardener myself), the scientific care of the great forests, the wit and brilliancy of the French theatre, the eloquence and beauty of the magnificent French literature—I had admired and enjoyed these great national treasures of France as all thoughtful Americans do. But now I began to study the people more closely, and to try to find out what slow accumulation of humble virtues had built the strong foundation of this brilliant flower of civilization that we call France.

My war-work naturally brought me in contact with people of all kinds—work-people, farmers, peasants, business men, artists—and I tried to profit by every talk, by every glimpse into their different lives, and to relate all I saw to the past life of the country. And gradually I learned, through my study of the present, why the history of France was what it was; why, in her long life of a thousand years, though she has often made mistakes in small things, she has always done certain great things—why she has always been headstrong and generous, why she has always led the way in moral and mental enlightenment,—why, in short, it was France who understood us before we were a nation, and came over and helped us to become one.

Considering these things, I began to see how important it was that we and the French should really get to know each other, and how it might be possible for some one like me, who has lived so long in both countries, to try to explain them to each other. And that is the reason why I want to talk to you about French ways and their meaning.

In doing so, I may tell you things that you know already; if I do, you must excuse me, and remember that I'd rather run that chance than leave out anything that might help the understanding between our countries.

I'm sure you agree with me that the best way of profiting by the study of a strange people is to see what we can learn from them, instead of picking out what we think there is to criticize in them. I hear a good deal in these days of the phrase: "What America can teach France." My idea is that we'd better leave it to the French to discover that, and apply ourselves to finding out what France can teach us; and we may be certain that at this very moment French lecturers, talking to French audiences, are

[missing page]

[fragment:] ["The]Germans we knew at home were easier people to get on with."

I wonder why? Well, for one thing, you knew the Germans *at home*, in *your* home, where they had to talk your language or not get on, where they had to be what you wanted them to be—or get out. And as we all know, no people on earth, when they settle in a new country, are more eager than the Germans to adopt its ways, and be taken for native-born citizens.

[missing page]

It was in summer, but there had been a cold rain storm all day, and as the Opera house was as cold as a vault, and it was not a full-dress occasion, but merely an out-of-season performance, with everybody wearing ordinary street clothes, I decided to keep on the light silk cloak I was wearing. But as I started for my seat I felt a tap on my shoulder, and one of those polite policemen requested me to take off my cloak.

"Thank you: but I prefer to keep it on."

"You can't, it's forbidden. *Es ist verboten.*"

"Forbidden? Why, what do you mean?"

"His Majesty the Emperor forbids any lady in the audience of the Royal and Imperial Opera-House to keep on her cloak."

"But I've a cold, and the house is so chilly—"

The polite policeman had grown suddenly stern and bullying. "Take off your cloak," he commanded.

"I won't," I said.

We looked at each other a minute—and I went in with my cloak on.

When I got back to the hotel, highly indignant, I met a German Princess, a Serene Highness, one of the greatest ladies in Germany, a cousin of his Imperial Majesty's.

I told her what had happened, and expected an echo of my indignation. But she showed no surprise. "Yes—I nearly always catch cold when I go to the Opera," she said resignedly.

"But do they make *you* take your cloak off?"

"Of course. It's the Emperor's order."

"Well—I kept mine on!" I said.

Her Serene Highness looked at me incredulously. Then she thought it over and said: "Ah, well—you're an American, and American travellers bring us so much money that the Emperor's orders are never to bully them."

What had puzzled me, by the way, when I looked about the crowded Opera-house, was that the Emperor should ever want the ladies of Berlin to take their cloaks off at the Opera. But that's a matter between them and their Maker—or their dressmaker. The interesting thing was that the German Princess did not in the least resent being bullied herself, or having neuralgia in consequence—but quite recognized that it was good business for her country not to bully Americans.

That little incident gave me a glimpse of what life in Germany must be like if you're a German; and also of the essential difference between the Germans and ourselves.

The fundamental difference is this: the German doesn't care to be free as long as he is well-fed, well-amused and making money. The Frenchman, and the American, wants to be free first of all, and free anyhow—free even when he might be better off, materially, if he were under a benevolent autocracy. The Frenchman and the American want to have a voice in governing their country, and the German prefers to be governed by professionals, as long as they make him comfortable and give him what he wants.

From the purely practical point of view this is not a bad plan, but it breaks down as soon as a moral issue is involved. They say corporations have no souls; neither have governments that are not answerable to a free people for their decisions in times of national danger.

But to come back to the point from which I started. What I want to make you see is this. [T]he differences between us and the French are mostly on the surface, and our feeling about the really important things is always the same, whereas the Germans, who seem less strange to many of us because we've been used to them at home, differ from us totally in all the important things.

But as to the superficial differences between us and the French, the things that may have struck and surprised you when you first came here: may I try to take up a few of the most obvious ones, and try to explain them away?

I daresay some of you, in America, had heard a good deal about French politeness—too much perhaps; you were inclined to think they were too polite to be really manly—like you. "A nation of dancing-masters—" and so on. (If they are, it's a pity everybody isn't taught dancing, since apparently it makes men the best fighters in the world).

Well—when you got here, and walked into the first shop to buy some chewing-gum, or Virginia tobacco, perhaps you found the people in the shop rather rude. Or you were annoyed that they didn't understand what you wanted, or didn't have it, when they finally did understand.

Now, in the first place, aren't you sometimes rather unreasonable in expecting France to be supplied with exactly the things you happen to be used to? If Germany had conquered Mexico, and invaded the United States—and it's a perfectly possible thing, as events have shown—the French would probably have come over to help us, as they did once before. And they would probably have been a good deal surprised to find that everything we ate and smoked and drank was different—and not nearly as nice, to their taste. But what should we have said if they had immediately begun by saying that it was France's mission to educate America? It seems rather more sensible to conclude that tastes are bound to differ in different countries—and, at any rate, that liking corn-beef hash for breakfast instead of a roll and butter is not a necessary proof of superiority.

But perhaps you will agree to this, and say that, nevertheless, you find the people you come in contact with in hotels and shops and trolleys are not always as pleasant as you had expected. Well—perhaps you don't always know the rules of the game—the game of politeness. You must remember that they are very different in Latin and Anglo-Saxon countries, and nine-tenths of the surface-misunderstandings are due to the fact that English and Americans don't realize what importance the Latin races attach to certain little ceremonious observances.

When you go into a shop, for instance, perhaps you just stroll in as you would in New York or London, and say: "I want so and so—"

Well, that is not the way it's done here. In France, in the humblest shop or restaurant, when a customer goes in he is expected to lift his hat and say:

"Bonjour, Monsieur," or "Bonjour, Madame," before he asks for what he wants; and if he does, the chances are he will get the article more quickly—and perhaps it will cost him less. And when it is handed to him, he is expected to say "Merci, Madame" or "Monsieur," and to repeat the bow and the "Bonjour" when he goes out.

If he omits all this, he will very likely meet glum faces, and get bad food; for there are many things that the French care for more than they care for making money or attracting customers; and one of these things is being treated with courtesy. They show courtesy to each other, and they expect it from strangers, and are so surprised when they don't get it that they often see a personal affront where none was intended.

You may regard this as making a lot of fuss about trifles; but our daily life is mostly made up of trifles, and I have always thought that politeness, though it sometimes takes a little longer, is in fact a short cut, since it carries us straight to the heart of the people to whom we show it . . . And it seems to me that politeness is most especially due when one is in a strange country—and most of all due when one has come to help that country in a terrible crisis, and when she is bound to bear with everything from the people who have come to her aid.

Please don't think, by the way, that I am suggesting you are not polite to the French; I am only reminding you that in foreign countries the truest courtesy is to be courteous in the way the foreigner is used to. To learn this takes a little patience and a little attention; but if you will remember "Bonjour" and "Merci" the other forms will come to you in time, and the smiles and friendliness you will get in return will make you feel much more at home than if you went on trying to din home habits into a foreign country.

It is not only in a shop or a restaurant that you are expected to lift your hat or to salute. In France every one uncovers before the dead. When you see one of those long funerals passing, with their sad procession of mourners on foot, salute the hearse as it goes by—a soldier's hearse, so often in these days—and you will see the look of sympathy in all those foreign eyes that are crying the same kind of tears that we do.

If there are any military motor drivers here this evening I should like to say a word to them on this point. I should like to ask them never to cut through a funeral procession. The French have a great reverence for the dead: they keep the anniversaries of their dead even more faithfully and tenderly than we do. Every year they have a memorial service, and go out to the grave with flowers; it is part of the intensely deep family feeling which is at the very root of French civilization.

The same feeling makes the French policeman check all traffic when a band of French school-children are crossing the street. The children are never stopped on the curb-stone while the motors go by: their rights come first in France. There is no country where they are more tenderly loved and cherished; whereas Germany, before the war, was the country in which the highest number of suicides occur[r]ed among school-children.

I spoke just now of the depth and sacredness of family feeling in France, and I want to insist on this, because it is perfectly evident that that side of the life of a country is the one which the stranger is slowest to discover. Even in ordinary times it must be so; and at this strange crisis in history, when two great foreign armies are pouring into France, and taking peaceful possession of her cities, her railways, her industries, it is inevitable that the side of life least visible to the newcomers is that of which France has most reason to be proud.

Wouldn't it be exactly the same in our country, if France and England had to send their armies to our aid? Do you think the first people the soldiers met when they landed would be the people you'd like your families to know?

When I spoke just now of the grumpiness of some French shopkeepers, and said it might be due to your not always knowing the French forms of politeness, I daresay you thought to yourselves: "*That* hasn't been our experience. The people we've dealt with have been polite enough, but they've cheated us in every way they could."

Well—mightn't that happen—just conceivably—in our American cities, if there were suddenly poured into them a few hundred thousand helpless foreigners with money in their pockets? Or has the millennium really come in America? I didn't know it had.

But you know better than I do the kind of people—the low international scum—that crops up in the wake of every army, ready to prey on ignorance and inexperience and good-nature. Such people exist in every country, they swarm wherever there is money to be made. Use all your wits to defend yourself against them, but don't judge France by what you see of them—or, if you do, don't be surprised if France judges *you* as unjustly.

I don't think either of these things will happen; for, as time passes, the force of circumstances will bring you in contact with the real French, the

French worth knowing; and I may almost say that it depends on you how soon you get to know them.

Indeed, I may assert that it depends on you; for ever since our first troops landed, French people of all classes and all situations in life have come to tell me how eager they were to welcome American officers and soldiers into their homes. Many, many of these homes are darkened by mourning; many belong to people who have been almost ruined by the war; but in spite of grief, in spite of straitened circumstances, these people are all eager to return the welcome that America gave to Lafayette and his men.

I say it depends on you—on every one of you. If you will take the trouble—the trifling trouble—to notice French rules of politeness, and to try to observe them, if you will show these hospitable people that you appreciate their hospitality, and want to be thought worthy of it, you will do something besides making your own life here less dull and lonely—you will be helping in the most lasting way to cement the old friendship between our two great countries.

These two countries, after the war, are destined to have very close commercial relations. Young men will be sent from France to America to study *our* ways, and from America to France to study French ways; and you can all help toward hastening the good results of this exchange—results so desirable for the future of peace and of civilization—if only you will try to understand the French, if you will try to make friends with the best ones, the ones you would like your wives and mothers an[d] sweethearts to know; and if you will go home after the war, and tell your own people what the people here are really like; not the sharpers, cheats and disreputable women, the rapscallions and dregs and sweepings of the land, but the honest decent self-respecting people, who haven't rushed to the dock to pick your pockets when you landed, but who are waiting, with open arms and grateful hearts, to give you back a hundredfold in kindness what the others may have taken from you in dollars.

It all depends on you. I know two young Frenchmen, who were in my employ before the war, and who have been at the front since it began, one in the artillery and the other in the infantry. Both of them, for the last months, have been with our troops; and if you could read the letters they wrote me when America declared war, and those they have written since they have been fighting side by side with our men, you would feel how close the real French heart is to the American heart.

This is what one of them writes, speaking of the fact that I hadn't left

Paris, which apparently he considers as much more exposed at present than the battlefield of the Somme. "I admire you for staying in Paris at this critical time, and I admire your American soldiers more than I can say for wishing to be at our sides in the terrible struggle."

And here is another, written only a few days ago: "We all feel here at the front that great things are soon going to happen that will turn the battle to our advantage, and we are confident in our gallant English allies, and in your brave countrymen, who have come of their own accord to fight at our sides. There is one thing you may be sure of; and that is that the Boche will never set foot in Paris as a victor. Long live France, long live the glorious United States, and all our Allies!"

That is a spirit I know you all feel and respond to; and I beg you to believe that hundreds of letters of the same kind are being written every day by the French soldier about his American comrade. And it's no small thing to be praised by a French soldier.

I said just now that I wanted to help you all to understand and appreciate the French. I want you to understand and appreciate their country too, and realize what a great inheritance it is for any people to have such a country. Perhaps many of you, in Paris, have not looked about you much yet, or felt the beauty of the city as you would have if you had not had so many other things on your minds. But I beg of you, now and then, to spare a little time to look at it—at the great buildings, the beautiful squares and avenues and parks and fountains and bridges.

We all take a pride in our cities at home—but sometimes we're inclined to think they're beautiful enough because we live there. The French think, on the contrary, that, because they live in Paris it's their duty to keep on making it more and more beautiful. They've been at it for nearly 2 thousand years—for Paris existed when Julius Caesar conquered Gaul—so we have every excuse if our own cities are not as finished and as full of fine monuments. But the great point about the French is that when they have any public improvement to make, they try to make it beautiful as well as useful. They don't allow hid[e]ous "elevateds" to straddle over their wide avenues, or overhead trolley wires to disfigure them; and those of you who have seen their gardens and parks and avenues in times of peace will remember how beautiful and how perfectly kept they all are.

Man is so made that the more he does to improve the place he lives in the more he loves it; you know that is true of your own house and lot, and it gets to be true of each village and town as the inhabitants take trouble and make sacrifices to beautify it. Every fine building or well-kept park that is added to a town makes that town something better worth being proud of.

The French have cultivated that kind of pride for a long time, and it is one of the roots of their intense and passionate patriotism.

I was told only today that not long ago one of the directors of the Museum of the Louvre was leaving the gallery of sculpture when a French officer came up and asked the man at the door if he could go in.

When he was told that it was closed he looked bitterly disappointed, and said he had to go back to the front the next morning, and had so wanted to look again at a few fine pieces of sculpture.

The director at once said that he would be delighted to take him about, and for an hour they walked through the gallery of French sculpture, and the director explained to the officer what they were seeing; and when it was over the officer simply said: "Thank you for giving me that hour. I know now better than ever how much I'm fighting for."

No man could have said that about a town that was all factory chimneys and gas-works and bar-rooms. We all learn in time that we must put something into our lives besides business and hustle; and France learned it a little sooner because she's seven or eight centuries older than we are. But we Americans are all capable of intense pride in our homes; it is growing in us every day, and we must all encourage it. And that is why I ask you to look about you here, and notice the beautiful things, and send home pictures of them, especially of the things we might all have—the splendid solid walls along the rivers, the beautiful bridges, the perfect roads, the exquisitely kept public parks and gardens.

Send home as many pictures of them as you can, and try to get the people at home to copy these things in the measure in which they can. The more beautiful our towns are the more we shall all love them; for every tiny bit of order and beauty and good taste which each citizen contributes to his town is like a fresh star added to the flag.

And I want to end by saying just this. You are seeing France in one way at a great advantage, because you are seeing her in the day of her great trial and her great glory. But you are also seeing her at a great disadvantage—as I'm sure you realize—because the whole regular life of the country has been disorganized for four years, and because the men who keep the country going in ordinary times are all at the front, giving their lives to save hers.

Therefore you must always remember, when you see things to criticize or regret, first that France is under a strain such as no other country has borne since the world began; and secondly, that even among the things that surprise or disappoint you, there are many you may find cause to admire when you come to know the language and the people better.

Anyhow, the safe thing is to say to yourselves, even when you don't understand, that nothing much can be wrong with a race of men who worship their old mothers, and love their children, and are always thinking how they can make the places they live in more beautiful—and who fight as the French are fighting now to defend all these things that are sacred to them.

(Spring 1918. Yale Collection of American Literature, Beinecke Rare Book and Manuscript Library.)

Capt. Ronald Simmons Dies on Active Service

Mrs. Edith Wharton Pays Stirring Tribute to Officer Who Was Always Ready.

To the Editor of the Herald:—

Sir,—Captain Ronald Simmons, of the American Army, died suddenly on August 12, in his thirty-fourth year, "on active service."

"Active service"—it is the phrase that best pictures him to the little group of friends among whom, in Paris, he had lived and worked for the last four years. Never was there any one who loved better to spend his tireless activity in serving others.

Ronald Simmons was born in Providence. He had lived in Paris, as a student at the Beaux-Arts, for several years before the war, and during those student years had made countless friends in many circles of Parisian life. For any one so shy and self-depreciatory he had a surprising gift of getting on with all sorts of people, and his military chiefs can attest to what degree his tact and good humor, and his exceptional understanding of French character and the French point of view, enhanced his usefulness in his branch of the service.

His friends would like to dwell on qualities more deeply concealed under his incurable modesty: on the responsive warmth of his sympathies, his joyous sense of humor, his sensitiveness to all things fine and rare, and the strange maturity of his judgments.

In 1914 he gave up everything to devote himself to various war charities, among others to the Comité des Etudiants Américains of the Beaux-Arts, which he made his own by his unflagging devotion, his administrative capacity and his ingenuity in devising new ways of interesting people in the work. As a member of the Committee of the Tuberculeux de la Guerre he collaborated with me till that charity was absorbed by the American Red Cross, and again and again I had occasion to profit by his wise advice, his tact and patience and discernment.

When America declared war he immediately volunteered, giving his whole energy to the task allotted him, but he was never too absorbed or hurried to find time for his friends, and whenever there was a problem to be solved, a difficulty to be met, a service to be rendered, it was still our old habit to "ring up Simmons."

He was always ready; every call found him, every distress appealed to him. If he had faults, his friends never discovered them; if he had lived long enough to give his full measure many more would have mourned him as we are mourning him to-day.

Edith Wharton
August 14th, 1918.
(Yale Collection of American Literature, Beinecke Rare Book and Manuscript Library.)

How Paris Welcomed the King.

By Edith Wharton.

It was a great pity that it rained so hard! Everybody, of course, tried to make the best of it. The facetious said it was "more English," and the sentimental that "all the sunshine was in our hearts."

But, all the same, there was a sense of general disappointment at Nature's strange oversight (her first since the signing of the Armistice) in neglecting to turn on the sunshine in honour of one of the greatest Days that civilization has ever known. Besides, the good people of Paris, who had been so lavish of their bunting, at a time when bunting costs as much as butter, would have liked King George to see their Union Jacks challenging the breeze instead of weeping into the gutters.

However, there it was; there the rain was. It came early, determined not to miss a moment of the show, and in fact arrived in time to spread a nice brown carpet of grease all the way from the end of the crimson carpet rolled down the steps of the Bois de Boulogne Station, to the beginning of the one rolled down the steps of the Ministry of Foreign Affairs.

There was one good thing, as it turned out, about this early-bird behaviour of the rain; for it set about with such matutinal zeal to drench decorations and spread mud that everybody knew from the first what was to be expected, and prepared accordingly. And, moreover, when the King actually arrived, the senseless extravagance of the downpour had led to bankruptcy (as any thrifty experienced cloud-committee could have told it); so that all umbrellas were furled before the crash of the first gun announced that the royal train had reached Paris.

Even if the rain had kept up, the high spirits of the crowd would have defied it; and to see it sneaking away just as the show began added to the general hilarity by reminding the lookers-on of a certain "strategical retreat" which had set it the example not so many weeks ago.

So, towards two o'clock of November 28, 1918, the rain left Paris just as King George reached it; and the royal and presidential and ministerial carriages rolled down the Avenue du Bois de Boulogne and the Champs Elysées under an inoffensive grey sky, and between thousands and thousands of dripping but rejoicing people.

Then, as the cannon roared (at last with such a peaceful roar!), and the crowds grew denser and the cheers louder, one began to be actually glad of the rain, glad of the wet flags, the demoralized wreaths, the wrecked decorations; for they left no semblance of a stage-setting between Paris and the guest she was greeting, no possibility of an idea that the public was "out for the fun," and not for the event that occasioned it.

No: Paris had stood there for hours in the rain for the conscious deliberate purpose of showing her great Ally how she loved him; and even to a spectator placed, as I was, on a balcony of the Ministry of Foreign Affairs, and cut off from a sight of the immense crowds in the Champs Elysées and the Place de la Concorde, there was no mistaking the unanimity of their welcome.

How many thousands and thousands of French throats must it not have taken to send up that mighty continuous roar that came to us through the trees and across the river in the thick, muffled, rainy air? The French are not natural-born cheerers; all Anglo-Saxons in Paris must have been surprised at their inarticulateness on Armistice Day. They can sing and talk and quarrel with the best, but they are too civilized to vent their emotions in mere shouting; yet when the King came they found their voices, and roared and roared as if they had been British or American, or both in one.

It was a magnificent and mighty show, that short quiet-coloured line of victorias and landaus driving slowly down between two walls of shouting spectators; a plain unadorned show, symbolic rather than pictorial, as democratic shows tend to be; but all the better for that, since it brought the public and the protagonist so much nearer to each other.

It was a magnificent and mighty show; and no one appreciated its significance and importance, or rejoiced in both, more than the Americans in Paris, who know how all-essential it is for the welfare of the world that the great sister nations facing each other across the Channel should unreservedly rejoice and be glad in each other's honour.

I lay a special stress on America's warm participation in the King's welcome because, as every one knows, one of the subtlest devices of recent German propaganda has been to play off American popularity in France against British. I suspect that, since our troops and the British have been on French soil, we have both of us been, in turn, popular and unpopular, and that the supposed general attitude towards us has really been, in most cases, the individual attitude of some particular Frenchman, soldier, civil servant, tradesman, shopkeeper, or whoever you choose, who happened to have a momentary grievance against a particular Briton or American, or a momentary reason for applauding one or the other of our races, and who aired his satisfaction or his grievance.

Most generalizations, when run to earth, turn out to have originated in some one person's drawing rash conclusions from his limited special experience, and handing them on in axiomatic form as the result of the wisdom of the ages. "They say" is usually "he" or "she says" at its source; and if it is depreciatory the stream widens quickly and soon becomes a flood.

It would have been a miracle if either Britons or Americans had been always and everywhere beloved during their sojourn on French soil. Some of them—individually—are not so very lovable at home, and we know that foreign travel does not always improve the temper. And think of France, so set in her ways, so self-centred, so perfectly satisfied to be France and nothing else—think of her having to entertain so many millions of guests, all full of goodwill no doubt, but knowing as a rule nothing whatever of the ways she is so set in, nothing of her religious, social, domestic, culinary or other peculiarities—fighting for her for all they were worth, but upsetting so many of her most cherished and peculiar little habits!

It would have been too stupid for German propaganda not to see its chance and insinuate, now: "Are the British doing all this just for love of you?" and now: "Don't you see how much easier it is to get on with the Americans than with the English?"

French individualism and conservatism too often meet such suggestions half way, and hand them on; but luckily France as a whole has always known better, and she showed it the other day when she made the grey clouds ring with her welcome to King George.

(Published in Reveille, London, England, Feb. 1919.)

Christmas Tinsel

My most memorable Christmas? It was in Paris, in 1916. We had been struggling for months with the insoluble refugee question: how to lodge, feed, clothe, doctor them, how to stop their squabbling and being ill and getting double rations, and slandering and beating each other, and wanting to go home when they had no homes and to stay in Paris when rescued and refurnished homes awaited them. Of course I allude only to the recalcitrant, impenitent and irreducible refugees; the others, the good ones, we had by the thousand too, but they caused us no gray hairs or sleepless nights and consequently are not stuff for drama.

Well: Among the refugees there were children innumerable, all likewise requiring to be clothed, fed, doctored, lodged—and also schooled and dentisted. And there were moments when, at grips day and night with this stern problem and struggling to get money, food, practical help in any shape, we used to be exasperated by little parcels of pop-corn and pink ribbon, of jacks-in-a-box, fancy pinafores and chewing-gum, each with a note from a "Happy Home in Oklahoma" or a "Bright Little American Girl," asking the recipient to send back a word of appreciation. (Of course such gifts were not the rule, any more than the bad refugees were; but we got too many of both.)

The result was to make us sternly utilitarian. The children must be clothed and fed before they had toys, even broken ones. But when the second Christmas came, we had got so fond of many of them that utilitarianism had to give way and everybody in the office said: "We *must* give them a Christmas tree!"

We did. We began to clamor for futilities and inutilities and in they poured at a rate the useful gifts never reached; and we got a big hall and a big tree and a big table groaning with presents, and everybody in the office was instructed to dole out a given number of tickets to the smallest, poorest, most pathetic of our children. It must have been one of the first Christmas trees in Paris since the war, and we were all thrilled by the preparations. So were the refugees, their children, their friends and the children of their friends. Applications for tickets poured in faster even than the gifts, and all the children who applied were apparently the smallest, poorest and most pathetic. Such at least was the defense afterward put in by the officials in whom the choice of candidates was vested.

The day came. Our ambassador, the ambassadress, all our honorary members, our benefactors and our well-wishers were there; and when they were seated, the doors were opened to the children. In they swarmed, small and poor, but not pathetic—not that day! Every face expressed a pent-up Christmas greed that made them look like little cannibals. And we had not known that there were so many refugee children in Paris, or even in the whole of France.

They came by twenties first, then by fifties and hundreds. Presently haggard helpers passed the word around: "No more toys." We stripped the tree, distributed stars, spangles, lanterns, tinsel and finally candle ends and tin candle-holders. One child got the crowning angel and barely escaped with its life.

By that time all the barriers were down. Some of us were forming a bodyguard around our valiant but bewildered guests, others battling with infuriated parents, silencing rapacious howls or dashing out to snatch more toys from the fast-closing shops. These emissaries, returning, reported that the street was packed with more children and the police expostulating about obstruction. Finally, through the raging mob, we fought a way out for the ambassador and his party, double-barred the doors to the approaching army and sat down aghast among the ruins. Then some one hysterically recalled that we had said: "Poor souls—we'll show them what an American Christmas tree is like."

They had turned the tables on us with a vengeance and shown us what a Franco-Belgian one is like when it is offered to people, young or old, whose lives have been uprooted, whose skies have been changed, who for two bewildered years have hung on the bitter edge of hunger, sickness and sorrow with their normal surplus of enjoyment suddenly cut off. If not a pretty sight, it was an instructive one; and when, for weeks afterward, aggrieved children in larger and larger numbers called to claim their quota of toys, they all received them, though at some cost to the useful part of our work; for we felt that once a year, and even on the brink of ruin, human nature needs Christmas tinsel more than coals and blankets.

(Published in The Delineator, December 1923.)

Notes

Introduction

1. For the most complete listing of adaptations of Wharton's work, see Appendix II, "Media Adaptations of Edith Wharton's Works" in *Edith Wharton: A to Z* by Sarah Bird Wright, 287–95.

2. This is not to say that scholars have completely ignored Wharton's life during the war years, nor the war's impact on her. Biographies by Lewis (*Edith Wharton: A Biography,* 1975) and Shari Benstock (*No Gifts from Chance: A Biography of Edith Wharton,* 1994) examine Wharton's life during the war years and its effects on her. Alan Price's *The End of the Age of Innocence: Edith Wharton and the First World War* (1996) is the most detailed biography of Wharton in the war years. These works, however, focus on the biography, rather than examining the writings from the war years. As of September 2002, the *MLA International Bibliography* includes about twenty items related to Wharton and war from 1975–2002, including a 1992 dissertation by Anne Marsh Fields focused on the war writings. Deborah Lindsay Williams's *Not in Sisterhood: Edith Wharton, Willa Cather, Zona Gale, and the Politics of Female Authorship* focuses on the three authors named, and gives Wharton's wartime publications more attention than they have usually received. In addition, recent panels at conferences (e.g., the Edith Wharton Society-sponsored conference at Newport in June 2000 and a panel at the 2001 convention of the Modern Language Association) have begun to address Wharton's war-related writings.

3. For a detailed listing of Wharton's magazine and newspaper publications during the war, see Stephen Garrison, *Edith Wharton: A Descriptive Bibliography,* especially 453–59.

4. Wharton also published *Xingu and Other Stories* in 1916. But she noted that "Coming Home" was the only new piece in the collection; the rest had been written before the war (*Letters* 385).

5. One text emerging from the war years that I do not address in this study is Wharton's 1920 travelogue, *In Morocco.* This book, which Wharton based on her trip to Morocco in 1917 under the protection of France's General Lyautey, is fascinating and complex; it also reveals Wharton's orientalist attitudes, and as such requires analysis beyond the scope of this book. Scholars are beginning to approach this text; coming studies of it will surely enrich Wharton scholarship.

6. I have not included Wharton's "Hymn of the Lusitania" in Appendix A, as the poem is not by Wharton but rather her translation of an unidentified original.

7. See, for instance, *Scars Upon My Heart: Women's Poetry and Verse of the First World War*, ed. Catherine Reilly, and *Lines of Fire: Women Writers of World War I*, ed. Margaret R. Higonnet.

8. Prime Minister Tony Blair of England stated in a speech to the House of Commons, "these attacks were not just attacks upon people and buildings; nor even merely upon the USA; these were attacks on the basic democratic values in which we all believe so passionately and on the civilised world." French President Jacques Chirac was quoted as saying, "'France . . will not stand aside' in combatting [*sic*] 'a scourge that defies all democracy'" (Neuffer); in another news report, "the German chancellor, Gerhard Schroder, called the attacks 'a declaration of war against the entire civilized world'" (Erlanger). In the United States, President George W. Bush declared, "We wage a war to save civilization, itself [*sic*]" ("President Discusses War on Terrorism").

Chapter 1. Edith Wharton and the Literary Legacy of the Great War

1. For the most detailed discussion of Wharton's wartime charities, see Alan Price, *The End of the Age of Innocence: Edith Wharton and the First World War*.

2. For a briefer version of the argument about Wharton's "wrong" attitude toward the war, see Kristin O. Lauer, "Can France Survive This Defender?" in Katherine Joslin and Alan Price, eds., *Wretched Exotic: Essays on Edith Wharton in Europe*, 88.

3. Peter Buitenhuis's *The Great War of Words: British, American, and Canadian Propaganda and Fiction 1914–1933* treats works like *Fighting France* and *A Son at the Front* thoughtfully, along with those of a number of other writers, male and female, who wrote during the war years but who are rarely, if ever, considered a part of the canon of "Great War" authors. (Buitenhuis employs the term *propaganda* neutrally, to designate efforts intended to persuade the United States to join the Allied forces.)

4. For a discussion of the relationship between the Great War and literary modernism, see Paul Fussell's *The Great War and Modern Memory* (whose argument regarding the war and modernism may be summarized in his remark that "it would take four years of trench warfare" to bring T. S. Eliot's *The Waste Land*—that landmark of modernism—into being [23]), as well as Samuel Hynes's *A War Imagined: The First World War and English Culture*. Dorothy Goldman, Jane Gledhill and Judith Hattaway summarize the general argument about the relationship between the war and modernism: "Although elements of the modernist style can be found prior to the war, it was during the war that writers embraced modernism as the form in which they could make concrete their experience of disjunction and fragmentation. The modernist's freedom from realism, traditional genre, and form became associated with notions of cultural apocalypse and disas-

ter" (79). See also the discussion of Wharton's postwar dislike of literary modernism in chapter six.

5. Owen may have been reacting to Jessie Pope's enthusiasm for the new roles the war made available to women, to her encouraging men to enlist for war, to her straightforward patriotism, or to all three. As Gilbert and Gubar make clear in *No Man's Land* (263), with regard to women's new roles in wartime, Pope celebrated "the girl who clips your ticket for the train, / And the girl who speeds the lift from floor to floor" ("War Girls," Reilly 90). She encouraged unenlisted men to go to war in lines like "Who's for the trench— / Are you, my laddie?" ("The Call," Reilly 88; see also Gilbert and Gubar 283). And, as the title of Owen's poem suggests, her straightforward patriotism may have offended him (see Welland 60).

6. See Paul Fussell regarding this famous passage from Hemingway: "In the summer of 1914 no one would have understood what on earth he was talking about" (21).

7. Hynes gives the credit for the creation of this style to a woman writer, May Sinclair, for her work *A Journal of Impressions in Belgium* (1915). As the war continued, however, the style became associated with male authors—Sassoon, Owen, and later Hemingway, among others.

8. Elshtain considers only *Fighting France* by Wharton, and apparently was unfamiliar with Wharton's thorough knowledge of France. See also the critique of Elshtain's work on Wharton in Goldman et al., 27.

9. See Claire Tylee: "although the First World War is seen and presented as the main determinant of modern British culture, the crucial area of that War, the experience of trench warfare and of one battle in particular, was a zone forbidden to women. Women were only attached to the Army as auxiliaries" (8).

10. In-text parenthetical references to Yale specify the Edith Wharton Collection, part of Yale's American Literature Collection, housed at the Beinecke Rare Book and Manuscript Library in New Haven, Connecticut. The Wharton Collection is organized into numbered, titled series, in turn comprised of numbered boxes that contain her papers. William K. Finley's comprehensive description of this collection and the complete contents of each series may be found at the Beinecke online: http://webtext.library.yale.edu/xm12html/beinecke.WHARTON.con.html#SV.

11. I am dating Wharton's residence from her settling in her apartment at 53 rue de Varenne (Lewis 258; Benstock *No Gifts* 318). Of course, Wharton had spent a great deal of time in France before 1909, including visits during her childhood.

12. For Wharton's affinity with France, see, for instance, "Landscapes of Desire: Edith Wharton and Europe" by Shari Benstock and "Edith Wharton in France" by Millicent Bell. Both are included in *Wretched Exotic: Essays on Edith Wharton in Europe*, ed. Katherine Joslin and Alan Price.

13. Wharton's harsh treatment of German-Americans is in marked contrast to the treatments of journalist Richard Harding Davis and novelist Willa Cather. In his preface to *With the Allies*, Davis distinguishes emphatically between Germans and

German-Americans: "This is not a war against Germans, as we know Germans in America, where they are among our sanest, most industrious, and most responsible countrymen. It is a war, as Winston Churchill has pointed out, against the military aristocracy of Germany" (vii). In *One of Ours*, Cather includes two scenes concerning the treatment of German-Americans. In the first scene, two German-American farmers are tried for "disloyal" utterances, as they have made remarks in favor of Germany and against the United States; Cather makes it clear that sentiment against them is inflated, but her reasonable judge advises them that they "have not recognized the element of appropriateness" in their remarks and fines each three hundred dollars (268–72). In the second scene, Cather depicts a group of farm boys who are taunting Mrs. Voigt, a German-American restaurant owner, simply because she is from Germany—and despite the fact that she has lived peacefully in their midst for years, and has, as she says, been "sell[ing] dem candy since dey was babies" (276).

14. For a detailed reading of these early stories, see my "Female Models and Male Mentors in Wharton's Early Fiction" in *American Literary Mentors*, Irene C. Goldman-Price and Melissa McFarland Pennell, eds., 84–95.

15. One might argue for a subcategory of the war novel called the "home front novel," or perhaps suggest that the term "war novel" be a larger category including both the "home front novel" and the "military" or "combat novel"—though almost inevitably, it seems, the "combat novel" would ascend to the status of the "real" war novel while the "home front novel" would become secondary. Certainly the current acceptance of many "war novels" as such is purely arbitrary, based almost entirely, it might seem, on the author's gender: for example, H.G. Wells' *Mr. Britling Sees It Through* is assuredly a home front novel, and the settings of Richard Aldington's *Death of a Hero* and Ernest Hemingway's *A Farewell to Arms* are also almost entirely domestic. A few of the best-known home front novels by women are Rebecca West's *The Return of the Soldier*, Virginia Woolf's *Jacob's Room*, and Willa Cather's *One of Ours*. *Lines of Fire: Women Writers of World War I*, ed. Margaret R. Higonnet, makes easily available a wide collection of writings by women, many of them focusing on the home front experience.

16. Many critics have felt that Wharton's postwar work is, in general, not up to the standard of her prewar work. R.W.B. Lewis, for instance, writes in his biography of Wharton that *The Glimpses of the Moon* "represent[s] certain weaknesses and dangerous temptations by which she was beginning to be beset" (*Edith Wharton* 445). He notes her "loosening grip upon the American idiom" in this period and claims that "even the portrait of American manners is unsure[,]" further speculating that in the postwar period Wharton "drove herself to write too fast and perhaps too much, because of financial need"(*Edith Wharton* 446, 447). Cynthia Griffin Wolff writes that Wharton's postwar novels focusing on parents and children (*A Son at the Front, The Mother's Recompense, The Children, Twilight Sleep*) "are not as strong as her earlier work, although there are exceptions. . . . One way to explain these failures would be to notice that now more than ever before Wharton wrote because she needed the money; another might be to suggest that as she aged, her

powers diminished. There is some truth to both claims" (331). She also argues that Wharton's lack of experience as a parent contributed to the weakness in these works, and that "increasingly, her satire lapses into an uncharacteristic querulousness, and everything about the postwar world is dismissed as vulgar and cheap" (331). Shari Benstock notes in *No Gifts from Chance* that "This final decade of [Wharton's] literary career was marked by mixed signals about the value of her writing. . . . [A]s critics revised upward the quality of her prewar writing, the more they demanded of her—and the less they agreed on what directions her work should take" (*No Gifts* 384). She notes that later critics faulted Wharton for writing too quickly, for writing "down" to a popular audience, and for losing touch with her American audience, and concedes that "An element of truth inheres in these assessments" (*No Gifts* 393). Dale Bauer provides a useful overview of the frequently negative reactions to Wharton's postwar novels (9–10).

Chapter 2. A Shaken Reality: Writings from Early in the War (1914–1915)

1. Wharton does not identify Vaudoyer by name in *Fighting France,* but does in her letter of March 11, 1915, to Henry James (*Letters* 353).

2. Mary Suzanne Schriber, "Introduction" to Wharton's *A Motor-Flight Through France,* xxvii. Wharton's enthusiasm for travel is well-known; see also her biographers R.W.B. Lewis and Shari Benstock. For a compilation of her travel writings, see Sarah Bird Wright, ed. and intro., *Edith Wharton Abroad: Selected Travel Writings, 1888–1920.* Significantly, this volume includes selections from both *Fighting France* and *French Ways and Their Meaning.* For Wharton, some facets of war writing overlapped with travel writing.

3. To *The Book of the Homeless,* the volume of poems, essays, artwork, and musical scores that Wharton edited in 1915 to raise money for her charities, Yeats contributed "A Reason for Keeping Silent," which begins, "I think it better that at times like these / We poets keep our mouths shut, for in truth / We have no gift to set a statesman right[.]" Yeats would reconsider the relationship between writers and war after seeing his countrymen under attack in the Easter Rebellion of 1916, though his attitude toward war would remain more ambivalent than Wharton's. "A Reason for Keeping Silent" was slightly revised, retitled "On Being Asked for a War Poem," and included in Yeats's 1919 volume, *The Wild Swans at Coole.*

4. Complete texts of all poems discussed in this chapter and later chapters are included in Appendix A. Sources of poems are in the bibliography.

5. Howells's contribution is a fourteen-line poem in rhyming couplets called "The Little Children," depicting the German army as "the arch-fiend" who "hurl[s]" children "from the tottering walls / Of their wrecked homes. . . ." In a letter to Wharton, Henry James (who transmitted Howells's manuscript for *The Book of the Homeless* to Wharton's publisher) called it "a fine & forcible & most feeling" poem, "really grim & strong & sincere" (Powers 352). Howells apparently had second thoughts about the poem "as being too crude & imperfect in form," according to James, but James believed that Howells was "utterly deluded" on this point, and

insisted "that we greatly admire it & in fine decline to give it up" (Powers 353). Thomas Hardy's poem was entitled "Cry of the Homeless." The poem addresses Germany as "Instigator of the ruin" and suggests that the appropriate response to Germany may be a curse (the "jolly Hardy malediction" to which James referred): "'May thy dearest ones be blighted / And forsaken,' be it said / By thy victims, / 'And thy children beg their bread!'" The final stanza of the poem withdraws this malediction, asking only somewhat more mildly "That compassion dew thy pillow / And absorb thy senses all / For thy victims, / Till death dark thee with his pall." This poem provides an interestingly different perspective on Fussell's commentary in *The Great War and Modern Memory.* Fussell begins by citing "Hardy's most recent volume of poems, *Satires of Circumstance*" as "establishing a terrible irony as the appropriate interpretive means" for understanding the war (3). An additional irony of literary history thus appears: judging by this contribution to *The Book of the Homeless,* Hardy's own initial response to the war was anything but ironic. (See Michael Millgate, *Thomas Hardy: A Biography,* especially 498–502, for Hardy's ambivalent reaction to the early months of the war.)

6. This is one of the earliest instances of Wharton referring to adoption, an important issue in much of her later work (perhaps most notably *The Children*).

7. In his notes on the eulogy, Wegener gives the date of du Breuil's death as Feb. 22 (*Uncollected Critical Writings* 204). I have been unable to reconcile this discrepancy.

8. For a discussion of the possibility of a sexual relationship between Yvonne Malo and Scharlach, see White 86, and Lewis, *Edith Wharton* 394.

9. Appendix B includes the war-related prose texts by Wharton that I discuss in this chapter and later chapters, including "My Work Among the Women Workers of Paris," Wharton's preface to *The Book of the Homeless,* and other selections.

Chapter 3. Work, Escape, and the Loss of Ambiguity: Writings from Later in the War (1916–1918)

1. The only significant exception to the critical neglect of *The Marne* and *French Ways and Their Meaning* is the amount of critical attention focused on one chapter in *French Ways,* "The New Frenchwoman," in which Wharton criticized American treatment of women and praised the responsibilities granted to Frenchwomen. See, for example, references to such passages in works by Susan Goodman, Janet Goodwyn, Penelope Vita-Finzi, Elizabeth Ammons, and Margaret McDowell.

2. See R.W.B. Lewis, *Edith Wharton* (422), Shari Benstock, *No Gifts from Chance* (346) and Alan Price, *The End of the Age of Innocence* (passim).

3. For a classic positive interpretation of Charity's marriage to Lawyer Royall, see Cynthia Griffin Wolff, *A Feast of Words,* especially 283–86; for a classic negative interpretation, see Elizabeth Ammons, *Edith Wharton's Argument with America,* 136–39.

4. This point is also made by Anne Marsh Fields in her dissertation, "Writing a War Story: Edith Wharton and World War I," 98.

5. Compare Shari Benstock: "Whatever truths about French, German, and American societies emerge in these essays (and there are many), their insights reflect most clearly Edith Wharton's personal values" (*No Gifts* 348).

6. It is difficult to establish exact dates of composition on *French Ways* and *The Marne*, though what evidence we have suggests that Wharton may have been working on them at the same time. The articles that were later published together as *French Ways* were published serially between April 1917 and June 1919 (see Garrison, 457–58). Benstock notes that Wharton "was at work on two projects," *The Marne* and *French Ways*, in 1918 (*No Gifts* 346).

7. For more on Cather's *One of Ours*, see Sharon O'Brien's "Combat Envy and Survivor Guilt: Willa Cather's 'Manly Battle Yarn'" in *Arms and the Woman: War, Gender, and Literary Representation*, ed. Helen M. Cooper, Adrienne Auslander Munich, and Susan Merrill Squier, 184–204.

8. For a useful discussion of the concept of war as an adventure, see Claire Tylee, *The Great War and Women's Consciousness*, especially pages 76–78.

9. Many reports of atrocities were fabricated by British propaganda in the Bryce Report. See, for example, Buitenhuis, who states that the Bryce Report "was largely a tissue of invention, unsubstantiated" (27).

10. For a fascinating and detailed account of Wharton's friendship with Ronald Simmons—including the most detailed account to date of Simmons himself—see Frederick Wegener, "Edith Wharton and Ronald Simmons: Documenting a Pivotal Wartime Friendship."

11. Wharton also wrote a number of essays for newspaper publication in these years, which (like *French Ways and Their Meaning*) embraced "the obvious." See Appendix B for one example, "Edith Wharton Tells of German Trail of Ruin."

12. See, for instance, Shari Benstock, who notes: "Intended to instruct American military men about French mores, the book [*French Ways*] was chosen by the United States Navy Department for ships' libraries" (*No Gifts* 348).

13. On Wharton's xenophobia, see, for instance, recent analyses in Millicent Bell, ed., *The Cambridge Companion to Edith Wharton*: Pamela Knights, "The Social Subject in *The Age of Innocence*" (20–46); Nancy Bentley, "Edith Wharton and the Science of Manners" (47–67); and Elizabeth Ammons, "Edith Wharton and Race" (68–86).

14. For more on Wharton's political conservatism, both before and after World War I, see Frederick Wegener, "'Rabid Imperialist': Edith Wharton and the Obligations of Empire in Modern American Fiction."

Chapter 4. Elegies and Satires: Works from the War's End (1919)

1. See *Letters* 423, n. 2, and Benstock, *No Gifts* 350.

2. The phrase "anxiety of authorship" comes, of course, from Sandra Gilbert and Susan Gubar's influential *The Madwoman in the Attic*. See especially chapter two, "Infection in the Sentence: The Woman Writer and the Anxiety of Authorship."

3. In 1918, Wharton had received a letter from Victor Solberg, an American sol-

dier asking for advice about some poems he had enclosed. She paraphrases his concern: "you seem to think that the risk of being subject to the influence of great poets is one that young writers should fear." On the contrary, she tells him, "the great object of the young writer should be, not to fear these influences, but to seek only the greatest, & to assimilate them so that they become part of his stock-in-trade" (*Letters* 411). Ivy's interest in avoiding influence is one Wharton found counterproductive. See also Deborah Lindsay Williams, *Not in Sisterhood: Edith Wharton, Willa Cather, Zona Gale, and the Politics of Female Authorship*, 126–27.

4. Barbara White also notes the recurrence of names in these short stories: "Ivy entitles her story 'His Letter Home' and names her hero Emile Durand; Wharton's first war story is titled 'Coming Home' and the hero of her second is Charles Durand" (87).

Chapter 5. Monument Building: *A Son at the Front*

1. See Lewis, *Edith Wharton*, 467; Wolff, 336–39; Benstock, *No Gifts*, 355–57. Two studies of the war—those by Peter Buitenhuis and Dorothy Goldman et al.— include brief but insightful analyses of the novel. The only extended analysis of *Son* is Judith Sensibar's "'Behind the Lines' in Edith Wharton's *A Son at the Front*: Re-Writing a Masculinist Tradition" (*Wretched Exotic: Essays on Edith Wharton in Europe*, ed. Katherine Joslin and Alan Price, 241–56). Sensibar focuses on a homosexual reading of Campton (see also note 7, below).

2. The back cover of the 1995 paperback reissue of *A Son at the Front* proclaims it "Wharton's antiwar masterpiece" (DeKalb: Northern Illinois University Press).

3. Shari Benstock also notes the link between Renoir's sketch and the topic of *A Son at the Front* (*No Gifts* 356).

4. Lewis (*Edith Wharton* 412) and Benstock ("Introduction" xi) also note that Wharton drew Boylston from Simmons. For more extensive evidence, as well as a detailed comparison of Boylston and Simmons, see Frederick Wegener, "Edith Wharton and Ronald Simmons: Documenting a Pivotal Wartime Friendship," especially 69–80.

5. For a detailed account of Wharton's vexed relationship with the American Red Cross, see Alan Price, *The End of the Age of Innocence*, Chapter 4.

6. In a letter of 26 February 1917 addressed only to "Chère Amie," Wharton describes the work of the committee: "Le Comité dont il s'agit s'occupe depuis plus de deux ans de recueillir aux Etats-Unis des secours pour les élèves des Beaux-Arts combattant au front et pour leurs familles. Il donne aussi de l'ouvrage aux mères et aux femmes des élèves et procure des commandes pour les artistes, anciens élèves des Beaux-Arts, qui sont dans l'impossibilité de gagner leur vie à cause de la guerre." [The committee in question has, for more than two years, collected from the United States aid for the students of the School of Beaux-Arts who are fighting at the front and for their families. It also gives work to the mothers and wives of these students, and secures orders for the artists, former students of the Beaux-Arts, who, because

of the war, find it impossible to make a living.] (26 Feb. 1917, *Wharton Collection* Yale)

7. Unlike Judith Sensibar (see note 1 above), I do not see Campton's possessiveness as incestuous homosexual possessiveness, nor his competitiveness with Brant as sexualized. Rather, Campton's sense of competition is financial and paternal: Brant has "proven" his masculinity by being able to provide for George, something Campton is only on the brink of doing as the novel opens. Further, I do not see Campton's repression of the word "effigy" in book I, chapter IV as a symptom of his self-inflicted punishment "for fantasies of incestuous, homoerotic desire" (Sensibar 249), but rather as a parent's automatic repression of that most horrifying of possibilities, the death of one's own child.

Chapter 6. Writing in the Wake of the War

1. See Price, *The End of the Age of Innocence,* 161–62, 169–71 and Benstock, *No Gifts,* 344, 347.

2. Wharton did not publish books in 1927, 1935, and 1937, the last year of her life; she left a partially completed novel, *The Buccaneers,* at her death.

3. William Lyon Phelps, writing for the *New York Times Book Review,* pointed out that Archer unpacks in the 1870s works by Guy de Maupassant, whose tales "began to appear" only in the "early eighties" (Tuttleton et al. 286); the anonymous reviewer for the *Times Literary Supplement* noted that "even the most advanced young people could not have been reading books by Vernon Lee or Huysmans or M. Paul Bourget in the early seventies"—though he or she concedes that "a few small anachronisms of fact are of no consequence" (Tuttleton et al. 290).

4. Several critics have compared Ellen's maturity to the immaturity of the American women in the novel. On the artificial preservation of the "innocence" of American women, see in particular Judith P. Saunders, "Becoming the Mask: Edith Wharton's Ingenues," reprinted in the New Riverside Edition of *The Age of Innocence,* ed. Carol J. Singley, 404–8.

5. For extensive excerpts from Wharton's plans for *Age,* as well as their discussion and analysis, see Alan Price, "The Composition of Edith Wharton's *The Age of Innocence.*"

6. Also indicative of Wharton's fundamental endorsement of Newland and May's marriage, whatever its limitations, is its contrast to the unstable marriages that were the focus of postwar novels like *The Mother's Recompense* and *The Children.* The latter novel in particular parodies adults whose belief is that marriage exists only to serve their personal happiness, regardless of the negative effects that serial marriages might have upon "the foundation of a home and the procreation of a family" (*French Ways* 128). For Wharton, individual happiness and the stability of the home were not necessarily compatible; as *French Ways and Their Meaning* implies, she believed that if any sacrifice had to be made, it was the duty of the individual to sacrifice happiness for the benefit of the family.

7. For classic discussions of the ending of *The Age of Innocence*, see Elizabeth Ammons, who interprets Archer's decision not to see Ellen as his preference for "May, dead, to Ellen Olenska, alive" (152), and Cynthia Griffin Wolff, who interprets this decision as a sign of his "genuine maturity" (325).

8. It is worth noting that the final chapter of *The Age of Innocence* is set in approximately 1905, which is also the setting of *The House of Mirth*, published in 1905. The world in which Dallas Archer and Fanny Beaufort thrive is also the world in which Lily Bart suffers—another indication of the limitations of that apparently golden age.

9. The exception is "The Old Maid." The first written of these novellas, it may not have lent itself to the use of a first-person narrator who is tangential to the central characters, particularly as Wharton was working with overflow material from *The Age of Innocence*. Alternately, Wharton may have realized only after completing "The Old Maid" that using a narrator from the 1920s would allow her to comment easily on changing mores. ("The Old Maid" was published serially in spring 1922; "New Year's Day" in July and August 1923; "False Dawn" in November 1923; and "The Spark" in May 1924 [see Garrison 460–61].)

10. Much discussion of *The Mother's Recompense* has focused on the quasi-incestuous triangle of Kate Clephane, Chris Fenno, and Anne Clephane (Kate's daughter). Shari Benstock notes that "the 'strong' theme of sexual desire between generations invokes the subject of incest (as in *The Reef* and *Summer*)" (*No Gifts* 384), and that "The incest theme remains a backdrop to the contradictory tensions that arise in Kate" (*No Gifts* 385). Wharton wrote to her friend John Hugh Smith, "I'm glad you like 'The Mother.' I felt, in writing it, all the force of what you say about the incest-element, & its importance in justifying her anguish—but I felt it wd be hardly visible in its exact sense to *her*, & wanted to try to represent the business as it seemed to her, culminating in the incest-vision when she sees the man holding Anne in his arms" (*Letters* 480).

11. Contemporary reviews of the novel included in *Edith Wharton: The Contemporary Reviews* (ed. Tuttleton, Lauer, and Murray) emphasize almost exclusively the social and psychological aspects of the novel, comparing Kate Clephane to Lily Bart of *The House of Mirth* and Anna Leath of *The Reef*, both prewar works.

12. This story is entitled "Behind the Government." It is undated, but the name of one character—Andrew Brant—suggests that Wharton may have written it before writing, or in the early stages of writing, *A Son at the Front*, with its important character Anderson ("Uncle Andy") Brant (typescript, *Wharton Collection* Yale).

13. On the Battle of Belleau Wood and the role of U.S. soldiers, see, for instance, John Keegan's account of the battle in *The First World War*, 407.

14. In manuscript, the story went under the title "Kouradjine Limited," again suggesting charm as a family business. This title was changed to "Bread Upon the Waters" when *Hearst's International-Cosmopolitan* accepted the story for magazine publication (Benstock, *No Gifts* 439); it was published as "Charm Incorporated" in Wharton's 1936 short story collection, *The World Over*.

Conclusion: Glancing Back at the War

1. Various portions of *A Backward Glance* were published serially between 1932 and 1934 (Garrison 465); one short section about Henry James was published in 1920 (Garrison 459).

2. Recent scholarship, particularly scholarship on women writers during the Great War, has begun to open up definitions of the literature of the Great War. For primary sources see, for instance, *Lines of Fire: Women Writers of World War I*, ed. Margaret R. Higonnet, and *Women, Men and the Great War: An Anthology of Stories*, ed. Trudi Tate. Secondary sources are also growing, including Clair Tylee, *The Great War and Women's Consciousness*; Dorothy Goldman et al., *Women Writers and the Great War*; Margaret R. Higonnet et al., eds., *Behind the Lines: Gender and the Two World Wars*; Helen M. Cooper et al., eds., *Arms and The Woman: War, Gender, and Literary Representation*.

3. To some extent the similarity of tone between Wharton and Tuchman is not a surprise: Tuchman lists Wharton's *Fighting France* as among her sources (450). Yet both Tuchman's consultation of Wharton's book and the similarity in tone between the two authors suggests the legitimacy of Wharton's work—a legitimacy, which, as we have seen, has been long questioned.

4. The *Percy Lubbock Material* comprises Series IX of the *Wharton Collection*, Yale Collection of American Literature, Beinecke Rare Book and Manuscript Library, New Haven, Connecticut.

5. The author of these remarks, according to Lubbock's *Portrait of Edith Wharton*, is Mrs. Walter Maynard. Lubbock identifies her as the author of a remark made earlier in the same document: "She had the rare gift of treating children like normal, human beings" (Lubbock 147).

6. On Wharton's falling-out with Percy Lubbock, see, for instance, Shari Benstock, *No Gifts from Chance*, 138, 416.

Appendix A

1. Wharton remarked that the sight of the "glorious ruins of Ypres . . . recalled a phrase used soon after the fall of Liège by Belgium's Foreign Minister—*"La Belgique ne regrette rien"* [Belgium regrets nothing]—which ought some day to serve as the motto of the renovated city" (*Fighting France* 154).

Bibliography

Aldington, Richard. *Death of a Hero.* 1929. London: Hogarth Press, 1984.

Aldrich, Mildred. *A Hilltop on the Marne.* Boston: Houghton Mifflin, 1915.

Ammons, Elizabeth. *Edith Wharton's Argument with America.* Athens: University of Georgia Press, 1980.

Bailey, Temple. "Made in Germany." *Scribner's Magazine* June 1915: 711–18.

Barbusse, Henri. *Under Fire [Le Feu].* 1916. Trans. Fitzwater Wray. New York: E. P. Dutton, 1917.

Bauer, Dale. *Edith Wharton's Brave New Politics.* Madison: University of Wisconsin Press, 1994.

Becker, Jean-Jacques. *The Great War and the French People.* Trans. Arnold Pomerans. New York: St. Martin's, 1986.

Bell, Millicent. "Edith Wharton in France." Joslin and Price. 61–73.

———, ed. *Cambridge Companion to Edith Wharton.* New York: Cambridge University Press, 1995.

Benstock, Shari. Introduction. *A Son at the Front.* By Edith Wharton. DeKalb: Northern Illinois University Press, 1995.

———. "Landscapes of Desire: Edith Wharton and Europe." Joslin and Price. 19–42.

———. *No Gifts from Chance: A Biography of Edith Wharton.* New York: Scribner's, 1994.

Binyon, Laurence. "The English Youth." *The New World: Poems.* London: Elkin Matthews, 1918. 30–31.

———. *For the Fallen.* London: Hodder and Stoughton, n.d. [1917?].

Blair, Tony. "Address by Tony Blair, Prime Minister of Great Britain Delivered to the House of Commons, London, England, September 14, 2001." *Vital Speeches of the Day* 67.24 (Oct. 1, 2001): 746–749. EBSCO Publishing. May 30, 2003. Available: http://search.epnet.com.

Buitenhuis, Peter. *The Great War of Words: British, American, and Canadian Propaganda and Fiction, 1914–1933.* Vancouver: University of British Columbia Press, 1987.

Cather, Willa. *One of Ours.* 1922. Boston: Houghton Mifflin, 1937.

Cooper, Helen M., Adrienne Auslander Munich, Susan Merrill Squier, eds. *Arms and the Woman: War, Gender, and Literary Representation.* Chapel Hill: University of North Carolina Press, 1989.

Cooperman, Stanley. *World War I and the American Novel.* Baltimore: Johns Hopkins Press, 1967.

cummings, e.e. *The Enormous Room.* 1922. New York: Modern Library, 1934.

Davis, Richard Harding. "'To Be Treated as a Spy.'" *Scribner's Magazine* Dec. 1914: 702–14.

———. *With the Allies.* New York: Charles Scribner's Sons, 1914.

Dos Passos, John. *One Man's Initiation: 1917.* 1920. Ithaca: Cornell University Press, 1969.

Edel, Leon, and Lyall Powers, eds. *The Complete Notebooks of Henry James.* New York: Oxford University Press, 1987.

Eliot, T. S. "Tradition and the Individual Talent." 1919. *Norton Anthology of American Literature.* 2nd ed. Ed. Nina Baym et al. Vol. 2. New York: W. W. Norton, 1985. 1201–8.

Elshtain, Jean Bethke. *Women and War.* New York: Basic Books, 1987.

Erlanger, Steven. "European Nations Stand With U.S., Ready to Respond." *The New York Times* Sept. 12, 2001: A23+. 10 June 2003. Available: http://0–proquest.umi.com.

Fields, Anne Marsh. "'Writing a War Story': Edith Wharton and World War I." Diss. University of North Carolina, Chapel Hill, 1992.

Ford, Ford Maddox. *A Man Could Stand Up.* 1926. London: Penguin, 1982.

Fussell, Paul. *The Great War and Modern Memory.* London: Oxford University Press, 1975.

Garrison, Stephen. *Edith Wharton: A Descriptive Bibliography.* Pittsburgh: University of Pittsburgh Press, 1990.

Gilbert, Martin. *The First World War: A Complete History.* New York: Henry Holt, 1994.

Gilbert, Sandra, and Susan Gubar. *The Madwoman in the Attic.* New Haven: Yale University Press, 1979.

———. *No Man's Land,* Vol. 2: *Sexchanges.* New Haven: Yale University Press, 1989.

Goldman, Dorothy, with Jane Gledhill and Judith Hattaway. *Women Writers and the Great War.* New York: Twayne Publishers, 1995.

Goldman-Price, Irene C., and Melissa McFarland Pennell, eds. *American Literary Mentors.* Gainesville: University Press of Florida, 1999.

Goodman, Susan. *Edith Wharton's Women: Friends and Rivals.* Hanover, N.H.: University Press of New England, 1990.

Goodwyn, Janet. *Edith Wharton: Traveller in the Land of Letters.* New York: St. Martin's, 1990.

Hall, Radclyffe. "Miss Ogilvy Finds Herself." 1926. *Norton Anthology of Literature by Women.* Ed. Sandra M. Gilbert and Susan Gubar. New York: Norton, 1985. 1443–57.

Hardy, Thomas. "Cry of the Homeless." *The Book of the Homeless.* Ed. Edith Wharton. 16.

Hartley, L. P. *The Go-Between.* 1953. London: Penguin, [1958].

Hause, Steven C. "More Minerva than Mars: The French Women's Rights Campaign and the First World War." Higonnet et al., eds., *Behind the Lines: Gender and the Two World Wars.* 99–113.

Hemingway, Ernest. *A Farewell to Arms.* 1929. New York: Charles Scribner's Sons, 1969.

Higonnet, Margaret R. Introduction. *Behind the Lines: Gender and the Two World Wars.* New Haven: Yale University Press, 1987. 1–17.

―――, ed. *Lines of Fire: Women Writers of World War I.* New York: Plume, 1999.

―――, Jane Jenson, Sonya Michel, Margaret Collins Weitz, eds. *Behind the Lines: Gender and the Two World Wars.* New Haven: Yale University Press, 1987.

Howells, William Dean. "The Little Children." *The Book of the Homeless.* Ed. Edith Wharton. 17.

Hynes, Samuel. *A War Imagined: The First World War and English Culture.* New York: Macmillan, 1990.

Joslin, Katherine, and Alan Price, eds. *Wretched Exotic: Essays on Edith Wharton in Europe.* New York: Peter Lang, 1993.

Keats, John. *Complete Poems and Selected Letters of John Keats.* Intro. Edward Hirsch. New York: Modern Library, 2001.

Keegan, John. *The First World War.* New York: Knopf, 1999.

―――. *A History of Warfare.* New York: Knopf, 1993.

Lewis, R.W.B. *Edith Wharton: A Biography.* New York: Harper and Row, 1975.

―――. Introduction. *The Age of Innocence.* By Edith Wharton. New York: Scribner's, 1968.

Lubbock, Percy. *Portrait of Edith Wharton.* 1947. New York: Krause Reprint, 1969.

de Margerie, Diane. Introduction. *French Ways and Their Meaning.* By Edith Wharton. Lenox and Lee, Mass.: Edith Wharton Restoration and Berkshire House Publishers, 1997.

McDowell, Margaret. *Edith Wharton.* Boston: Twayne Publishers, 1976.

Millgate, Michael. *Thomas Hardy: A Biography.* New York: Random House, 1982.

Moore, Marianne. "Poetry." *Norton Anthology of American Literature.* 2nd ed. Ed. Nina Baym et al. Vol. 2. New York: W. W. Norton, 1985. 1182–83.

Neuffer, Elizabeth. "Chirac, in New York, Calls for UN Push to Fight Terror." *Boston Globe* 20 Sept. 2001: A30+. 10 June 2003. Available: http://0–proquest.umi.com.

Nevius, Blake. *Edith Wharton: A Study of Her Fiction.* Berkeley: University of California Press, 1953.

Olin-Ammentorp, Julie. "Female Models and Male Mentors in Wharton's Early Fiction." Goldman-Price and Pennell 84–95.

Owen, Wilfred. "Dulce et Decorum Est." *The Penguin Book of World War I Poetry.* 2nd ed. Ed. Jon Silkin. New York: Penguin, 1981. 182–83.

Perrot, Michelle. "The New Eve and the Old Adam: French Women's Condition at the Turn of the Century." Higonnet et al., eds., *Behind the Lines*. 51–60.

Pound, Ezra. "Hugh Selwyn Mauberly: E.P. Ode pour l'election de Son Sepulchre." 1920. *Norton Anthology of American Literature*. 2nd ed. Ed. Nina Baym et al. Vol. 2. New York: W. W. Norton, 1985. 1129–42.

Powell, E. Alexander. "On the British Battle Line." *Scribner's Magazine* Oct. 1915: 456–69.

Powers, Lyall H., ed. *Henry James and Edith Wharton: Letters: 1900–1915*. New York: Scribner's, 1990.

"President Discusses War on Terrorism." Nov. 8, 2001. *SIRS*. Government Sources via SIRS Knowledge Source. May 30, 2003. Available: http://www.sirs.com.

Price, Alan. "The Composition of Edith Wharton's *The Age of Innocence.*" *The Yale University Library Gazette* 55 (1980): 22–30.

———. *The End of the Age of Innocence: Edith Wharton and the First World War*. New York: St. Martin's, 1996.

Reilly, Catherine, ed. *Scars Upon My Heart: Women's Poetry and Verse of the First World War*. London: Virago, 1982.

Sarolea, Charles. *The Anglo-German Problem*. 1912. New York: G. P. Putnam's Sons, 1915.

Sassoon, Siegfried. "Glory of Women." *The Penguin Book of First World War Poetry*. 2nd ed. Ed. Jon Silkin. London: Penguin, 1981. 132.

Saunders, Judith P. "Becoming the Mask: Edith Wharton's Ingenues." *The Age of Innocence*. By Edith Wharton. Ed. Carol J. Singley. Boston: Houghton Mifflin-New Riverside, 2000. 404–8.

Schinz, Albert. *French Literature of the Great War*. New York: Appleton, 1920.

Sensibar, Judith. "'Behind the Lines' in Edith Wharton's *A Son at the Front:* Rewriting a Masculinist Tradition." Joslin and Price. 241–56.

Showalter, Elaine. "Rivers and Sassoon: The Inscription of Male Gender Anxieties." Higonnet et al., eds., *Behind the Lines*. 61–69.

Sinclair, May. *A Journal of Impressions in Belgium*. New York: Macmillan, 1915.

Tate, Trudi. *Women, Men, and the Great War: An Anthology of Stories*. Manchester: Manchester University Press, 1995.

Thoreau, Henry David. *Walden and Selected Essays*. Ed. George Whicher. New York: Hendricks House, 1973.

Trumbell, Annie Eliot. "The Sinews of War." *Scribner's Magazine* May 1915: 624–35.

Tuchman, Barbara W. *The Guns of August*. 1962. New York: Ballantine, 1994.

Tuttleton, James, Kristin O. Lauer, and Margaret P. Murray, eds. *Edith Wharton: The Contemporary Reviews*. Cambridge: Cambridge University Press, 1992.

Tylee, Claire. *The Great War and Women's Consciousness: Images of Militarism and Womanhood in Women's Writings, 1914–64*. Iowa City: University of Iowa Press, 1990.

Vita-Finzi, Penelope. *Edith Wharton and the Art of Fiction*. New York: St. Martin's, 1990.

Waddington, Mary King. "In War Times." *Scribner's Magazine* Jan. 1915: 35–47.

Waid, Candace. *Edith Wharton's Letters from the Underworld*. Chapel Hill: University of North Carolina Press, 1991.

———. Introduction. *Summer*. By Edith Wharton. New York: Penguin Signet Classic, 1993.

Ward, Mrs. Humphry. *England's Effort: Letters to an American Friend*. New York: Scribner's, 1916.

Wegener, Frederick. "Edith Wharton and Ronald Simmons: Documenting a Pivotal Wartime Friendship." *The Yale University Library Gazette* 77 (2002): 51–85.

———. "'Rabid Imperialist': Edith Wharton and the Obligations of Empire in Modern American Fiction." *American Literature* 72 (2000): 783–812.

Welland, D.S.R. *Wilfred Owen: A Critical Study*. London: Chatto and Windus, 1960.

Wells, H. G. *Mr. Britling Sees It Through*. New York: MacMillan, 1916.

West, Rebecca. *The Return of the Soldier*. New York: Penguin Books, 1998.

Wharton, Edith. *The Age of Innocence*. 1920. Intro. R.W.B. Lewis. New York: Scribner's, 1968.

———. *A Backward Glance*. 1934. Intro. Louis Auchincloss. New York: Scribner's, 1985.

———. "Battle Sleep." *The Century* Sept. 1915: 736.

———. "Belgium." *King Albert's Book: A Tribute to the Belgian King and People from Representative Men and Women Throughout the World*. New York: Hearst's International Library Co., 1915, p. 165.

———. "Beaumetz, Feb. 23$^{rd.}$ 1915." Wharton mss. Lilly Library, Indiana University, Bloomington.

———. "Charm Incorporated." 1934. *Collected Short Stories* 2: 743–62.

———. "Christmas Tinsel." *Delineator* Dec. 1923: 11.

———. *The Collected Short Stories of Edith Wharton*. 2 vols. Ed. R.W.B. Lewis. New York: Macmillan-Scribner's, 1968.

———. "Coming Home." 1915. *Collected Short Stories* 2: 230–56.

———. *The Custom of the Country*. 1913. Ed. and intro. Stephen Orgel. Oxford: Oxford University Press, 1995.

———. *Edith Wharton Abroad: Selected Travel Writings, 1888–1920*. Ed. Sarah Bird Wright. New York: St. Martin's, 1996.

———. "Edith Wharton Tells of German Trail of Ruin." *New York Sun* April 6, 1917: 1, 4.

———. "Elegy." *Twelve Poems*. London: Medici Society, 1926. 33.

———. *"Fast and Loose" and "The Buccaneers."* 1938 and 1977. Ed. and intro. Viola Hopkins Winner. Charlottesville: University Press of Virginia, 1993.

———. *Fighting France*. New York: Scribner's, 1919.

———. *French Ways and Their Meaning*. New York: D. Appleton, 1919.

———. "The Great Blue Tent." *The New York Times* Aug. 25, 1915: 10.

———. *The House of Mirth*. 1905. New York: Scribner's, 1969.

———. "How Paris Welcomed the King." *Reveille* (London, England) Feb. 1919: 367–69.

———. *The Letters of Edith Wharton*. Ed. R.W.B. Lewis and Nancy Lewis. New York: Scribner's, 1988.

———. "The Looking Glass." 1933. *Collected Short Stories* 2: 844–58.

———. *The Marne*. New York: Appleton, 1918.

———. "Miss Mary Pask." 1925. *Collected Short Stories* 2: 373–84.

———. *The Mother's Recompense*. 1925. Intro. Louis Auchincloss. New York: Scribner's, 1986.

———. *A Motor-Flight Through France*. 1908. Intro. Mary Suzanne Schriber. DeKalb: Northern Illinois University Press, 1991.

———. "My Work Among the Women Workers of Paris." *New York Times Magazine Section* 28 Nov. 1915: 1–2.

———. *Old New York*. 1924. Intro. Marilyn French. London: Virago, 1985.

———. "'On Active Service': American Expeditionary Force (R.S., August 12th, 1918)." *Scribner's Magazine* Nov. 1918: 619.

———. "Permanent Values in Fiction." *The Uncollected Critical Writings of Edith Wharton*. 175–79.

———. "The Refugees." 1919. *Collected Short Stories* 2: 570–93.

———. *A Son at the Front*. New York: Scribner's, 1923.

———. *Summer*. 1917. Intro. Candace Waid. New York: Penguin-Signet, 1993.

———. "Tendencies in Modern Fiction." *The Uncollected Critical Writings of Edith Wharton*. 170–74.

———. "The Tryst." *The Book of the Homeless*. 41–42.

———. *Twilight Sleep*. New York: Appleton, 1927.

———. *The Uncollected Critical Writings of Edith Wharton*. Ed. and intro. Frederick Wegener. Princeton: Princeton University Press, 1996.

———. *The Valley of Decision*. 2 vols. New York: Scribner's, 1902.

———. "Velvet Ear Pads." 1925. *Collected Short Stories* 2: 473–500.

———. "With the Tide." *Saturday Evening Post* March 29, 1919: 8.

———. "Writing a War Story." 1919. *Collected Short Stories* 2: 359–70.

———. *The Writing of Fiction*. 1925. New York: Simon and Schuster, 1997.

———. "You and You." *Pittsburgh Chronicle Telegraph* Jan. 1919: 6.

———, ed., [trans., contributor]. *The Book of the Homeless*. New York: Scribner's, 1916.

White, Barbara A. *Edith Wharton: A Study of the Short Fiction*. New York: Twayne, 1991.

Whitman, Walt. *Complete Poetry and Collected Prose*. New York: Library of America, 1982.

Williams, Deborah Lindsay. *Not in Sisterhood: Edith Wharton, Willa Cather, Zona Gale, and the Politics of Female Authorship*. New York: Palgrave, 2001.

Wolff, Cynthia Griffin. *A Feast of Words: The Triumph of Edith Wharton*. 2nd ed. Reading, MA: Addison-Wesley, 1995.

Woolf, Virginia. *Jacob's Room*. 1922. New York: Harvest-Harcourt Brace Jovanovich, 1960.

Wright, Sarah Bird. *Edith Wharton: A to Z*. New York: Facts on File, 1988.

X, Captain, of the French Staff [pseudonym of Raymond Recouly]. "General Joffre: The Victor of the Marne." *Scribner's Magazine* Oct. 1915: 389–403.

Yeats, William Butler. "Easter 1916." *The Collected Poems of W. B. Yeats*. New York: Macmillan, 1956. 177–80.

———. "A Reason for Keeping Silent." *The Book of the Homeless*. Ed. Edith Wharton. New York: Scribner's, 1916. 45.

Index

Page numbers of principal discussions are in **boldface.**

Adorno, Theodor, 161
Akins, Zoe, 164
Aldington, Richard, 282n15
Aldrich, Mildred, 24, 216
Ammons, Elizabeth, 64, 284nn1, 3, 285n13, 288n7
Angell, Norman: *The Great Illusion*, 137

Bagnold, Enid, 34
Bahlmann, Anna, 56
Bailey, Temple: "Made in Germany," 35–36
Barbusse, Henri: *Le Feu* (*Under Fire*), 36, 227
Bauer, Dale, 160, 161, 282–83n16
Becker, Jean-Jacques, 23–24, 224, 225
Beerbohm, Max, 122, 157, 210
Bell, Clive, 132
Bell, Millicent, 221, 227, 281n12
Bennett, Arnold, 13
Benstock, Shari, 159, 196–97, 232, 279n2, 282–83n16, 283n2; on EW and France, 23, 281n12; on *French Ways and Their Meaning*, 285nn5, 6, 12; on *The Marne*, 89, 284n2, 285n6; on *The Mother's Recompense*, 288n10; on *A Son at the Front*, 286nn3, 4 (chap. 5)
Bentley, Nancy, 285n13
Berenson, Bernard, 21, 22, 28, 29, 48, 57, 58
Berenson, Mary, 54
Berry, Walter, 17, 21, 54, 162
Binyon, Laurence, 151–52
Bliss, Mildred, 156
The Book of the Homeless (ed. EW), 2, 111, 118, 119, 122, 283n3, 283–84n5; preface, 55, 284n9. *See also* Wharton, Edith: works (poems: "The Tryst")
Bourget, Paul, 24
du Breuil de Saint-Germain, Jean, 46–48, 56, 84–85, 113, 284n7; death as heroic, 46, 142, 206, 224; Wharton's elegy for, 46–48, 87, 93
Brooke, Rupert, 11
Buitenhuis, Peter, 13, 280n3, 285n9, 286n1

Canby, Henry Seidel, 169
"Captain X" (Raymond Recouly), 37, 104
Cather, Willa, 73, 281–82n13, 282n15, 285n7
Chanler, Margaret (Daisy), 115, 123, 143
Charities, EW's involvement in, 6, 29, 55, 111, 217, 227; after the war, 154–55, 212, 232; not a "vocation," 14, 98; reflected in "Christmas Tinsel," 218–19; in *A Son at the Front*, 125–28, 286–87n6; in "Velvet Ear Pads," 199. *See also* Refugees
Conrad, Joseph, 60, 119–20, 123, 158, 200
Cooper, Helen M., 289n2
cummings, e.e., 72, 123

Davis, Richard Harding, 36, 37, 38, 104, 281–82n13
Defense of the Realm Act (DORA), 65, 97, 105
Dos Passos, John, 72, 123
"Dulce et decorum est . . . ," 9, 10, 142; in EW, 9–10; in *The Marne*, 76, 142; in *Son at the Front*, 142. *See also* Owen, Wilfred

Eliot, T. S., 7, 8, 13; "Tradition and the Individual Talent," 158, 159–60; "The Waste Land," 159, 280n4
Elshtain, Jean Bethke, 15, 281n8

Faivre, Abel, 17, 219
Farrand, Beatrix, 155
Feminism. *See* Great War writing: feminist approaches to, gender and
Fields, Anne Marsh, 279n2, 284n4
Fitzgerald, F. Scott, 123
Ford, Ford Madox, 73
Fullerton, Morton, 58
Fussell, Paul, 3, 14, 41–42; on Thomas Hardy, 8, 283–84n5; on Horace, 10; literary ambiguity, 56, 59, 82, 223; literary style influenced by the war, 8, 11, 280n4, 281n6; literature as escape from war, 60; Myth of the War, 7–12 passim, 73, 226; prewar years as idyllic, 45; soldiers' legends, 52, 77

Galsworthy, John, 13
Garrison, Stephen, 279n3
Gender and war writing. *See* Great War writing: feminist approaches to, gender and; Myth of the War; Wharton, Edith: frontline experience as the "real" experience
Gerhardie, William, 214
Gilbert, Sandra, 13–15, 24, 281n5, 285n2
Gledhill, Jane, 15, 280n4, 281n8, 286n1, 289n2
Goldman, Dorothy, 15, 280n4, 281n8, 286n1, 289n2
Goodman, Susan, 284n1
Goodwyn, Janet, 284n1
Grant, Robert, 59, 115, 141, 157
Graves, Robert, 16, 118
Great War writing: canon of, 4, 7–12, 219, 223, 226; feminist approaches to, 3, 13–15, 26, 234; gender and, 3, 4, 15, 16–20, 24–25, 34–37; relative to works by EW, 71, 105, 110, 141, 149. *See also* Wharton, Edith: war (difficulties writing about)
Gubar, Susan, 13–15, 24, 281n5, 285n2

Hall, Radclyffe, 103
Hardley, L. P., 182
Hardy, Thomas, 8, 43, 283–84n5
Hattaway, Judith, 15, 280n4, 281n8, 286n1, 289n2
Hemingway, Ernest, 7, 19, 72, 123, 282n15; and literary style, 12, 138, 139, 281nn6, 7
Henri (EW's footman), 47–48, 56, 87–88
Higonnet, Margaret, 86, 280n7, 282n15, 289n2
Horace, 9, 10, 142. *See also* "Dulce et decorum est . . ."
Howells, William Dean, 43, 105, 283–84n5
d'Humières, Robert, 47–48, 56
Hynes, Samuel, 3, 118; and literary style influenced by the war, 8, 12, 106, 280n4, 281n7; and Myth of the War, 7–12 passim, 14, 73, 223, 226; prewar years as idyllic, 45; soldiers as artists and critics, 16; women and war, 19–20, 34

Inglis, Elsie, 19

James, Henry, 66, 106, 210, 227, 289n1; death of, 56, 57; historical novel as escape from the present, 123, 161, 169–70; letters from EW, 16, 22, 24, 30, 156, 283n1; letters to EW, 43, 46, 283–84n5; on language in wartime, 12, 139; relative to *A Son at the Front*, 120–21, 122–23, 125–26
Jewett, Rutger, 143, 212
Jones, Mary (Minnie) Cadwalader, 25, 91, 155, 164, 199
Joyce, James, 13, 159

Keegan, John, 20, 225–26, 227, 232, 288n13
Kipling, Rudyard, 13
Knights, Pamela, 285n13

Lapsley, Gaillard, 27, 59
Lauer, Kristin O., 280n2
Lawrence, D. H., 13, 159
Lewis, R. W. B., 135, 161–62, 279n2, 282n16, 283n2, 284n2; on "Coming Home," 284n8; on *A Son at the Front*, 286n4

(chap. 5); on war's effect on imagination, 1, 210, 234

Lewis, Sinclair, 123, 214

Lubbock, Percy, 98, 230, 289nn5–6

Macauley, Rose, 19

Maeterlinck, Maurice, 220

Masculinity: and war, 18, 71, 121, 132

Masefield, John, 10, 32

McDowell, Margaret, 284n1

Millgate, Michael, 283–84n5

Modernism, 8, 12, 13, 281n6; EW and, 13, 158–62, 215, 280n4

Monuments: to war, 91, 152–53. See also Wharton, Edith: works (novels: A Son at the Front)

Moore, Marianne, 226

Munich, Adrienne Auslander, 289n2

Myth of the War, 7–13, 19. See also Fussell, Paul; Hynes, Samuel; Great War writing

Nevius, Blake, 58, 61, 149

Northcliffe, Lord, 10–11, 32

Norton, Elizabeth (sister of Sara Norton), 230

Norton, Robert, 139

Norton, Sara (Sally), 21, 22, 50, 56, 59, 70, 123, 230

O'Brien, Sharon, 285n7

Olin-Ammentorp, Julie, 282n14

Owen, Wilfred, 8, 9–10, 11, 38, 281nn5, 7

Pope, Jessie, 10, 281n5

Pound, Ezra, 7, 8, 13, 219

Powell, E. Alexander, 36

Powers, Lyall H., 123

Price, Alan, 12, 279n2, 280n1, 284n2; American Red Cross and EW, 126, 286n5; on EW's war works, 48, 54

Proust, Marcel, 158

Refugees, 33, 38, 43, 55, 57, 58, 98, 228–29; in EW's "The Refugees," 101, 111; in The Age of Innocence, 168, 169; in "Velvet Ear Pads," 199–200; in "Charm Incorpo-

rated," 208–9; in "Christmas Tinsel," 228–29

Reilly, Catherine: Scars Upon My Heart: Women's Poetry and Verse from the First World War, 280n7

Reims Cathedral, 4, 35, 37, 38, 39

Renan, Ernest: L'Abbesse de Jouarre, 99

Rheims Cathedral. See Reims Cathedral

Renoir, Pierre-Auguste, 118–19, 123, 286n1

Rhinelander, Newbold, 119, 132; death of, 57, 150, 197, 202–3; grave site of, 155, 198; reflected in A Son at the Front, 123–25, 147

Rhinelander, Thomas, 124, 132, 150–51, 155, 156, 203

Roosevelt, Theodore, 90, 95–97, 113

Sargent, John Singer, 122

Sarolea, Charles: The Anglo-German Problem, 21

Sassoon, Siegfried, 8, 12, 16, 18, 38, 281n7; "Glory of Women," 222–23, 227

Saunders, Judith P., 287n4

Schriber, Mary Suzanne, 283n2

Scribner, Charles, 6, 7, 34, 157, 200, 210

Scribner's Magazine, 24, 29, 35, 36, 38, 98, 104, 217

Sears, Joseph, 115–16

de Séguier, Comte de, 48

Sensibar, Judith, 286n1, 287n7

Showalter, Elaine, 18

Simmons, Ronald, 87–88, 93; death of, 57, 197; friendship with EW, 285n10; grave site of, 155, 198; reflected in EW's The Marne, 78; in A Son at the Front, 123–25, 127, 147, 202. See also Wharton, Edith: works (poems: "'On Active Service'")

Sinclair, May, 7, 19, 34, 281n7

Sitwell, Edith, 7

Soldiers: as artists and critics, 16; as artists and critics in works by EW, 108–10, 184–85, 185–87; EW's experience with, 123–24, 156, 192, 230–32; works addressed to, 78–80, 91–92, 94

Squier, Susan Merrill, 289n2

Stevens, Ebenezer (EW's great-grandfather), 232

Survivor guilt, 15; in EW's poem "Elegy," 113; in *A Son at the Front*, 121

"Talk to American Soldiers" (speech by EW), 78–80, 92
Tate, Trudi: *Women, Men, and the Great War*, 289n2
Thoreau, Henry David: *Walden*, 181
Tolstoy, Leo: *War and Peace*, 39–40
Troy: as war, myth, name, 72
Trumbell, Annie Eliot: "Sinews of War," 35
Tuchman, Barbara, 224–25, 289n3
Tylee, Claire, 18, 26, 281n9, 285n8, 289n2
Tyler, Elisina, 57, 217

Volunteer Aid Detachment (VAD), 19, 34
Vita-Finzi, Penelope, 284n1

Waddington, Mary King, 24, 104, 216
Waid, Candace, 61
Ward, Mrs. Humphry, 18, 24, 50, 122, 214
War novel: definition of, 7, 25–26; broadening definition of, 289n2; relative to EW's *A Son at the Front*, 115–16, 141, 143
Wegener, Frederick, 284n7, 285nn10, 14, 286n4 (chap. 5)
Wells, H. G., 137, 282n15
West, Rebecca: *Return of the Soldier*, 282n15
Wharton, Edith: civilization as an issue in postwar works of, 220–21; France, attitude toward, 2, 21, 23, 67, 77, 79, 81, 132; Germans and German-Americans, attitude toward, 41–42, 80–81, 82, 281n13; increasing conservatism reflected in writings of, 15, 83, 130–31, 195–96, 285n14; on roles of women, 14, 52, 84–85, 200, 221; and writing as a vocation, 14, 98, 156, 224–32; xenophobia of, 80–81, 285n13
—American moral superiority, dislike of: in *The Marne*, 69, 75, 81; in "Talk to American Soldiers," 78–79
—and frontline experience as "real" war, 34–35, 133, 153, 184, 217; fear of missing "real" experience of war reflected in fic-

tion, 71, 99, 100, 101, 174, 198; relative to gender roles, 85–86. *See also* Great War writing: gender and
—Great War, attitude toward, 2, 16–17, 28–34, passim; in *A Backward Glance*, 219–20; in *The Marne*, 66, 70, 72–74; in *A Son at the Front*, 118, 136, 141–42. *See also* Wharton, Edith: United States, attitude toward
—and ideals, idealistic language, 9–12, 29, 48, 91; in *The Marne*, 76, 142; in poems, 42, 44–45, 55, 92–93, 97; in *A Son at the Front*, 118; on use of, by Laurence Binyon, 151–52. *See also* "Dulce et decorum est . . ."
—inactivity, frustration with, 19; reflected in fiction, 50, 67, 128–29
—incapacitated male characters, creation of, 67, 112, 218–19, 222–23, 227; in "Coming Home," 50; in "The Refugees," 101
—reality, sense of a shaken, 28–29; in *Fighting France*, 29–31; reflected in fiction, 62–63, 99, 100, 129, 172–74, 198
—United States, attitude toward, 21–22, 66, 141; in "The Great Blue Tent," 44; in "Her Son," 203; in *The Mother's Recompense*, 189; in "The Refugees," 102; in *A Son at the Front*, 136
—war, difficulties writing about, 18–19, 24–26, 34–38, 99, 222–23; reflected in "Writing a War Story," 103–12, 184–85
—war, belief in transformative effects of, 20, 39–40, 152, 192, 228; in *The Age of Innocence*, 169; in *The Marne*, 75–76; in *The Mother's Recompense*, 192–94; in *A Son at the Front*, 20, 39, 133–35; in "The Spark," 182–84
—war treated as social event by: in "Her Son," 202; in *The Marne*, 68–69; in *The Mother's Recompense*, 188, 190–91, 194; in "The Refugees," 99, 102; in *A Son at the Front*, 111, 126–27, 128
WORKS
—**Nonfiction.** *See also The Book of the Homeless*; "Talk to American Soldiers"
A Backward Glance, 1, 3, 128, 162, 218, 232, 289n1; discussion of war years in,

213–22; end of war in, 90–91, 154; self-presentation in, 214, 216–18, 221–22; war's destruction of world of EW's youth, 27, 160–61, 213–16, 220–22, 226; writing after the war, 118, 233
"Christmas Tinsel," 228–29
Edith Wharton Abroad: Selected Travel Writings, 1888–1920, 283n2
"Edith Wharton Tells of German Trail of Ruin," 285n
Fighting France, 2, 3, 11, 13, 14, **29–34,** 35, 55, 59, 210, 225, 233, 280n3, 281n8, 283nn1–2, 289n3; difficulties as a woman writing about war in, 37–42; literary tropes in, 31–32; reflected in EW's other nonfiction, 82–83, 87, 94–95, 215–19 (in *The Age of Innocence,* 168–71 passim, 183; in *The Marne,* 74; in *The Mother's Recompense,* 192, 193; in *A Son at the Front,* 129, 131, 133; shaken reality in, 29–31; in short stories, 48, 101, 107, 183–84, 204, 205; in *Summer,* 61–63 passim, 65)
French Ways and Their Meaning, 2, 3, 21, 29, 43, 59, **78–86,** 233, 283n2, 285n6; attitude toward marriage in, 88, 131, 174–76; attitude toward women in, 14, 84–85, 169, 284n1; compared to *The Age of Innocence,* 168–71 passim, 174–76, 287n6; compared to *Fighting France,* 82–83; compared to "Her Son," 204; compared to "How Paris Welcomed the King," 93; compared to *The Marne,* 66, 68, 75; compared to *A Son at the Front,* 131, 141; compared to *Summer,* 61, 65, 88; genesis in "Talk to American Soldiers," 78–81; in historical context, 23, 83–86; idealistic language in, 9, 11; tone in, 5, 41, 58, 89, 91, 165, 285n12
"How Paris Welcomed the King," 90, 93–95. *See also* "How Victory Came to Paris"
"How Victory Came to Paris," 91, 93. *See also* "How Paris Welcomed the King"
"In Morocco," 5, 157, 279n5
"Italian Backgrounds," 68
"The Look of Paris," 29, 37–38

A Motor-Flight Through France, 34, 283n2
"My Work Among the Women Workers of Paris," 55, 284n9
"Permanent Values in Fiction," 158, 159
Preface to *The Book of the Homeless,* 55, 284n9
"Tendencies in Modern Fiction," 158–60
The Writing of Fiction, 157, **158–61,** 229
—Novels and novellas
The Age of Innocence, 3, 26, 115, 138, 157, **161–80,** 233; composition of, 162, 179, 287n5, 288n9; as escape from war years, 123, 162; influence of war years on, 168–77; marriage in, 174–76; treatment of the past as a lost world in, 161–68, 179–80, 211, 287n3; women in, 169–71, 287n4
The Buccaneers (unfinished novel), 287n2
The Children, 143, 161, 174, 195, 200, 233, 282n16; adoption in, 284n6; compared to *The Age of Innocence,* 287n6; issues of civilization in, 220
The Custom of the Country, 13, 26, 34; compared to *The Age of Innocence,* 164, 167; compared to *A Backward Glance,* 220; compared to *The Marne,* 68; compared to *A Son at the Front,* 133, 144–45; compared to stories by EW, 106, 206; compared to *Summer,* 61
Ethan Frome, 13, 26, 60
False Dawn, 288n9. *See also* Old New York
The Fruit of the Tree, 149
The Glimpses of the Moon, 115, 138, 157, 162, 282n16
Homo Sapiens (projected sequel to *The Age of Innocence*), 179
The House of Mirth, 8–9, 13, 26, 135, 160; compared to *The Age of Innocence,* 167, 288n8; compared to *A Backward Glance,* 220, 233; compared to *The Mother's Recompense,* 288n11; compared to "The Refugees," 102; compared to *A Son at the Front,* 130, 144–45, 148; compared to *Summer,* 61; compared to "Writing a War Story," 105

Wharton, Edith: works—*continued*
Literature (unfinished novel), 6, 233
The Marne, 2, 3, 13, 45, 58, **65–78,** 98,
210, 233, 284n1; American cultural
superiority in, 81; American soldiers
depicted in, 70–71; Troy Belknap compared to EW, 66–67, 78, 159; compared to *A Backward Glance*, 215,
216; compared to *French Ways and
Their Meaning*, 66, 67, 89; compared
to "Her Son," 205, 206; compared to
"How Paris Welcomed the King," 94;
compared to *The Mother's Recompense*, 189, 191, 192, 193; compared to
poems by EW, 45, 96; compared to *A
Son at the Front*, 125, 127, 131–38
passim, 141, 147, 148; compared to
Summer, 61, 65, 88–89, 196; composition of, 65–66, 114, 285n6; front lines
depicted in, 25, 37, 48, 110; gender
roles in, 67–71; as historical novel,
135; idealism in, 9, 10, 11, 76, 91, 96,
142; reception of, 89, 226, 284n2; and
Ronald Simmons, 57, 78; tone in, 5,
29, 59, 74–75, 165
The Mother's Recompense, 157, **187–97,**
210, 288nn10–11; compared to *The
Age of Innocence*, 287n6; compared to
A Backward Glance, 220; compared to
"Her Son," 203; compared to "The
Looking Glass," 208; contrasted with
wartime writings, 187, 188–89, 191,
193–94; Kate Clephane in, 190–91,
194–96; Chris Fenno in, 191–94; gender roles in, 192; incest issue in,
288n10; parent-child relationships in,
143, 176, 196–97, 282n16; social function of war in, 188, 190–91, 194, 202;
war as backdrop for, 161, 187–88, 198,
211, 233
"New Year's Day," 201–2, 288n9. *See also
Old New York*
"The Old Maid," 202, 288n9. *See also
Old New York*
Old New York, 3, 157, 182, 201, 202, 211,
233; compared to *The Age of Inno-

cence*, 179–80, 194; compared to *A
Backward Glance*, 213, 214, 216, 221,
222; compared to "Her Son," 205;
compared to "The Looking Glass," 208;
compared to *The Mother's Recompense*, 194; and history, 123, 161, 179–
81, 208, 288n9. *See also* "New Year's
Day"; "The Old Maid"; "The Spark"
The Reef, 288n11
A Son at the Front, 2, 3, 45, **115–53,**
156, 162, 178, 210, 211, 219, 226, 227,
233, 280n3; biographical sources of,
118–27, 286n3, 286–87n6; John
Campton, central analysis of, 142–48,
286n1, 287n7; canon of WWI works,
relative to, 10, 11, 12, 14–15, 20, 25–
26, 110; compared to *The Age of Innocence*, 175, 178; compared to "Behind the Government," 288n12;
compared to "Belgium," 42–43; compared to "Her Son," 201–6 passim;
compared to "How Paris Welcomed
the King," 94; compared to "The Looking Glass," 207; compared to *The
Marne*, 76, 78; compared to *The
Mother's Recompense*, 188–97 passim;
compared to "The Spark," 182, 183;
composition of, 114, 115, 138, 142,
146–47; as EW's final statement on the
war, 89, 111–12, 118, 125–35; and gender roles, 131–33; and Ronald
Simmons, 57, 78, 123–25, 127, 147,
286n4 (chap. 5); war depicted as transformative in, 39, 133–35, 146, 147; as
war novel, 115–16, 141, 143
"The Spark," **181–87;** compared to "Her
Son," 204; compared to *The Mother's
Recompense*, 193–94; compared to
"The Refugees," 187; compared to *A
Son at the Front*, 182, 183; compared
to "Writing a War Story," 184–87; and
genre, 186; narrator in, 181–82; war as
transformative in, 182–84. *See also
Old New York*
Summer, 2, 3, 26, 35, **59–65,** 119, 177;
Charity's marriage, 60, 63–64, 284n3;

compared to *The Age of Innocence,* 167, 173, 177; compared to *French Ways and Their Meaning,* 81, 82, 89; compared to *The Marne,* 88–89; compared to *A Son at the Front,* 129; composition of, 59, 162; as escape from the war years, 59, 60–61, 88, 89; gender and maturation in, 88, 196; war's influence on, 61–65, 88

Twilight Sleep, 61, 161, 195, 197–98, 233; issues of civilization in, 220; parent-child relationships in, 282n16

The Valley of Decision, 61, 135, 162

—**Poems:** "Battle Sleep," 44–45, 155, 212; "Beaumetz, Feb. 23rd. 1915," 46–47, 87, 93, 113, 141; "Belgium," 42, 45, 47, 289n1 (app. A); "Elegy," 112–13, 198; "The Great Blue Tent," 11, 44, 45, 96; "Hymn of the Lusitania" (trans. EW), 280n6; "'On Active Service,'" 47, 87–88, 89, 93, 112, 141, 147; "The Tryst," 43–44, 55, 223; "With the Tide," 90, 95–97, 113, 114; "You and You," 90, 91–93, 95, 97, 112, 141, 192, 223

—**Short stories**

"April Showers," 24, 104

"Behind the Government" (unfinished story), 288n12

"Bread Upon the Waters." *See* "Charm Incorporated"

"Charm Incorporated," 200, 205, 206, 208–11, 288n14

"Coming Home," 2, 3, **48–54,** 112, 210, 219, 279n4, 284n8, 286n4 (chap. 4); compared to *The Age of Innocence,* 169, 171–72; compared to "Her Son," 205; compared to *The Marne,* 65, 67; compared to *A Son at the Front,* 128–32 passim, 140, 142; compared to "The Spark," 186; compared to *Summer,* 61, 64; reality in, 29, 33; style in, 11, 27, 102, 107

"The Day of the Funeral," 198

"Diagnosis," 198

"A Glimpse," 198

"Her Son," **200–206,** 211; compared to "Charm Incorporated," 208; compared to "The Looking Glass, 207; compared to *A Son at the Front,* 201–6 passim

"Joy in the House," 198

"The Looking Glass," 205, **206–8**

"Miss Mary Pask," 198, 199

"The Pelican," 24

"The Refugees," 2, 3, 67, 91, 97, **98–103,** 112, 210, 219, 227, 286n4 (chap.4); and actual refugees, 98, 101, 111; compared to *The Age of Innocence,* 174; compared to *The Mother's Recompense,* 188; compared to *A Son at the Front,* 126, 130, 132, 141; compared to stories by EW, 105, 187, 199, 202, 209; and romance, 101–2; tone in, 89; war as social event in, 99, 102, 126

"Roman Fever," 176

"Souls Belated," 191

"Velvet Ear Pads," 198–200, 208, 211

"Writing a War Story," 2, 3, 37, 97, 98, 103–12, 156, 210; compared to "Her Son," 204; compared to "The Refugees," 105; compared to *A Son at the Front,* 133, 141; compared to "The Spark," 184–87, 204; names in, 109, 112, 286n4 (chap. 4)

"Xingu," 102

White, Barbara, 104, 284n8, 286n4 (chap. 4)

Whitman, Walt, 134; in EW's "The Spark," 182, 185–87 passim

Williams, Deborah Lindsay, 279n2, 285–86n3

Winthrop, Egerton, 56, 57

Wolff, Cynthia Griffin, 118, 142, 149, 282n16, 284n3, 288n7

Women: and war, 15, 18–20; exclusion of, from war, 18, 19. *See also* Great War writing: gender and

Woolf, Virginia, 7, 8, 13, 159; *Jacob's Room,* 282n15; *A Room of One's Own,* 158

Wright, Sarah Bird, 279n1, 238n2

Yeats, William Butler, 40, 283n3

Julie Olin-Ammentorp is professor of English at Le Moyne College in Syracuse, New York. She is the author of several essays on Edith Wharton, including articles published in *Studies in American Fiction, Women's Studies,* and *The Edith Wharton Review,* and has contributed to collections of essays such as *Wretched Exotic: Essays on Edith Wharton in Europe* and *American Literary Mentors.* She has served as president of the Edith Wharton Society.